D1225059

The BOOK of DOOMS

ARTESIA
ARTESIA AFIELD
ARTESIA AFIRE

forthcoming

ARTESIA BESIEGED

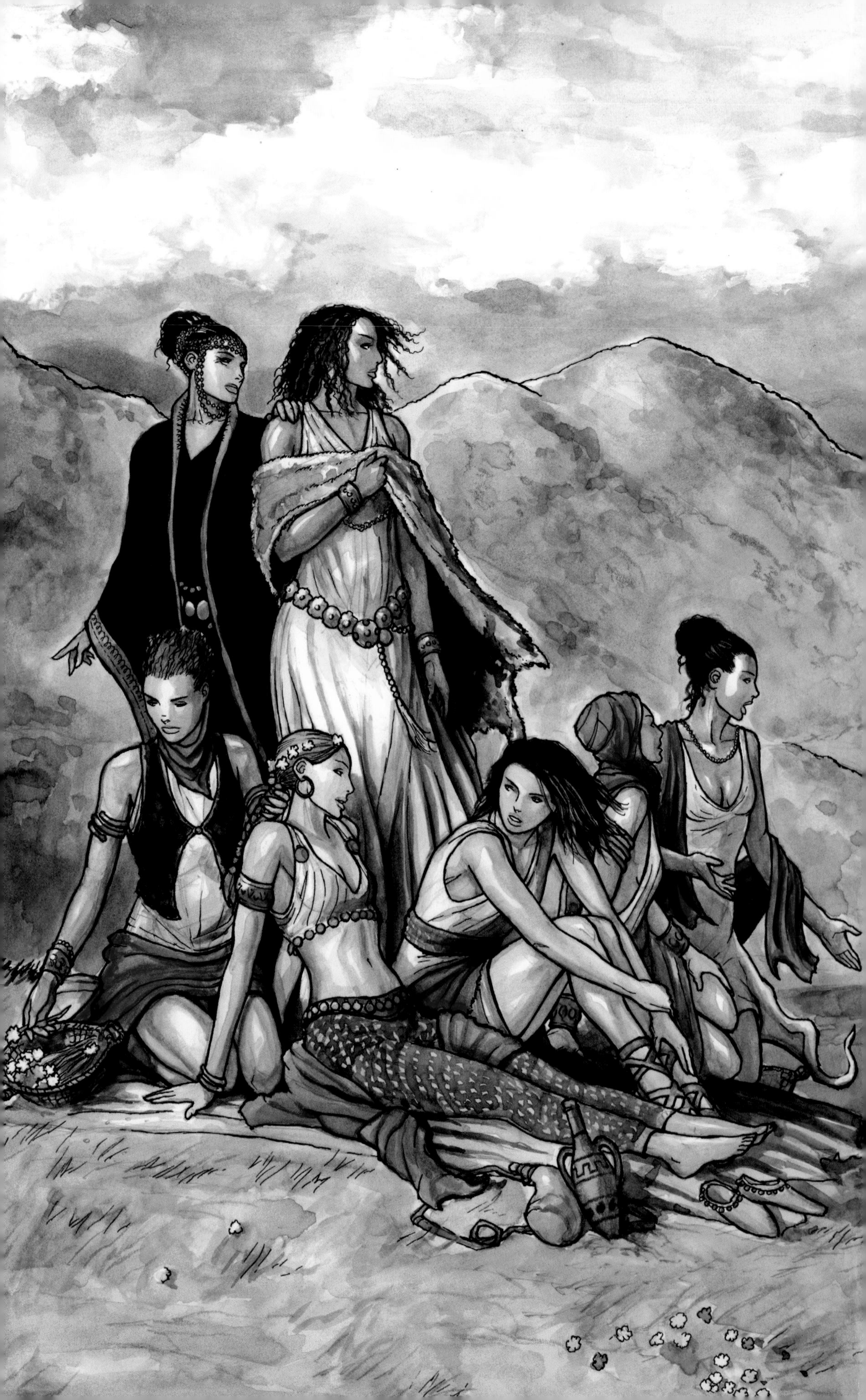

ARTESIA

written & illustrated
by MARK SMYLIE

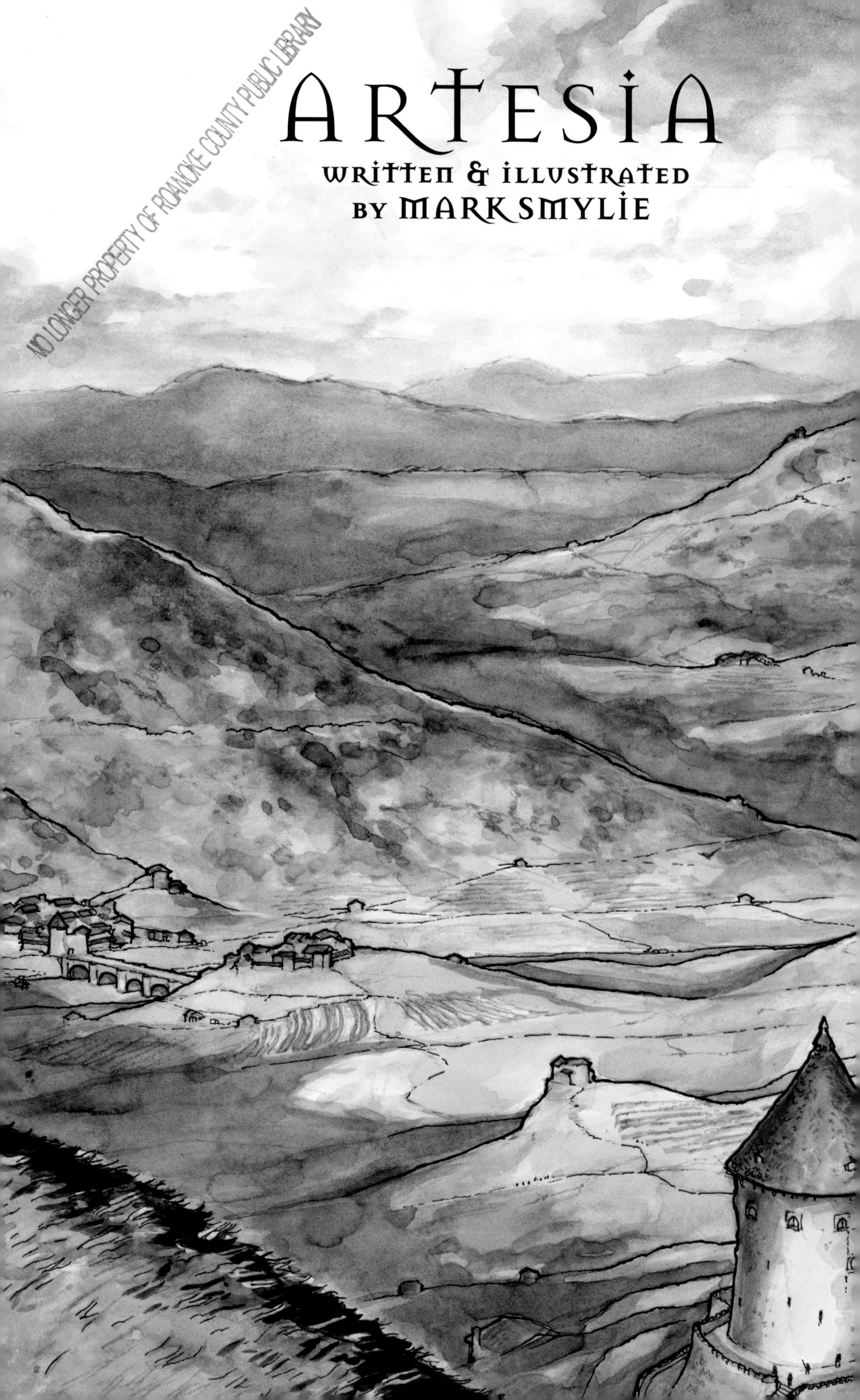

ARCHAIA STUDIOS PRESS

ARTESIA
Written and Illustrated by
Mark Smylie

Edited by
Mark Bellis
for *Sirius Entertainment*

Production Assistance by
Mark McNabb
at *McNabb Studios*

Management Consultant
Brian Petkash
at *Sphinx Group*

Published by Archaia Studios Press.
96 Linwood Plaza PMB 360
For Lee, NJ 07024-3701
www.archaiasp.com

November 2006
Third (Hardcover) Edition
ISBN: 1-932386-22-X
ISBN-13: 978-1-932386-22-6
previous ISBN: 1-932386-02-5

Printed in China.

TABLE OF CONTENTS

APPENDIXES

LIST OF PLATES

**PLATES BY MARK McNABB
BASED ON ILLUSTRATIONS
BY MARK SMYLIE**

THE FIRST
BOOK OF DOOMS

In Memory of My Mother

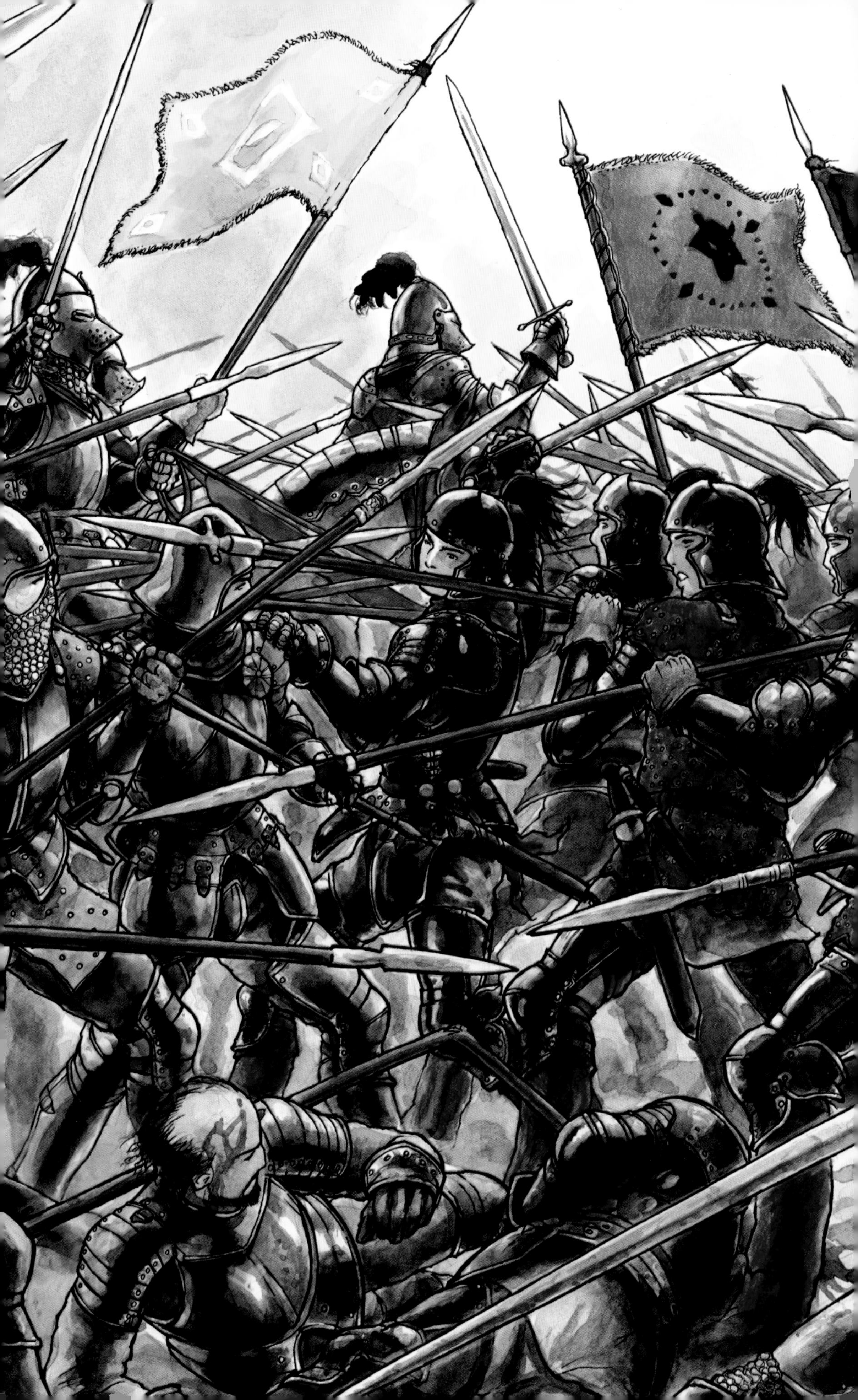

CHAPTER ONE

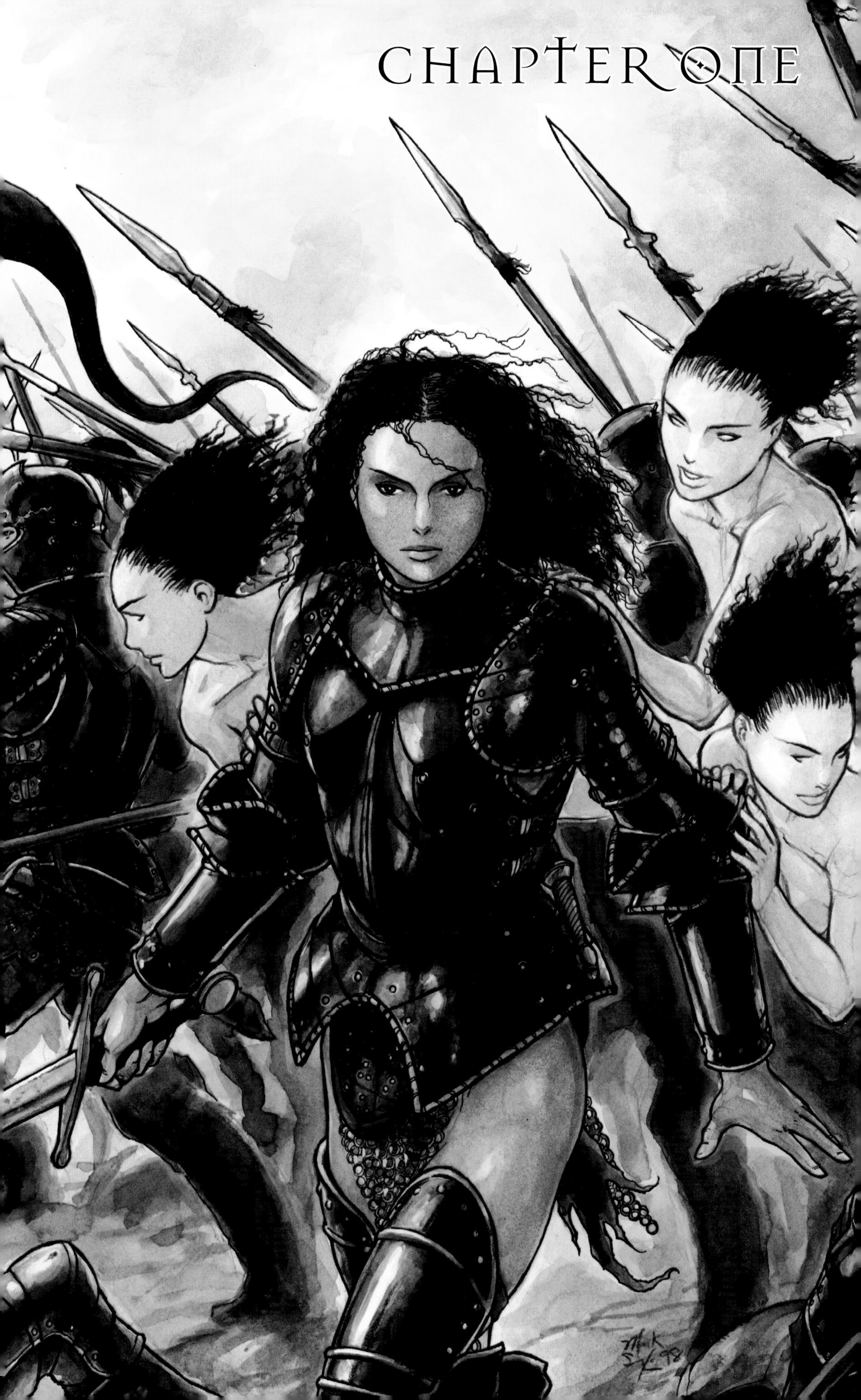

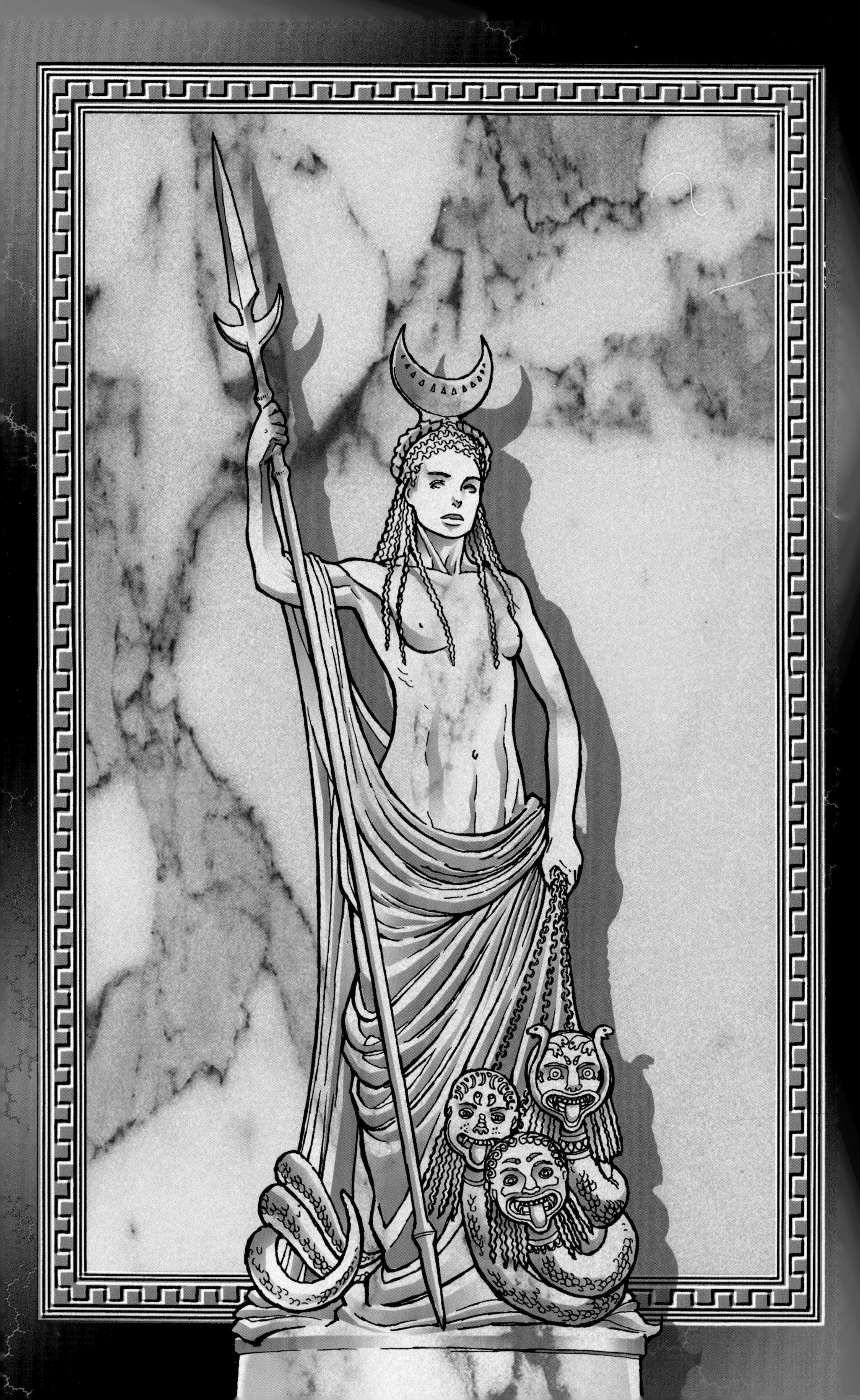

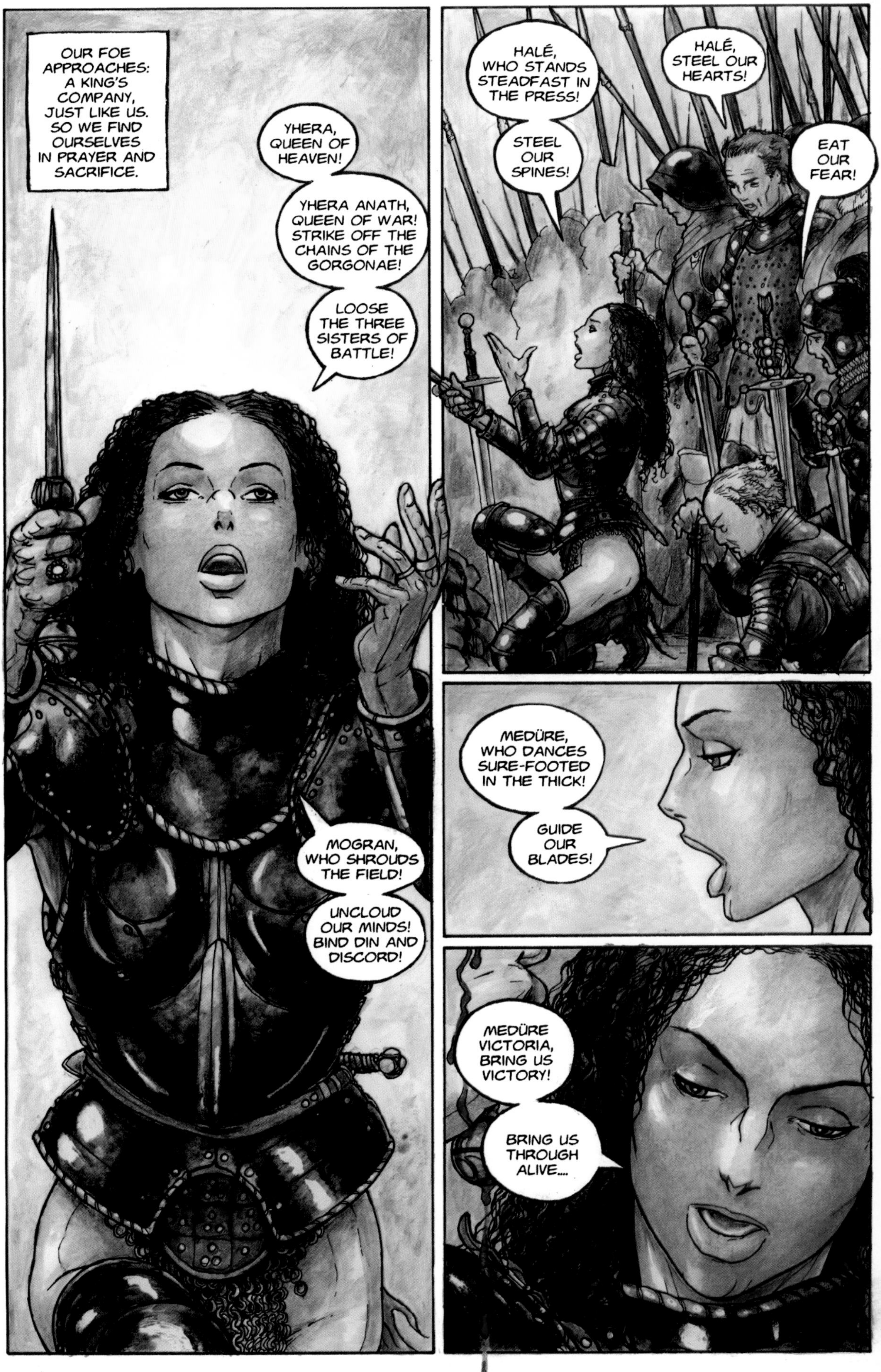
OUR FOE APPROACHES: A KING'S COMPANY, JUST LIKE US. SO WE FIND OURSELVES IN PRAYER AND SACRIFICE.
YHERA, QUEEN OF HEAVEN!
YHERA ANATH, QUEEN OF WAR! STRIKE OFF THE CHAINS OF THE GORGONAE!
LOOSE THE THREE SISTERS OF BATTLE!
MOGRAN, WHO SHROUDS THE FIELD!
UNCLOUD OUR MINDS! BIND DIN AND DISCORD!
HALÉ, WHO STANDS STEADFAST IN THE PRESS!
STEEL OUR SPINES!
HALÉ, STEEL OUR HEARTS!
EAT OUR FEAR!
MEDÜRE, WHO DANCES SURE-FOOTED IN THE THICK!
GUIDE OUR BLADES!
MEDÜRE VICTORIA, BRING US VICTORY!
BRING US THROUGH ALIVE....

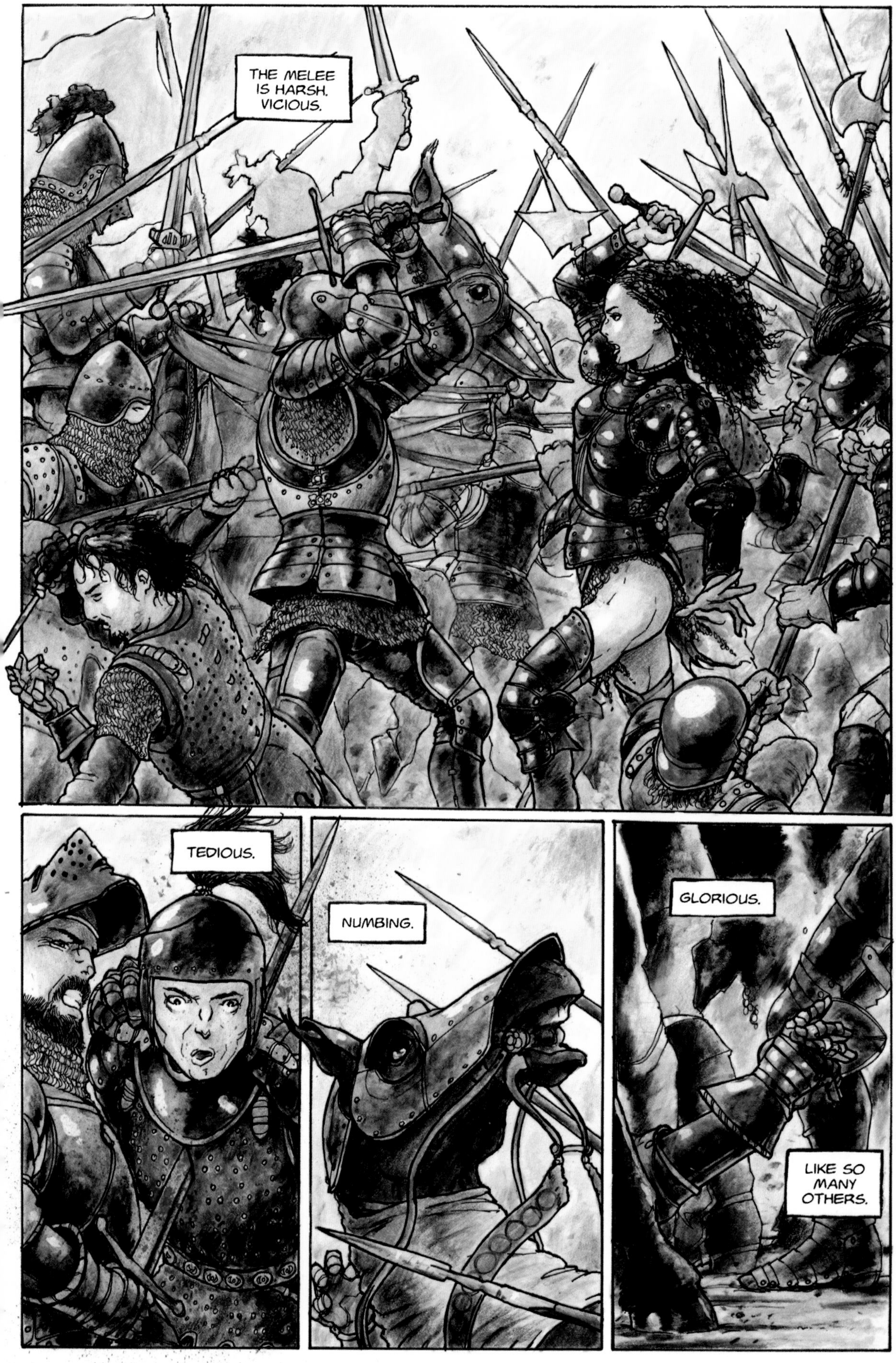
THE MELEE IS HARSH. VICIOUS.
TEDIOUS.
NUMBING.
GLORIOUS.
LIKE SO MANY OTHERS.

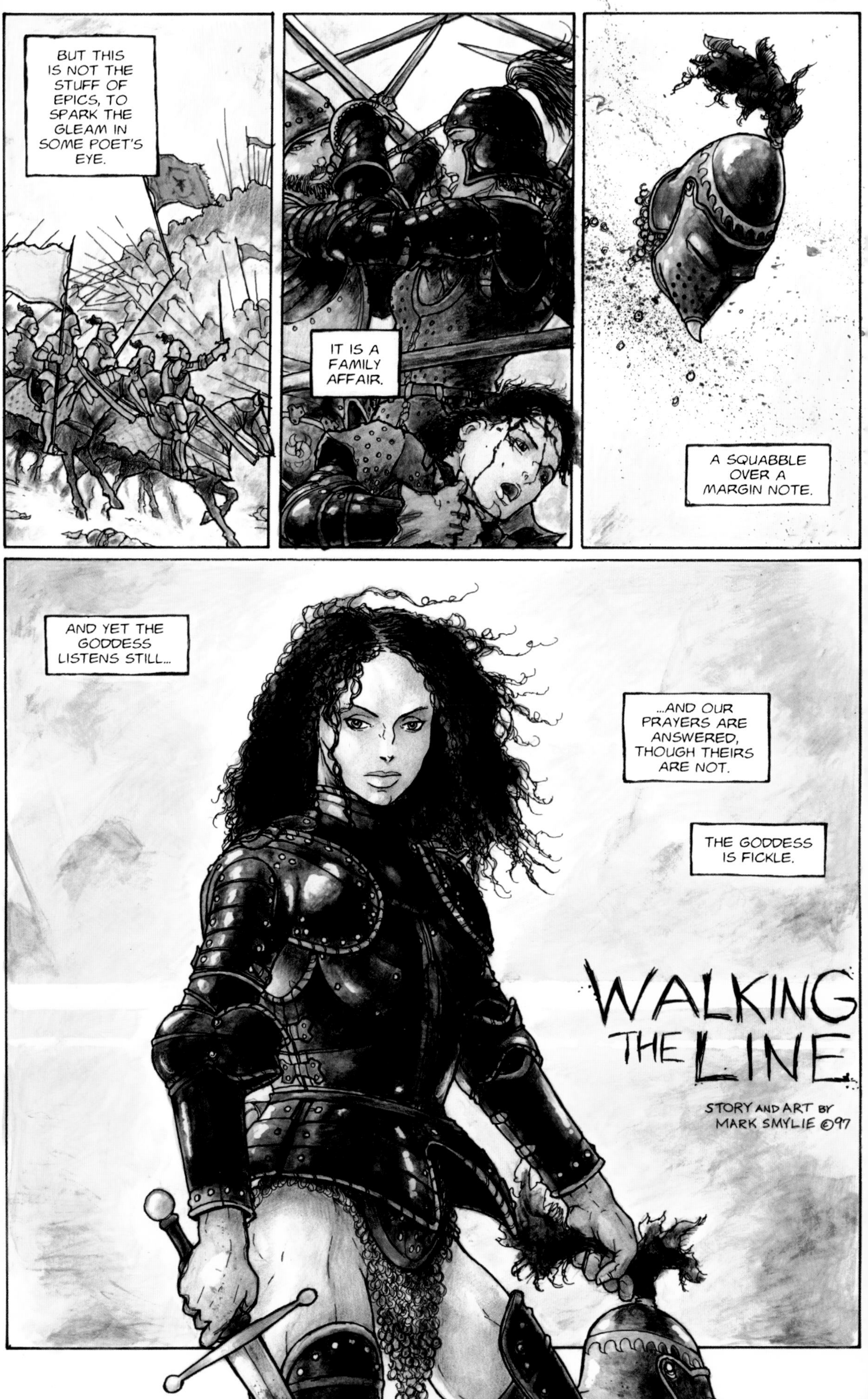
BUT THIS IS NOT THE STUFF OF EPICS, TO SPARK THE GLEAM IN SOME POET'S EYE.
IT IS A FAMILY AFFAIR.
A SQUABBLE OVER A MARGIN NOTE.
AND YET THE GODDESS LISTENS STILL...
...AND OUR PRAYERS ARE ANSWERED, THOUGH THEIRS ARE NOT.
THE GODDESS IS FICKLE.
WALKING THE LINE
STORY AND ART BY MARK SMYLIE ©97

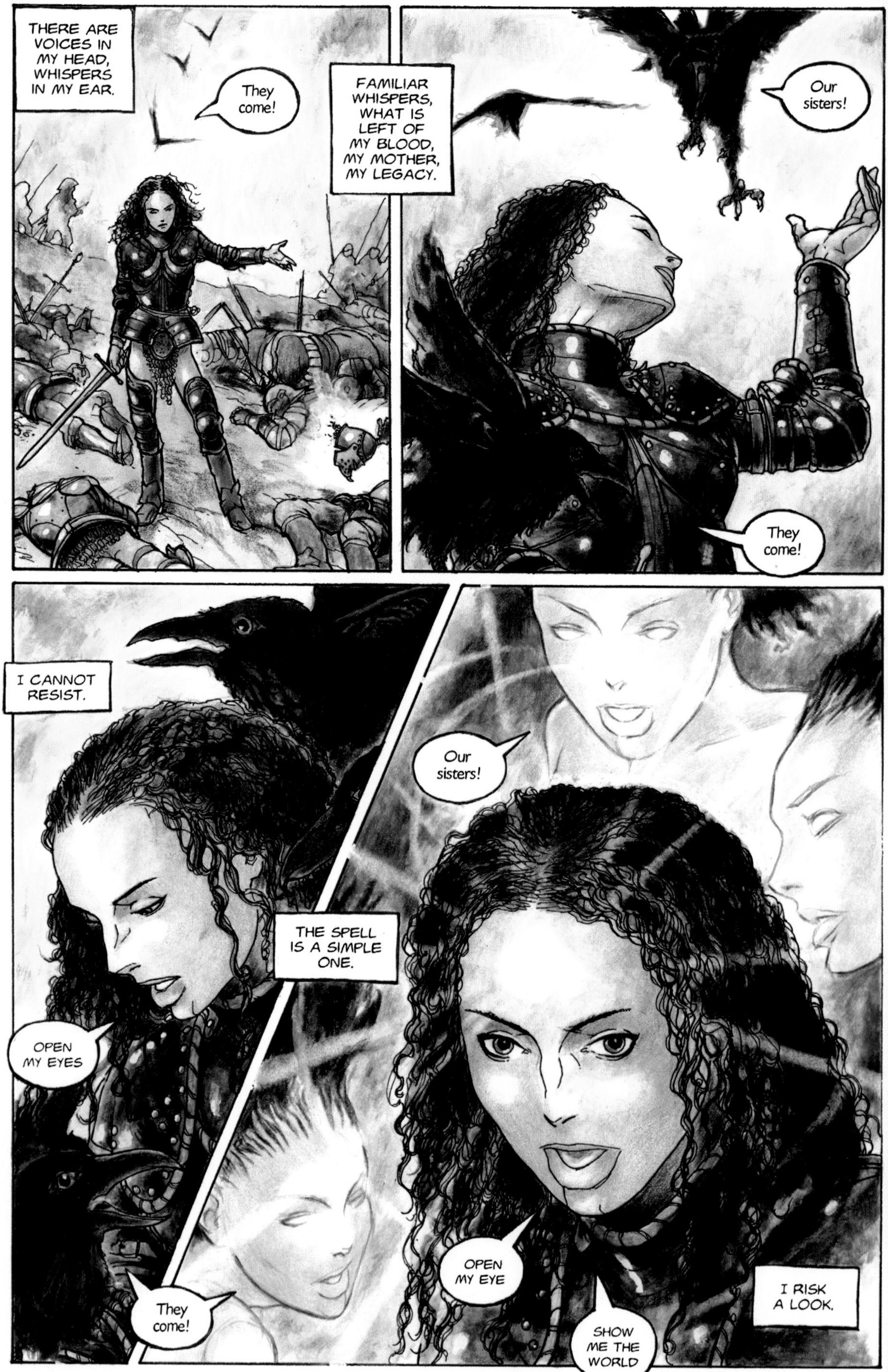
THERE ARE VOICES IN MY HEAD, WHISPERS IN MY EAR.
They come!
FAMILIAR WHISPERS, WHAT IS LEFT OF MY BLOOD, MY MOTHER, MY LEGACY.
Our sisters!
They come!
I CANNOT RESIST.
Our sisters!
THE SPELL IS A SIMPLE ONE.
OPEN MY EYES
They come!
OPEN MY EYE
SHOW ME THE WORLD
I RISK A LOOK.

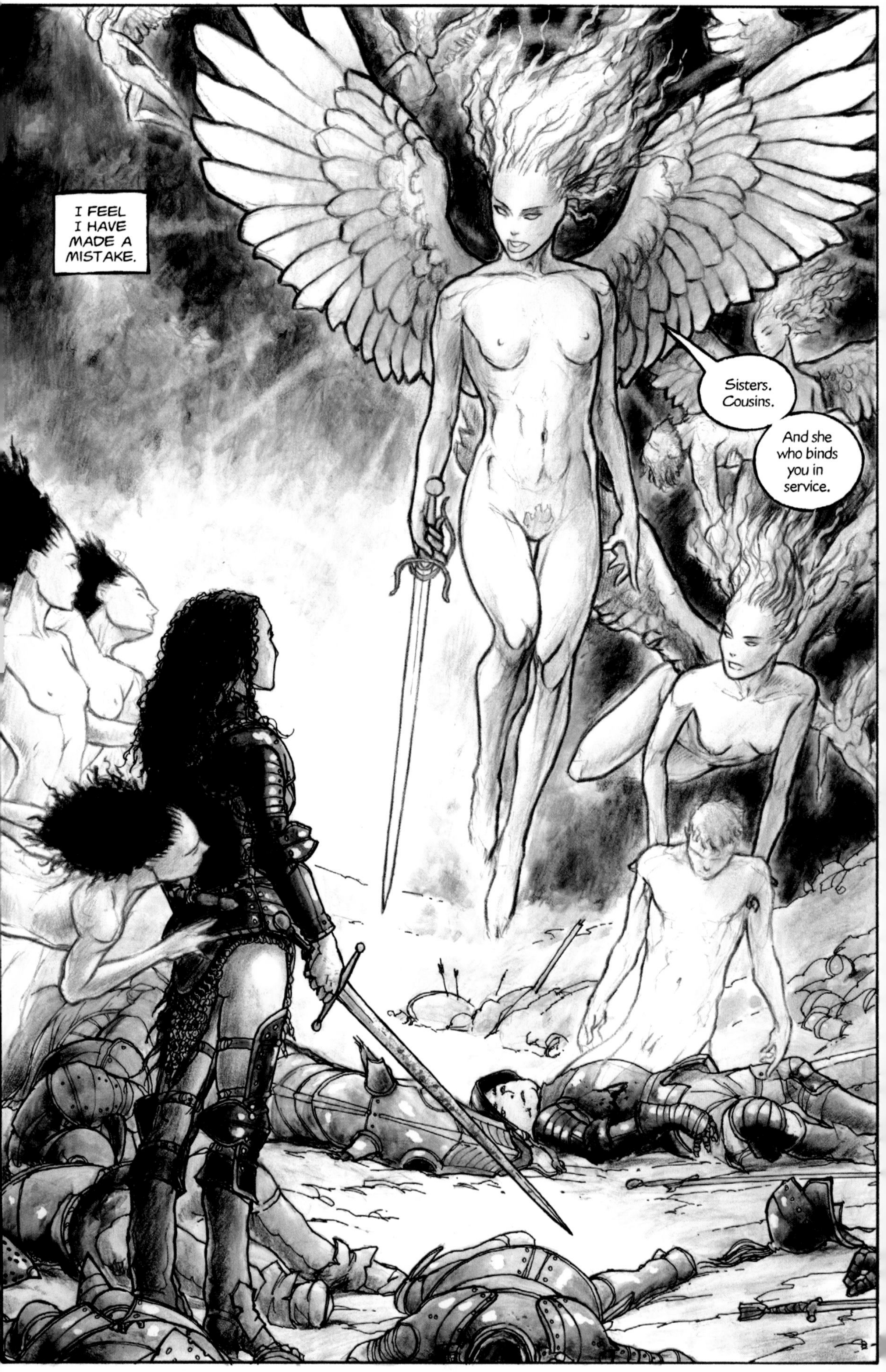
I FEEL I HAVE MADE A MISTAKE.
Sisters. Cousins.
And she who binds you in service.

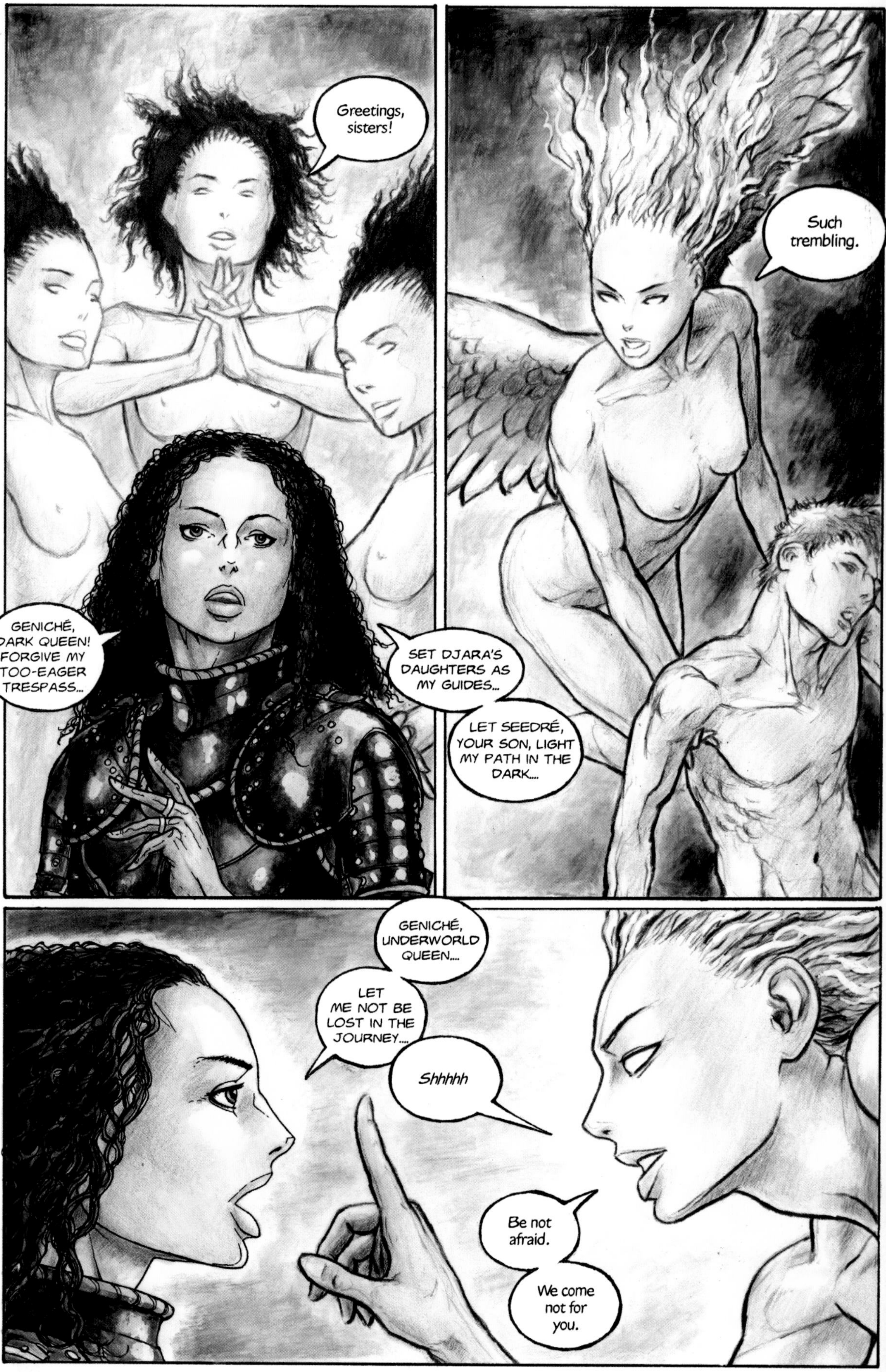
Greetings, sisters!
GENICHÉ, DARK QUEEN! FORGIVE MY TOO-EAGER TRESPASS...
SET DJARA'S DAUGHTERS AS MY GUIDES...
LET SEEDRÉ, YOUR SON, LIGHT MY PATH IN THE DARK....
Such trembling.
GENICHÉ, UNDERWORLD QUEEN....
LET ME NOT BE LOST IN THE JOURNEY....
Shhhhh
Be not afraid.
We come not for you.

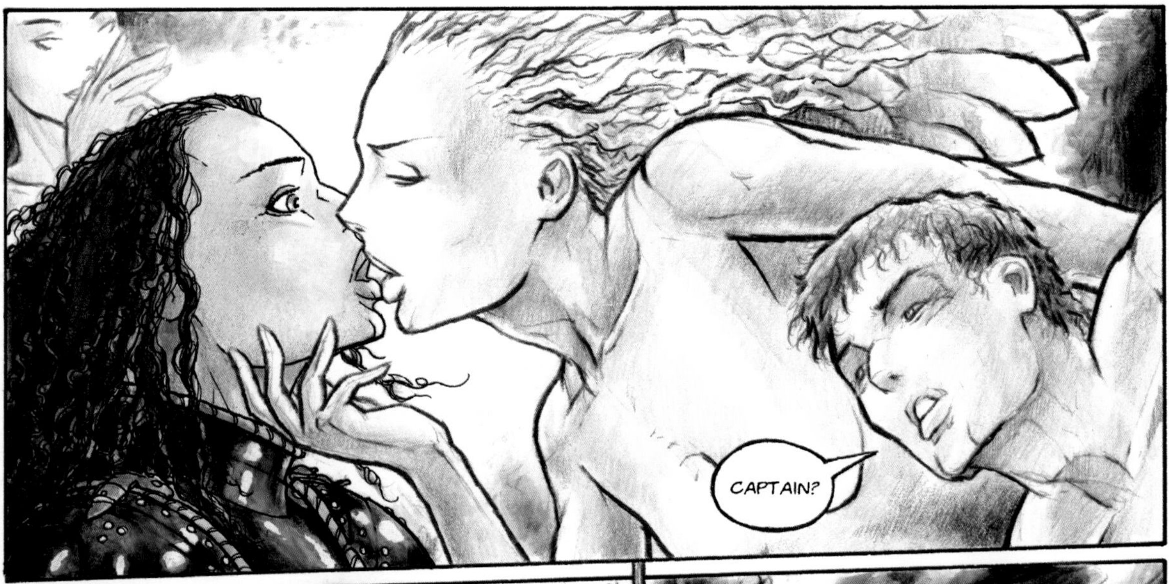
CAPTAIN?

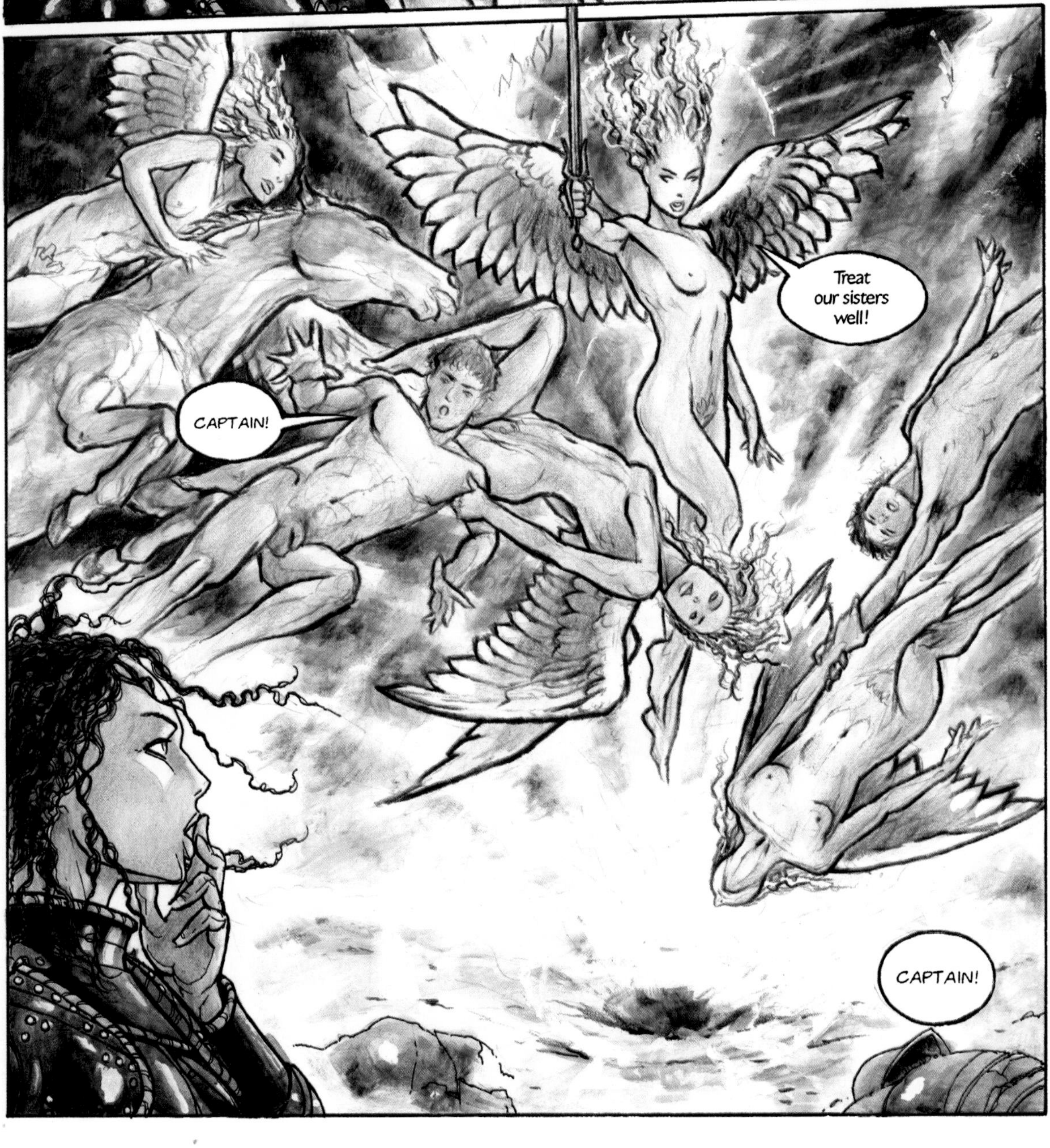
Treat our sisters well!
CAPTAIN!
CAPTAIN!

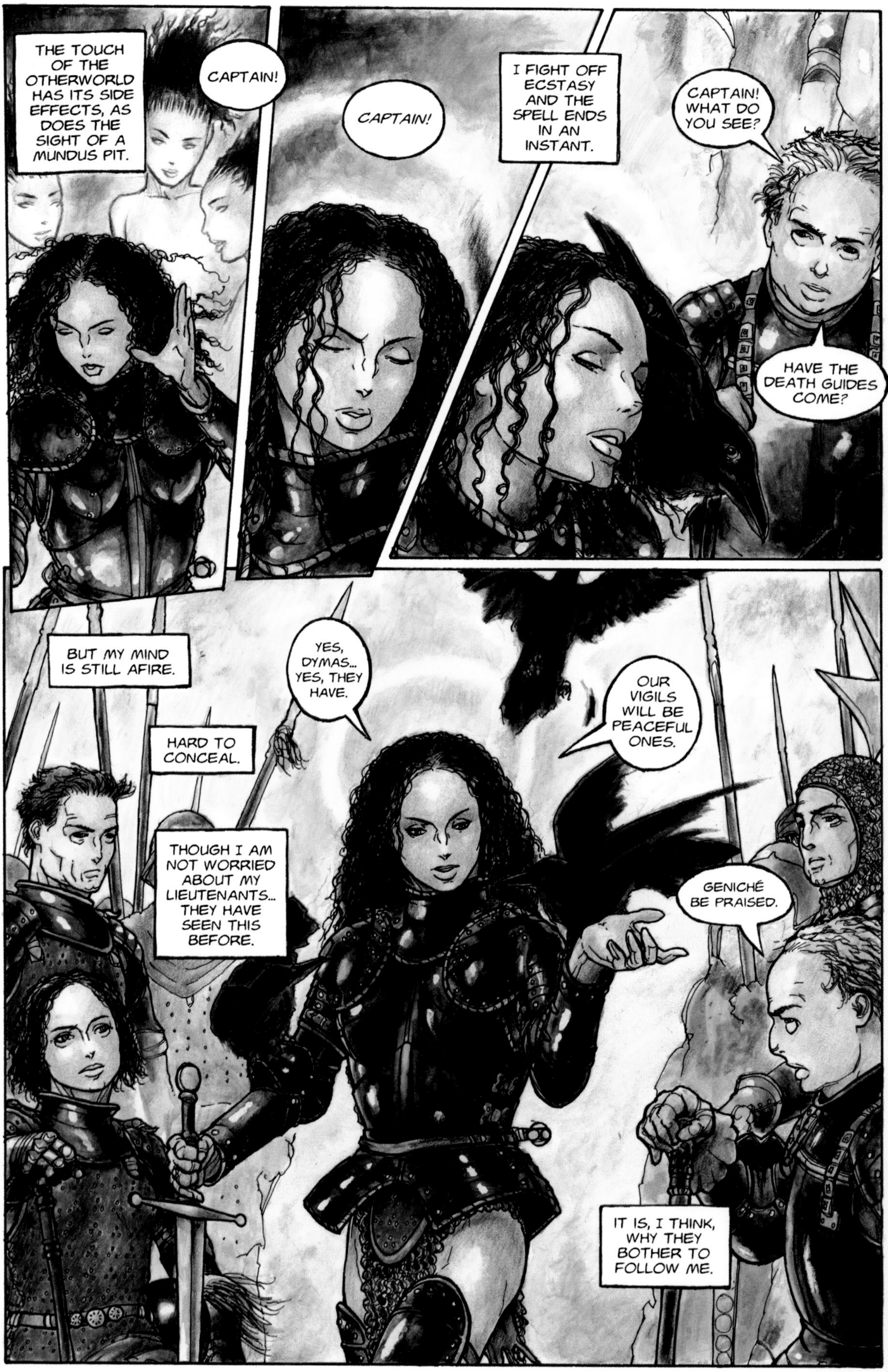
THE TOUCH OF THE OTHERWORLD HAS ITS SIDE EFFECTS, AS DOES THE SIGHT OF A MUNDUS PIT.
CAPTAIN!
CAPTAIN!
I FIGHT OFF ECSTASY AND THE SPELL ENDS IN AN INSTANT.
CAPTAIN! WHAT DO YOU SEE?
HAVE THE DEATH GUIDES COME?
BUT MY MIND IS STILL AFIRE.
HARD TO CONCEAL.
YES, DYMAS... YES, THEY HAVE.
OUR VIGILS WILL BE PEACEFUL ONES.
THOUGH I AM NOT WORRIED ABOUT MY LIEUTENANTS... THEY HAVE SEEN THIS BEFORE.
GENICHÉ BE PRAISED.
IT IS, I THINK, WHY THEY BOTHER TO FOLLOW ME.

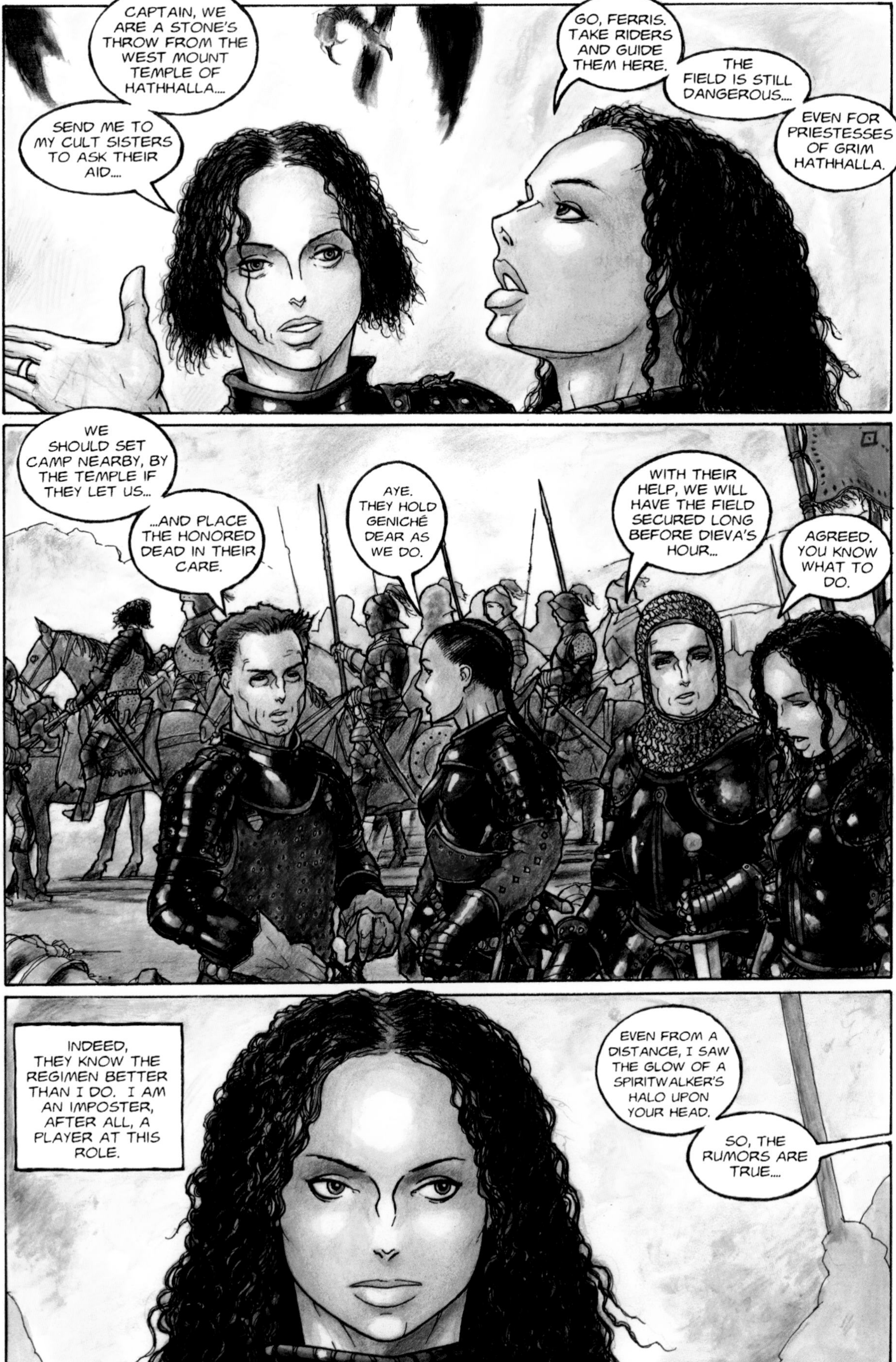
CAPTAIN, WE ARE A STONE'S THROW FROM THE WEST MOUNT TEMPLE OF HATHHALLA....
SEND ME TO MY CULT SISTERS TO ASK THEIR AID....
GO, FERRIS. TAKE RIDERS AND GUIDE THEM HERE.
THE FIELD IS STILL DANGEROUS....
EVEN FOR PRIESTESSES OF GRIM HATHHALLA.
WE SHOULD SET CAMP NEARBY, BY THE TEMPLE IF THEY LET US...
...AND PLACE THE HONORED DEAD IN THEIR CARE.
AYE. THEY HOLD GENICHÉ DEAR AS WE DO.
WITH THEIR HELP, WE WILL HAVE THE FIELD SECURED LONG BEFORE DIEVA'S HOUR...
AGREED. YOU KNOW WHAT TO DO.
INDEED, THEY KNOW THE REGIMEN BETTER THAN I DO. I AM AN IMPOSTER, AFTER ALL, A PLAYER AT THIS ROLE.
EVEN FROM A DISTANCE, I SAW THE GLOW OF A SPIRITWALKER'S HALO UPON YOUR HEAD.
SO, THE RUMORS ARE TRUE....

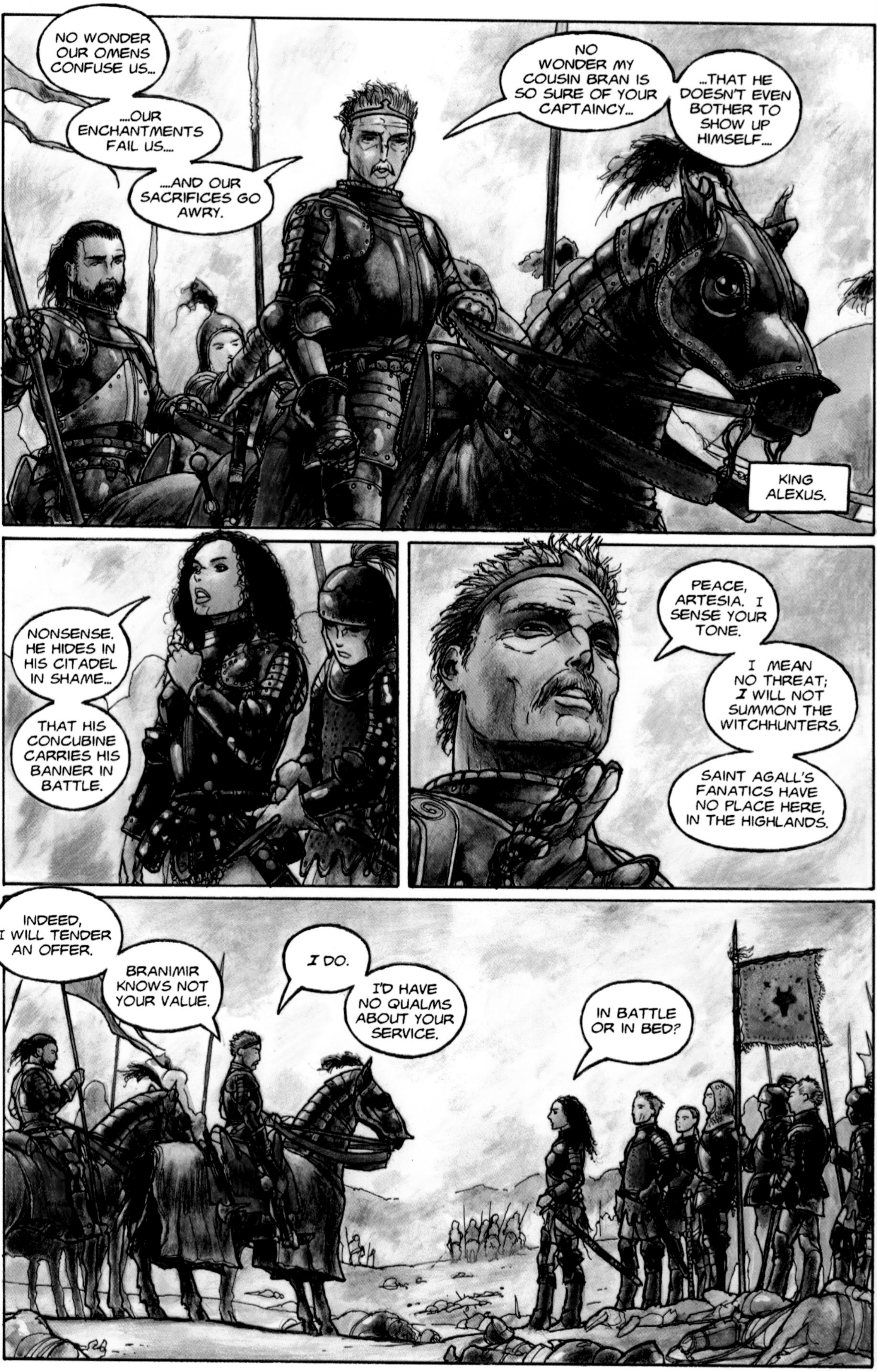
NO WONDER OUR OMENS CONFUSE US...
....OUR ENCHANTMENTS FAIL US....
....AND OUR SACRIFICES GO AWRY.
NO WONDER MY COUSIN BRAN IS SO SURE OF YOUR CAPTAINCY...
...THAT HE DOESN'T EVEN BOTHER TO SHOW UP HIMSELF....
KING ALEXUS.
NONSENSE. HE HIDES IN HIS CITADEL IN SHAME...
THAT HIS CONCUBINE CARRIES HIS BANNER IN BATTLE.
PEACE, ARTESIA. I SENSE YOUR TONE.
I MEAN NO THREAT; *I* WILL NOT SUMMON THE WITCHHUNTERS.
SAINT AGALL'S FANATICS HAVE NO PLACE HERE, IN THE HIGHLANDS.
INDEED, I WILL TENDER AN OFFER.
BRANIMIR KNOWS NOT YOUR VALUE.
I DO.
I'D HAVE NO QUALMS ABOUT YOUR SERVICE.
IN BATTLE OR IN BED?

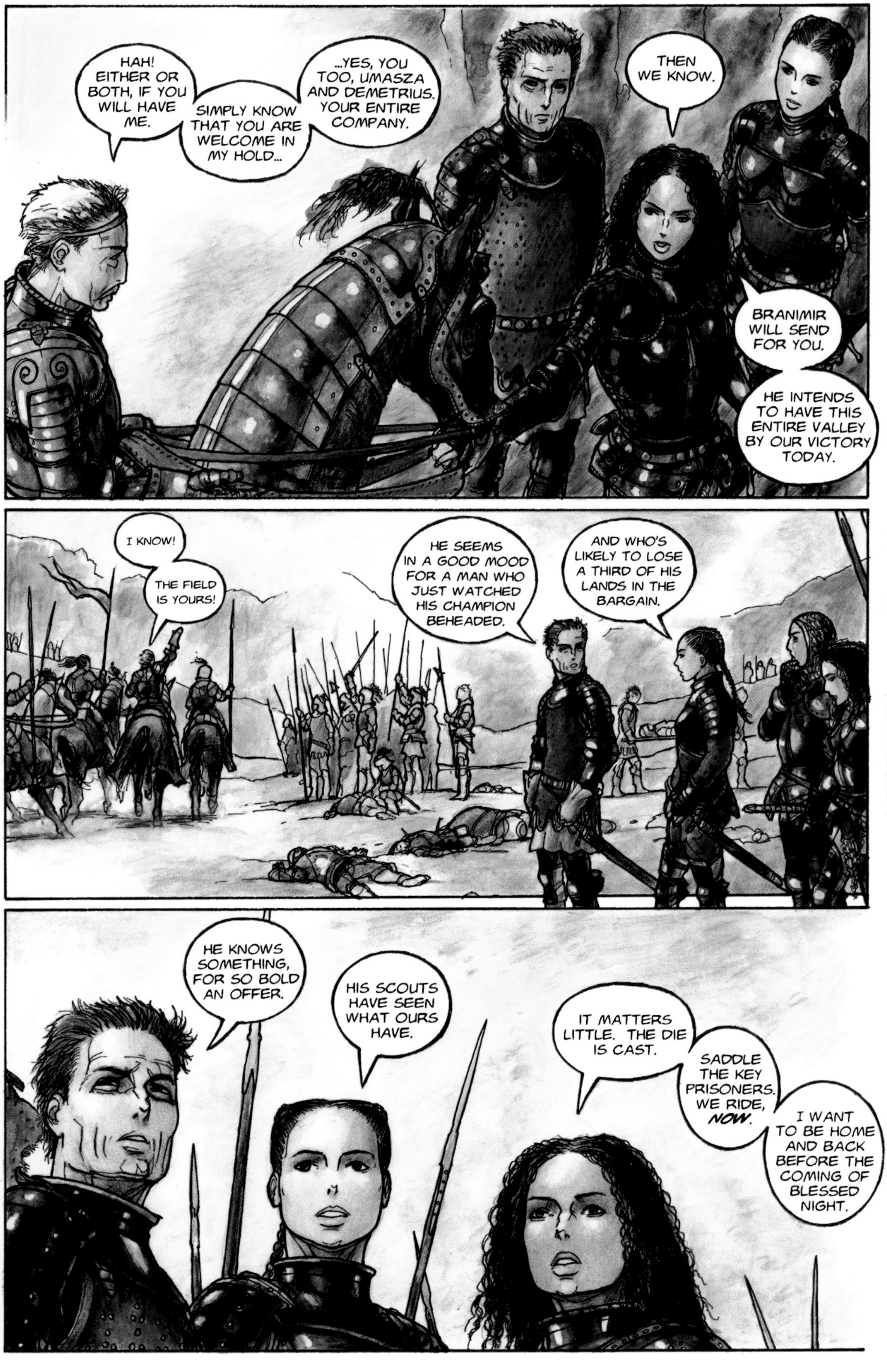
HAH! EITHER OR BOTH, IF YOU WILL HAVE ME.
SIMPLY KNOW THAT YOU ARE WELCOME IN MY HOLD...
...YES, YOU TOO, UMASZA AND DEMETRIUS. YOUR ENTIRE COMPANY.
THEN WE KNOW.
BRANIMIR WILL SEND FOR YOU.
HE INTENDS TO HAVE THIS ENTIRE VALLEY BY OUR VICTORY TODAY.
I KNOW!
THE FIELD IS YOURS!
HE SEEMS IN A GOOD MOOD FOR A MAN WHO JUST WATCHED HIS CHAMPION BEHEADED.
AND WHO'S LIKELY TO LOSE A THIRD OF HIS LANDS IN THE BARGAIN.
HE KNOWS SOMETHING, FOR SO BOLD AN OFFER.
HIS SCOUTS HAVE SEEN WHAT OURS HAVE.
IT MATTERS LITTLE. THE DIE IS CAST.
SADDLE THE KEY PRISONERS. WE RIDE, NOW.
I WANT TO BE HOME AND BACK BEFORE THE COMING OF BLESSED NIGHT.

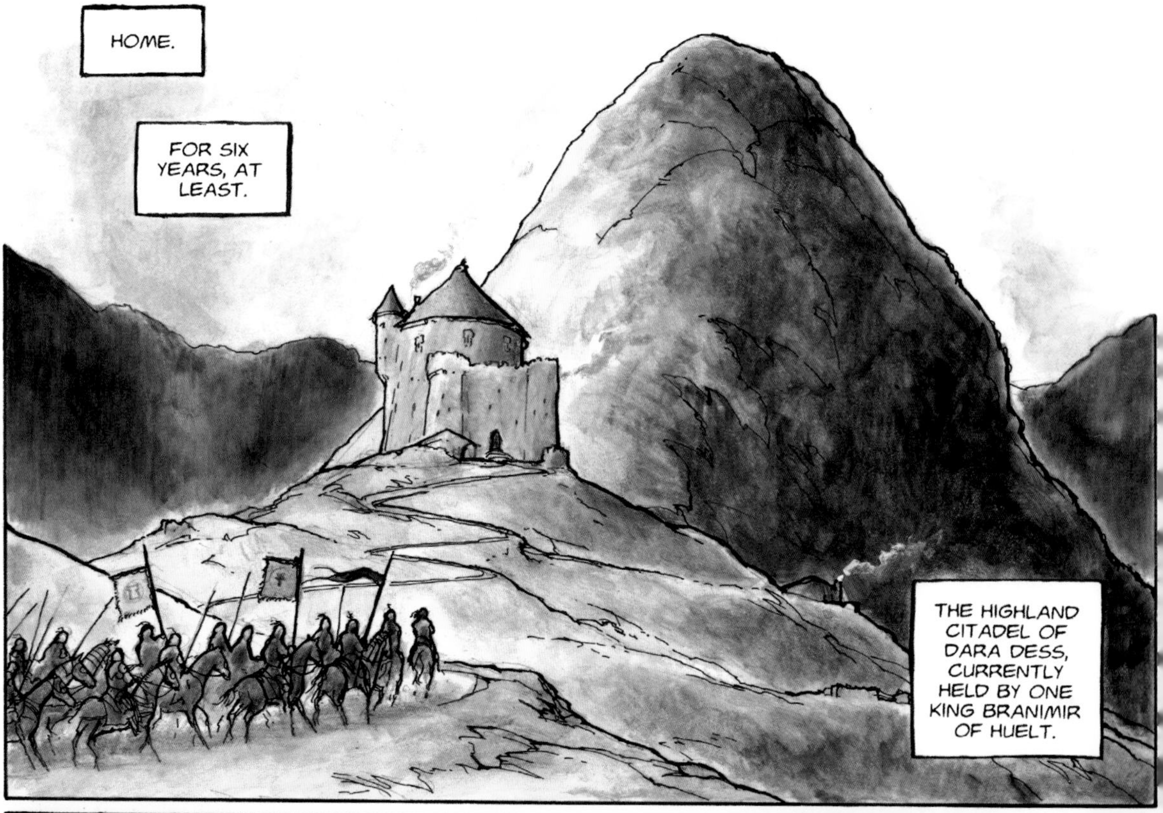
HOME.
FOR SIX YEARS, AT LEAST.
THE HIGHLAND CITADEL OF DARA DESS, CURRENTLY HELD BY ONE KING BRANIMIR OF HUELT.

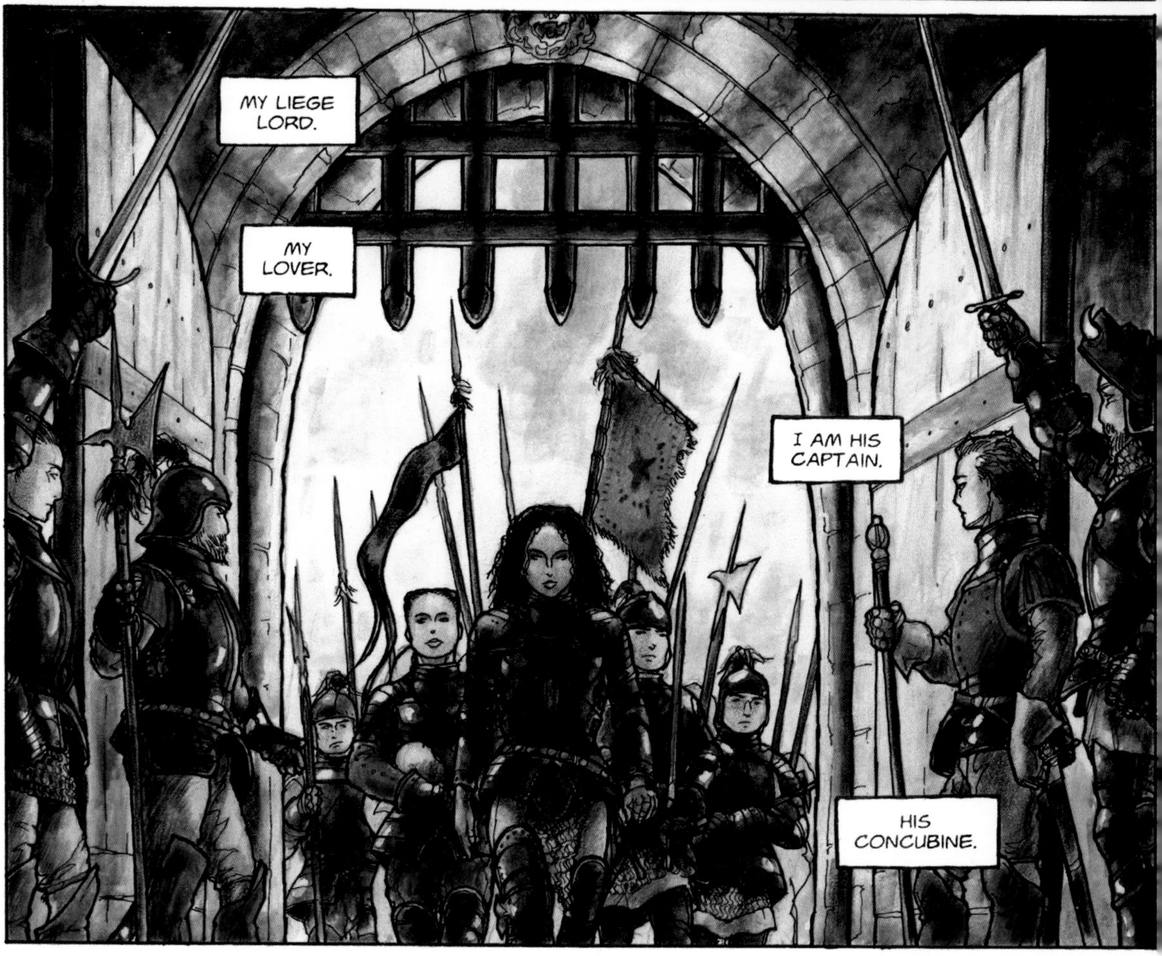
MY LIEGE LORD.
MY LOVER.
I AM HIS CAPTAIN.
HIS CONCUBINE.

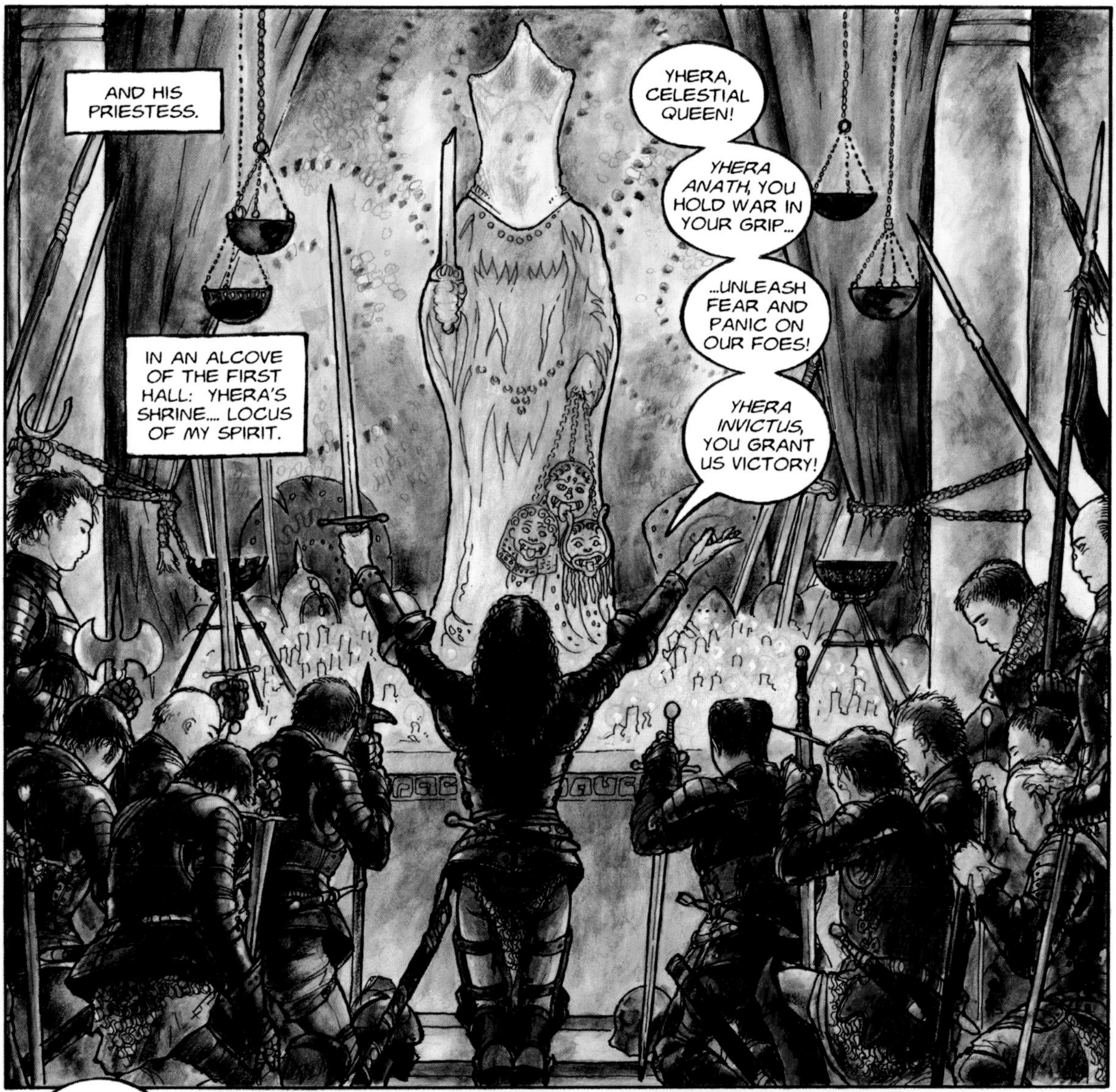
AND HIS PRIESTESS.
IN AN ALCOVE OF THE FIRST HALL: YHERA'S SHRINE.... LOCUS OF MY SPIRIT.
YHERA, CELESTIAL QUEEN!
YHERA ANATH, YOU HOLD WAR IN YOUR GRIP...
...UNLEASH FEAR AND PANIC ON OUR FOES!
YHERA INVICTUS, YOU GRANT US VICTORY!

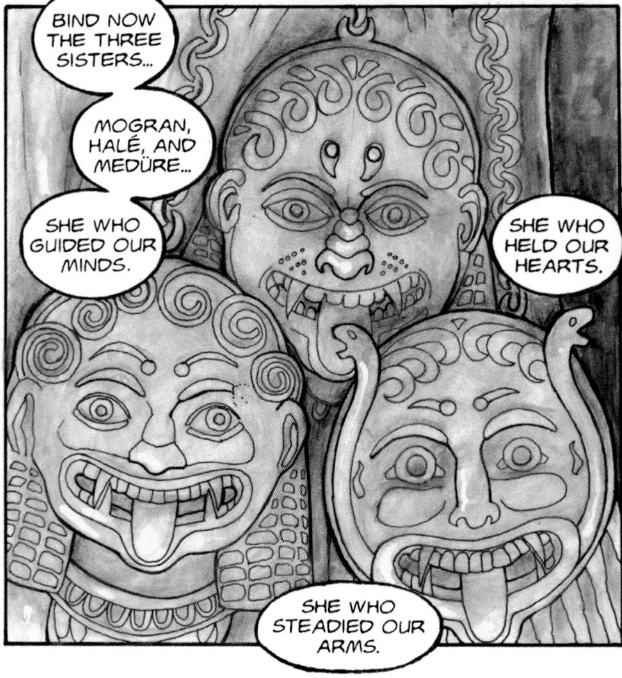
BIND NOW THE THREE SISTERS...
MOGRAN, HALÉ, AND MEDÜRE...
SHE WHO GUIDED OUR MINDS.
SHE WHO HELD OUR HEARTS.
SHE WHO STEADIED OUR ARMS.

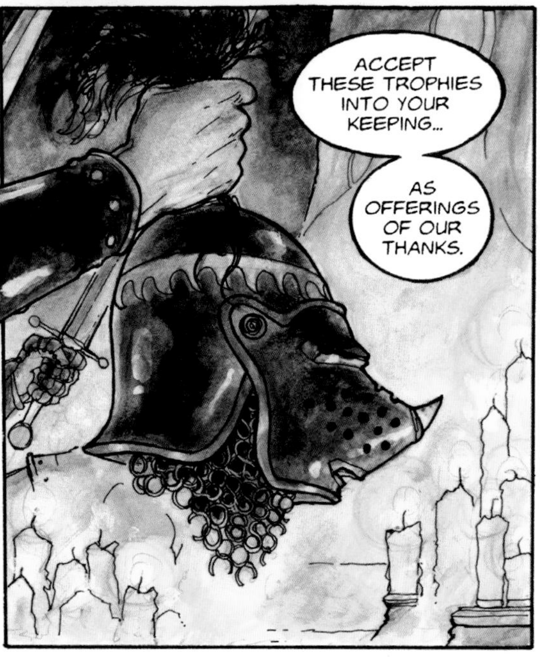
ACCEPT THESE TROPHIES INTO YOUR KEEPING...
AS OFFERINGS OF OUR THANKS.

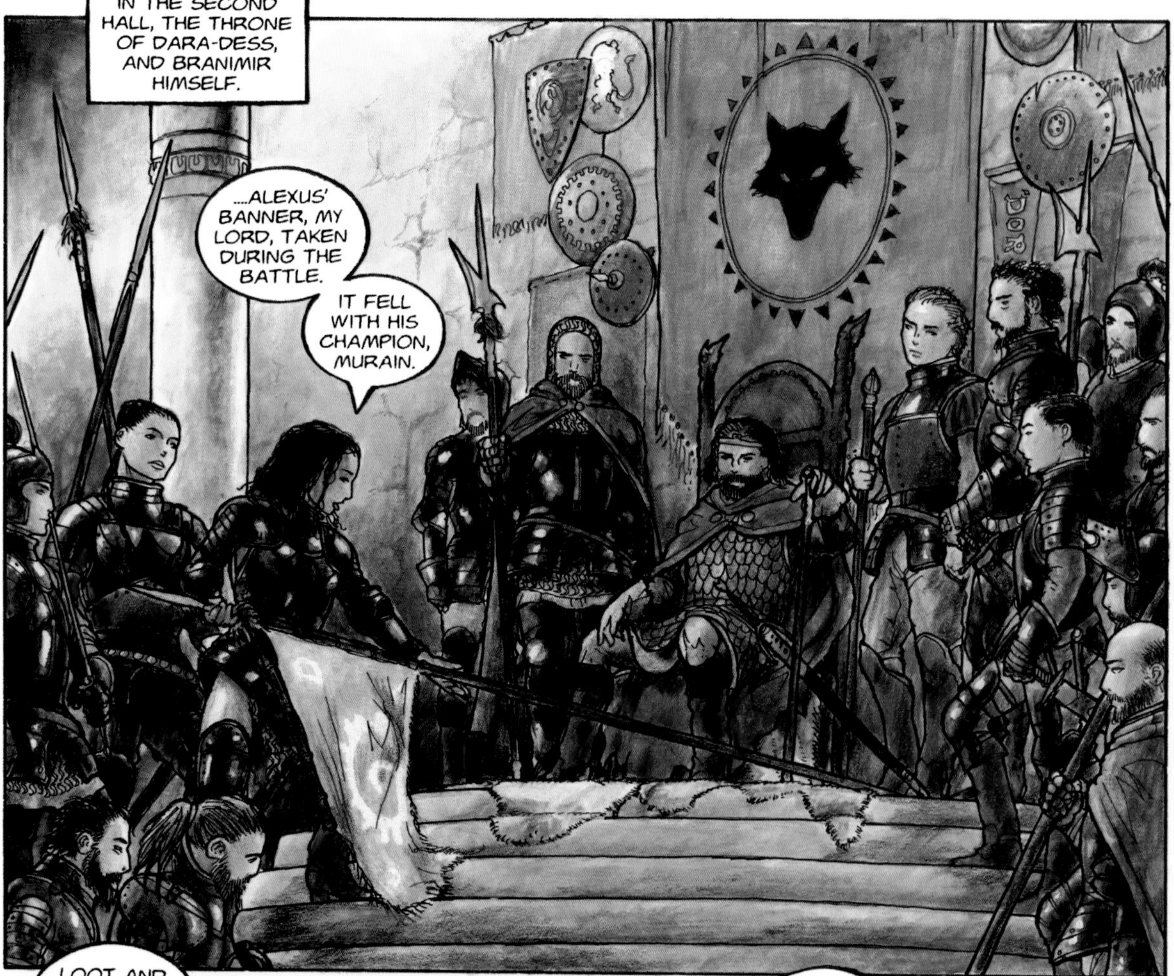
IN THE SECOND HALL, THE THRONE OF DARA-DESS, AND BRANIMIR HIMSELF.
....ALEXUS' BANNER, MY LORD, TAKEN DURING THE BATTLE.
IT FELL WITH HIS CHAMPION, MURAIN.

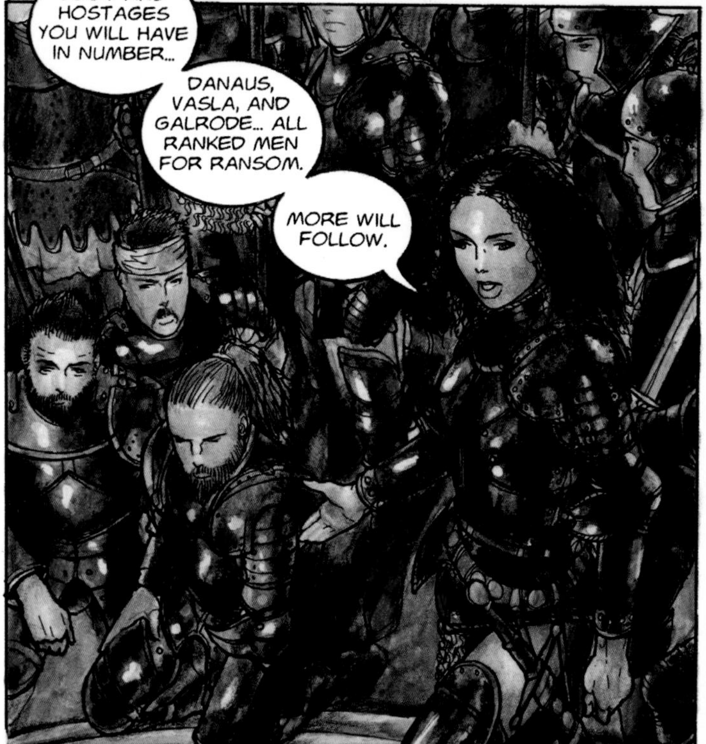
LOOT AND HOSTAGES YOU WILL HAVE IN NUMBER...
DANAUS, VASLA, AND GALRODE... ALL RANKED MEN FOR RANSOM.
MORE WILL FOLLOW.

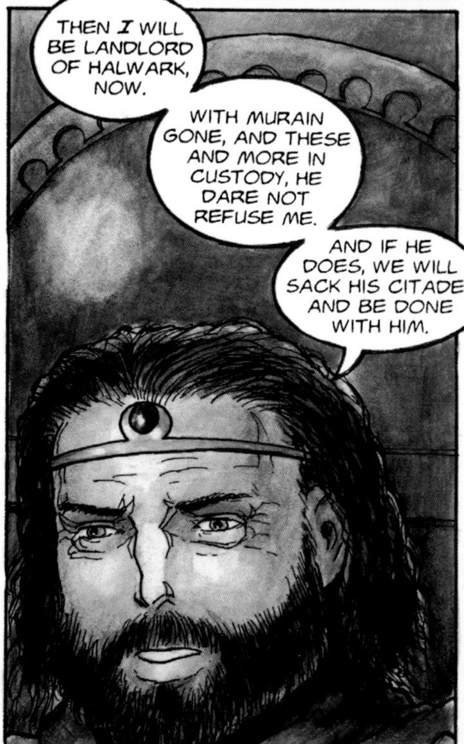
THEN *I* WILL BE LANDLORD OF HALWARK, NOW.
WITH MURAIN GONE, AND THESE AND MORE IN CUSTODY, HE DARE NOT REFUSE ME.
AND IF HE DOES, WE WILL SACK HIS CITADE AND BE DONE WITH HIM.

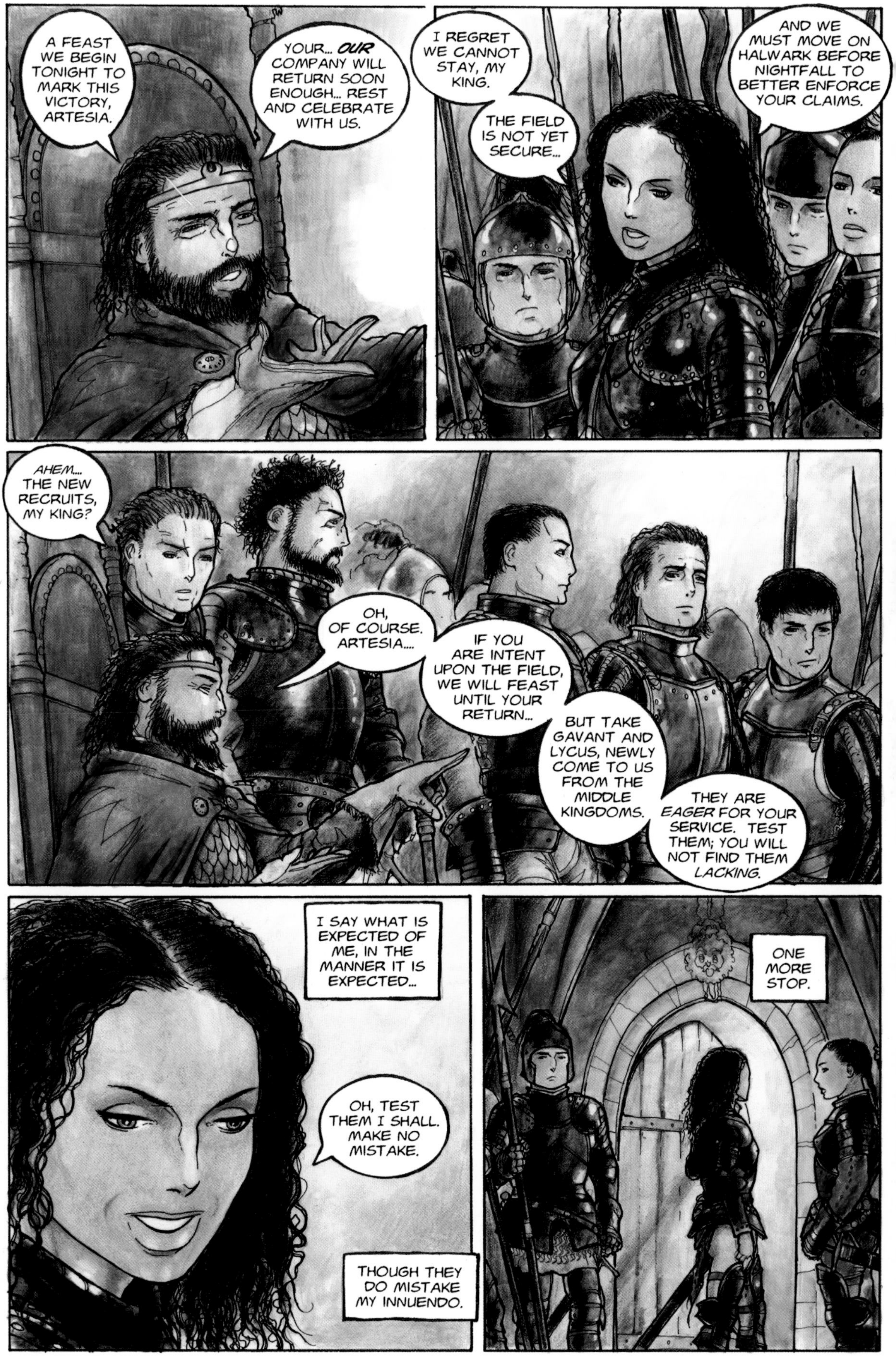
A FEAST WE BEGIN TONIGHT TO MARK THIS VICTORY, ARTESIA.
YOUR... OUR COMPANY WILL RETURN SOON ENOUGH... REST AND CELEBRATE WITH US.
I REGRET WE CANNOT STAY, MY KING.
THE FIELD IS NOT YET SECURE...
AND WE MUST MOVE ON HALWARK BEFORE NIGHTFALL TO BETTER ENFORCE YOUR CLAIMS.
AHEM.... THE NEW RECRUITS, MY KING?
OH, OF COURSE. ARTESIA....
IF YOU ARE INTENT UPON THE FIELD, WE WILL FEAST UNTIL YOUR RETURN...
BUT TAKE GAVANT AND LYCUS, NEWLY COME TO US FROM THE MIDDLE KINGDOMS.
THEY ARE EAGER FOR YOUR SERVICE. TEST THEM; YOU WILL NOT FIND THEM LACKING.
I SAY WHAT IS EXPECTED OF ME, IN THE MANNER IT IS EXPECTED...
OH, TEST THEM I SHALL. MAKE NO MISTAKE.
THOUGH THEY DO MISTAKE MY INNUENDO.
ONE MORE STOP.

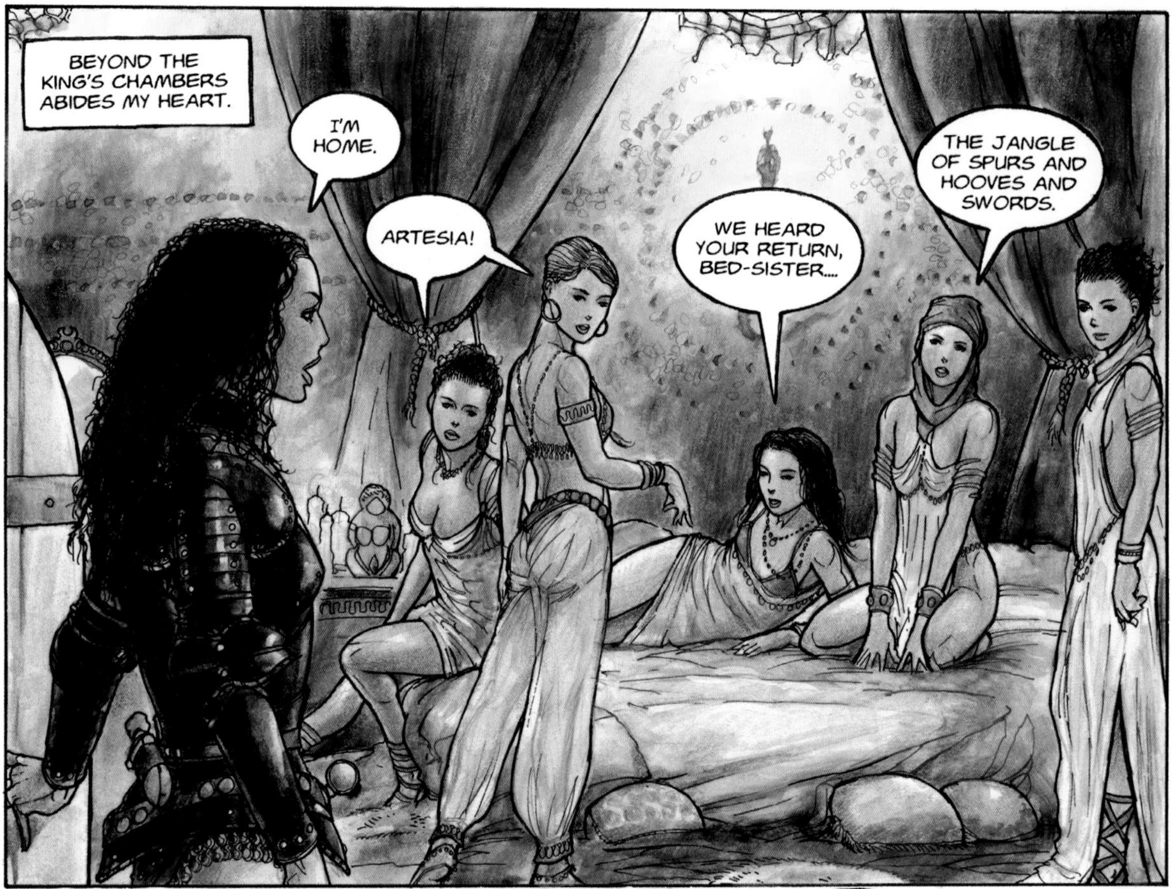
BEYOND THE KING'S CHAMBERS ABIDES MY HEART.
I'M HOME.
ARTESIA!
WE HEARD YOUR RETURN, BED-SISTER....
THE JANGLE OF SPURS AND HOOVES AND SWORDS.

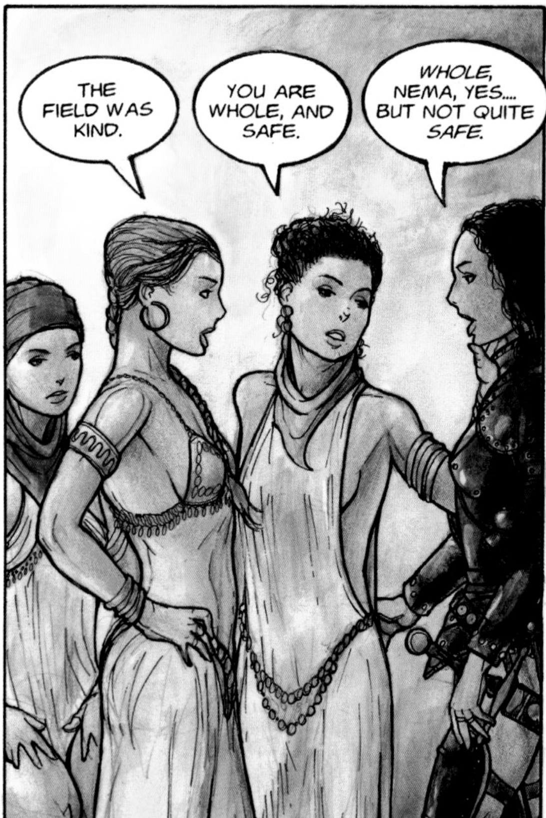
THE FIELD WAS KIND.
YOU ARE WHOLE, AND SAFE.
WHOLE, NEMA, YES.... BUT NOT QUITE SAFE.

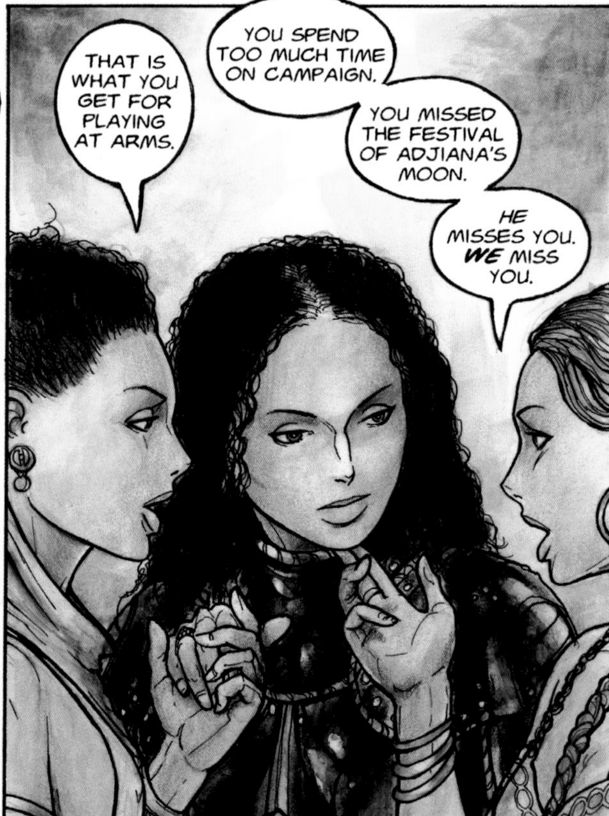
THAT IS WHAT YOU GET FOR PLAYING AT ARMS.
YOU SPEND TOO MUCH TIME ON CAMPAIGN.
YOU MISSED THE FESTIVAL OF ADJIANA'S MOON.
HE MISSES YOU. WE MISS YOU.

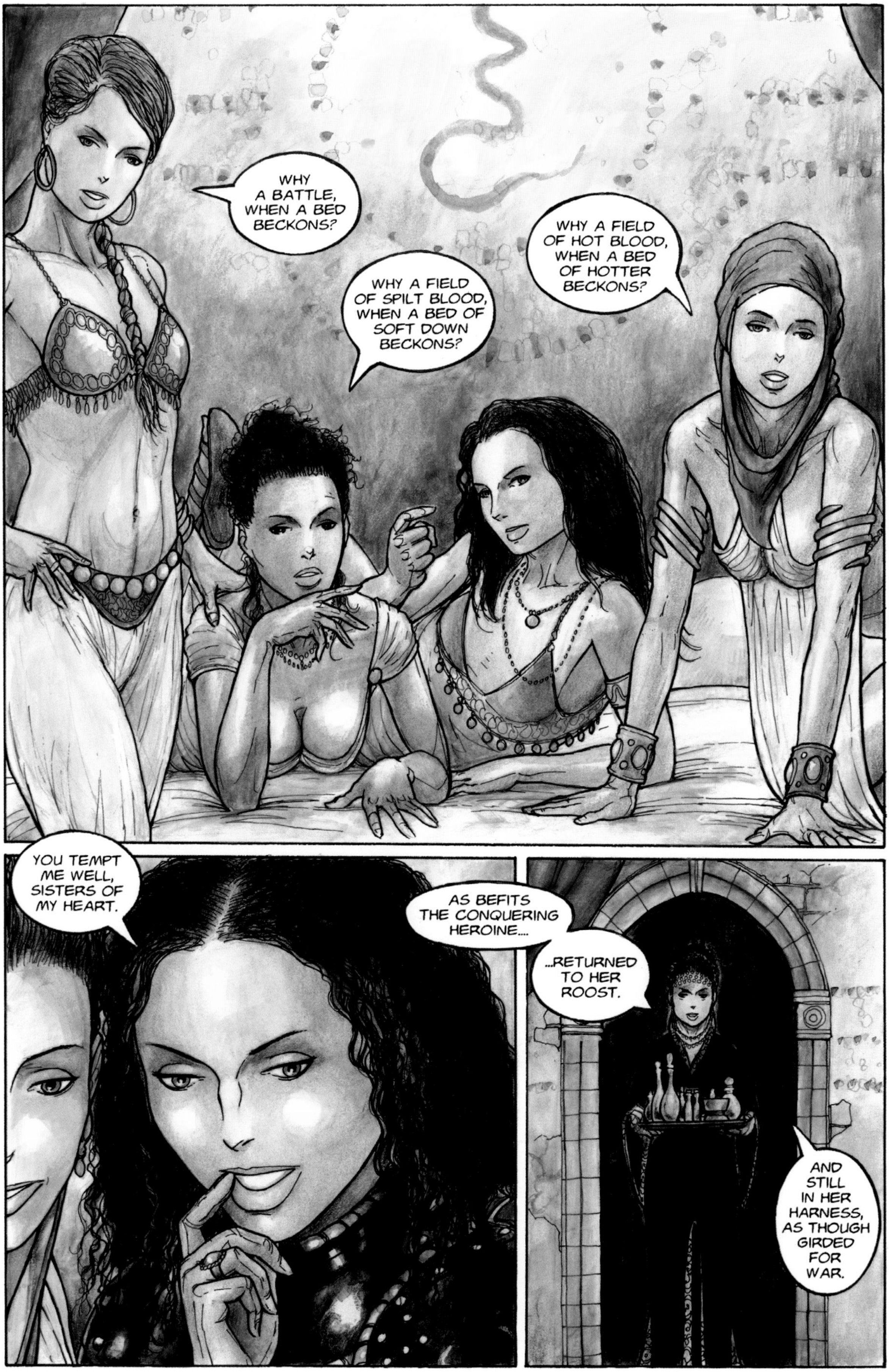
WHY A BATTLE, WHEN A BED BECKONS?
WHY A FIELD OF SPILT BLOOD, WHEN A BED OF SOFT DOWN BECKONS?
WHY A FIELD OF HOT BLOOD, WHEN A BED OF HOTTER BECKONS?
YOU TEMPT ME WELL, SISTERS OF MY HEART.
AS BEFITS THE CONQUERING HEROINE....
...RETURNED TO HER ROOST.
AND STILL IN HER HARNESS, AS THOUGH GIRDED FOR WAR.

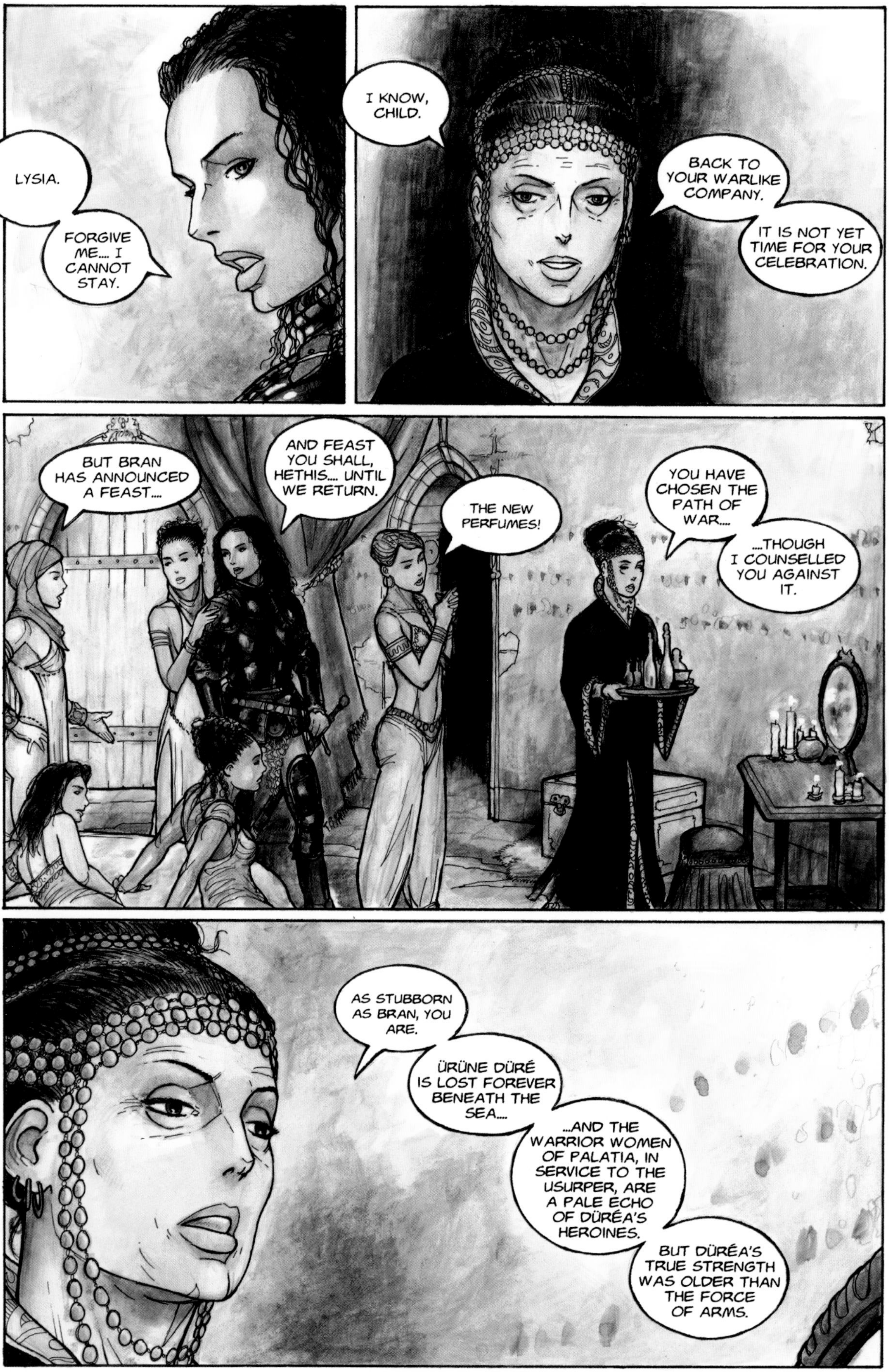
LYSIA.
FORGIVE ME.... I CANNOT STAY.
I KNOW, CHILD.
BACK TO YOUR WARLIKE COMPANY.
IT IS NOT YET TIME FOR YOUR CELEBRATION.
BUT BRAN HAS ANNOUNCED A FEAST....
AND FEAST YOU SHALL, HETHIS.... UNTIL WE RETURN.
THE NEW PERFUMES!
YOU HAVE CHOSEN THE PATH OF WAR....
....THOUGH I COUNSELLED YOU AGAINST IT.
AS STUBBORN AS BRAN, YOU ARE.
ÜRÜNE DÜRÉ IS LOST FOREVER BENEATH THE SEA....
...AND THE WARRIOR WOMEN OF PALATIA, IN SERVICE TO THE USURPER, ARE A PALE ECHO OF DÜRÉA'S HEROINES.
BUT DÜRÉA'S TRUE STRENGTH WAS OLDER THAN THE FORCE OF ARMS.

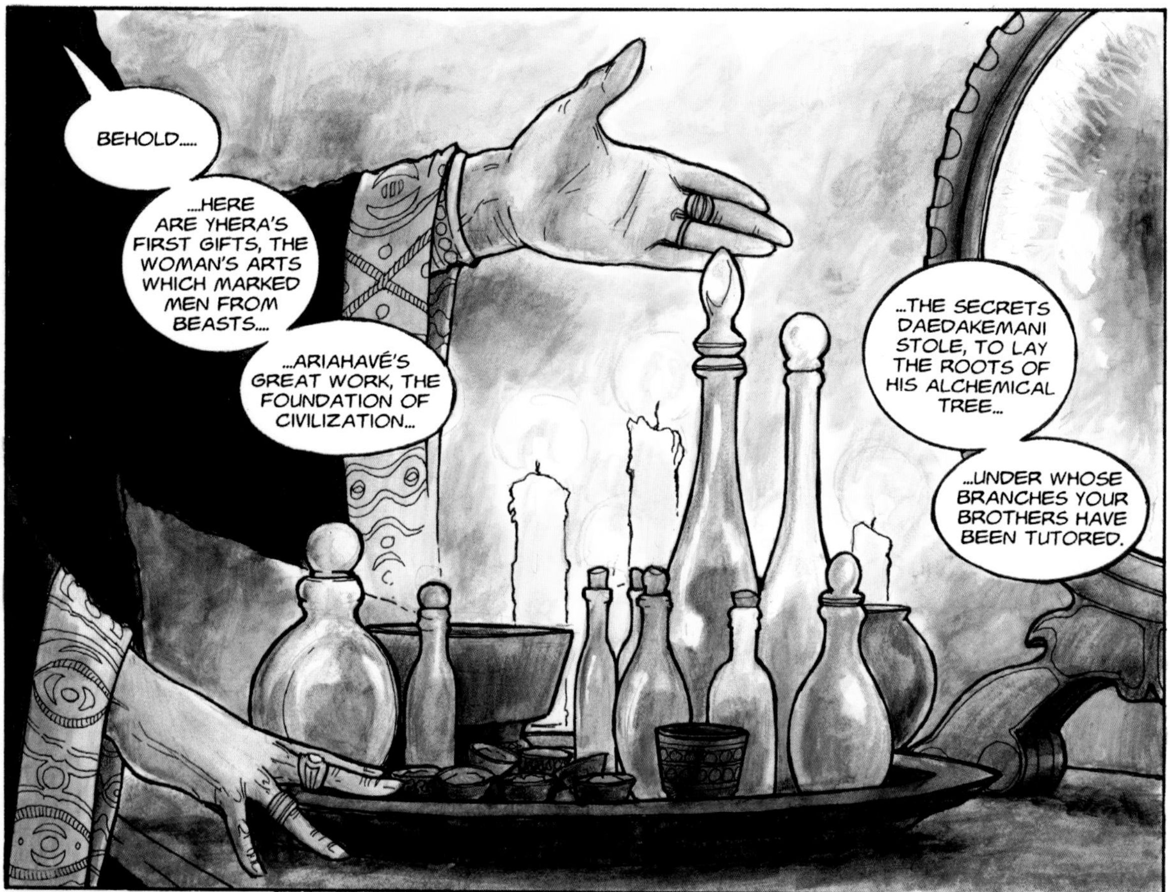
BEHOLD.....
...HERE ARE YHERA'S FIRST GIFTS, THE WOMAN'S ARTS WHICH MARKED MEN FROM BEASTS....
...ARIAHAVÉ'S GREAT WORK, THE FOUNDATION OF CIVILIZATION...
...THE SECRETS DAEDAKEMANI STOLE, TO LAY THE ROOTS OF HIS ALCHEMICAL TREE...
...UNDER WHOSE BRANCHES YOUR BROTHERS HAVE BEEN TUTORED.

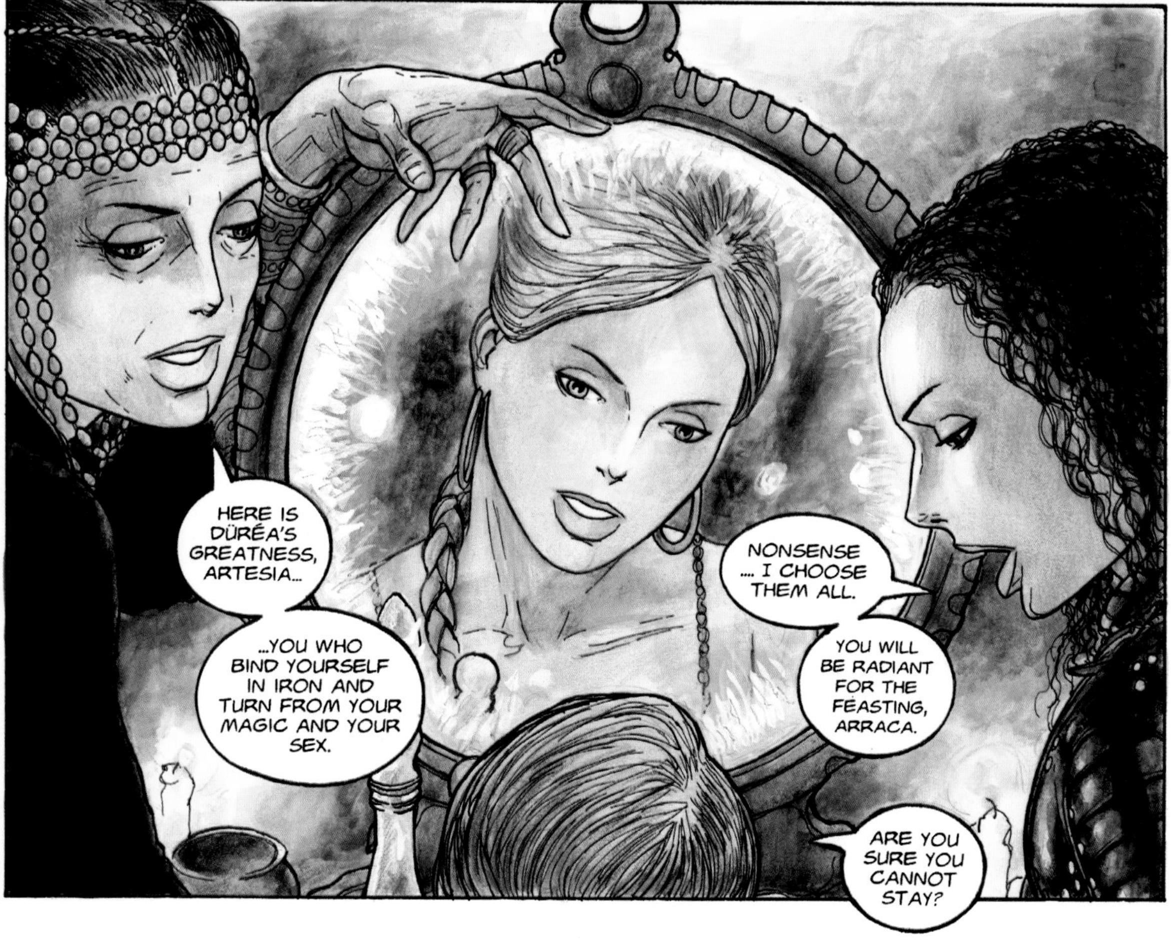
HERE IS DÜRÉA'S GREATNESS, ARTESIA...
...YOU WHO BIND YOURSELF IN IRON AND TURN FROM YOUR MAGIC AND YOUR SEX.
NONSENSE .... I CHOOSE THEM ALL.
YOU WILL BE RADIANT FOR THE FEASTING, ARRACA.
ARE YOU SURE YOU CANNOT STAY?

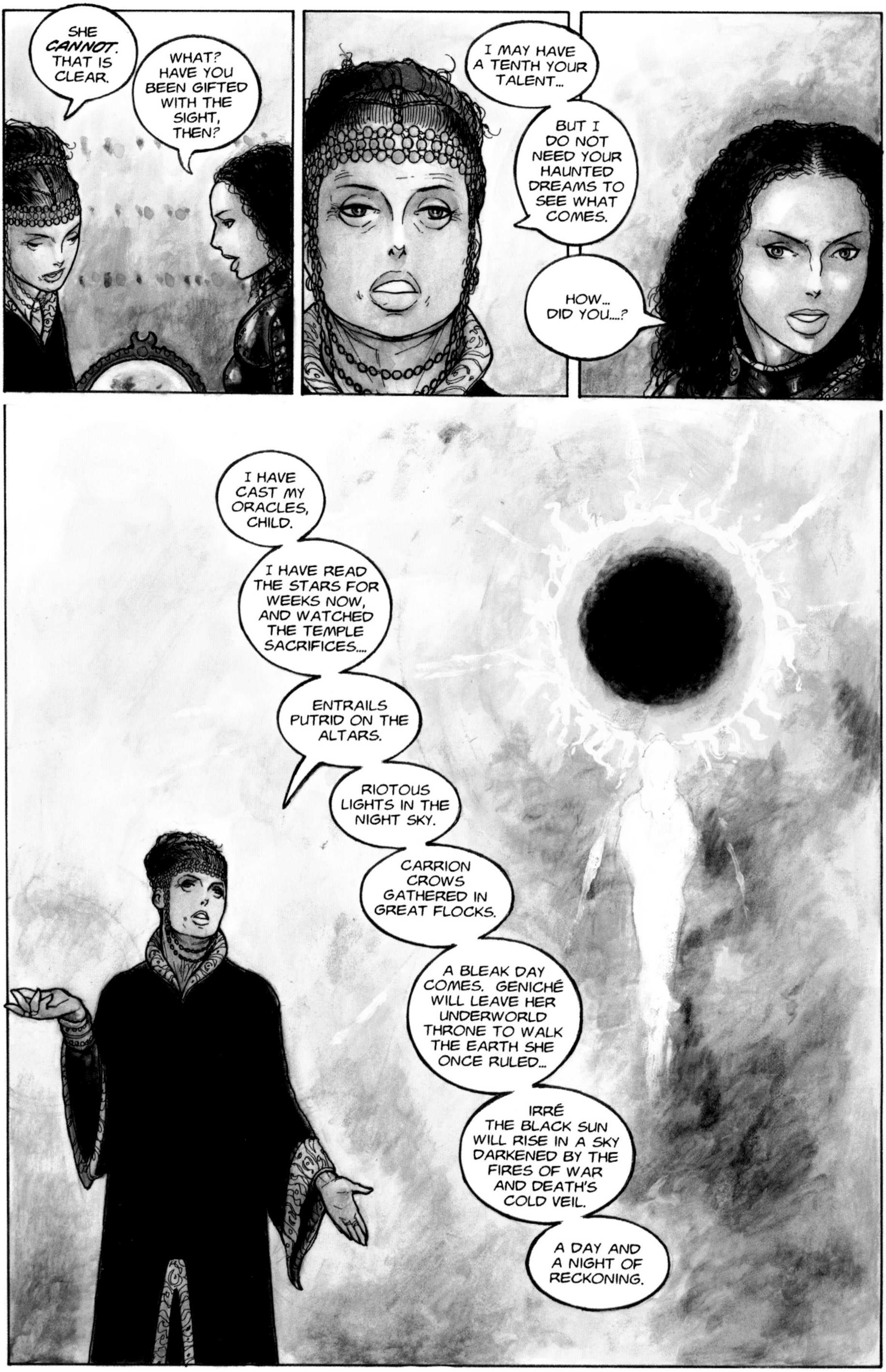
SHE *CANNOT.* THAT IS CLEAR.
WHAT? HAVE YOU BEEN GIFTED WITH THE SIGHT, THEN?
I MAY HAVE A TENTH YOUR TALENT...
BUT I DO NOT NEED YOUR HAUNTED DREAMS TO SEE WHAT COMES.
HOW... DID YOU....?
I HAVE CAST MY ORACLES, CHILD.
I HAVE READ THE STARS FOR WEEKS NOW, AND WATCHED THE TEMPLE SACRIFICES....
ENTRAILS PUTRID ON THE ALTARS.
RIOTOUS LIGHTS IN THE NIGHT SKY.
CARRION CROWS GATHERED IN GREAT FLOCKS.
A BLEAK DAY COMES. GENICHÉ WILL LEAVE HER UNDERWORLD THRONE TO WALK THE EARTH SHE ONCE RULED...
IRRÉ THE BLACK SUN WILL RISE IN A SKY DARKENED BY THE FIRES OF WAR AND DEATH'S COLD VEIL.
A DAY AND A NIGHT OF RECKONING.

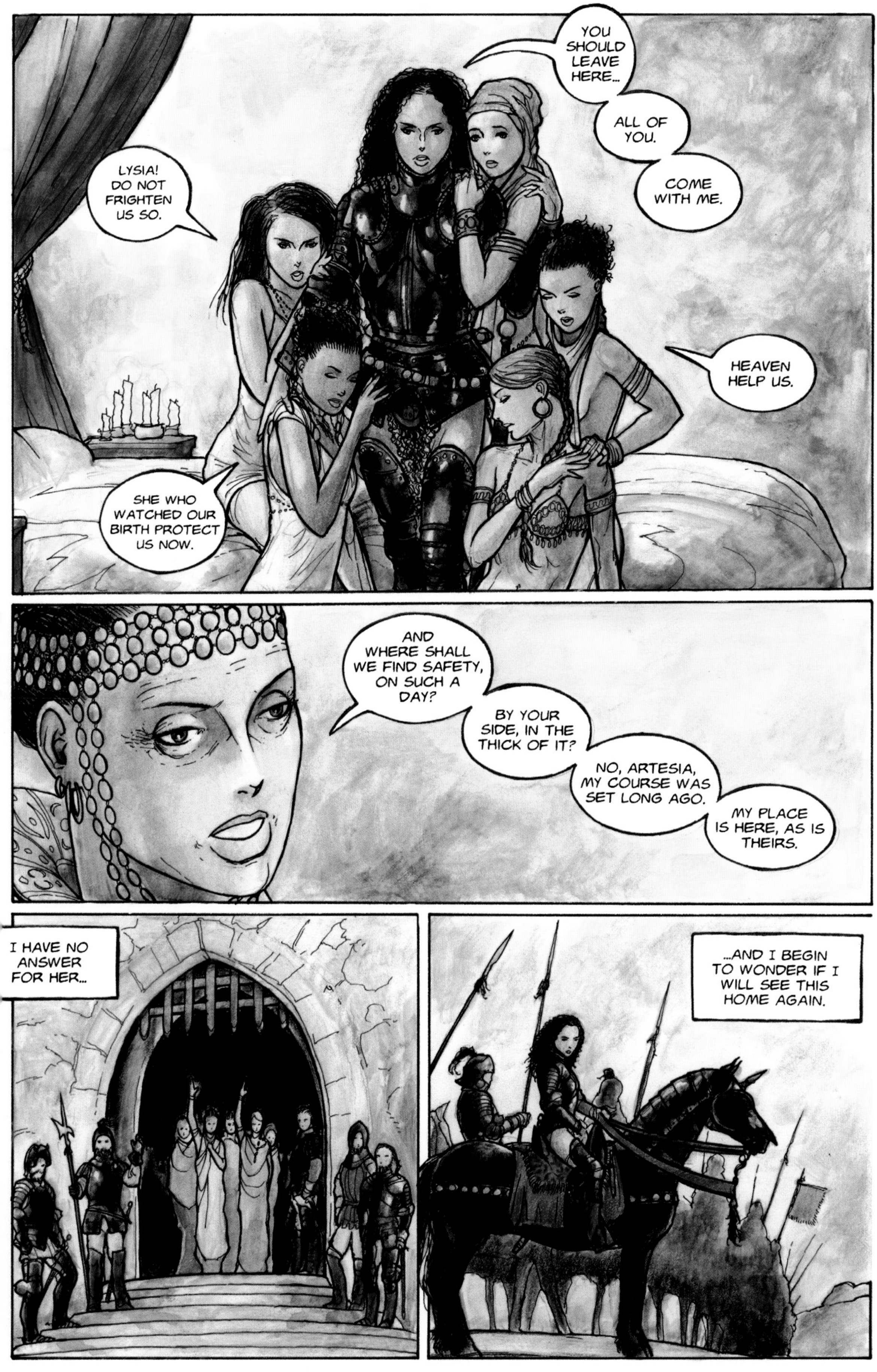
YOU SHOULD LEAVE HERE...
ALL OF YOU.
COME WITH ME.
LYSIA! DO NOT FRIGHTEN US SO.
HEAVEN HELP US.
SHE WHO WATCHED OUR BIRTH PROTECT US NOW.
AND WHERE SHALL WE FIND SAFETY, ON SUCH A DAY?
BY YOUR SIDE, IN THE THICK OF IT?
NO, ARTESIA, MY COURSE WAS SET LONG AGO.
MY PLACE IS HERE, AS IS THEIRS.
I HAVE NO ANSWER FOR HER...
...AND I BEGIN TO WONDER IF I WILL SEE THIS HOME AGAIN.

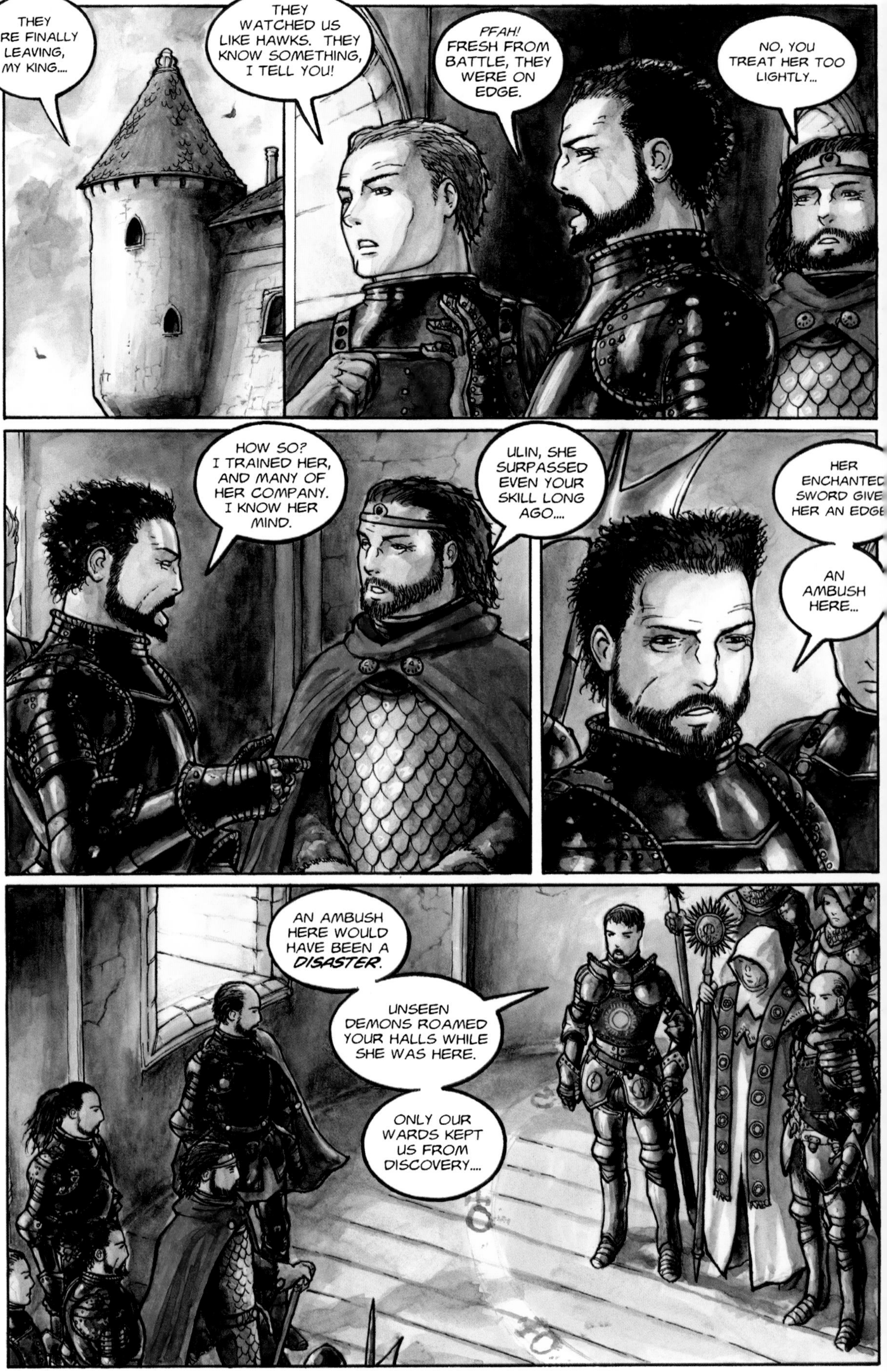
THEY ARE FINALLY LEAVING, MY KING....
THEY WATCHED US LIKE HAWKS. THEY KNOW SOMETHING, I TELL YOU!
PFAH! FRESH FROM BATTLE, THEY WERE ON EDGE.
NO, YOU TREAT HER TOO LIGHTLY...
HOW SO? I TRAINED HER, AND MANY OF HER COMPANY. I KNOW HER MIND.
ULIN, SHE SURPASSED EVEN YOUR SKILL LONG AGO....
HER ENCHANTED SWORD GIVE HER AN EDGE
AN AMBUSH HERE...
AN AMBUSH HERE WOULD HAVE BEEN A ***DISASTER***.
UNSEEN DEMONS ROAMED YOUR HALLS WHILE SHE WAS HERE.
ONLY OUR WARDS KEPT US FROM DISCOVERY....

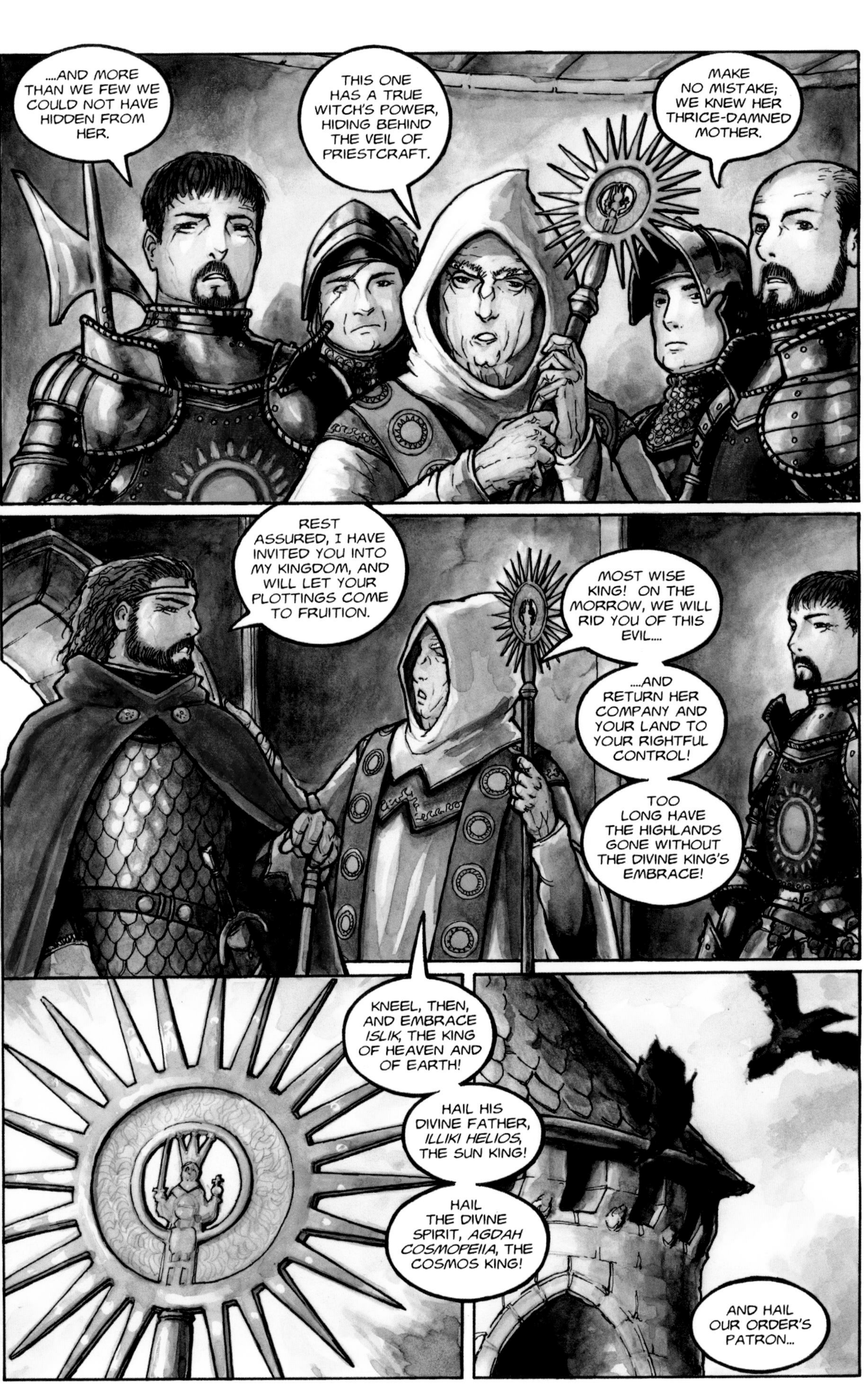
....AND MORE THAN WE FEW WE COULD NOT HAVE HIDDEN FROM HER.
THIS ONE HAS A TRUE WITCH'S POWER, HIDING BEHIND THE VEIL OF PRIESTCRAFT.
MAKE NO MISTAKE; WE KNEW HER THRICE-DAMNED MOTHER.
REST ASSURED, I HAVE INVITED YOU INTO MY KINGDOM, AND WILL LET YOUR PLOTTINGS COME TO FRUITION.
MOST WISE KING! ON THE MORROW, WE WILL RID YOU OF THIS EVIL....
....AND RETURN HER COMPANY AND YOUR LAND TO YOUR RIGHTFUL CONTROL!
TOO LONG HAVE THE HIGHLANDS GONE WITHOUT THE DIVINE KING'S EMBRACE!
KNEEL, THEN, AND EMBRACE *ISLIK*, THE KING OF HEAVEN AND OF EARTH!
HAIL HIS DIVINE FATHER, *ILLIKI HELIOS*, THE SUN KING!
HAIL THE DIVINE SPIRIT, *AGDAH COSMOPEIIA*, THE COSMOS KING!
AND HAIL OUR ORDER'S PATRON...

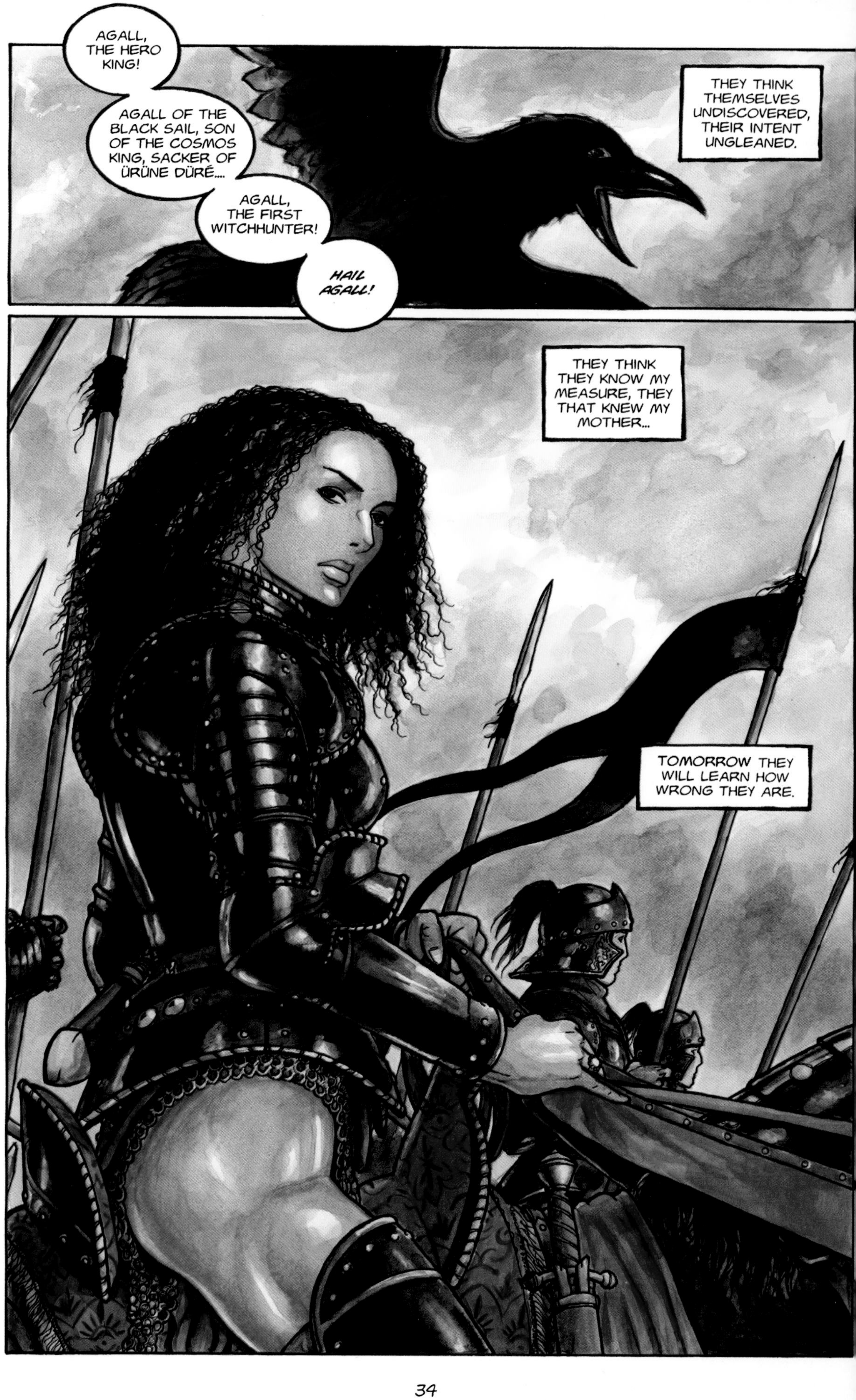
AGALL, THE HERO KING!
AGALL OF THE BLACK SAIL, SON OF THE COSMOS KING, SACKER OF ÜRÜNE DÜRÉ....
AGALL, THE FIRST WITCHHUNTER!
HAIL AGALL!
THEY THINK THEMSELVES UNDISCOVERED, THEIR INTENT UNGLEANED.
THEY THINK THEY KNOW MY MEASURE, THEY THAT KNEW MY MOTHER...
TOMORROW THEY WILL LEARN HOW WRONG THEY ARE.

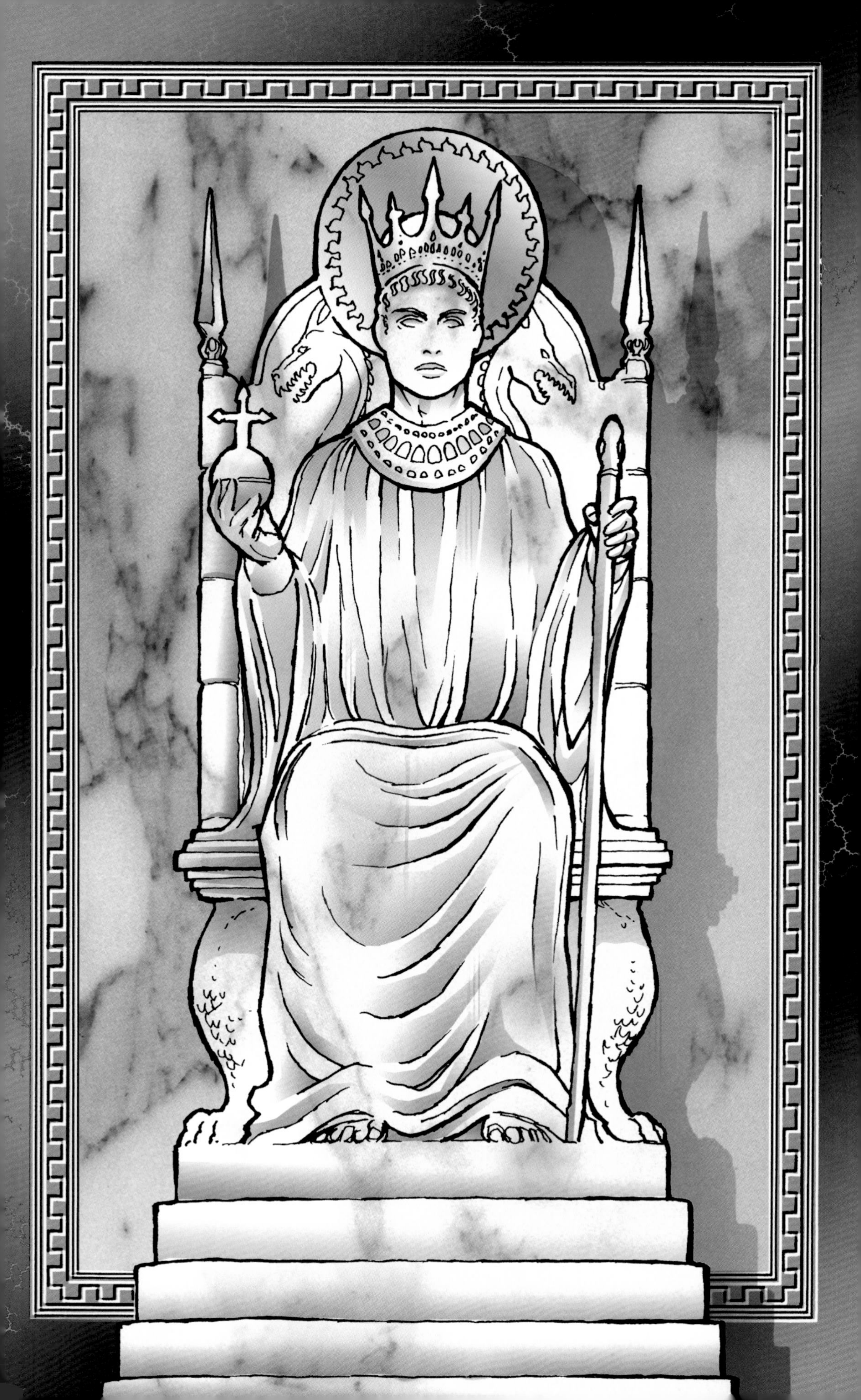

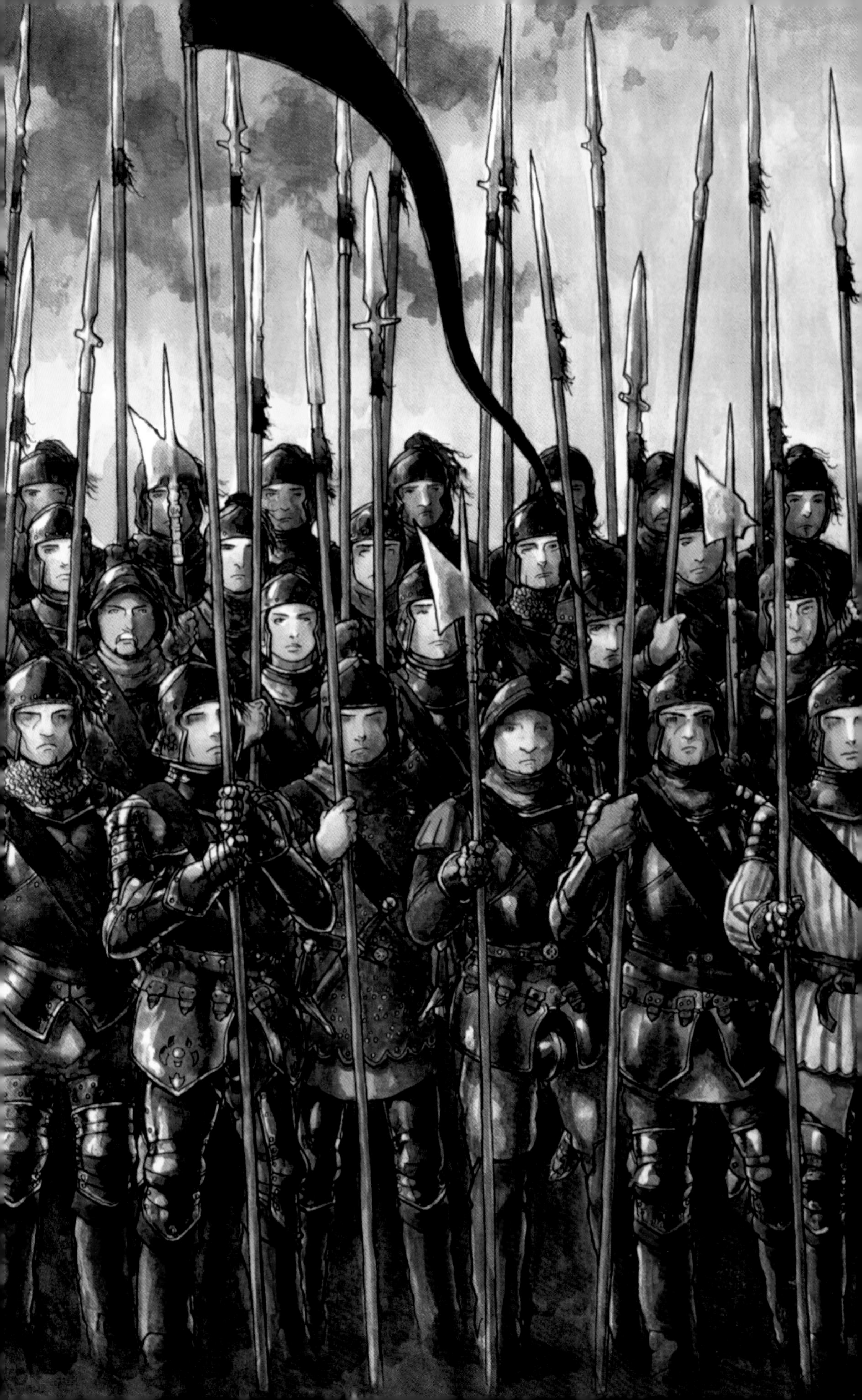

CHAPTER TWO

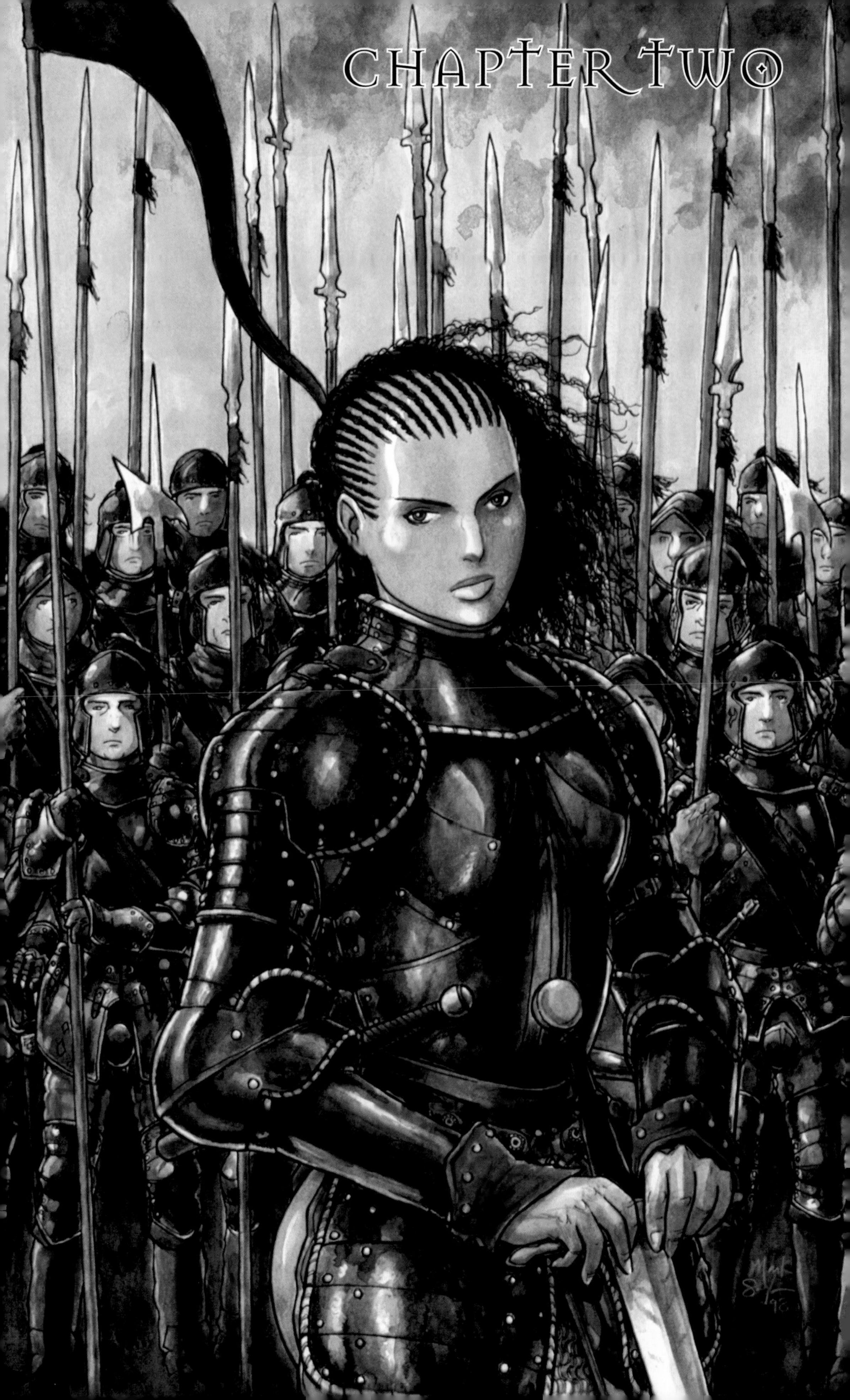

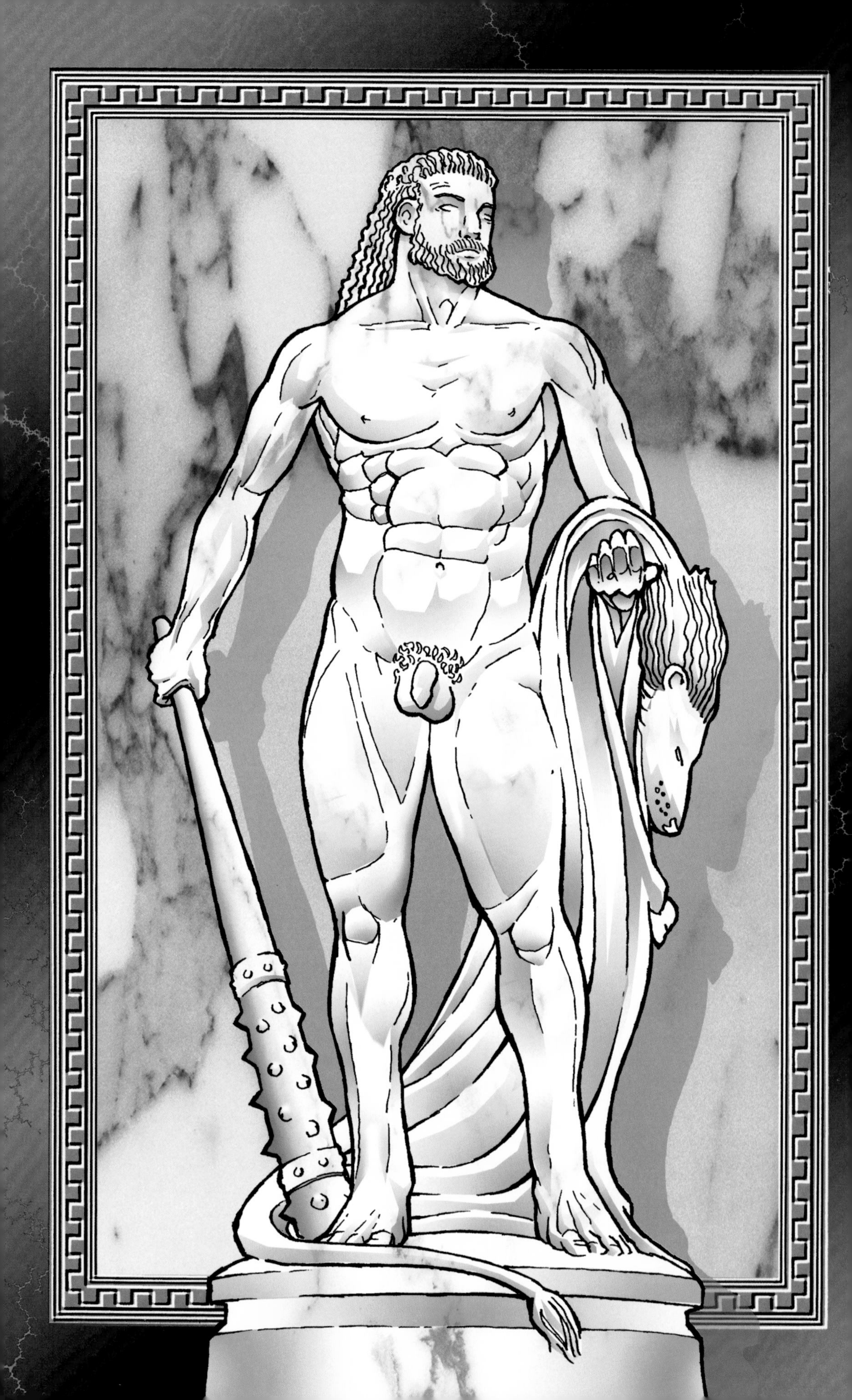

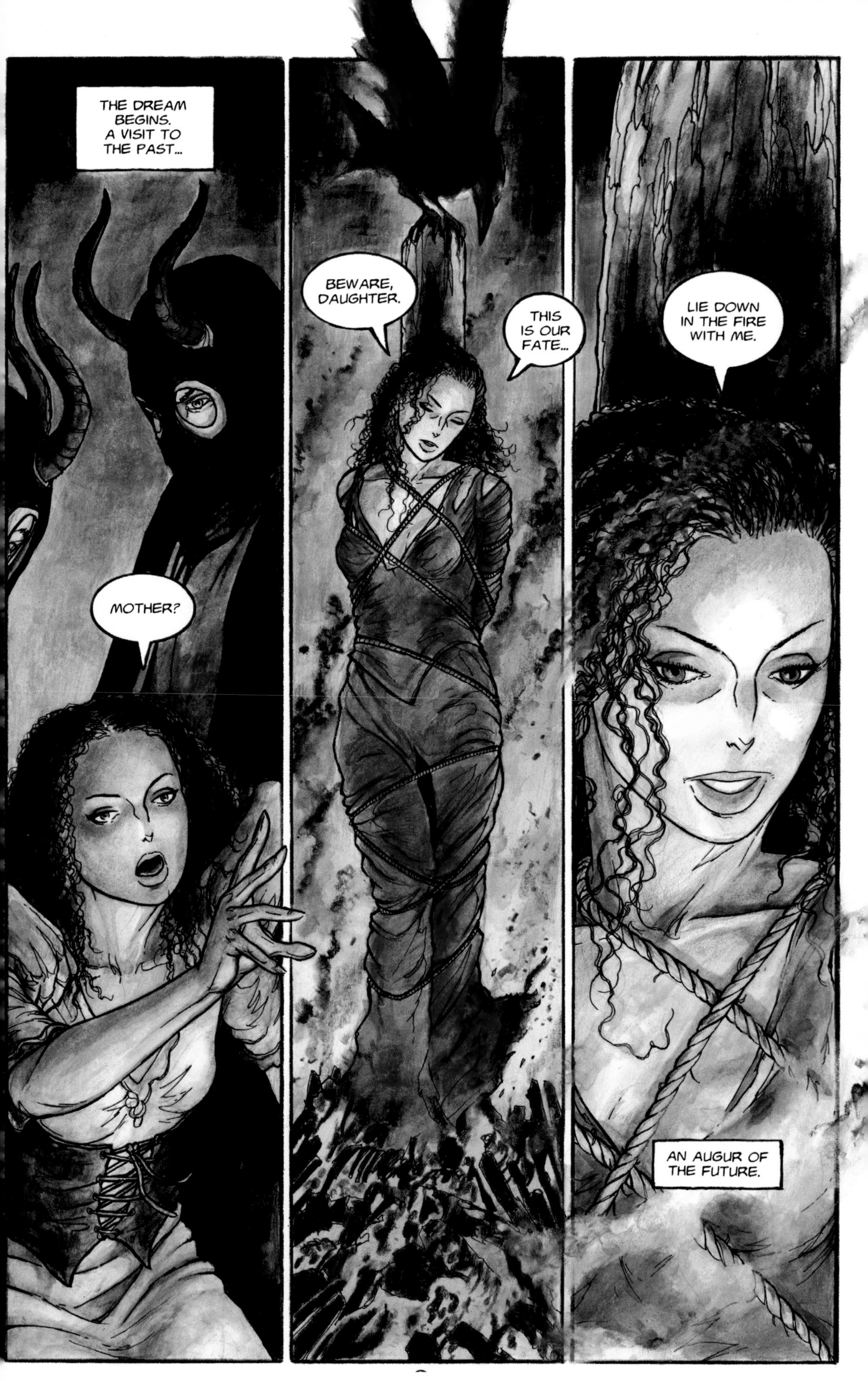
THE DREAM BEGINS. A VISIT TO THE PAST...
MOTHER?
BEWARE, DAUGHTER.
THIS IS OUR FATE...
LIE DOWN IN THE FIRE WITH ME.
AN AUGUR OF THE FUTURE.

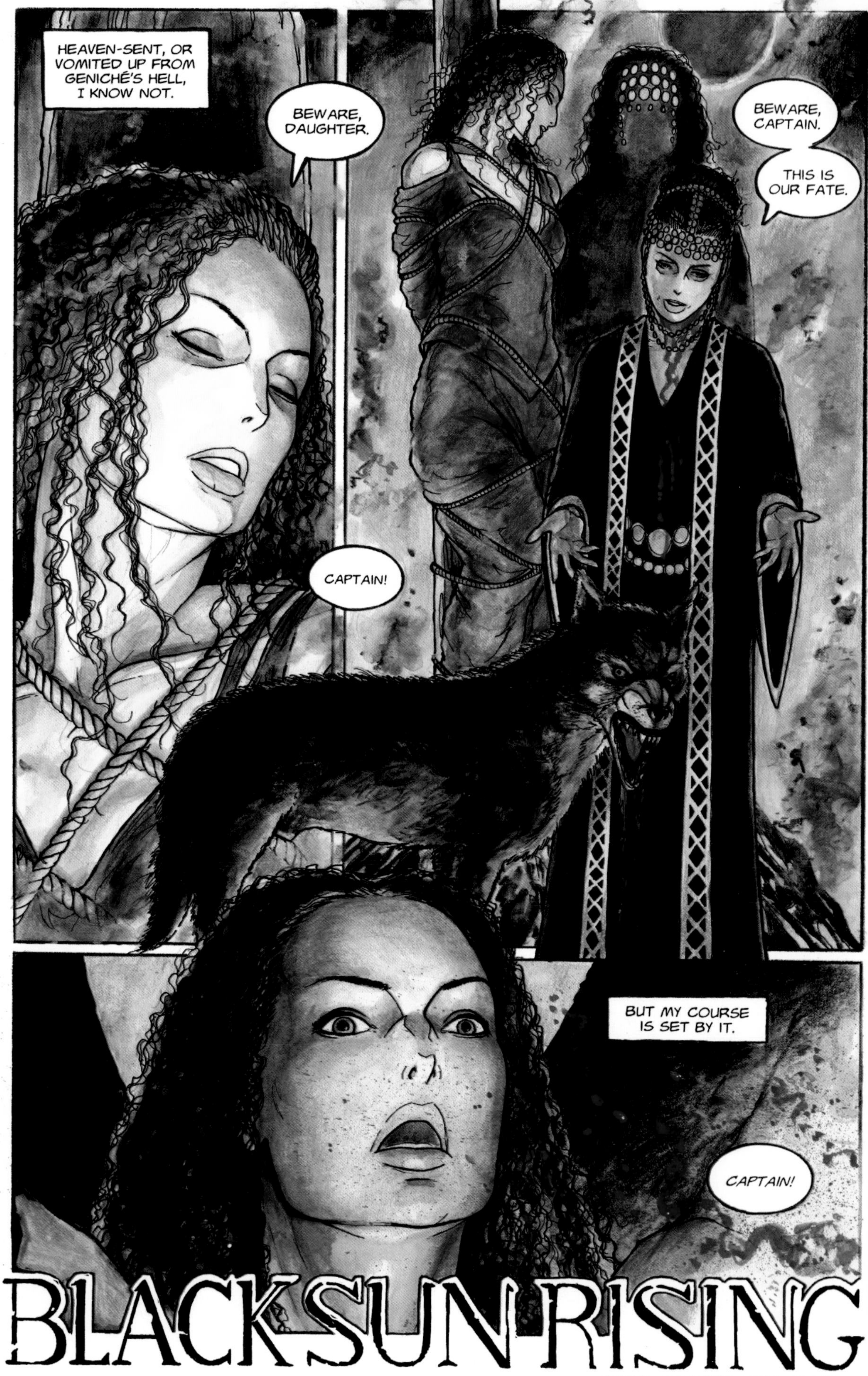
HEAVEN-SENT, OR VOMITED UP FROM GENICHÉ'S HELL, I KNOW NOT.
BEWARE, DAUGHTER.
BEWARE, CAPTAIN.
THIS IS OUR FATE.
CAPTAIN!
BUT MY COURSE IS SET BY IT.
CAPTAIN!
BLACK SUN RISING
STORY & ART © 1997 MARK SMYLIE

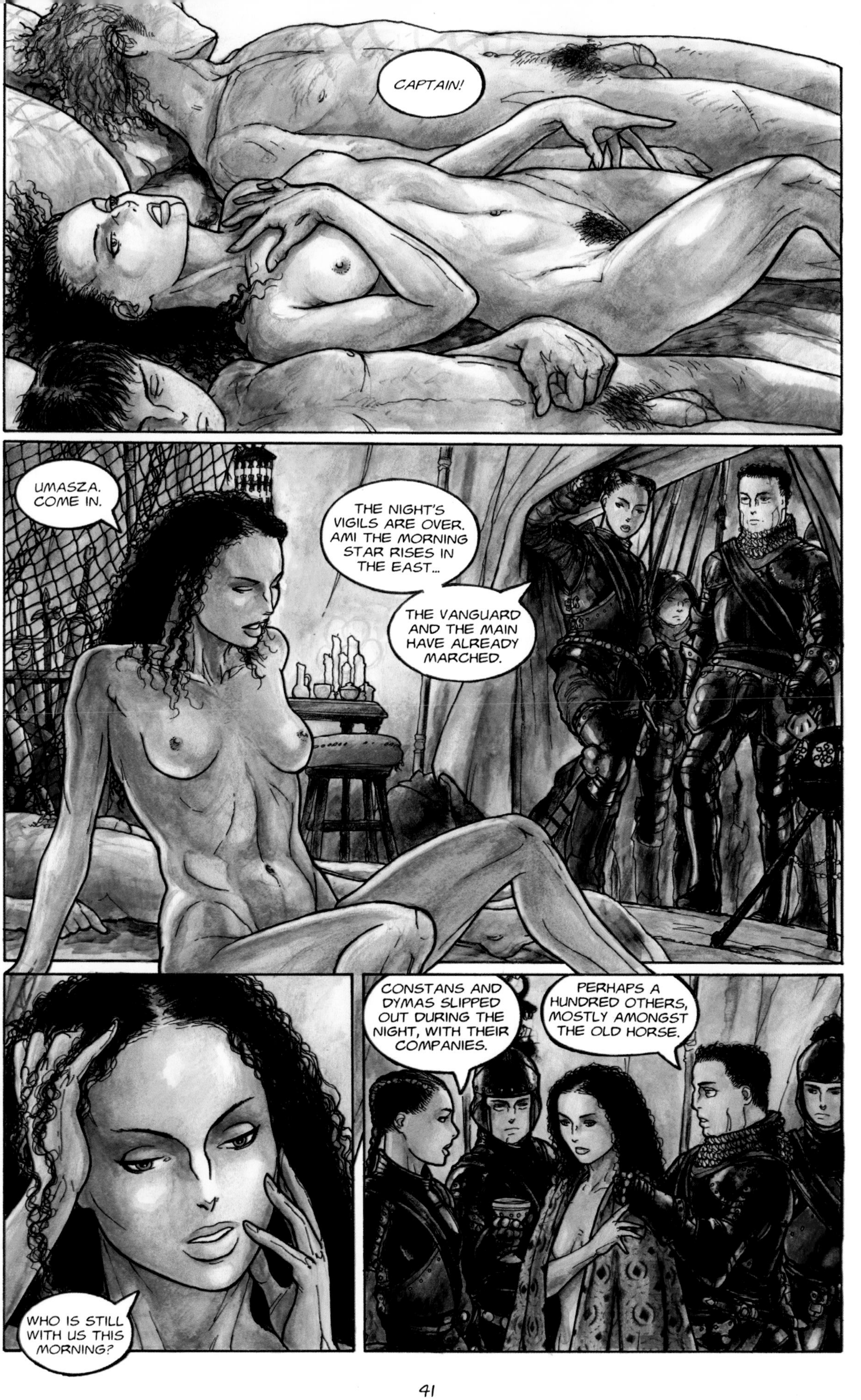
CAPTAIN!
UMASZA. COME IN.
THE NIGHT'S VIGILS ARE OVER. AMI THE MORNING STAR RISES IN THE EAST...
THE VANGUARD AND THE MAIN HAVE ALREADY MARCHED.
WHO IS STILL WITH US THIS MORNING?
CONSTANS AND DYMAS SLIPPED OUT DURING THE NIGHT, WITH THEIR COMPANIES.
PERHAPS A HUNDRED OTHERS, MOSTLY AMONGST THE OLD HORSE.

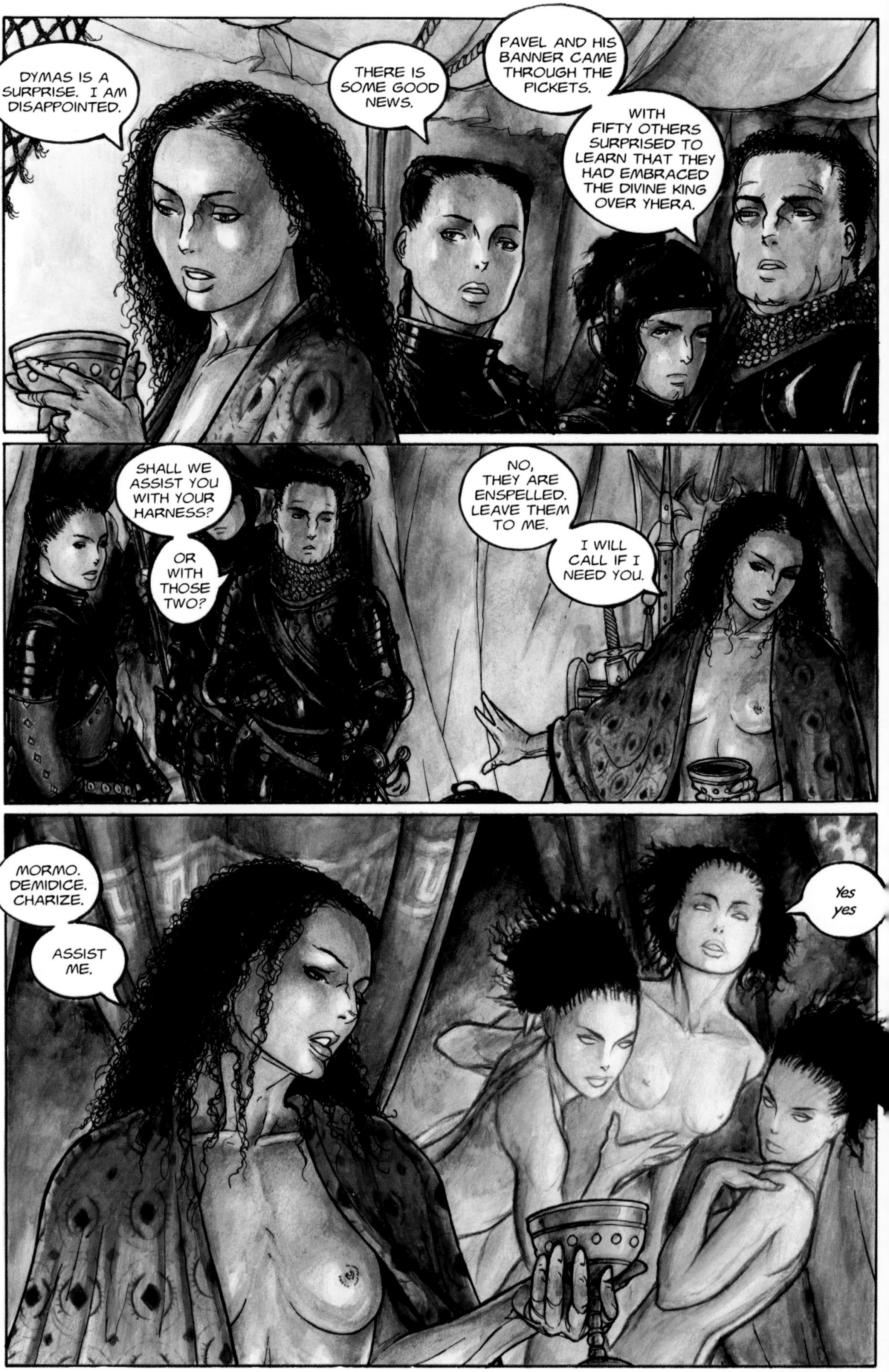
DYMAS IS A SURPRISE. I AM DISAPPOINTED.
THERE IS SOME GOOD NEWS.
PAVEL AND HIS BANNER CAME THROUGH THE PICKETS.
WITH FIFTY OTHERS SURPRISED TO LEARN THAT THEY HAD EMBRACED THE DIVINE KING OVER YHERA.
SHALL WE ASSIST YOU WITH YOUR HARNESS?
OR WITH THOSE TWO?
NO, THEY ARE ENSPELLED. LEAVE THEM TO ME.
I WILL CALL IF I NEED YOU.
MORMO. DEMIDICE. CHARIZE.
ASSIST ME.
Yes yes

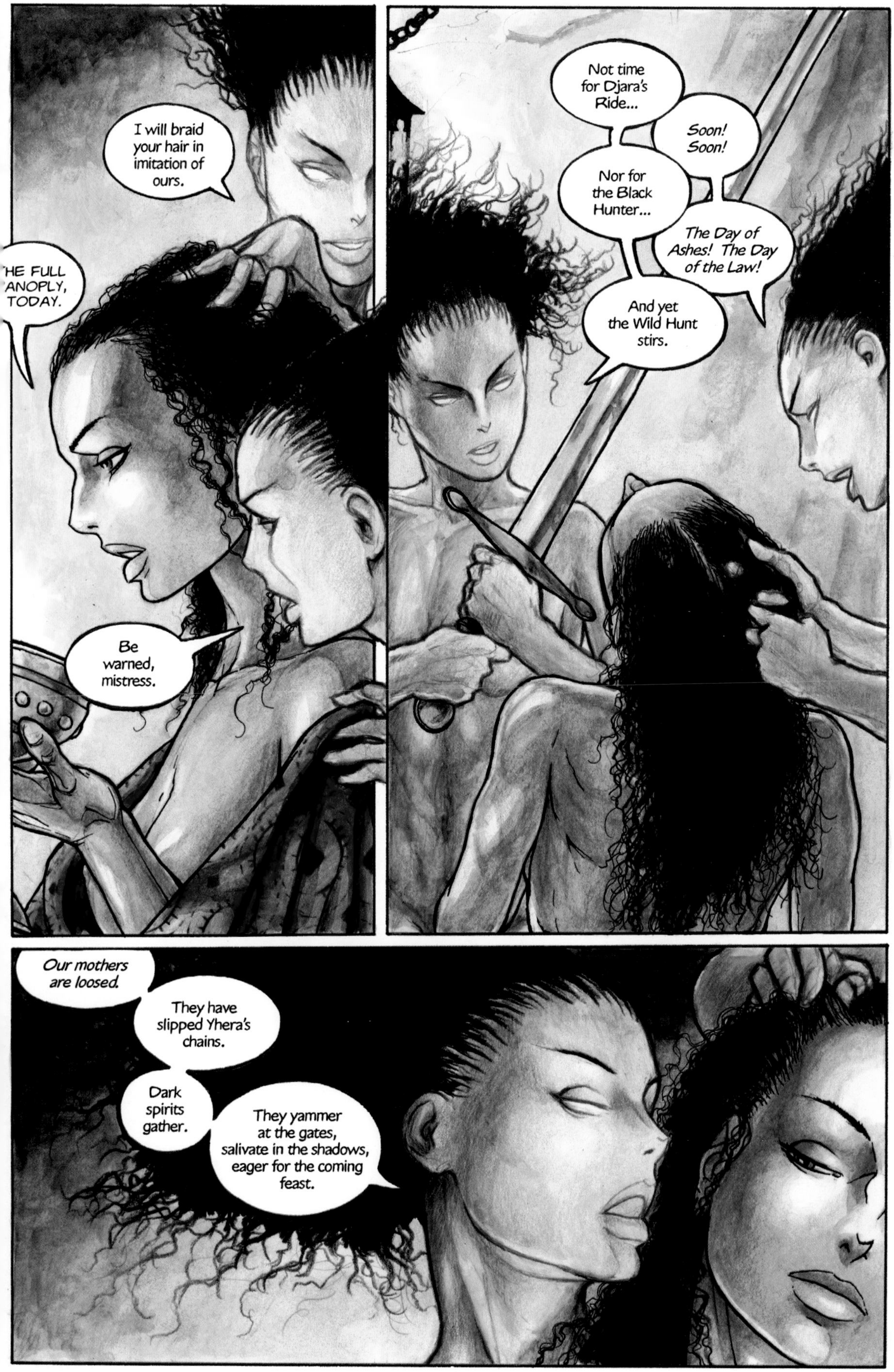

I will braid your hair in imitation of ours.
HE FULL ANOPLY, TODAY.
Be warned, mistress.
Not time for Djara's Ride...
Nor for the Black Hunter...
And yet the Wild Hunt stirs.
Soon! Soon!
The Day of Ashes! The Day of the Law!
Our mothers are loosed.
They have slipped Yhera's chains.
Dark spirits gather.
They yammer at the gates, salivate in the shadows, eager for the coming feast.

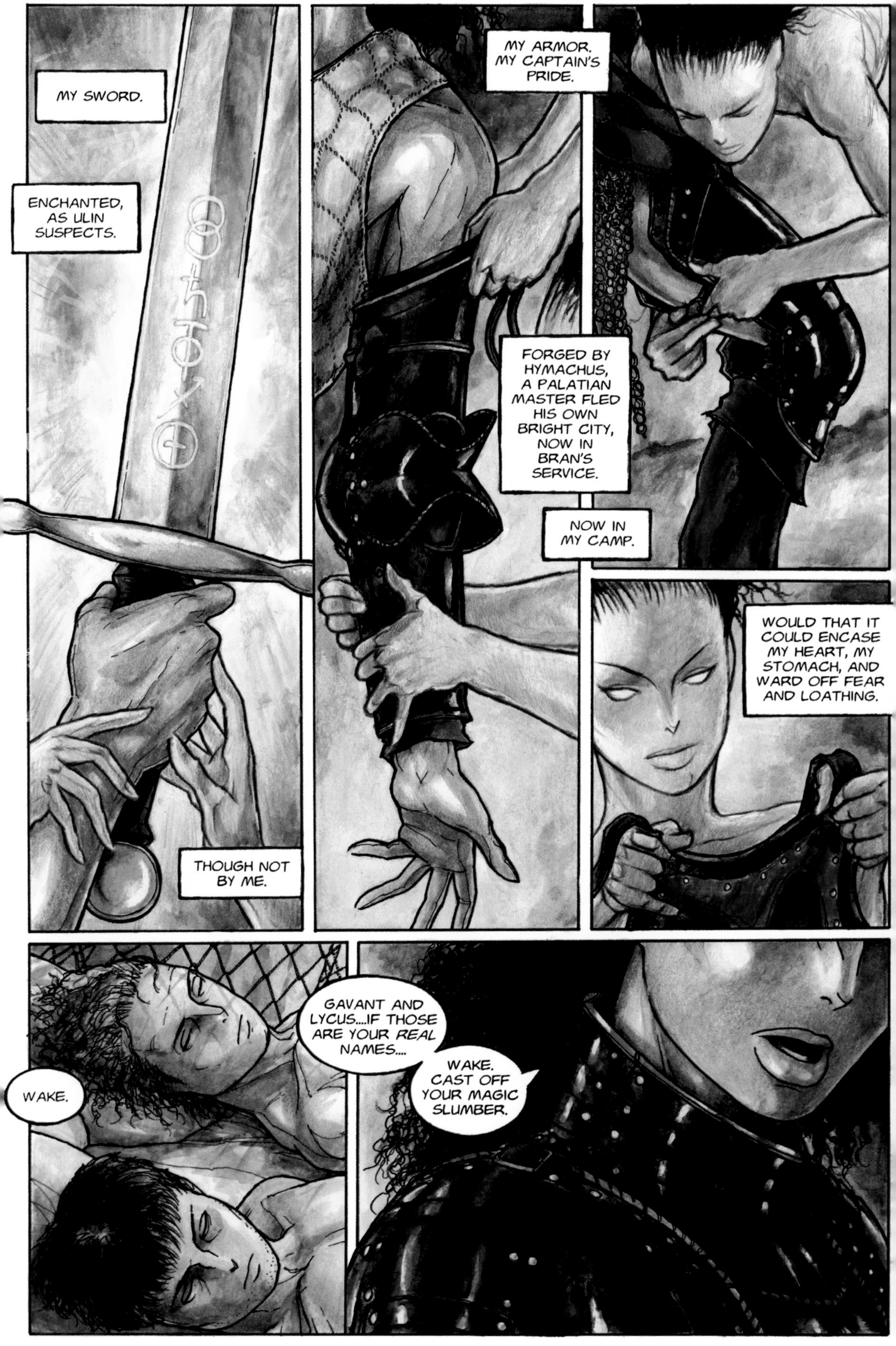
MY SWORD.
ENCHANTED, AS ULIN SUSPECTS.
THOUGH NOT BY ME.
MY ARMOR. MY CAPTAIN'S PRIDE.
FORGED BY HYMACHUS, A PALATIAN MASTER FLED HIS OWN BRIGHT CITY, NOW IN BRAN'S SERVICE.
NOW IN MY CAMP.
WOULD THAT IT COULD ENCASE MY HEART, MY STOMACH, AND WARD OFF FEAR AND LOATHING.
WAKE.
GAVANT AND LYCUS....IF THOSE ARE YOUR *REAL* NAMES....
WAKE. CAST OFF YOUR MAGIC SLUMBER.

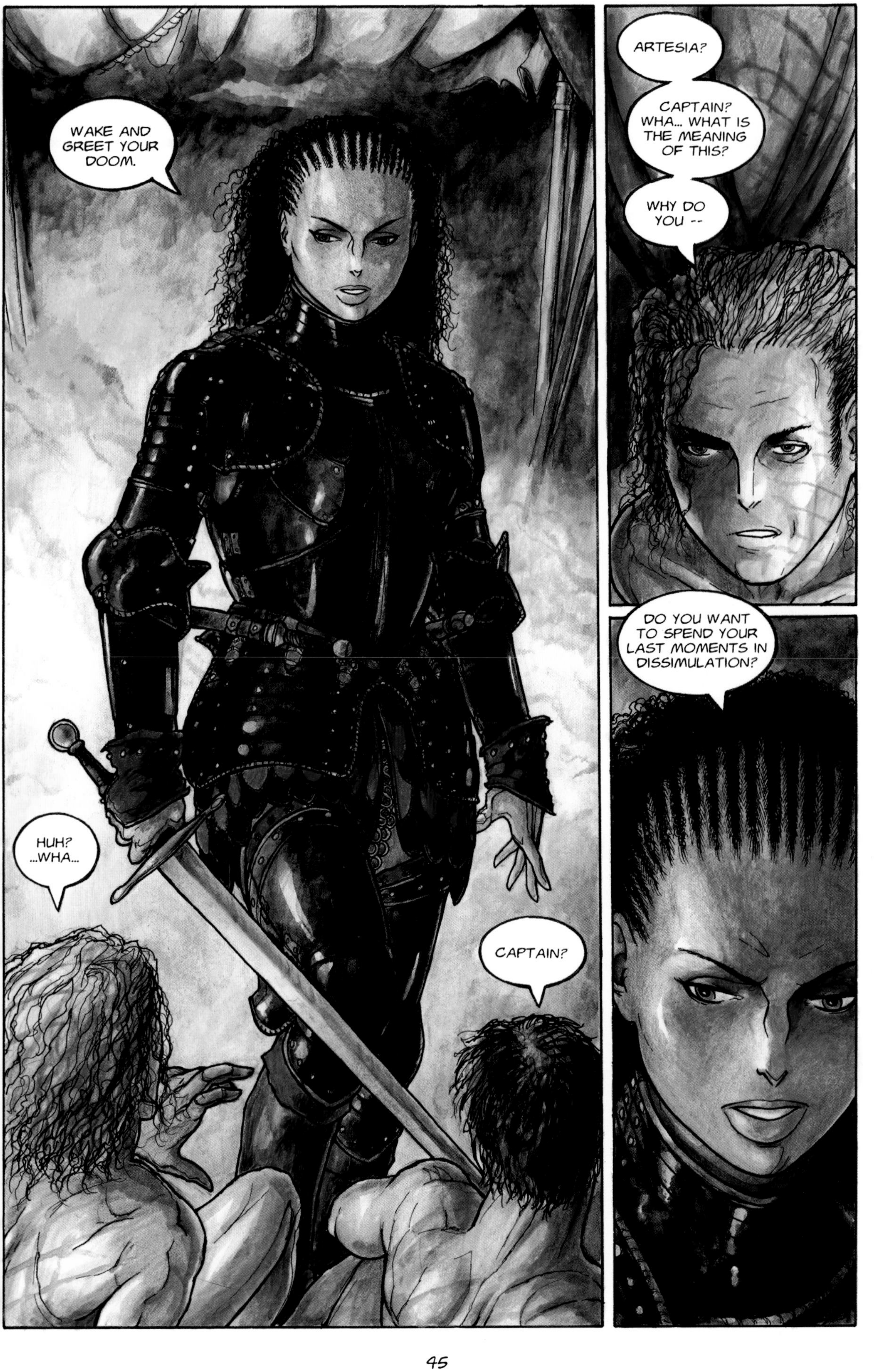
WAKE AND GREET YOUR DOOM.
HUH? ...WHA...
CAPTAIN?
ARTESIA?
CAPTAIN? WHA... WHAT IS THE MEANING OF THIS?
WHY DO YOU --
DO YOU WANT TO SPEND YOUR LAST MOMENTS IN DISSIMULATION?

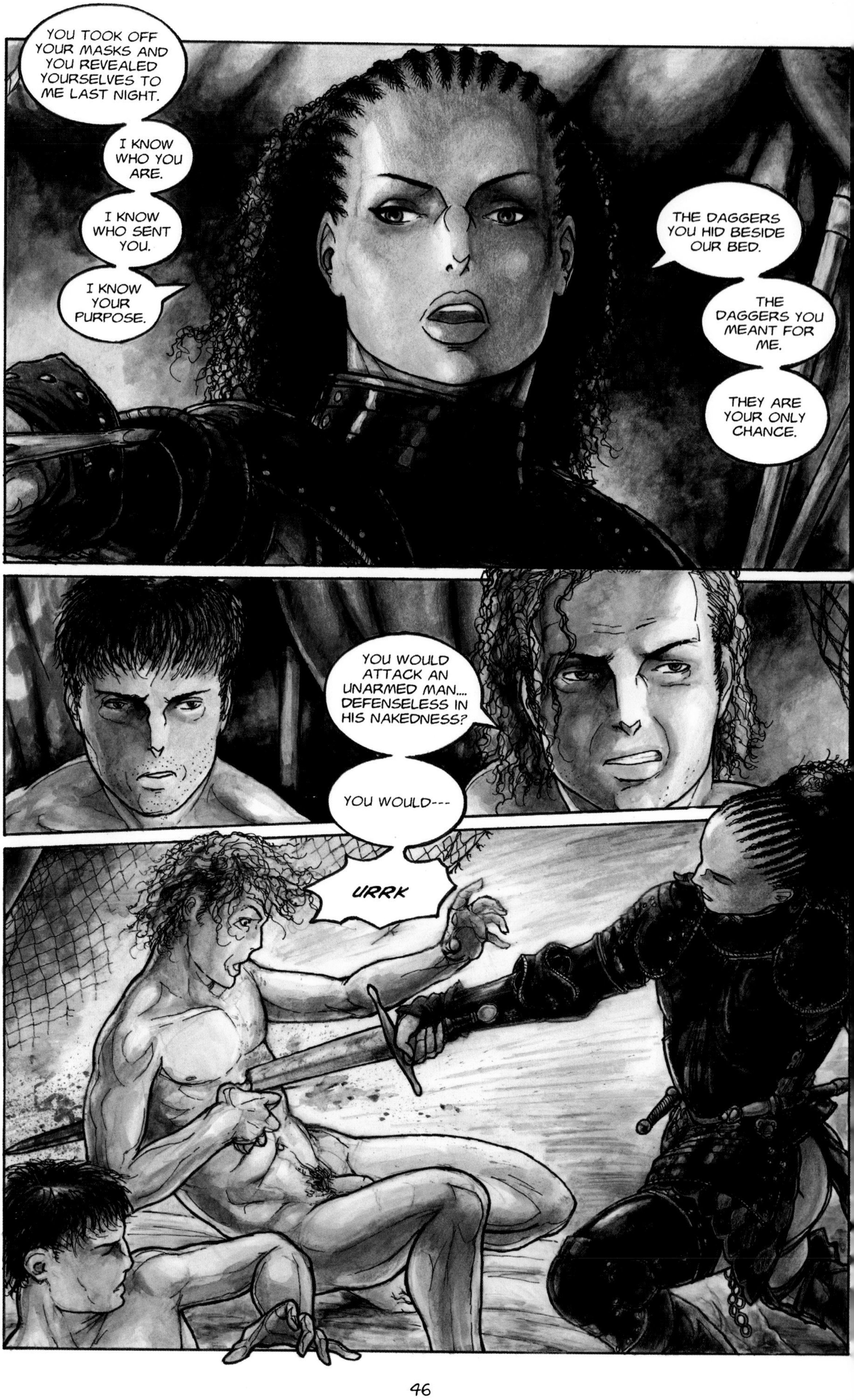
YOU TOOK OFF YOUR MASKS AND YOU REVEALED YOURSELVES TO ME LAST NIGHT.
I KNOW WHO YOU ARE.
I KNOW WHO SENT YOU.
I KNOW YOUR PURPOSE.
THE DAGGERS YOU HID BESIDE OUR BED.
THE DAGGERS YOU MEANT FOR ME.
THEY ARE YOUR ONLY CHANCE.
YOU WOULD ATTACK AN UNARMED MAN.... DEFENSELESS IN HIS NAKEDNESS?
YOU WOULD---
URRK

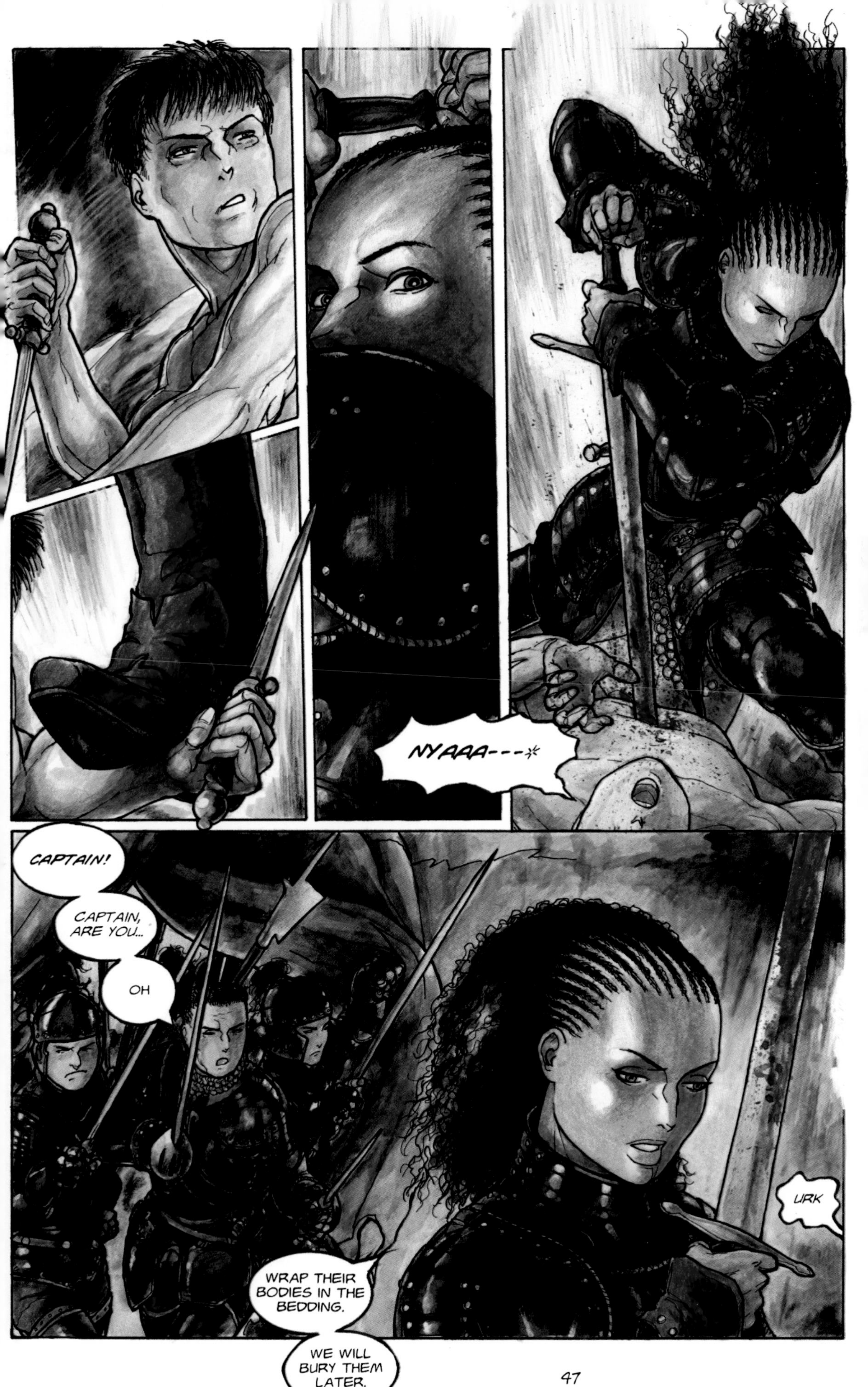
NYAAA---
CAPTAIN!
CAPTAIN, ARE YOU...
OH
URK
WRAP THEIR BODIES IN THE BEDDING.
WE WILL BURY THEM LATER.

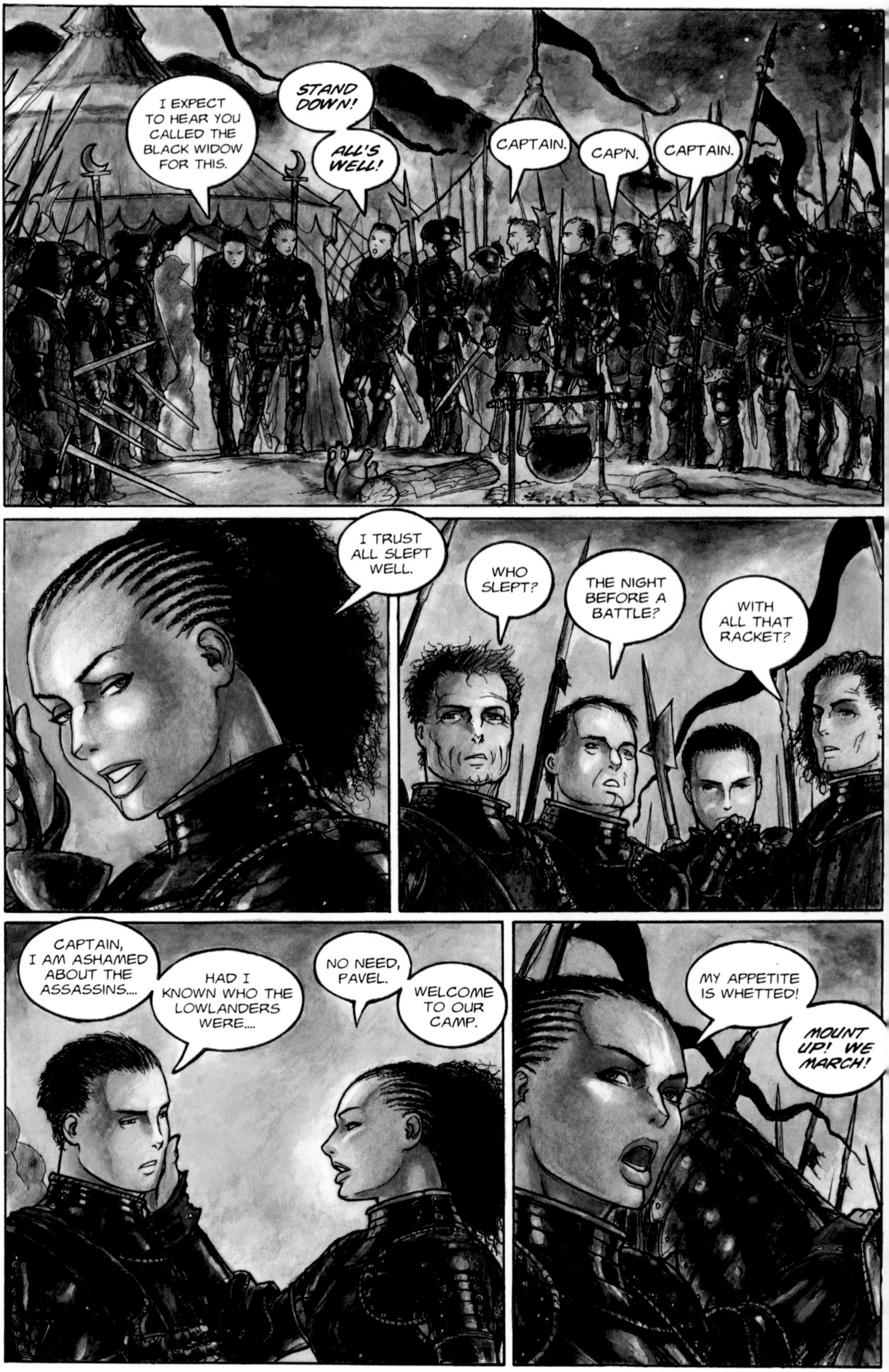
I EXPECT TO HEAR YOU CALLED THE BLACK WIDOW FOR THIS.
STAND DOWN!
ALL'S WELL!
CAPTAIN.
CAP'N.
CAPTAIN.
I TRUST ALL SLEPT WELL.
WHO SLEPT?
THE NIGHT BEFORE A BATTLE?
WITH ALL THAT RACKET?
CAPTAIN, I AM ASHAMED ABOUT THE ASSASSINS....
HAD I KNOWN WHO THE LOWLANDERS WERE....
NO NEED, PAVEL.
WELCOME TO OUR CAMP.
MY APPETITE IS WHETTED!
MOUNT UP! WE MARCH!

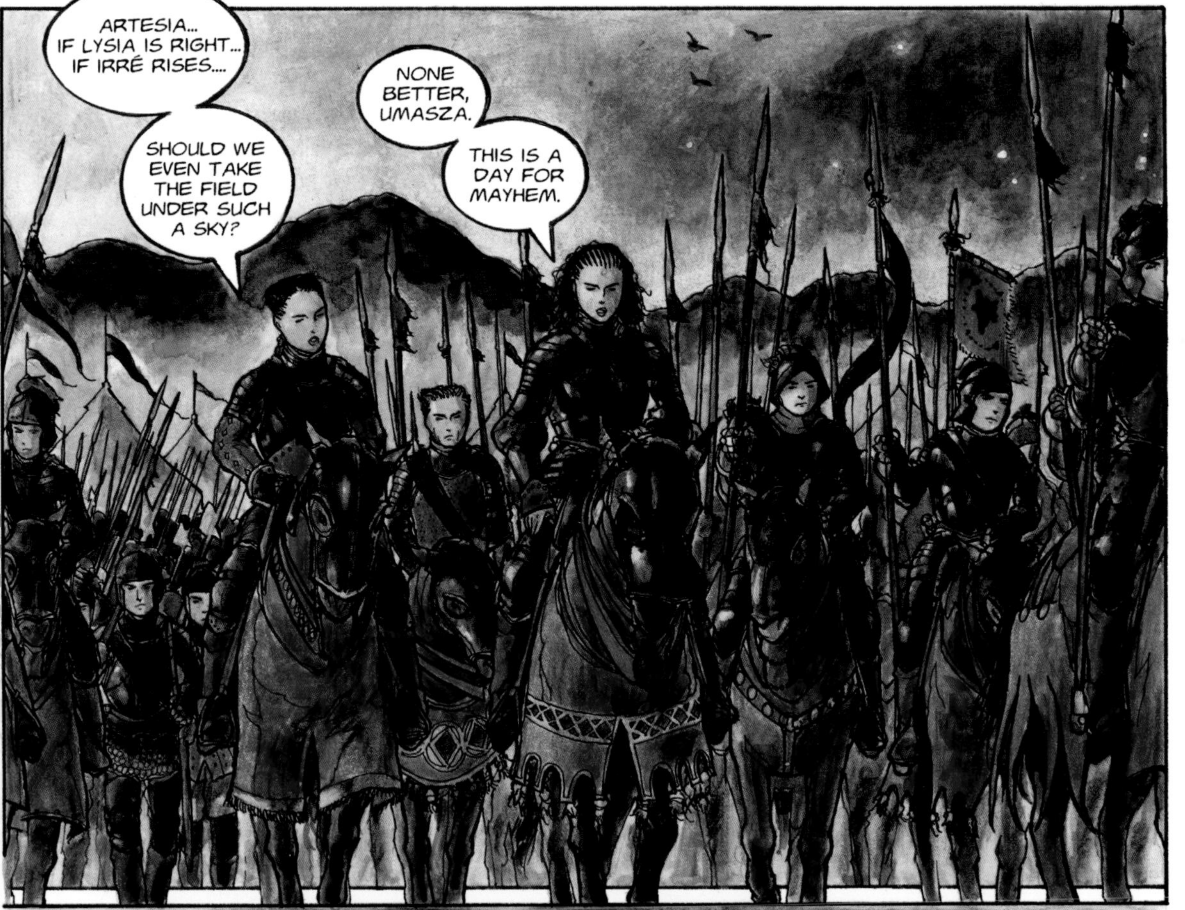
ARTESIA... IF LYSIA IS RIGHT... IF IRRÉ RISES....
SHOULD WE EVEN TAKE THE FIELD UNDER SUCH A SKY?
NONE BETTER, UMASZA.
THIS IS A DAY FOR MAYHEM.

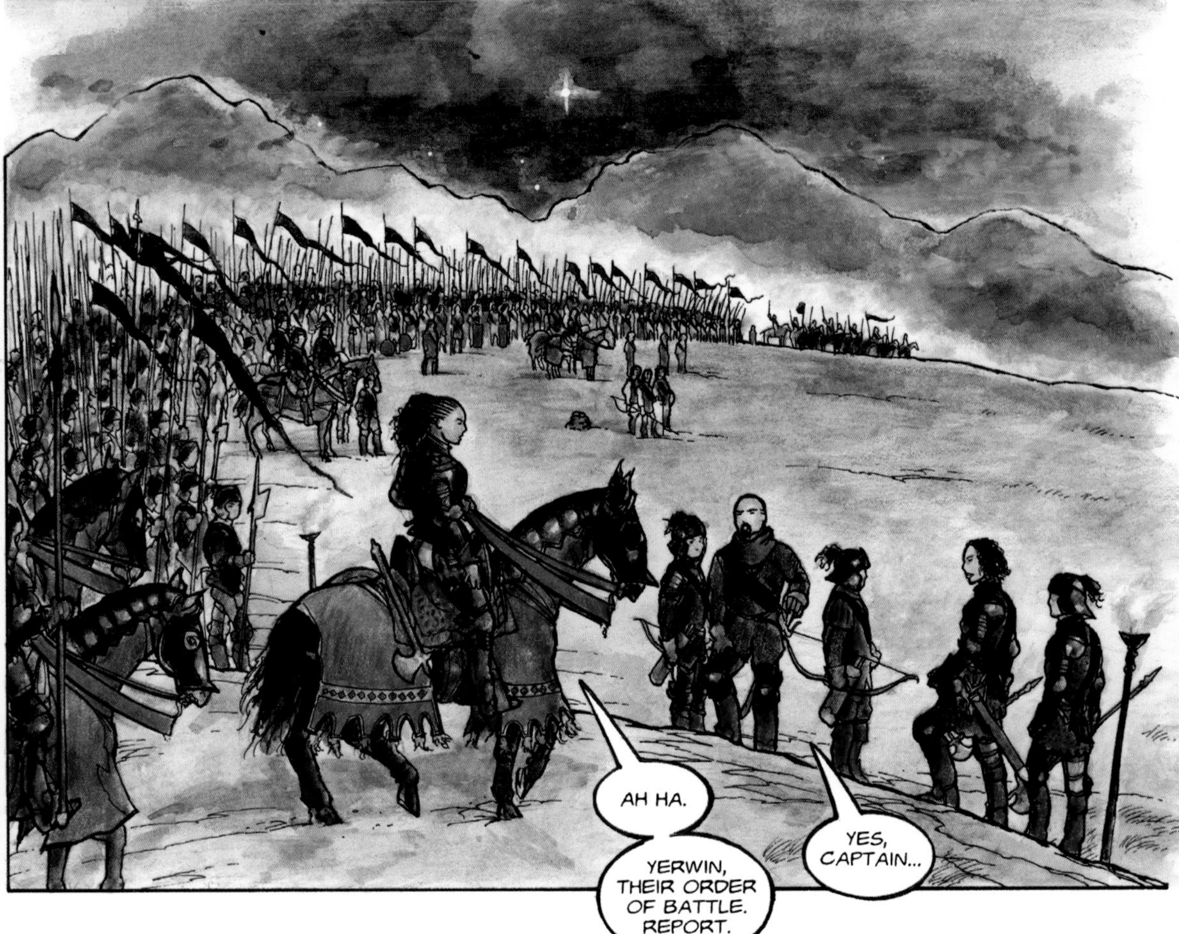
AH HA.
YERWIN, THEIR ORDER OF BATTLE. REPORT.
YES, CAPTAIN...

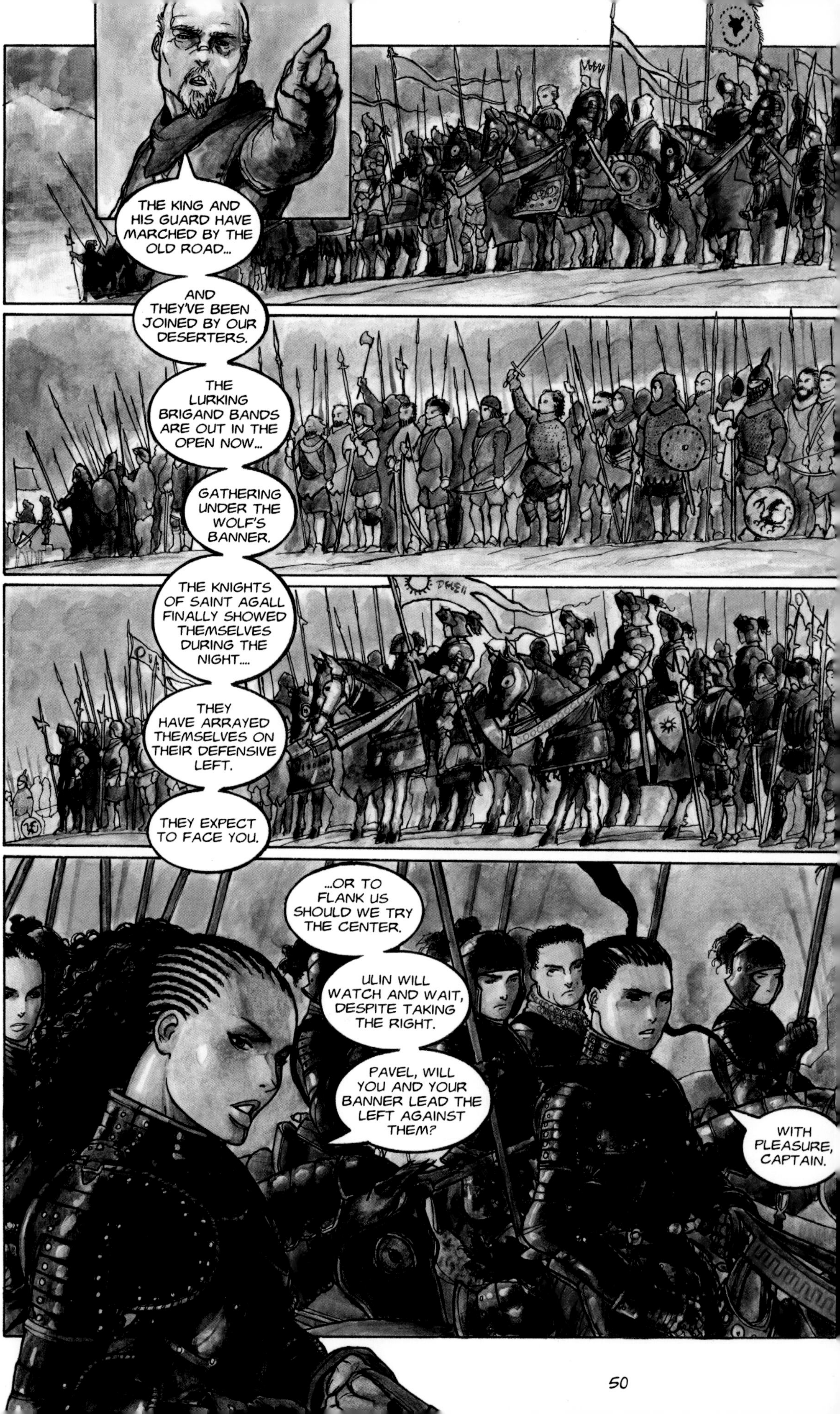
THE KING AND HIS GUARD HAVE MARCHED BY THE OLD ROAD...
AND THEY'VE BEEN JOINED BY OUR DESERTERS.
THE LURKING BRIGAND BANDS ARE OUT IN THE OPEN NOW...
GATHERING UNDER THE WOLF'S BANNER.
THE KNIGHTS OF SAINT AGALL FINALLY SHOWED THEMSELVES DURING THE NIGHT....
THEY HAVE ARRAYED THEMSELVES ON THEIR DEFENSIVE LEFT.
THEY EXPECT TO FACE YOU.
...OR TO FLANK US SHOULD WE TRY THE CENTER.
ULIN WILL WATCH AND WAIT, DESPITE TAKING THE RIGHT.
PAVEL, WILL YOU AND YOUR BANNER LEAD THE LEFT AGAINST THEM?
WITH PLEASURE, CAPTAIN.

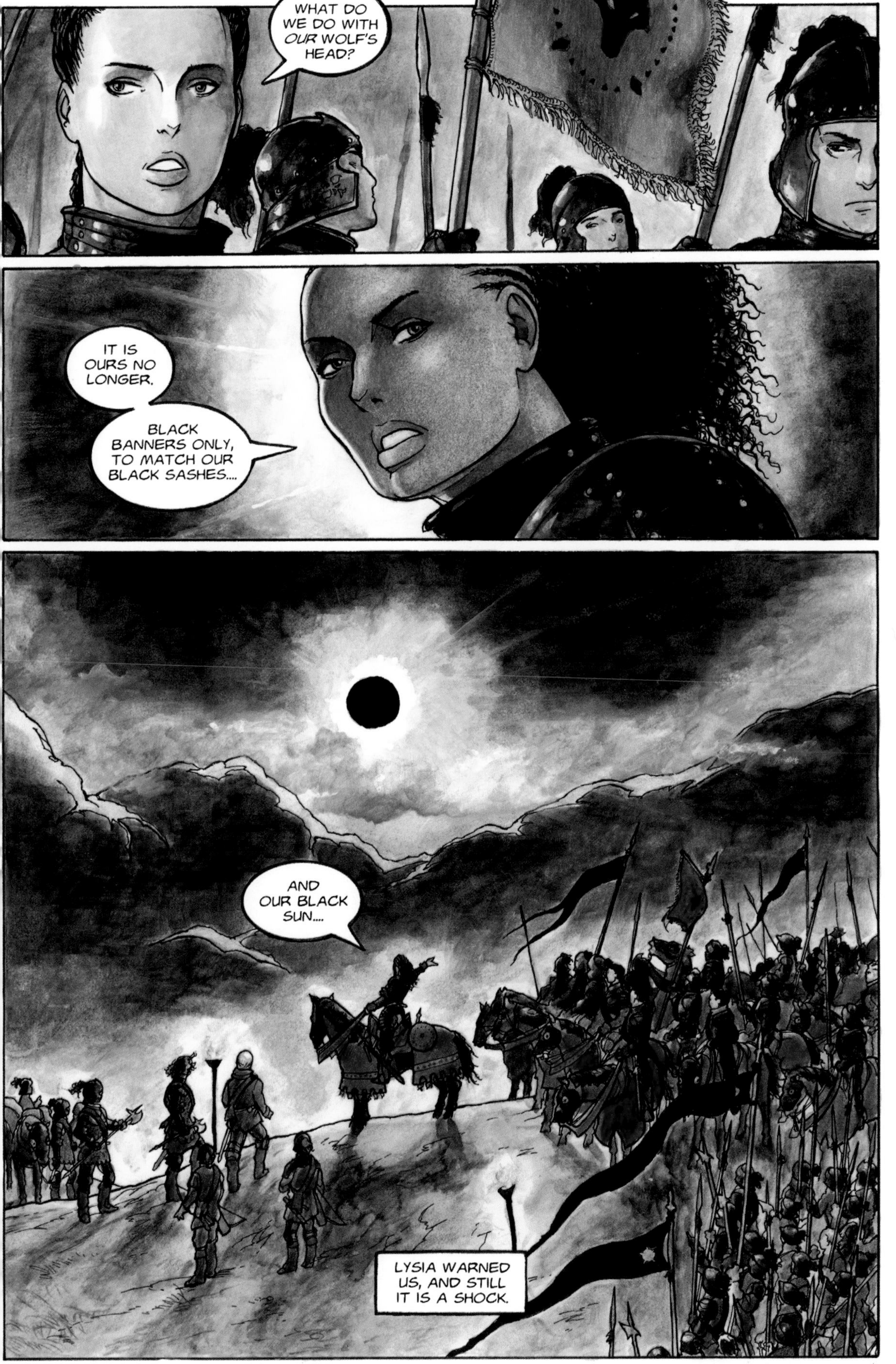
WHAT DO WE DO WITH OUR WOLF'S HEAD?
IT IS OURS NO LONGER.
BLACK BANNERS ONLY, TO MATCH OUR BLACK SASHES....
AND OUR BLACK SUN....
LYSIA WARNED US, AND STILL IT IS A SHOCK.

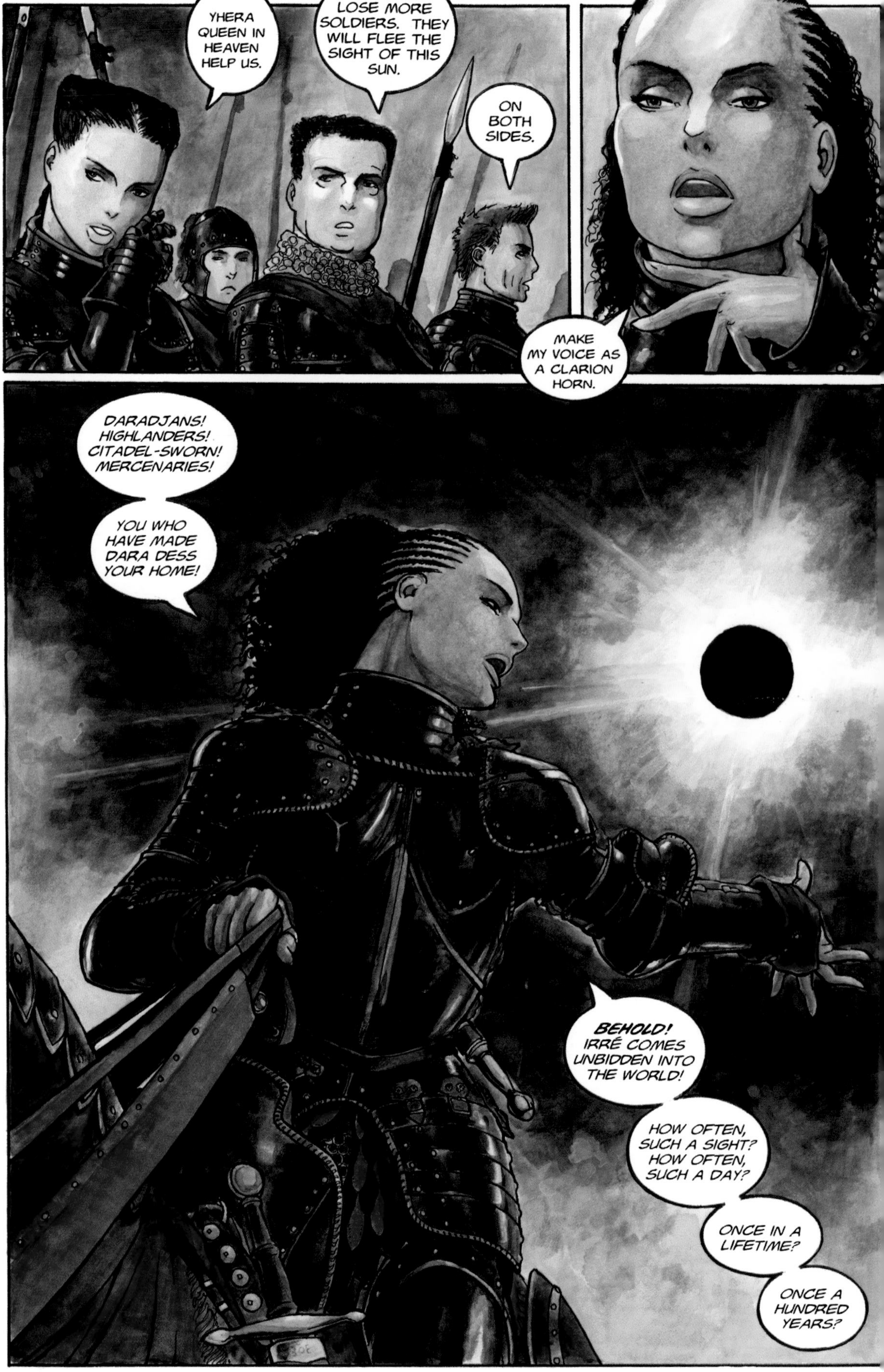
YHERA QUEEN IN HEAVEN HELP US.
WE WILL LOSE MORE SOLDIERS. THEY WILL FLEE THE SIGHT OF THIS SUN.
ON BOTH SIDES.
MAKE MY VOICE AS A CLARION HORN.
DARADJANS! HIGHLANDERS! CITADEL-SWORN! MERCENARIES!
YOU WHO HAVE MADE DARA DESS YOUR HOME!
BEHOLD! IRRÉ COMES UNBIDDEN INTO THE WORLD!
HOW OFTEN, SUCH A SIGHT? HOW OFTEN, SUCH A DAY?
ONCE IN A LIFETIME?
ONCE A HUNDRED YEARS?

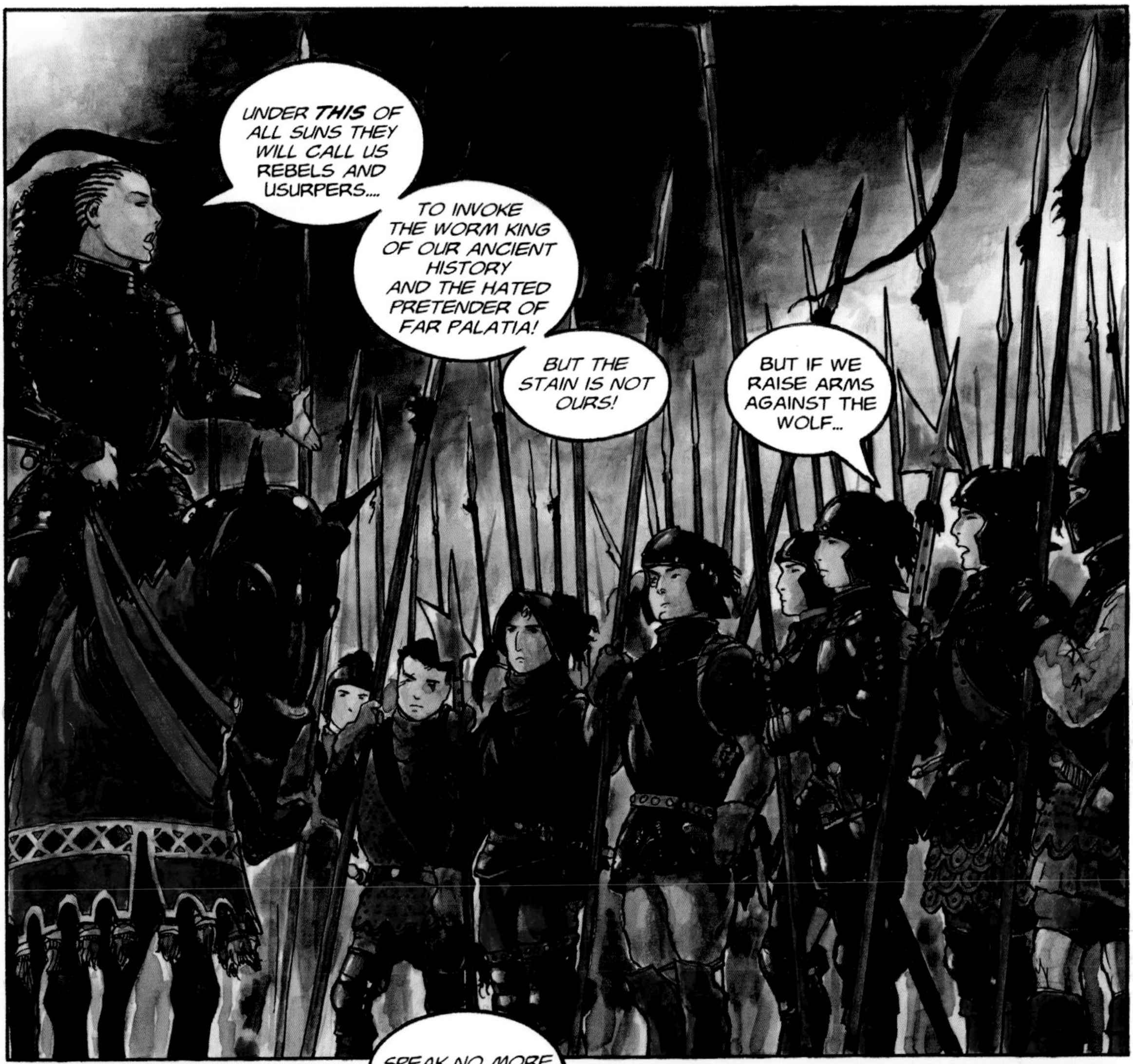
UNDER THIS OF ALL SUNS THEY WILL CALL US REBELS AND USURPERS....
TO INVOKE THE WORM KING OF OUR ANCIENT HISTORY AND THE HATED PRETENDER OF FAR PALATIA!
BUT THE STAIN IS NOT OURS!
BUT IF WE RAISE ARMS AGAINST THE WOLF...

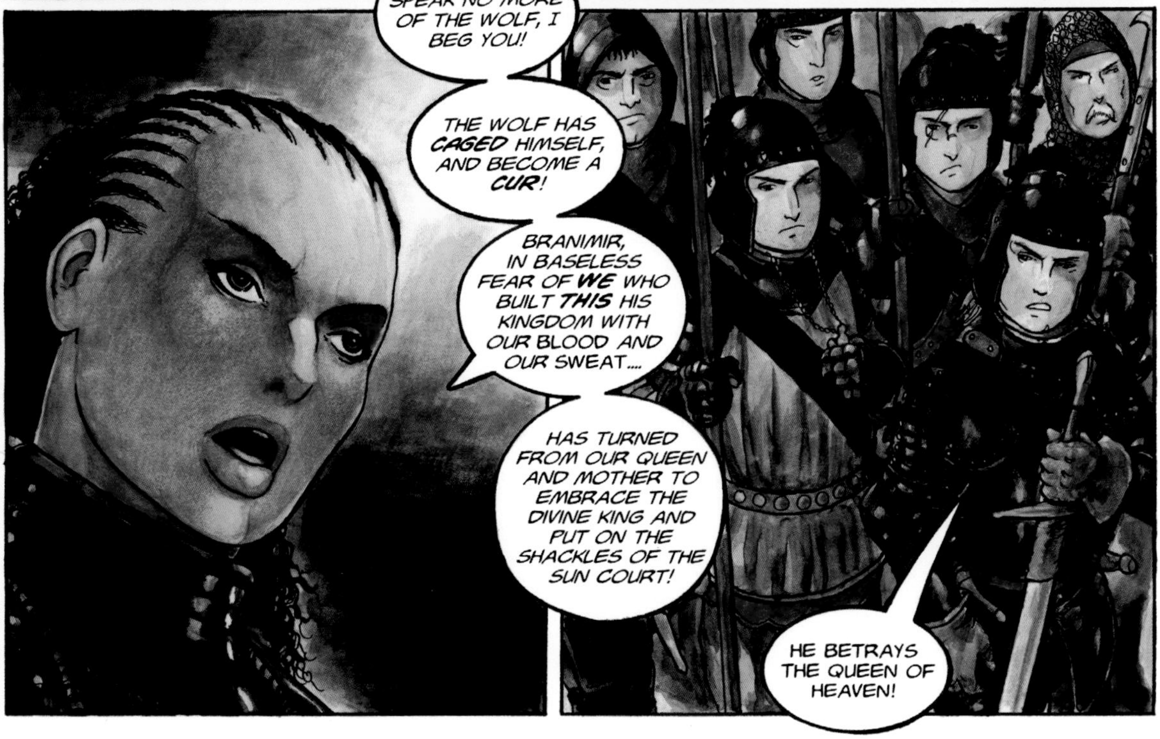
SPEAK NO MORE OF THE WOLF, I BEG YOU!
THE WOLF HAS CAGED HIMSELF, AND BECOME A CUR!
BRANIMIR, IN BASELESS FEAR OF WE WHO BUILT THIS HIS KINGDOM WITH OUR BLOOD AND OUR SWEAT....
HAS TURNED FROM OUR QUEEN AND MOTHER TO EMBRACE THE DIVINE KING AND PUT ON THE SHACKLES OF THE SUN COURT!
HE BETRAYS THE QUEEN OF HEAVEN!

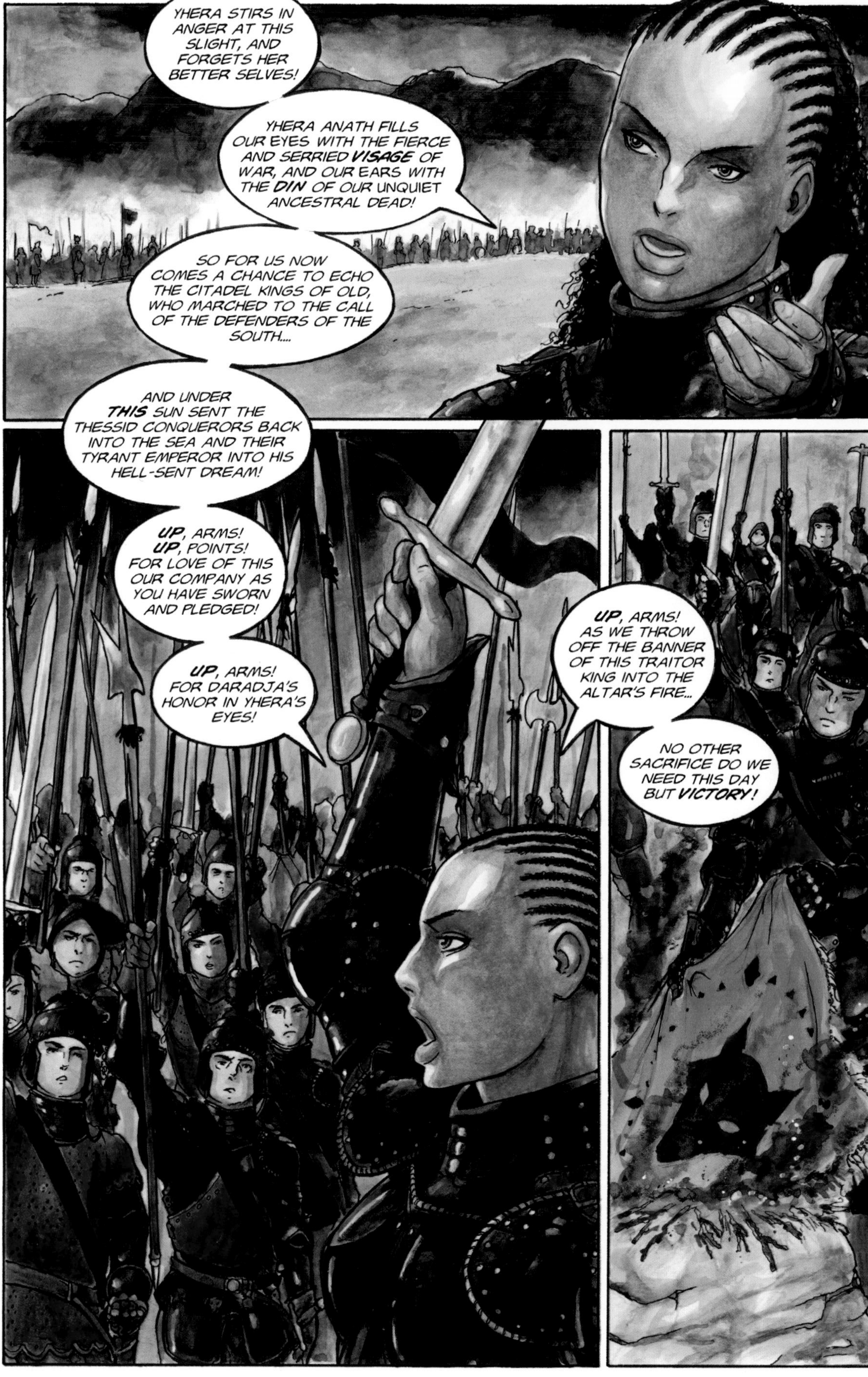
YHERA STIRS IN ANGER AT THIS SLIGHT, AND FORGETS HER BETTER SELVES!
YHERA ANATH FILLS OUR EYES WITH THE FIERCE AND SERRIED VISAGE OF WAR, AND OUR EARS WITH THE DIN OF OUR UNQUIET ANCESTRAL DEAD!
SO FOR US NOW COMES A CHANCE TO ECHO THE CITADEL KINGS OF OLD, WHO MARCHED TO THE CALL OF THE DEFENDERS OF THE SOUTH....
AND UNDER THIS SUN SENT THE THESSID CONQUERORS BACK INTO THE SEA AND THEIR TYRANT EMPEROR INTO HIS HELL-SENT DREAM!
UP, ARMS! UP, POINTS! FOR LOVE OF THIS OUR COMPANY AS YOU HAVE SWORN AND PLEDGED!
UP, ARMS! FOR DARADJA'S HONOR IN YHERA'S EYES!
UP, ARMS! AS WE THROW OFF THE BANNER OF THIS TRAITOR KING INTO THE ALTAR'S FIRE...
NO OTHER SACRIFICE DO WE NEED THIS DAY BUT VICTORY!

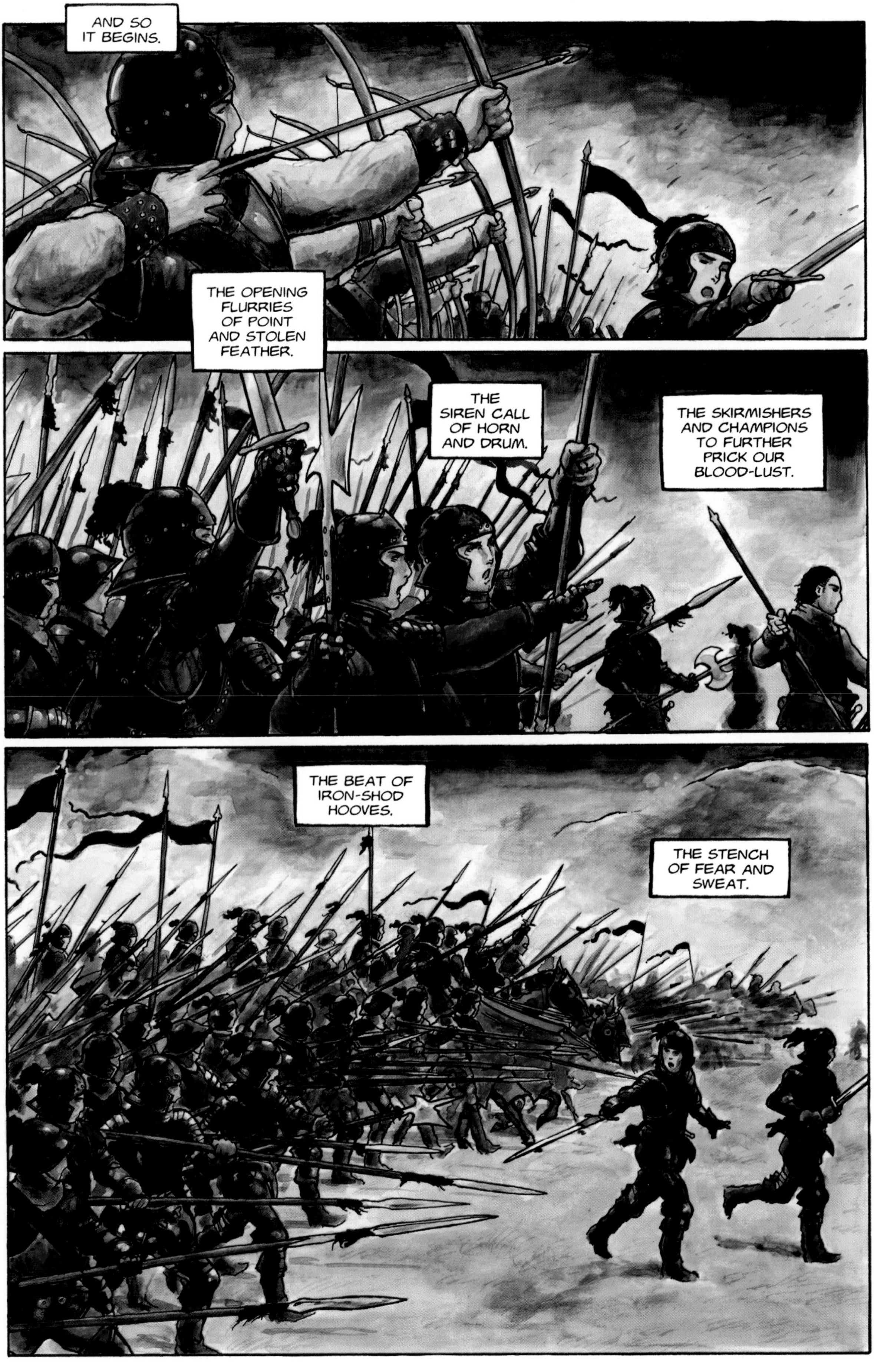
AND SO IT BEGINS.
THE OPENING FLURRIES OF POINT AND STOLEN FEATHER.
THE SIREN CALL OF HORN AND DRUM.
THE SKIRMISHERS AND CHAMPIONS TO FURTHER PRICK OUR BLOOD-LUST.
THE BEAT OF IRON-SHOD HOOVES.
THE STENCH OF FEAR AND SWEAT.

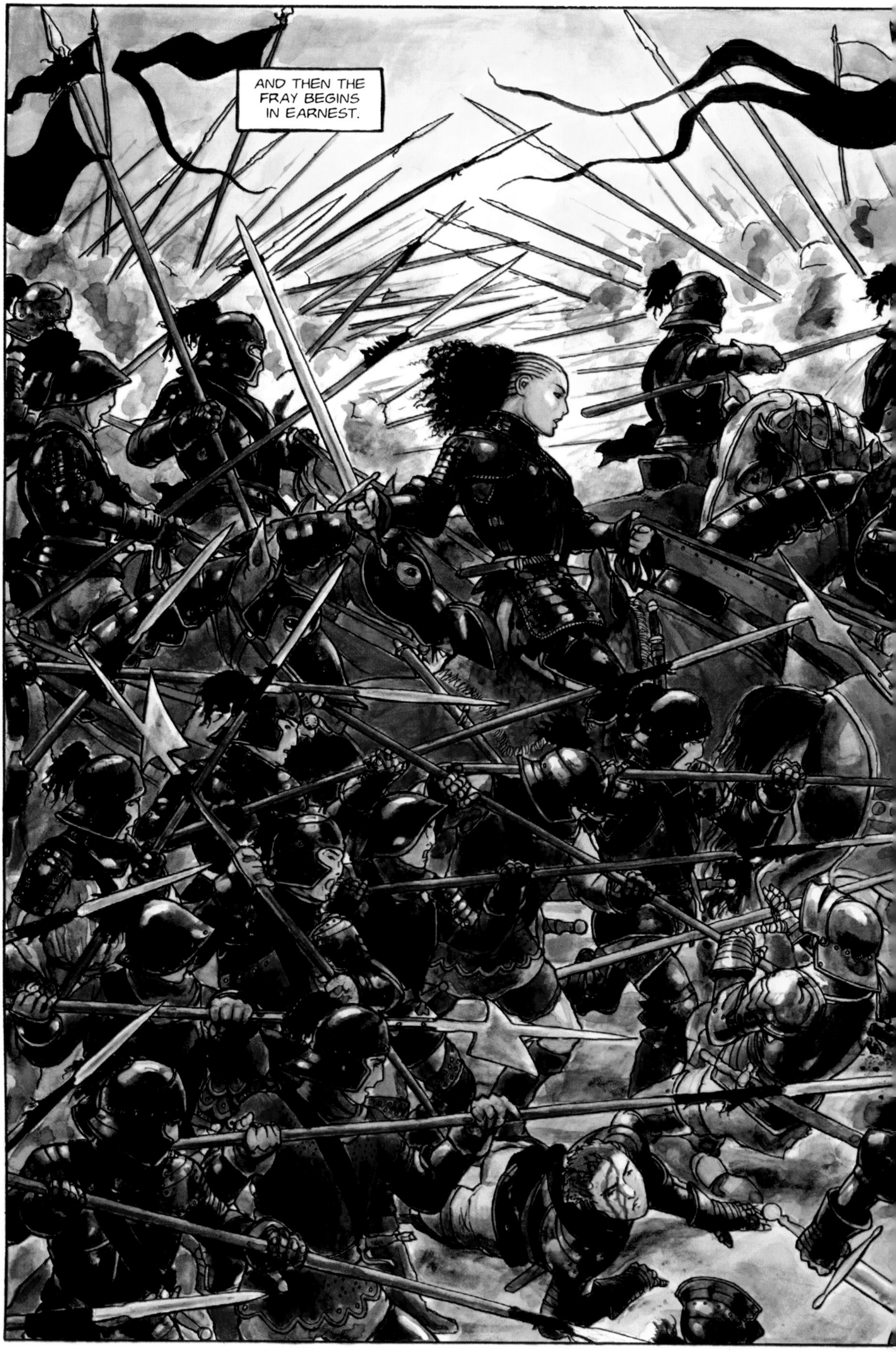
AND THEN THE FRAY BEGINS IN EARNEST.

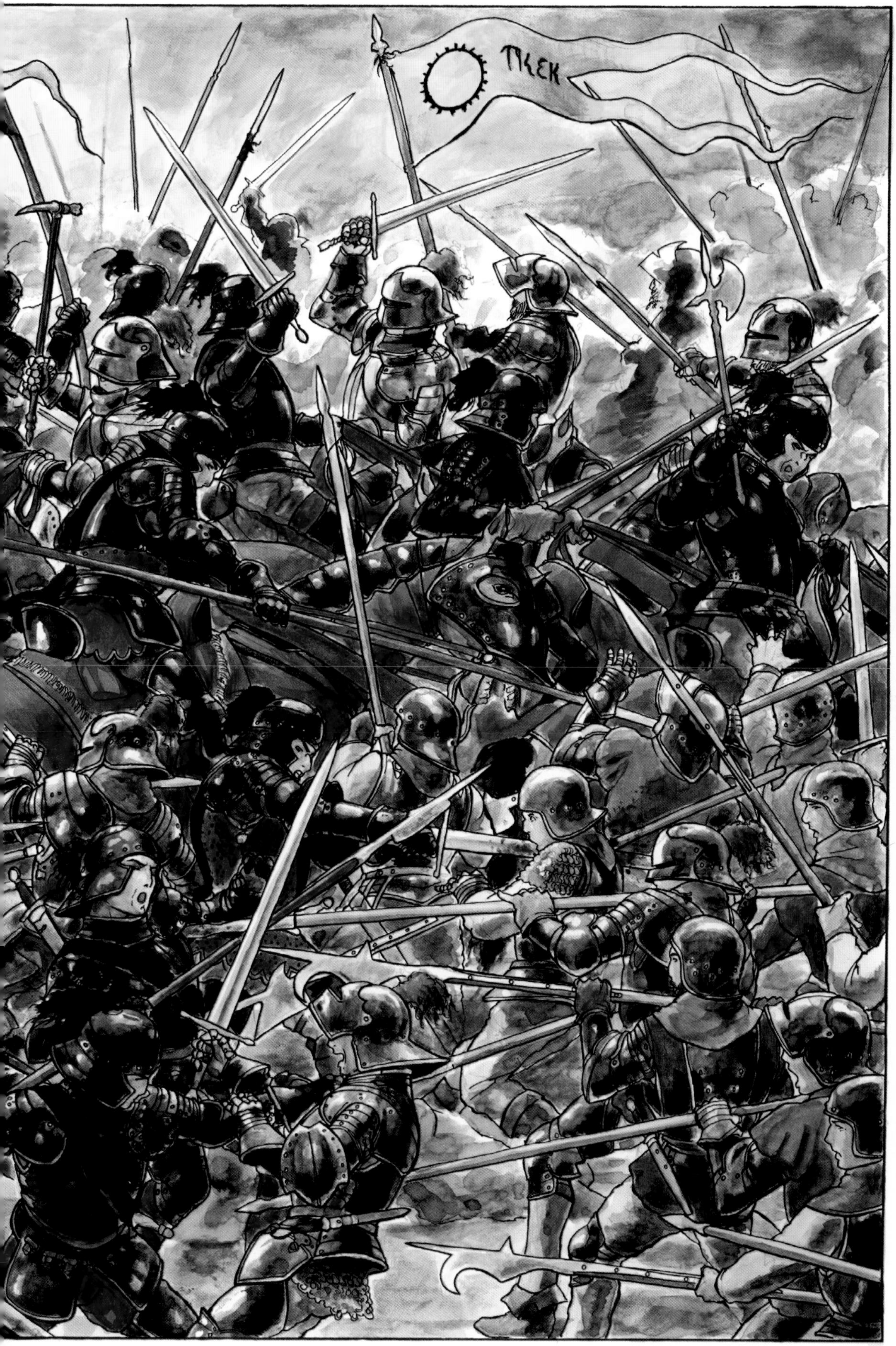

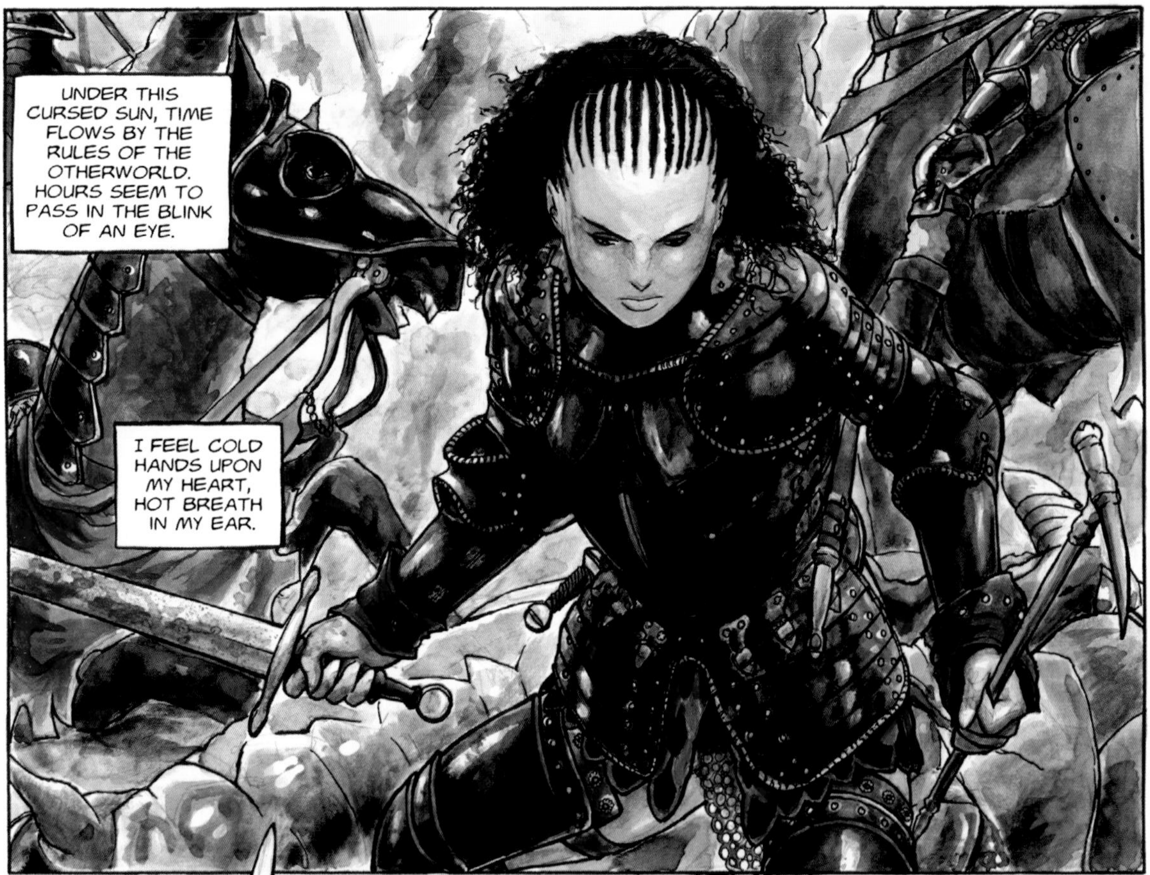
UNDER THIS CURSED SUN, TIME FLOWS BY THE RULES OF THE OTHERWORLD. HOURS SEEM TO PASS IN THE BLINK OF AN EYE.
I FEEL COLD HANDS UPON MY HEART, HOT BREATH IN MY EAR.

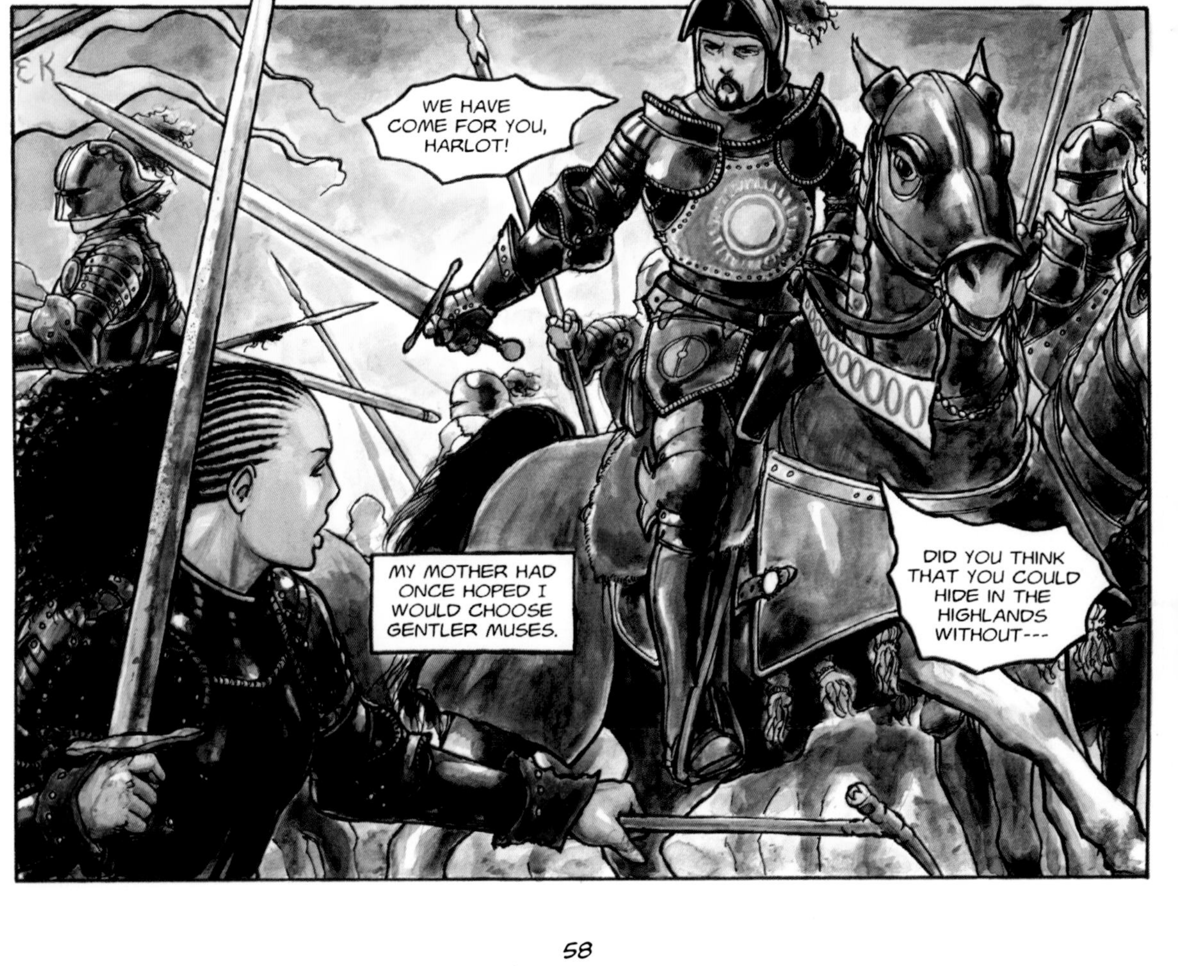
WE HAVE COME FOR YOU, HARLOT!
MY MOTHER HAD ONCE HOPED I WOULD CHOOSE GENTLER MUSES.
DID YOU THINK THAT YOU COULD HIDE IN THE HIGHLANDS WITHOUT---

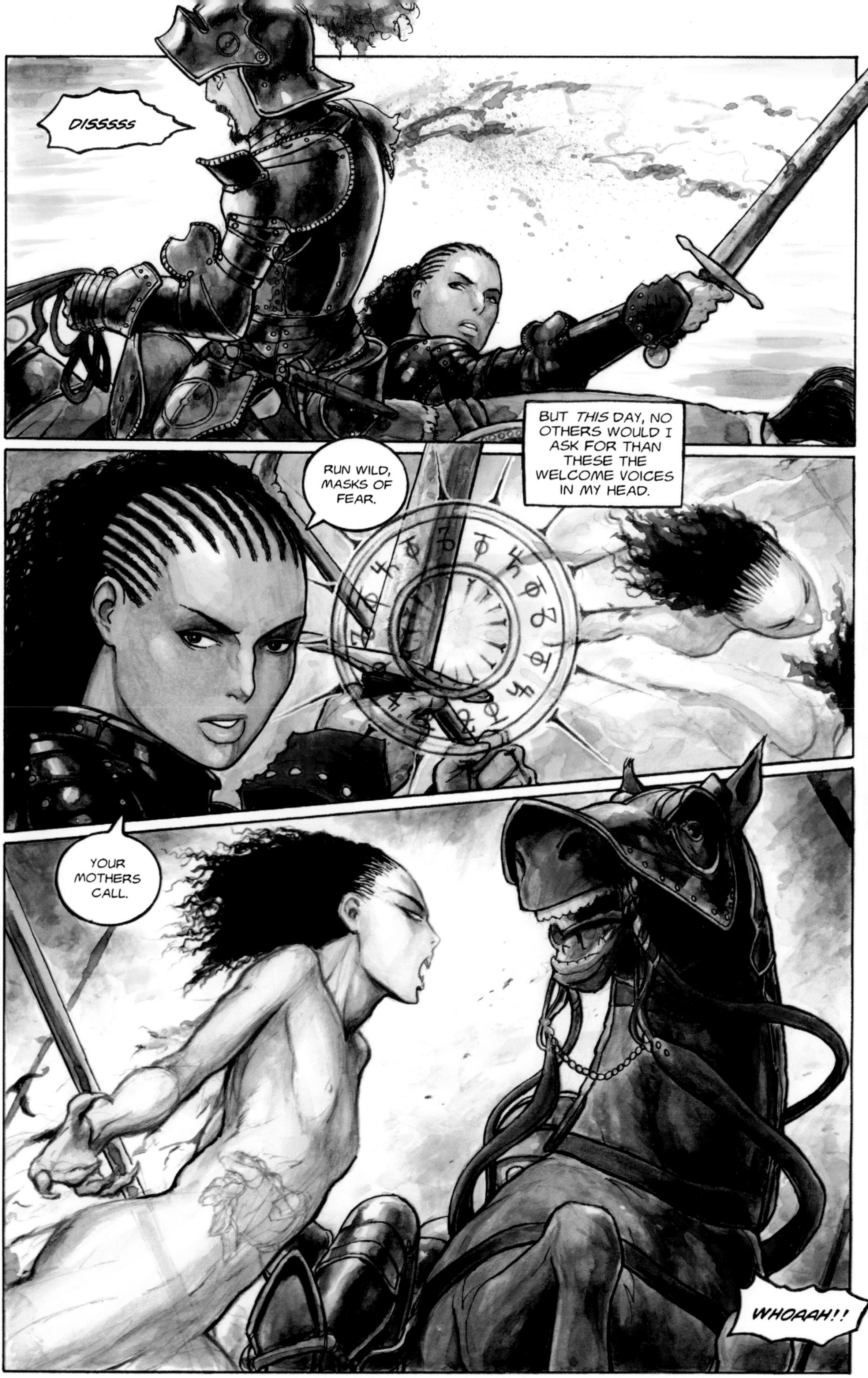
DISSSSS
RUN WILD, MASKS OF FEAR.
BUT *THIS* DAY, NO OTHERS WOULD I ASK FOR THAN THESE THE WELCOME VOICES IN MY HEAD.
YOUR MOTHERS CALL.
WHOAAH!!

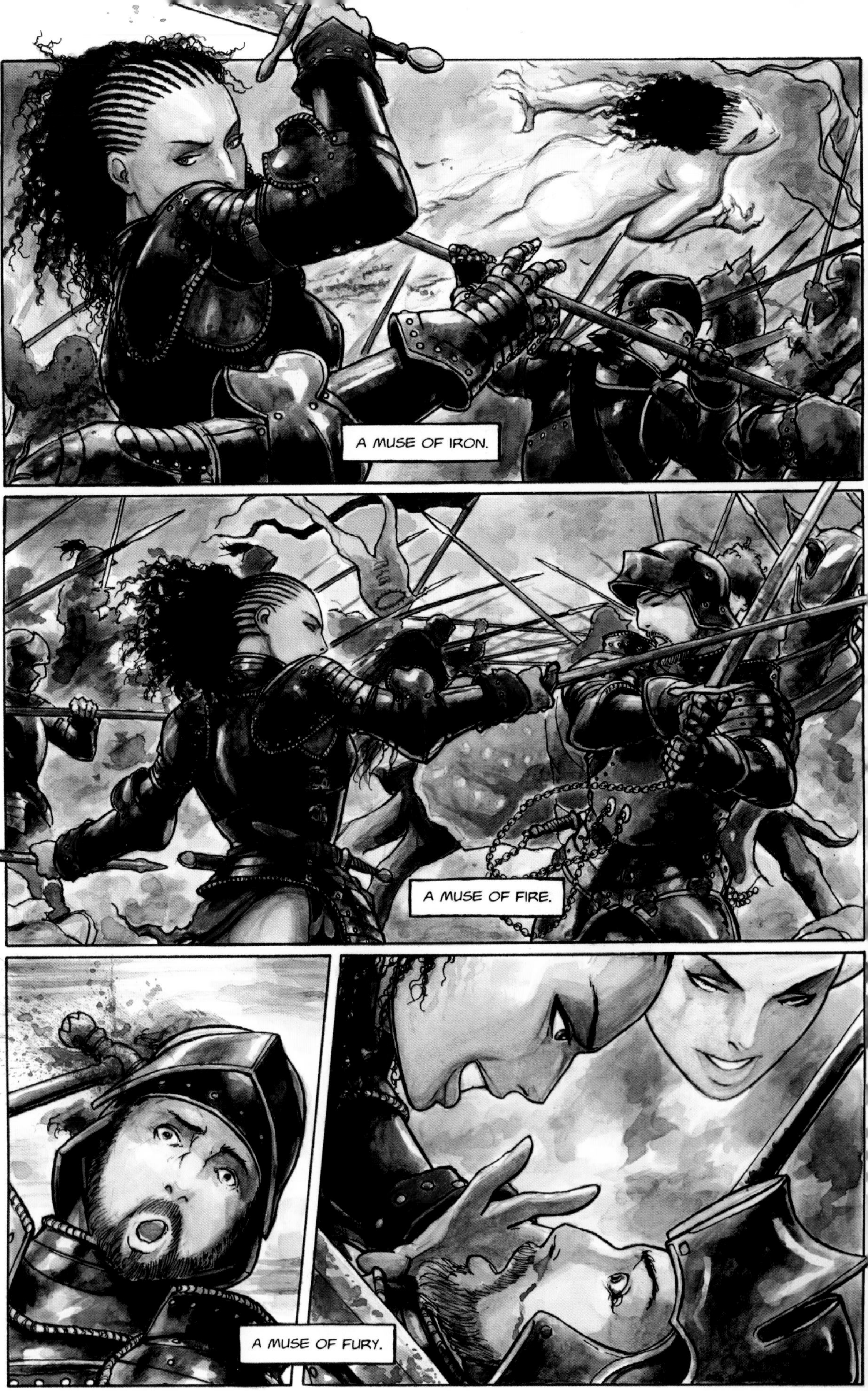
A MUSE OF IRON.
A MUSE OF FIRE.
A MUSE OF FURY.

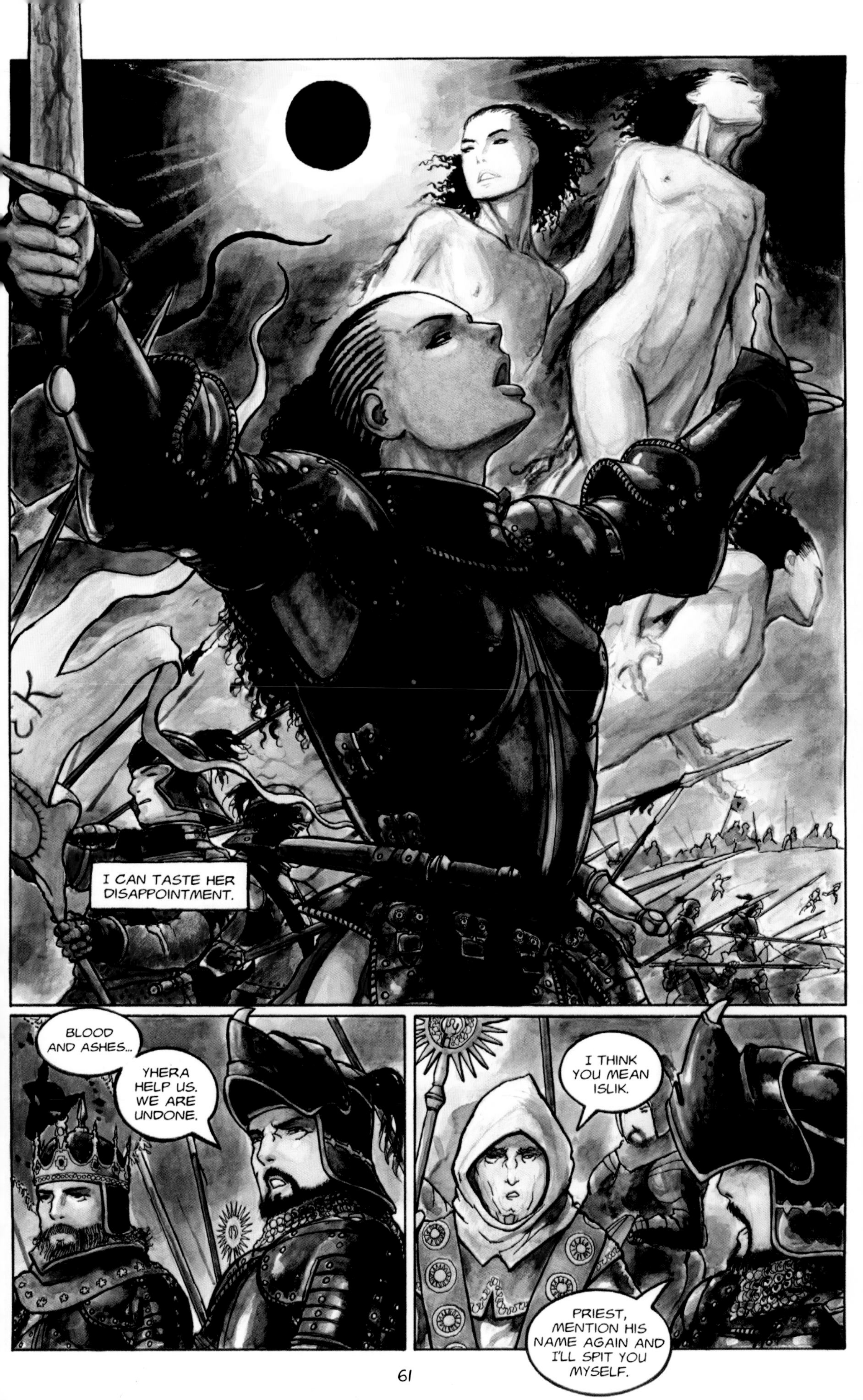
I CAN TASTE HER DISAPPOINTMENT.
BLOOD AND ASHES...
YHERA HELP US. WE ARE UNDONE.
I THINK YOU MEAN ISLIK.
PRIEST, MENTION HIS NAME AGAIN AND I'LL SPIT YOU MYSELF.

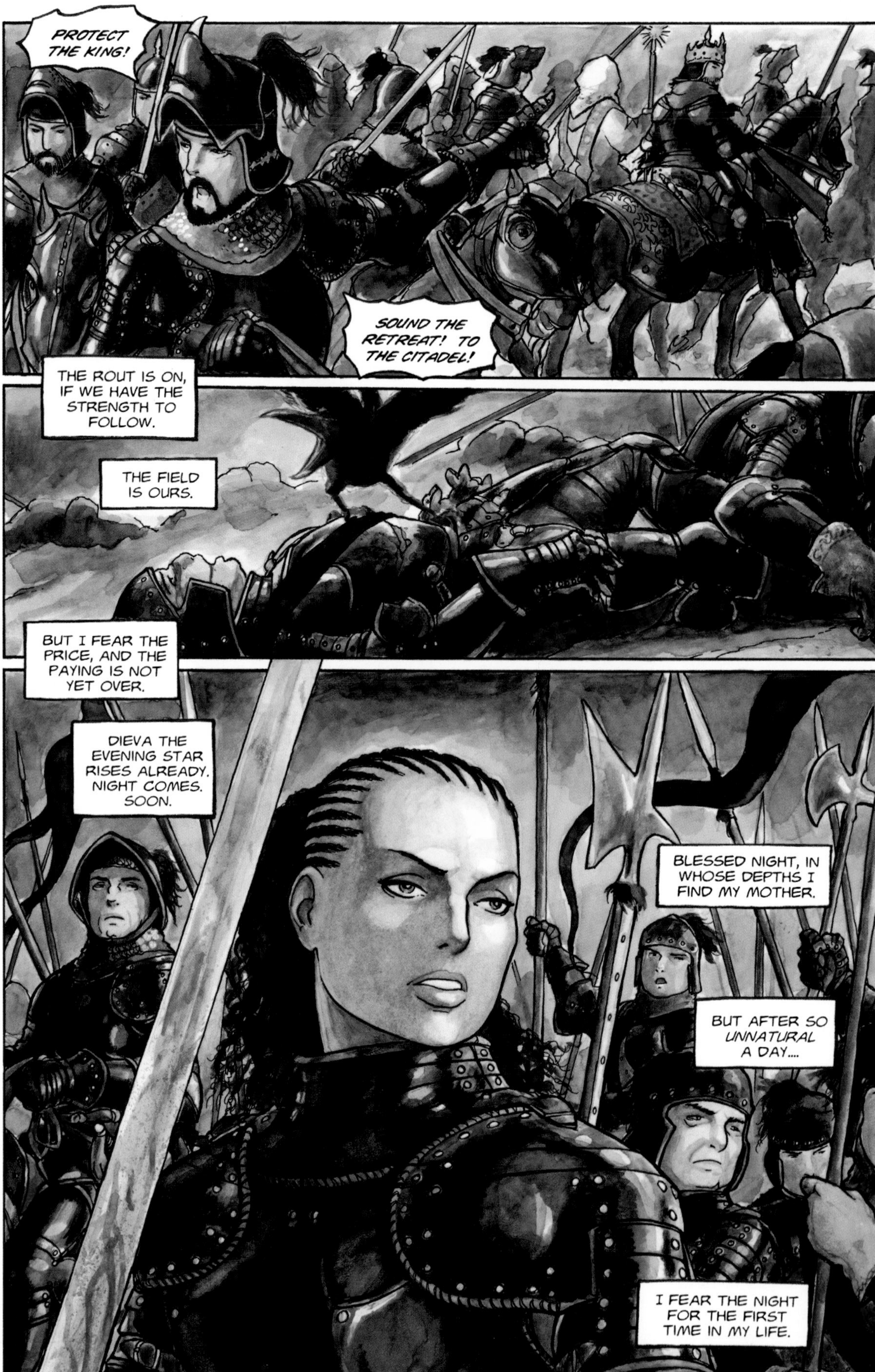
PROTECT THE KING!
SOUND THE RETREAT! TO THE CITADEL!
THE ROUT IS ON, IF WE HAVE THE STRENGTH TO FOLLOW.
THE FIELD IS OURS.
BUT I FEAR THE PRICE, AND THE PAYING IS NOT YET OVER.
DIEVA THE EVENING STAR RISES ALREADY. NIGHT COMES. SOON.
BLESSED NIGHT, IN WHOSE DEPTHS I FIND MY MOTHER.
BUT AFTER SO *UNNATURAL* A DAY....
I FEAR THE NIGHT FOR THE FIRST TIME IN MY LIFE.

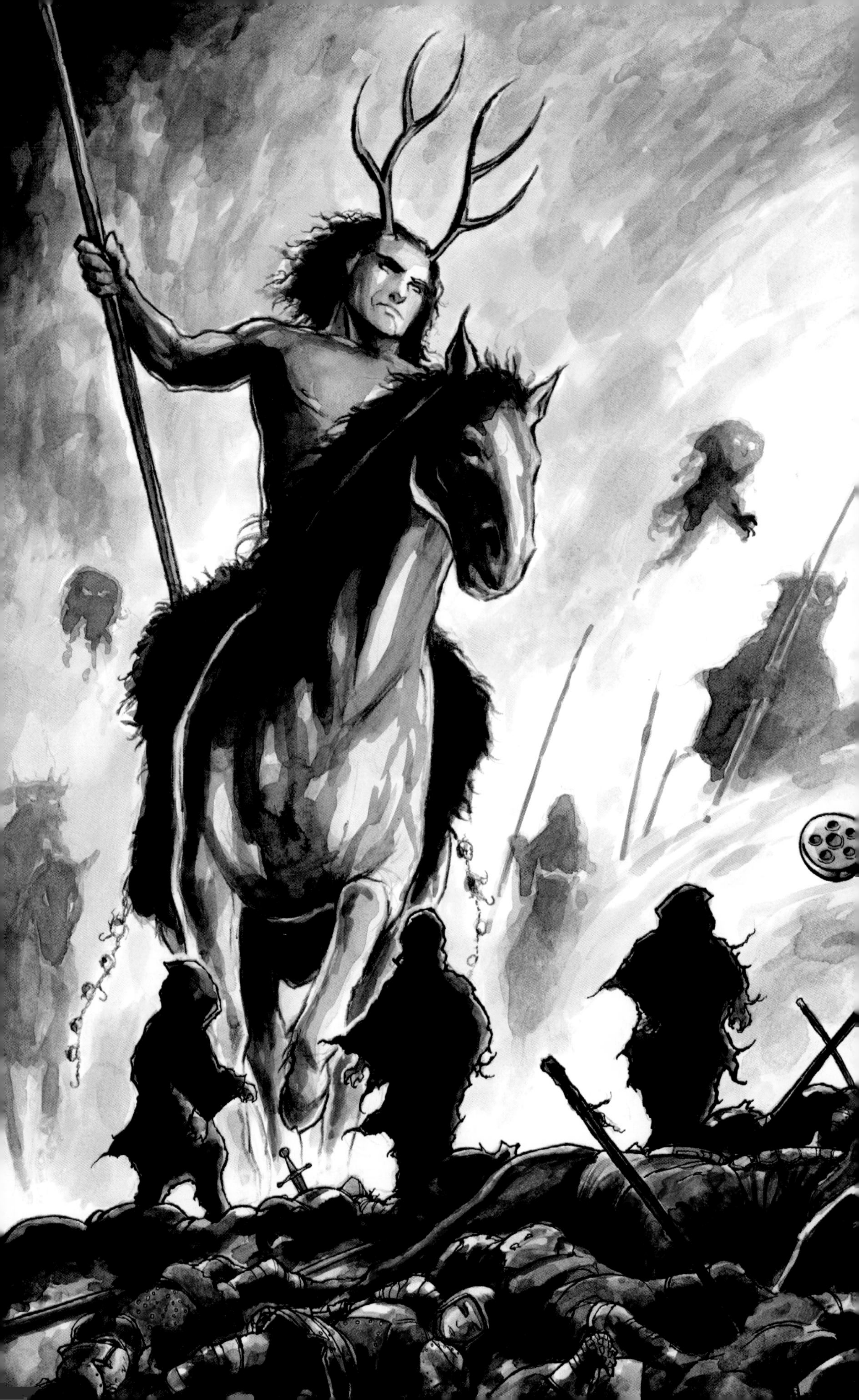

CHAPTER THREE

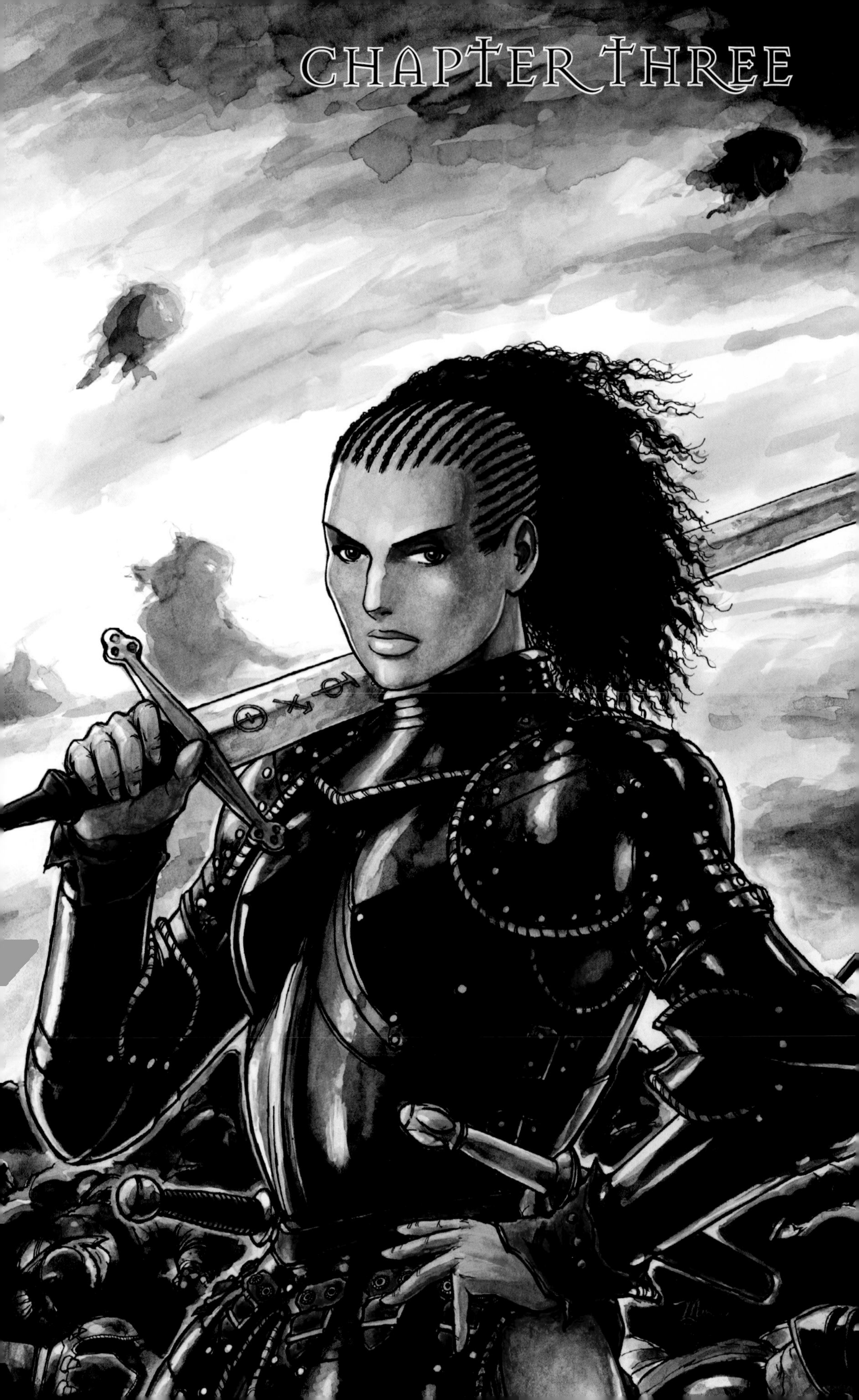

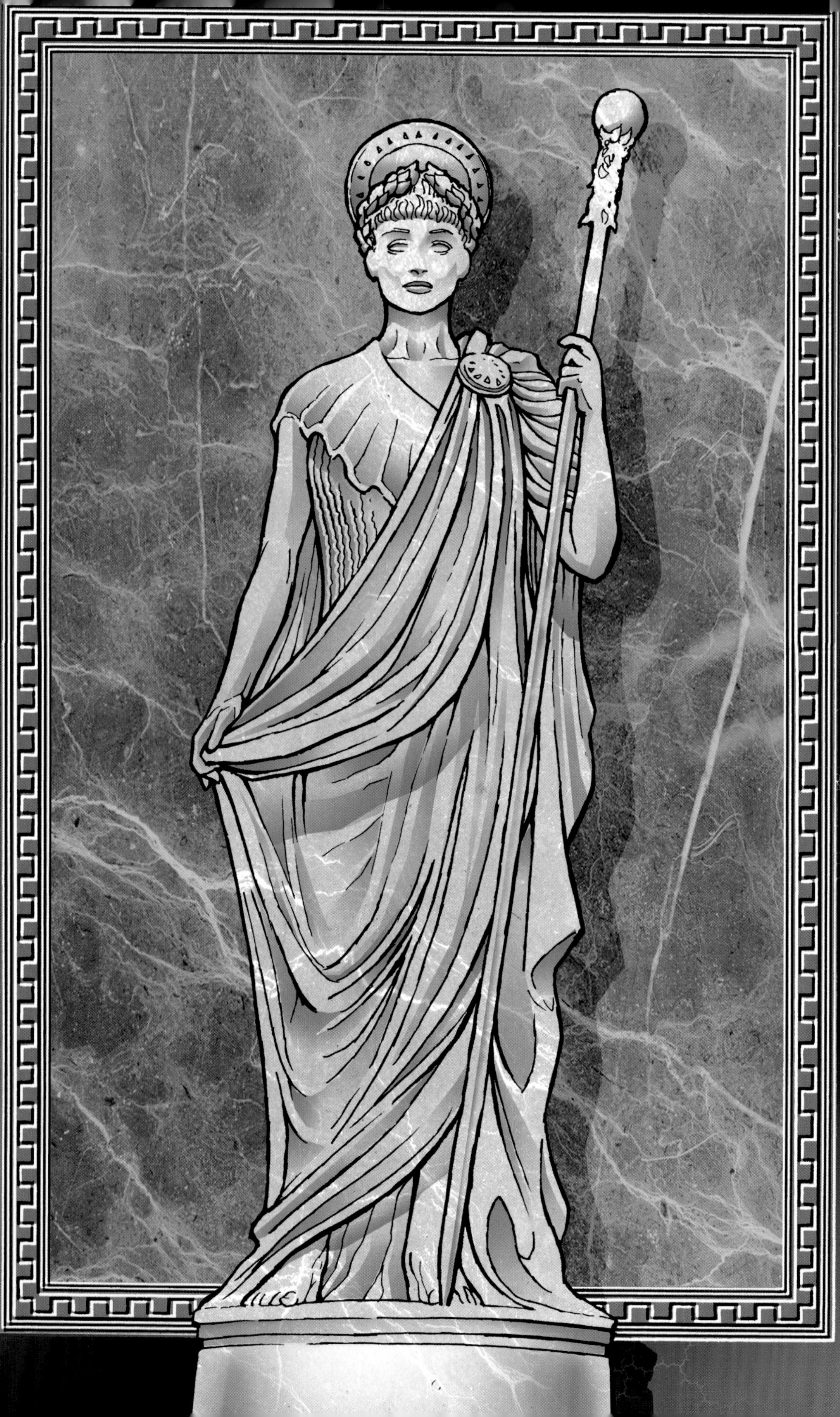

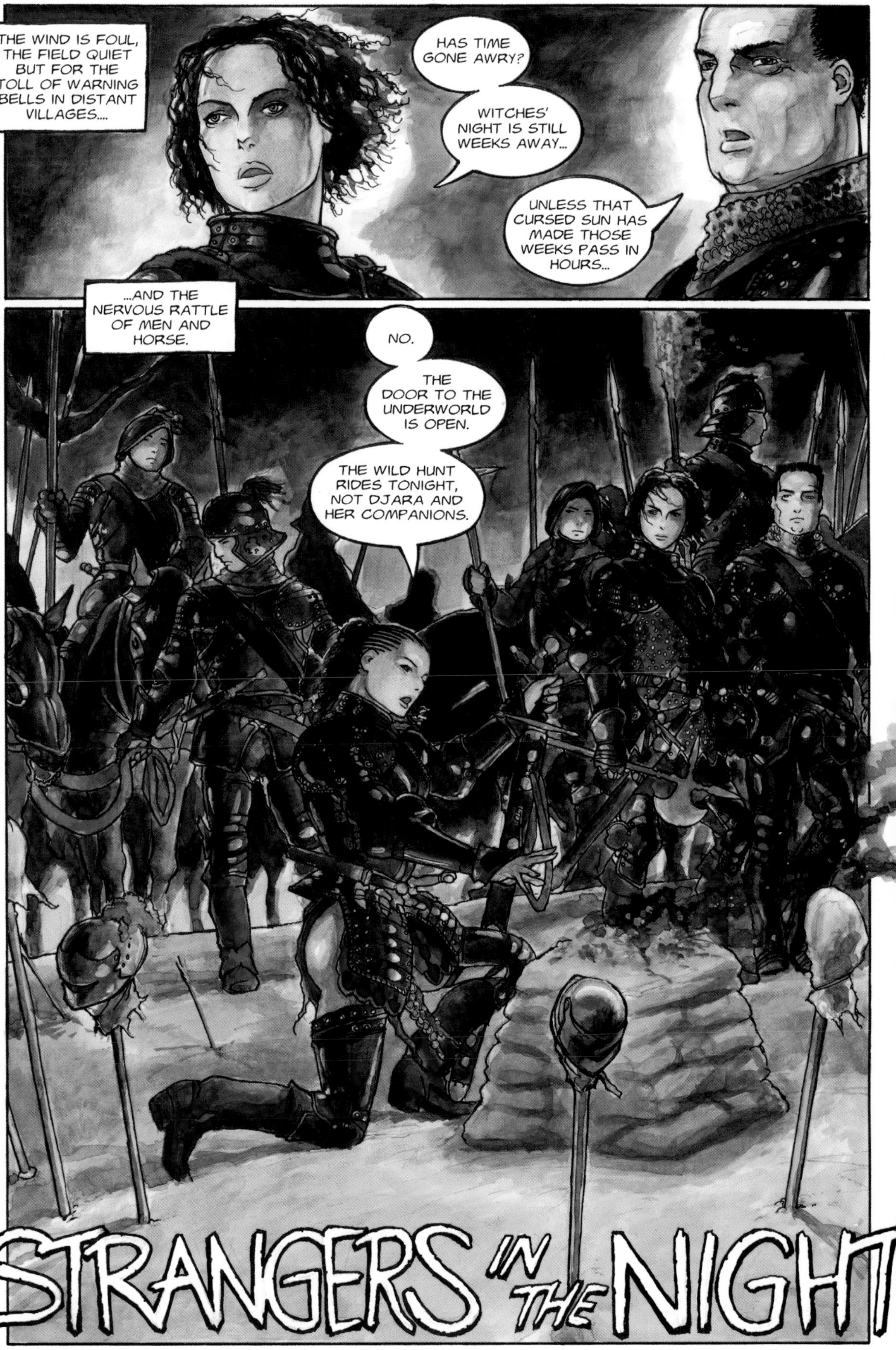
THE WIND IS FOUL, THE FIELD QUIET BUT FOR THE TOLL OF WARNING BELLS IN DISTANT VILLAGES....
HAS TIME GONE AWRY?
WITCHES' NIGHT IS STILL WEEKS AWAY...
UNLESS THAT CURSED SUN HAS MADE THOSE WEEKS PASS IN HOURS...
...AND THE NERVOUS RATTLE OF MEN AND HORSE.
NO.
THE DOOR TO THE UNDERWORLD IS OPEN.
THE WILD HUNT RIDES TONIGHT, NOT DJARA AND HER COMPANIONS.
STRANGERS IN THE NIGHT

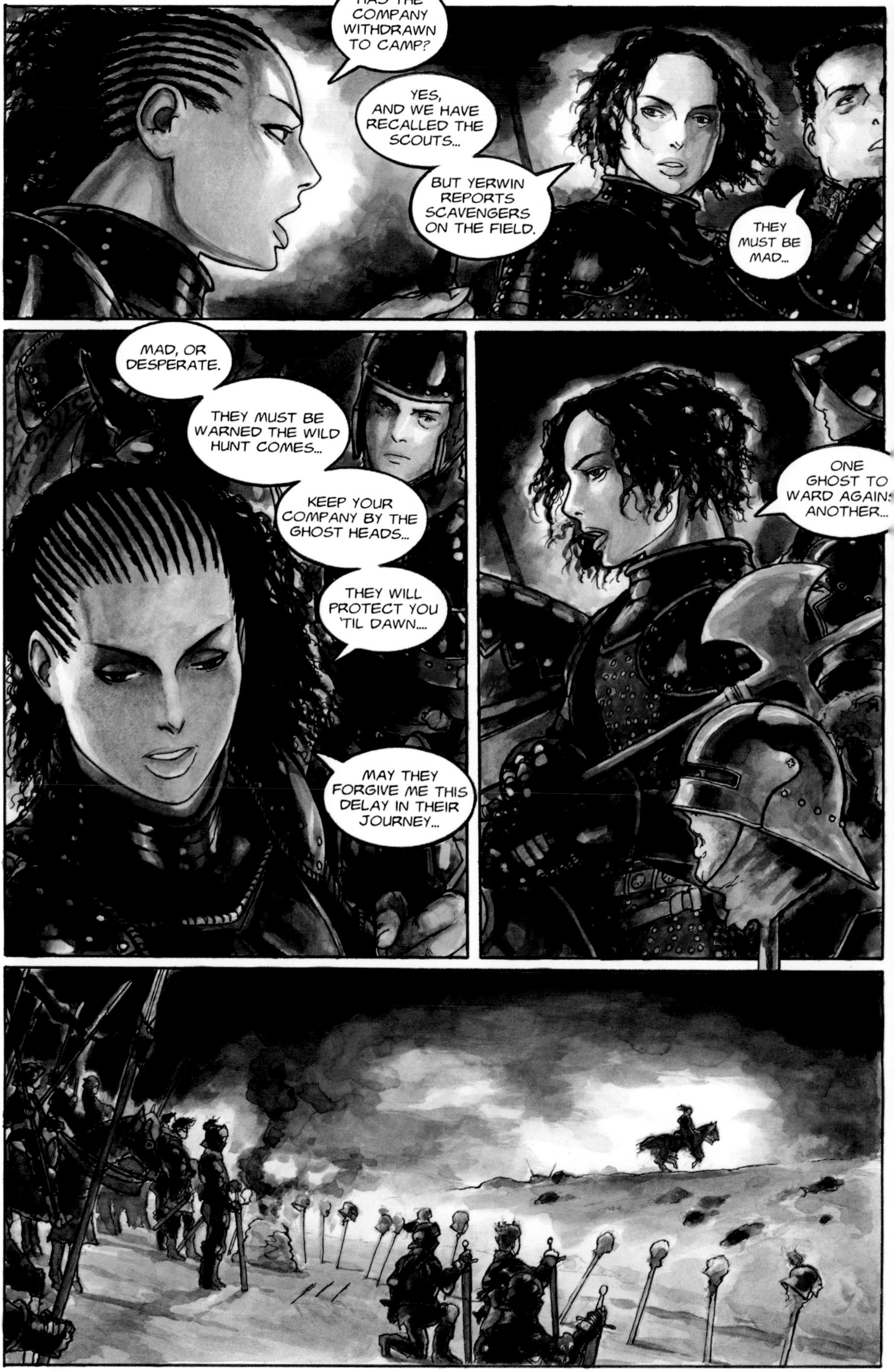
HAS THE COMPANY WITHDRAWN TO CAMP?
YES, AND WE HAVE RECALLED THE SCOUTS...
BUT YERWIN REPORTS SCAVENGERS ON THE FIELD.
THEY MUST BE MAD...
MAD, OR DESPERATE.
THEY MUST BE WARNED THE WILD HUNT COMES...
KEEP YOUR COMPANY BY THE GHOST HEADS...
THEY WILL PROTECT YOU 'TIL DAWN....
MAY THEY FORGIVE ME THIS DELAY IN THEIR JOURNEY...
ONE GHOST TO WARD AGAIN: ANOTHER...

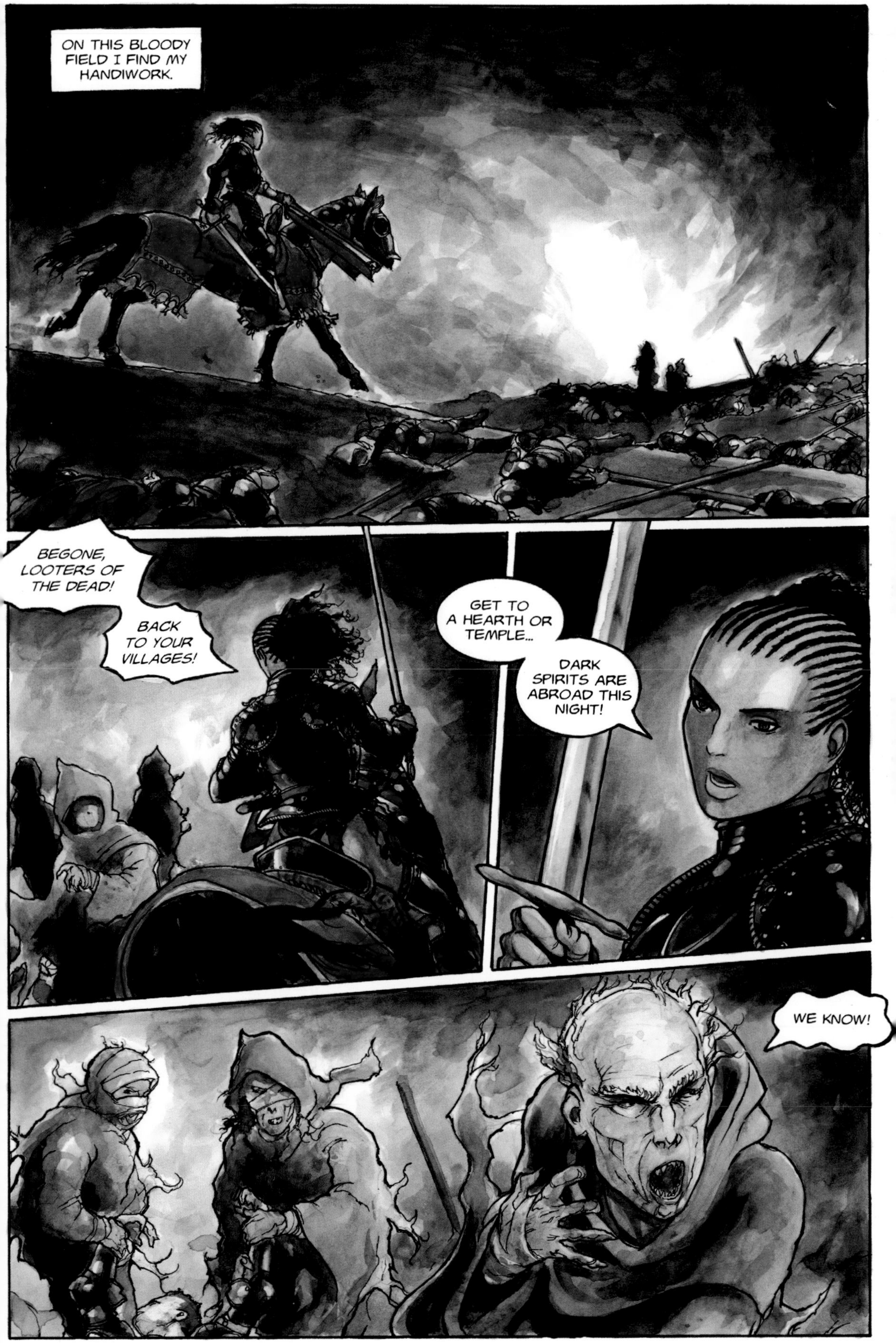
ON THIS BLOODY FIELD I FIND MY HANDIWORK.
BEGONE, LOOTERS OF THE DEAD!
BACK TO YOUR VILLAGES!
GET TO A HEARTH OR TEMPLE...
DARK SPIRITS ARE ABROAD THIS NIGHT!
WE KNOW!

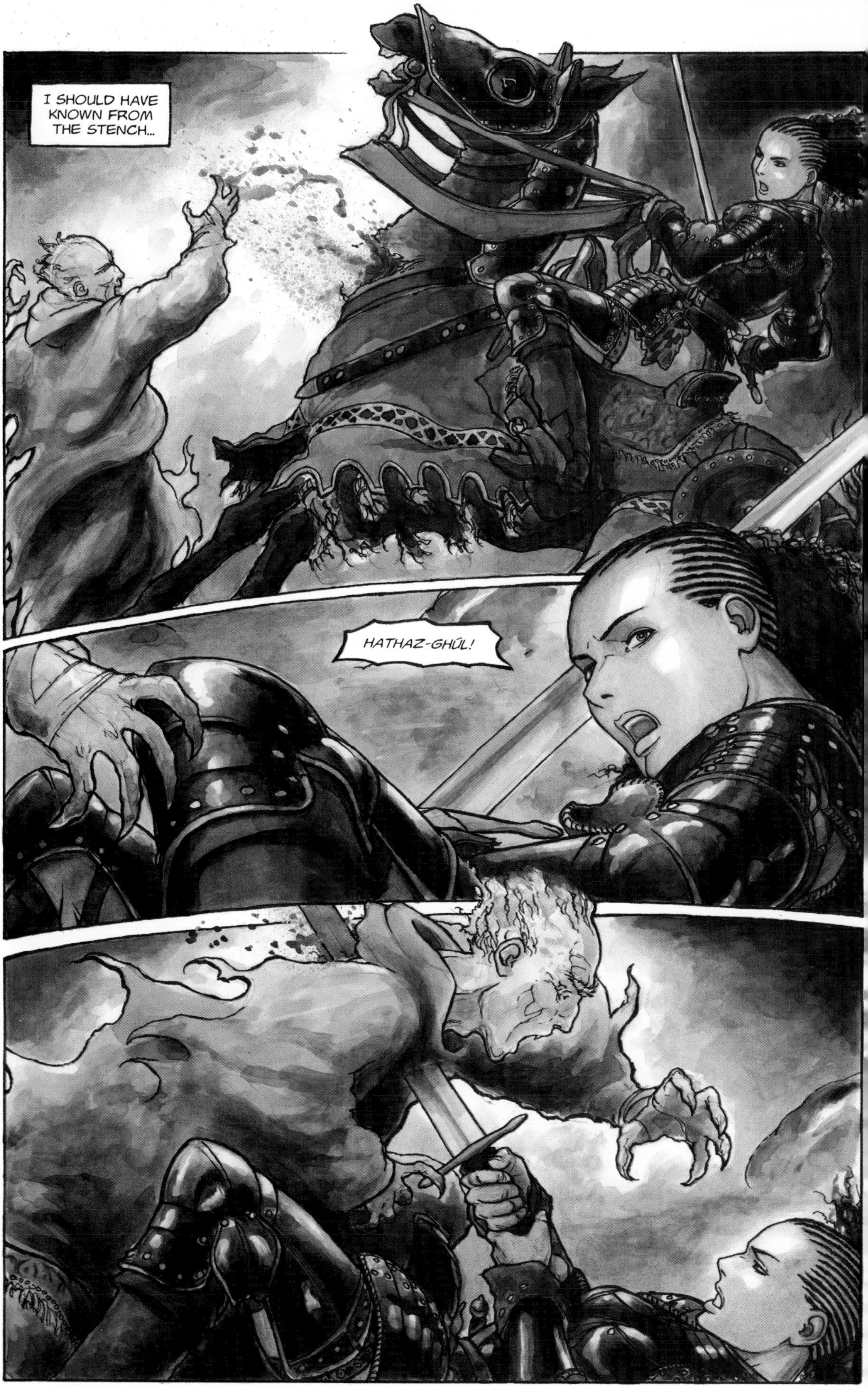
I SHOULD HAVE KNOWN FROM THE STENCH...
HATHAZ-GHÚL!

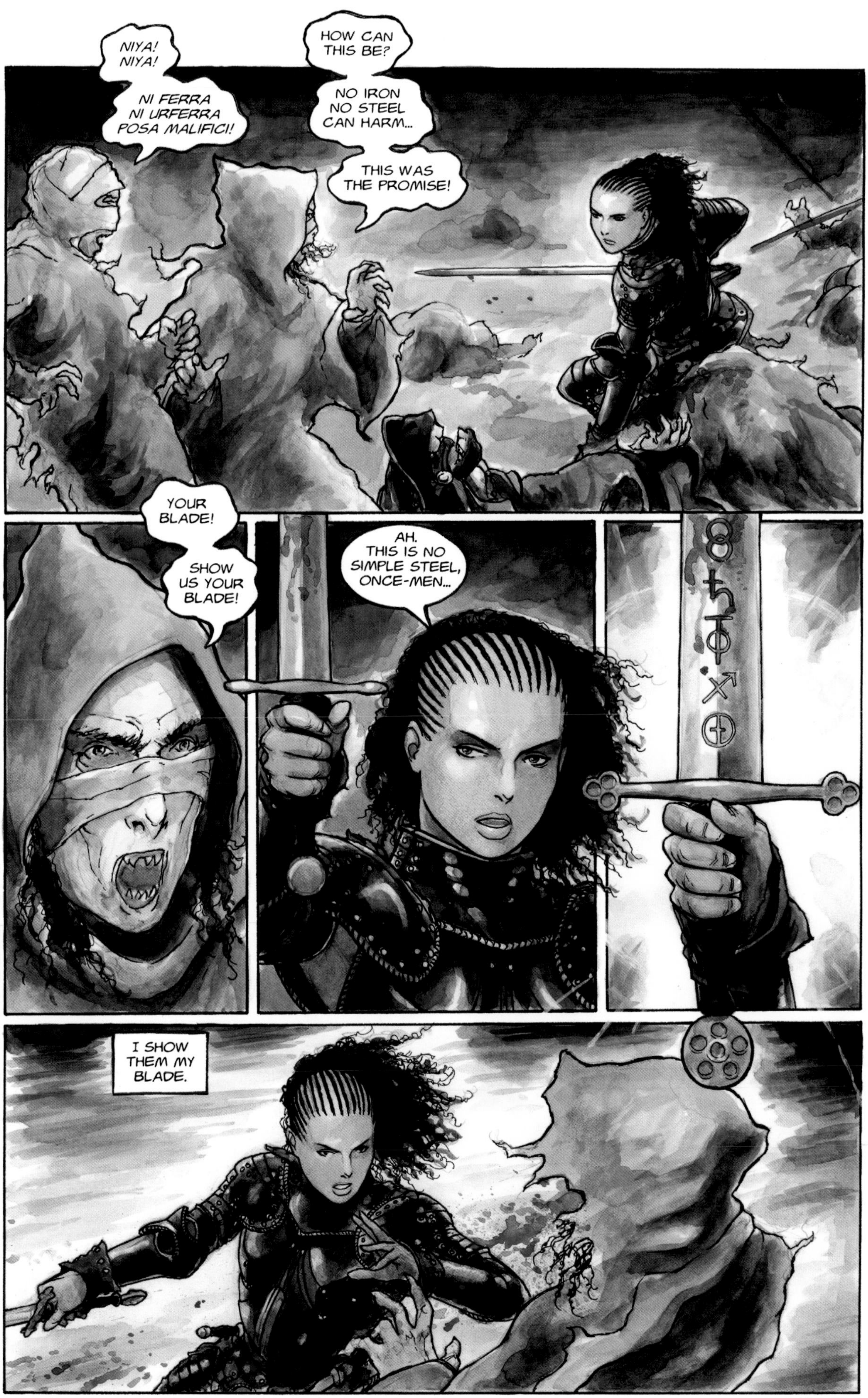
NIYA! NIYA!
NI FERRA NI URFERRA POSA MALIFICI!
HOW CAN THIS BE?
NO IRON NO STEEL CAN HARM...
THIS WAS THE PROMISE!
YOUR BLADE!
SHOW US YOUR BLADE!
AH. THIS IS NO SIMPLE STEEL, ONCE-MEN...
I SHOW THEM MY BLADE.

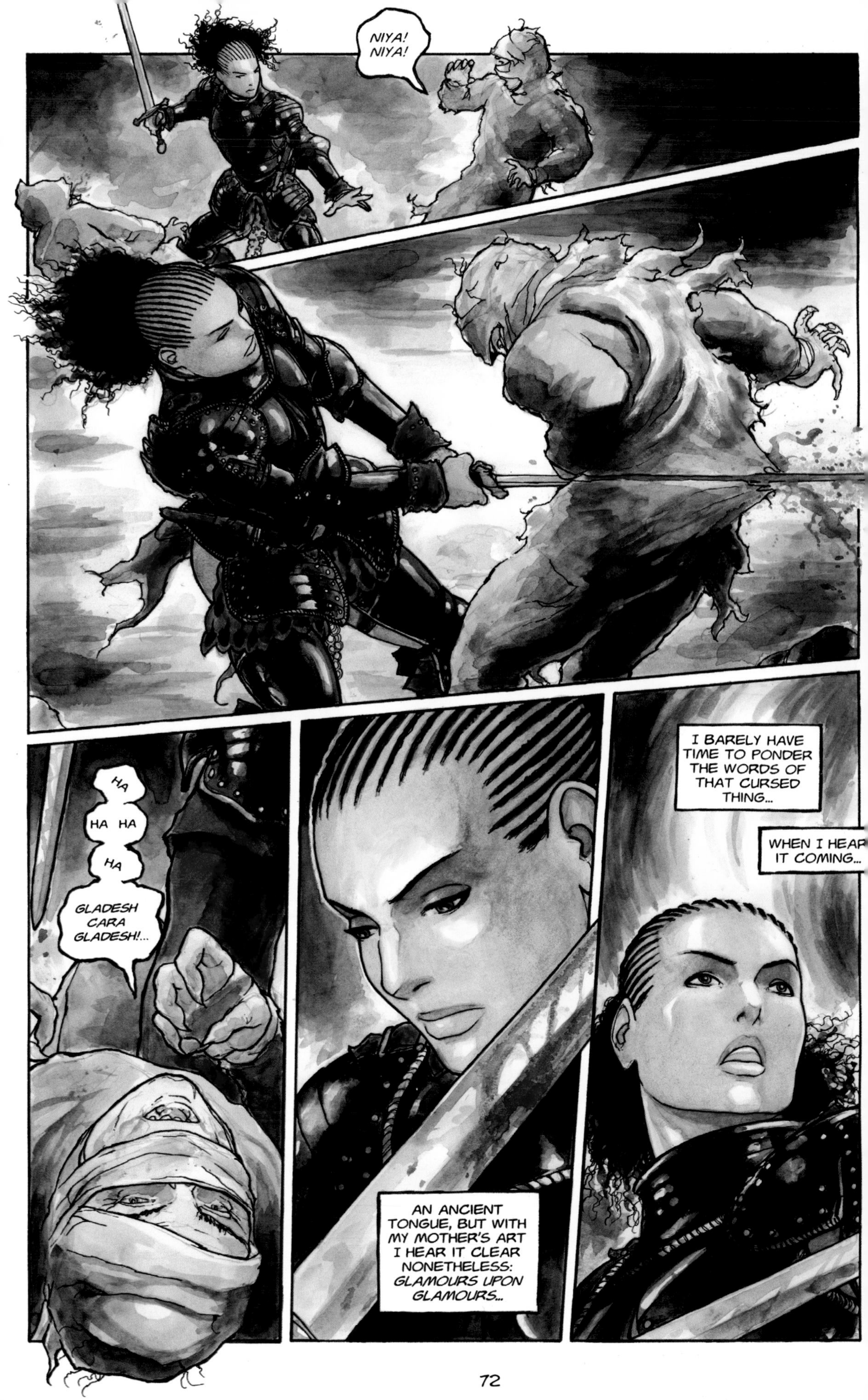

NIYA! NIYA!
HA
HA HA
HA
GLADESH CARA GLADESH!...
AN ANCIENT TONGUE, BUT WITH MY MOTHER'S ART I HEAR IT CLEAR NONETHELESS: GLAMOURS UPON GLAMOURS...
I BARELY HAVE TIME TO PONDER THE WORDS OF THAT CURSED THING...
WHEN I HEAR IT COMING...

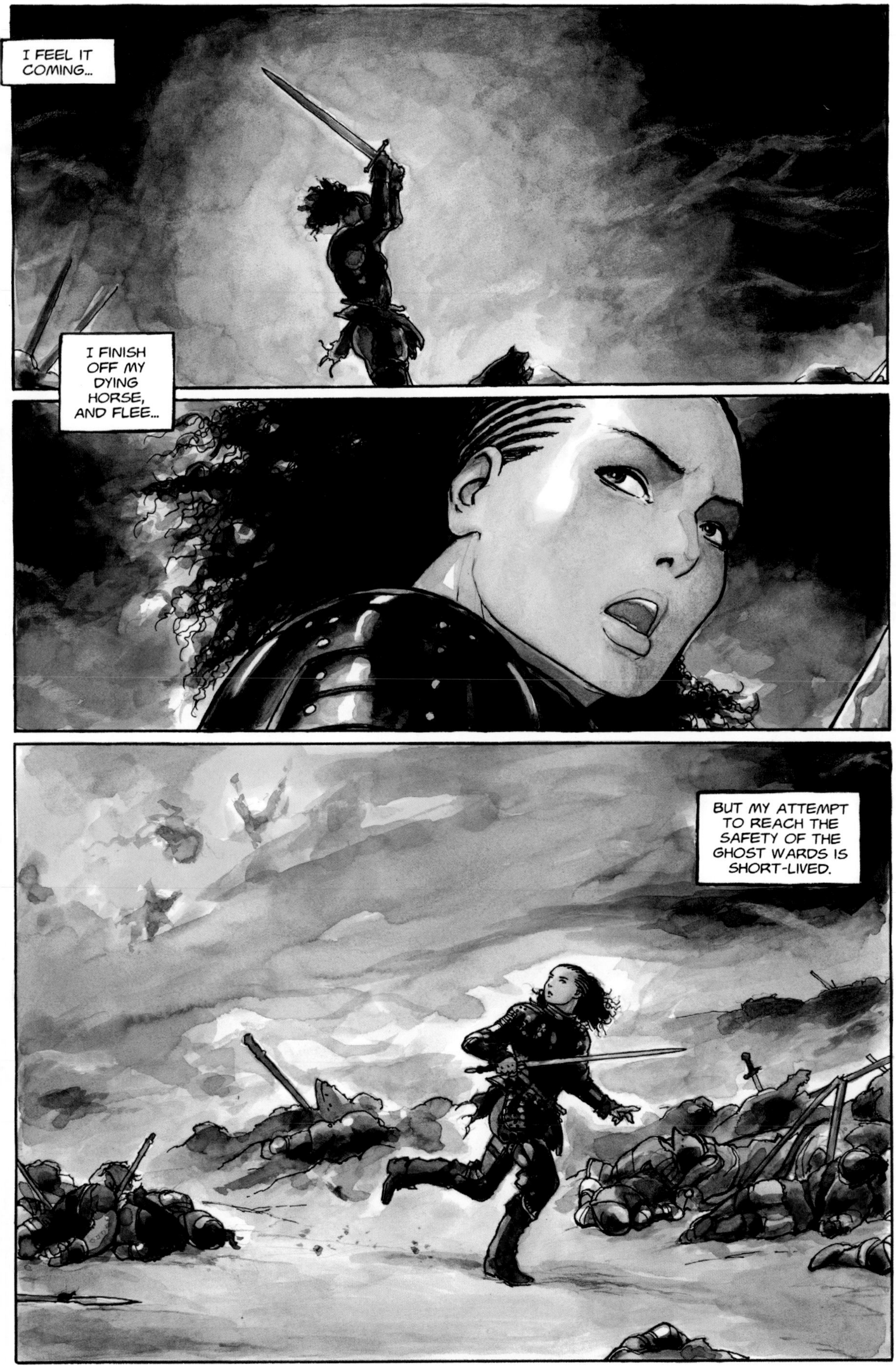
I FEEL IT COMING...
I FINISH OFF MY DYING HORSE, AND FLEE...
BUT MY ATTEMPT TO REACH THE SAFETY OF THE GHOST WARDS IS SHORT-LIVED.

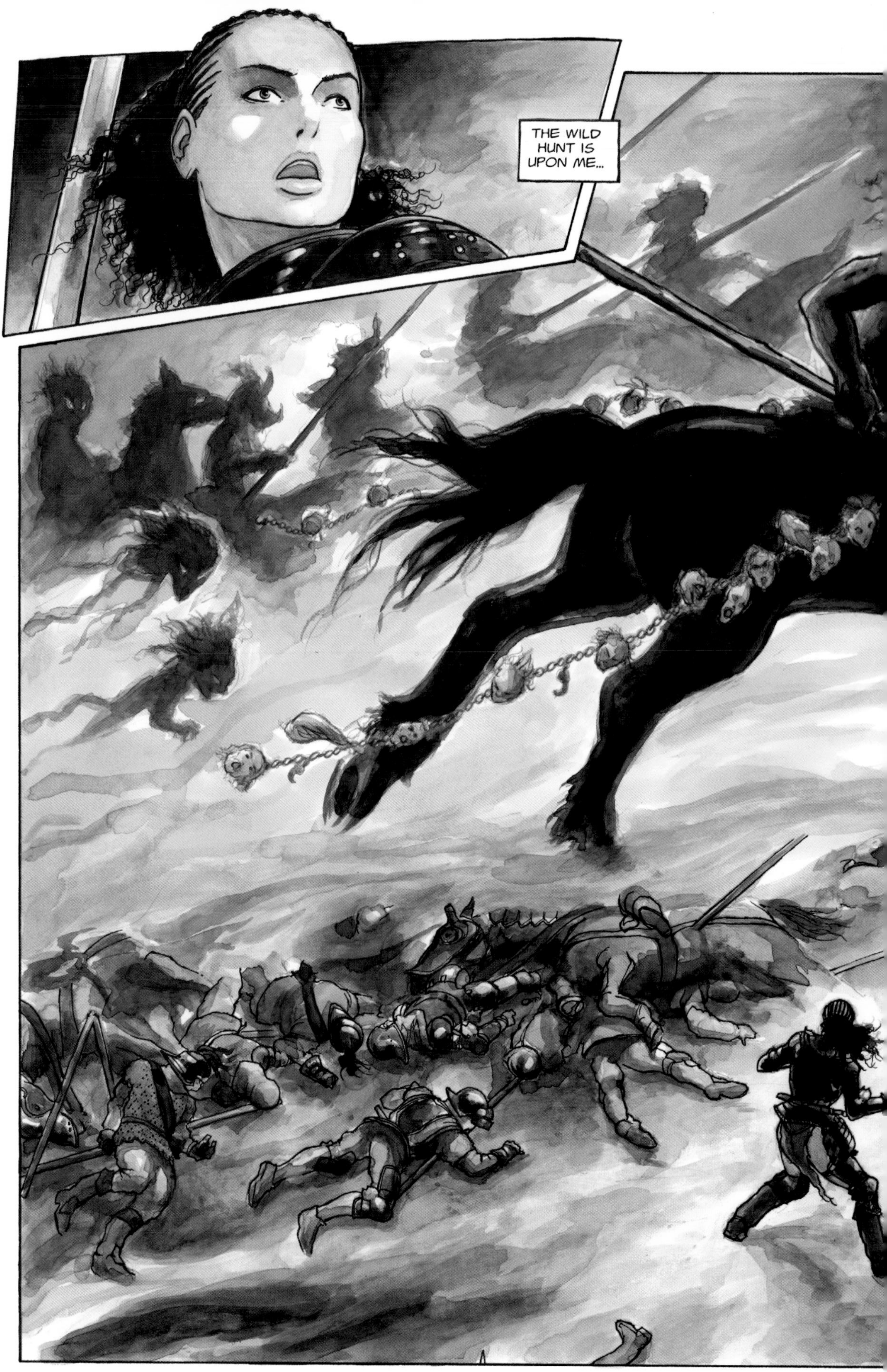
THE WILD HUNT IS UPON ME...

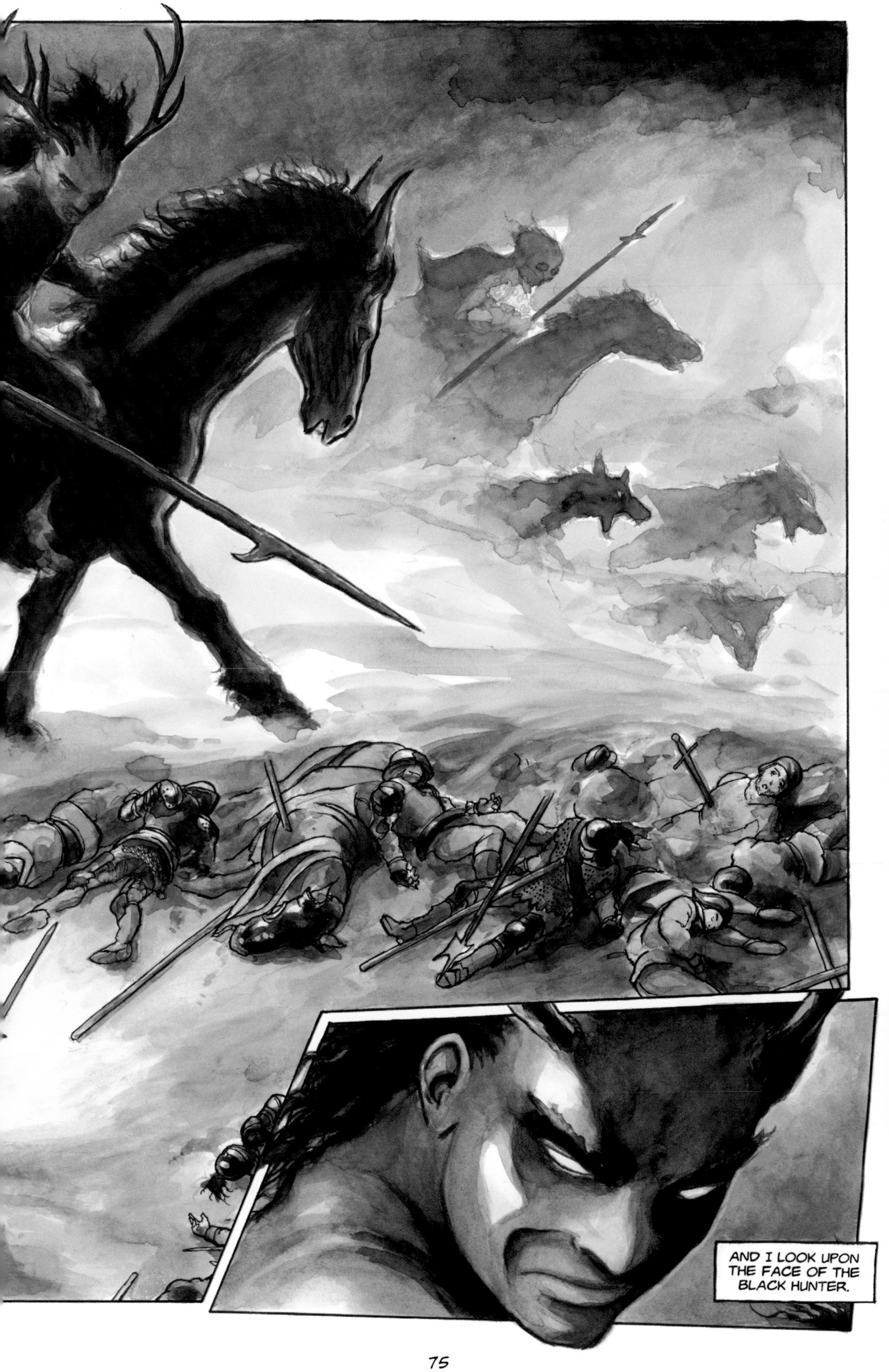
AND I LOOK UPON THE FACE OF THE BLACK HUNTER.

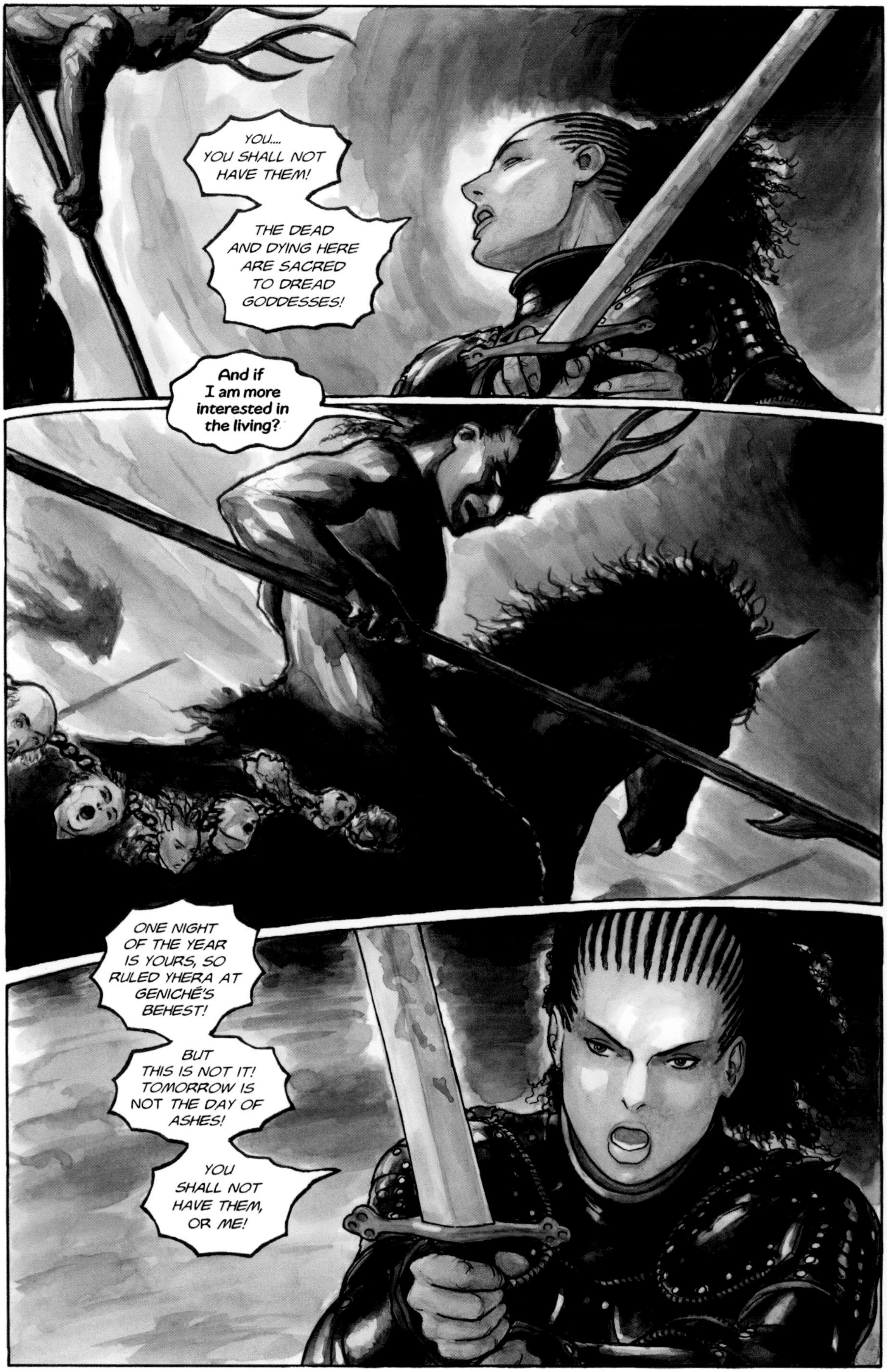

YOU.... YOU SHALL NOT HAVE THEM!
THE DEAD AND DYING HERE ARE SACRED TO DREAD GODDESSES!
And if I am more interested in the living?
ONE NIGHT OF THE YEAR IS YOURS, SO RULED YHERA AT GENICHÉ'S BEHEST!
BUT THIS IS NOT IT! TOMORROW IS NOT THE DAY OF ASHES!
YOU SHALL NOT HAVE THEM, OR ME!

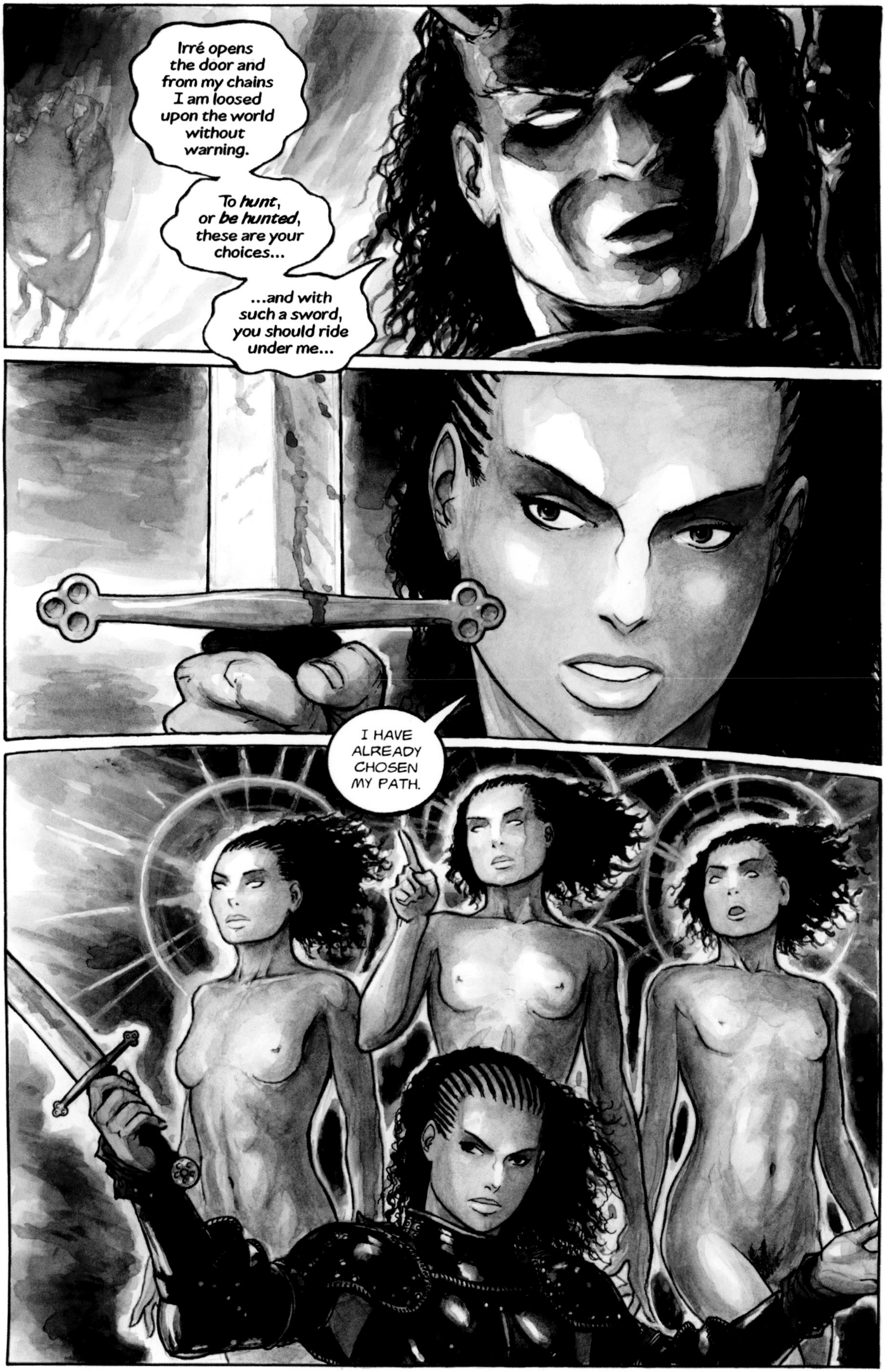
Irré opens the door and from my chains I am loosed upon the world without warning.
To hunt, or be hunted, these are your choices...
...and with such a sword, you should ride under me...
I HAVE ALREADY CHOSEN MY PATH.

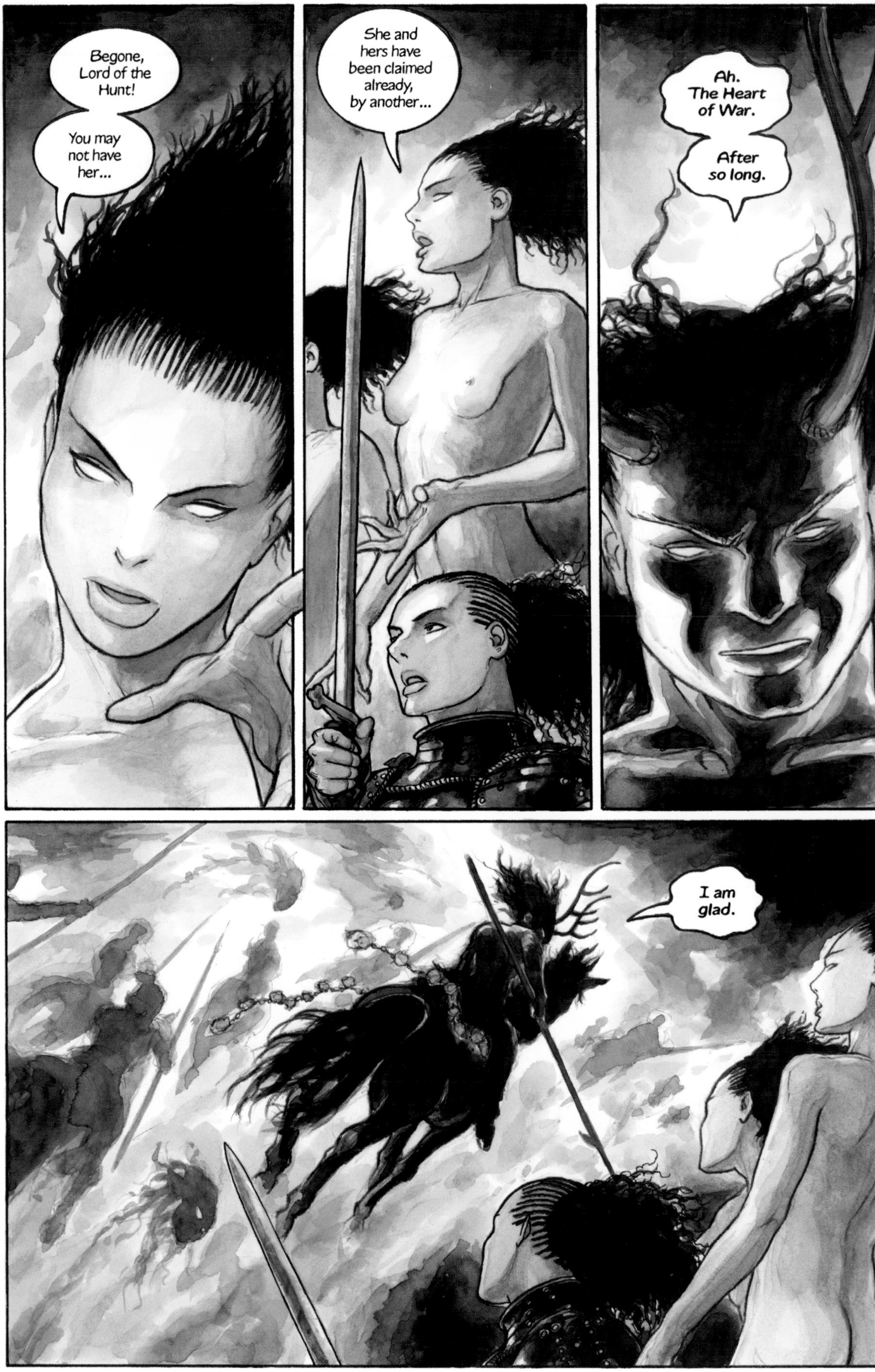
Begone, Lord of the Hunt!
You may not have her...
She and hers have been claimed already, by another...
Ah. The Heart of War.
After so long.
I am glad.

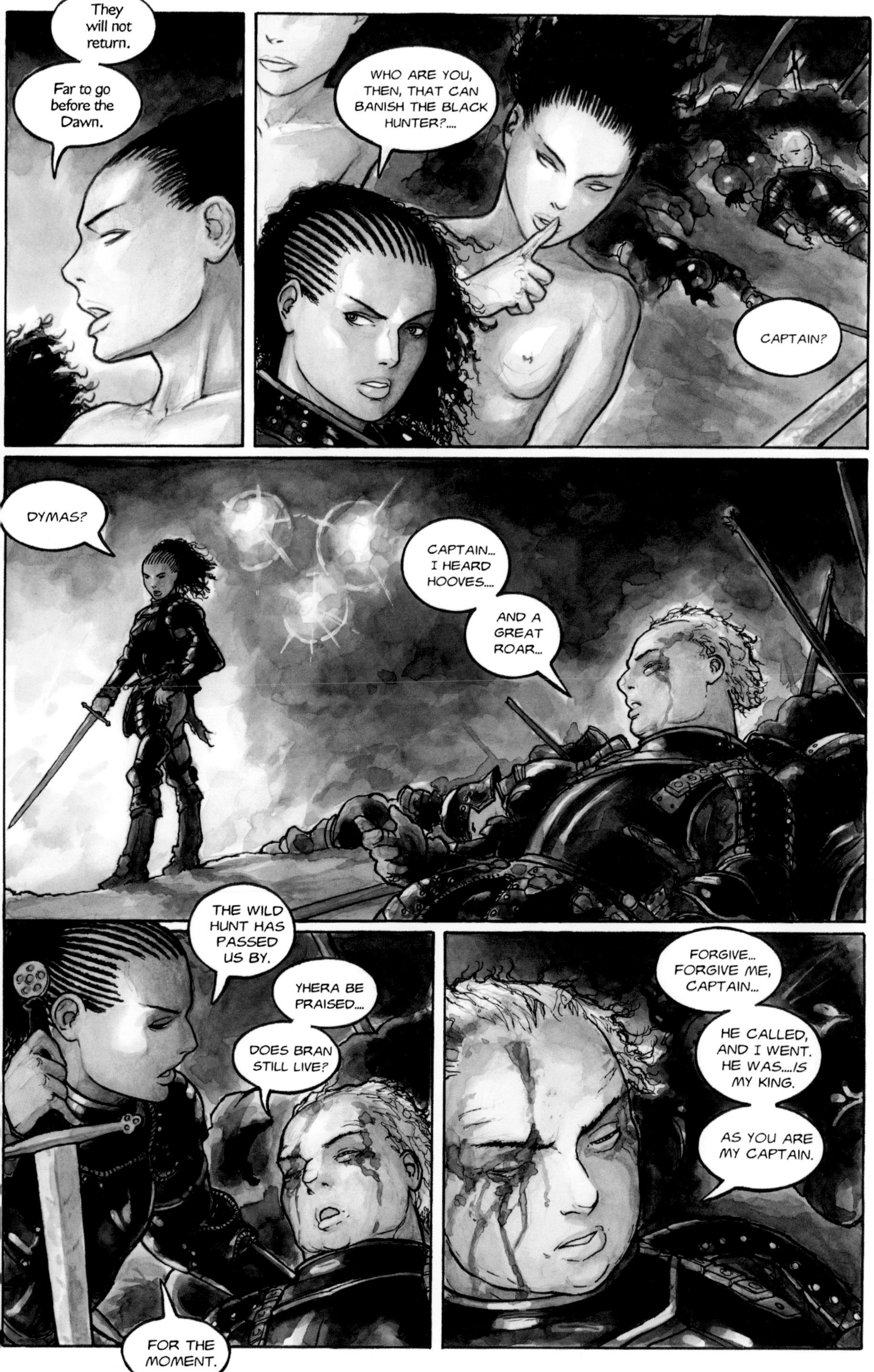
They will not return.
Far to go before the Dawn.
WHO ARE YOU, THEN, THAT CAN BANISH THE BLACK HUNTER?....
CAPTAIN?
DYMAS?
CAPTAIN... I HEARD HOOVES....
AND A GREAT ROAR...
THE WILD HUNT HAS PASSED US BY.
YHERA BE PRAISED....
DOES BRAN STILL LIVE?
FOR THE MOMENT.
FORGIVE... FORGIVE ME, CAPTAIN...
HE CALLED, AND I WENT. HE WAS....IS MY KING.
AS YOU ARE MY CAPTAIN.

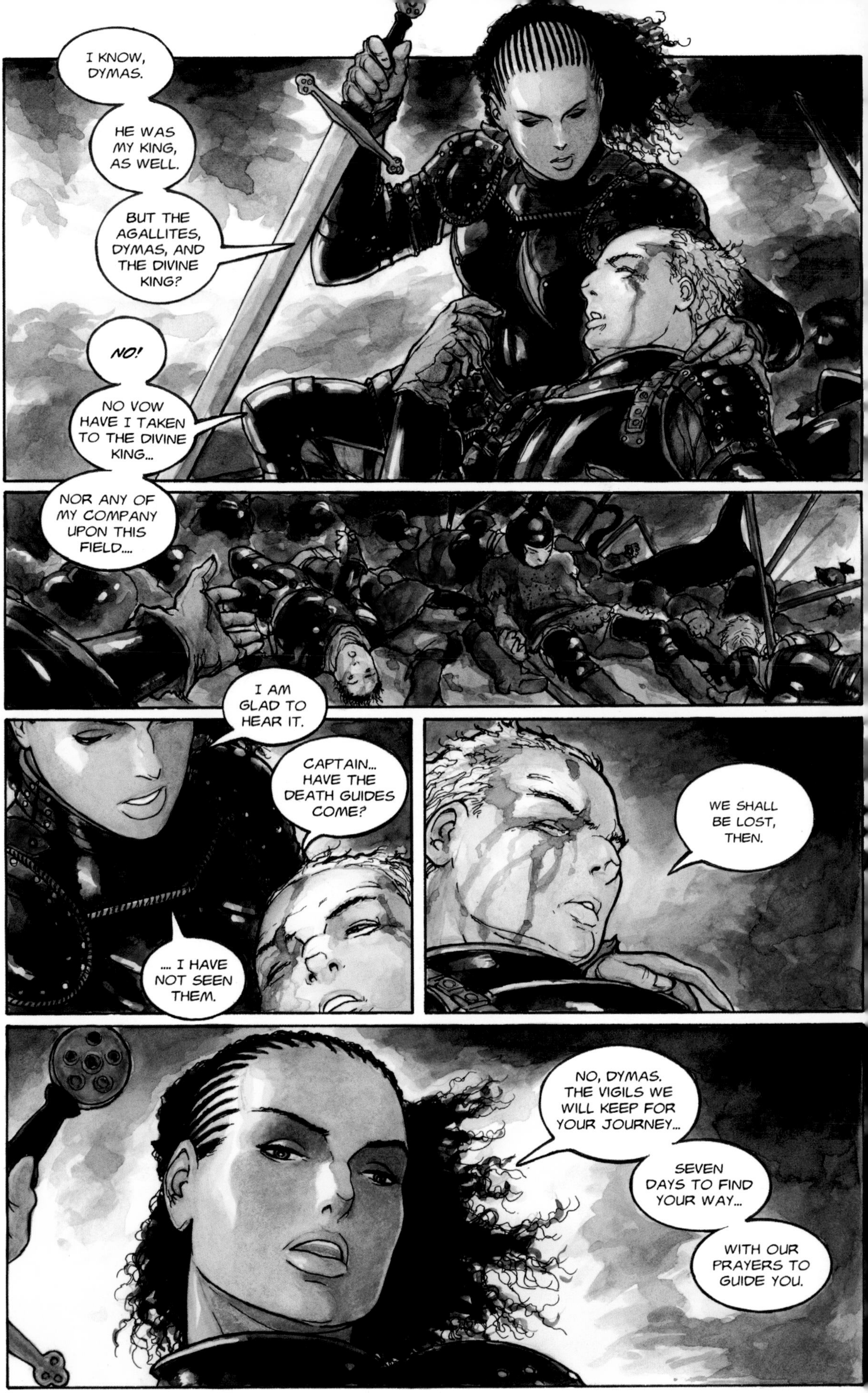
I KNOW, DYMAS.
HE WAS MY KING, AS WELL.
BUT THE AGALLITES, DYMAS, AND THE DIVINE KING?
NO!
NO VOW HAVE I TAKEN TO THE DIVINE KING...
NOR ANY OF MY COMPANY UPON THIS FIELD....
I AM GLAD TO HEAR IT.
CAPTAIN... HAVE THE DEATH GUIDES COME?
.... I HAVE NOT SEEN THEM.
WE SHALL BE LOST, THEN.
NO, DYMAS. THE VIGILS WE WILL KEEP FOR YOUR JOURNEY...
SEVEN DAYS TO FIND YOUR WAY...
WITH OUR PRAYERS TO GUIDE YOU.

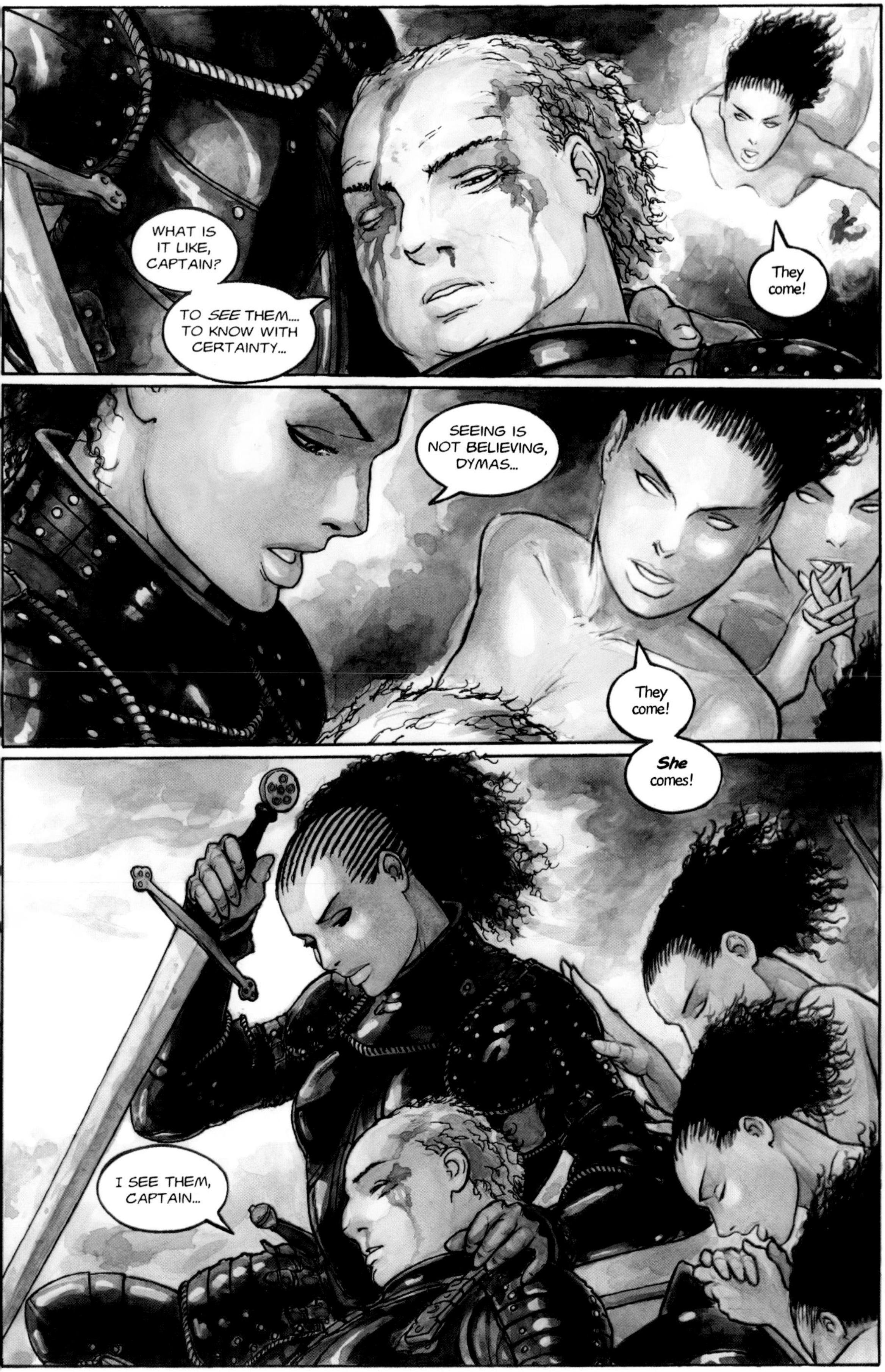
WHAT IS IT LIKE, CAPTAIN?
TO SEE THEM.... TO KNOW WITH CERTAINTY...
They come!
SEEING IS NOT BELIEVING, DYMAS...
They come!
She comes!
I SEE THEM, CAPTAIN...

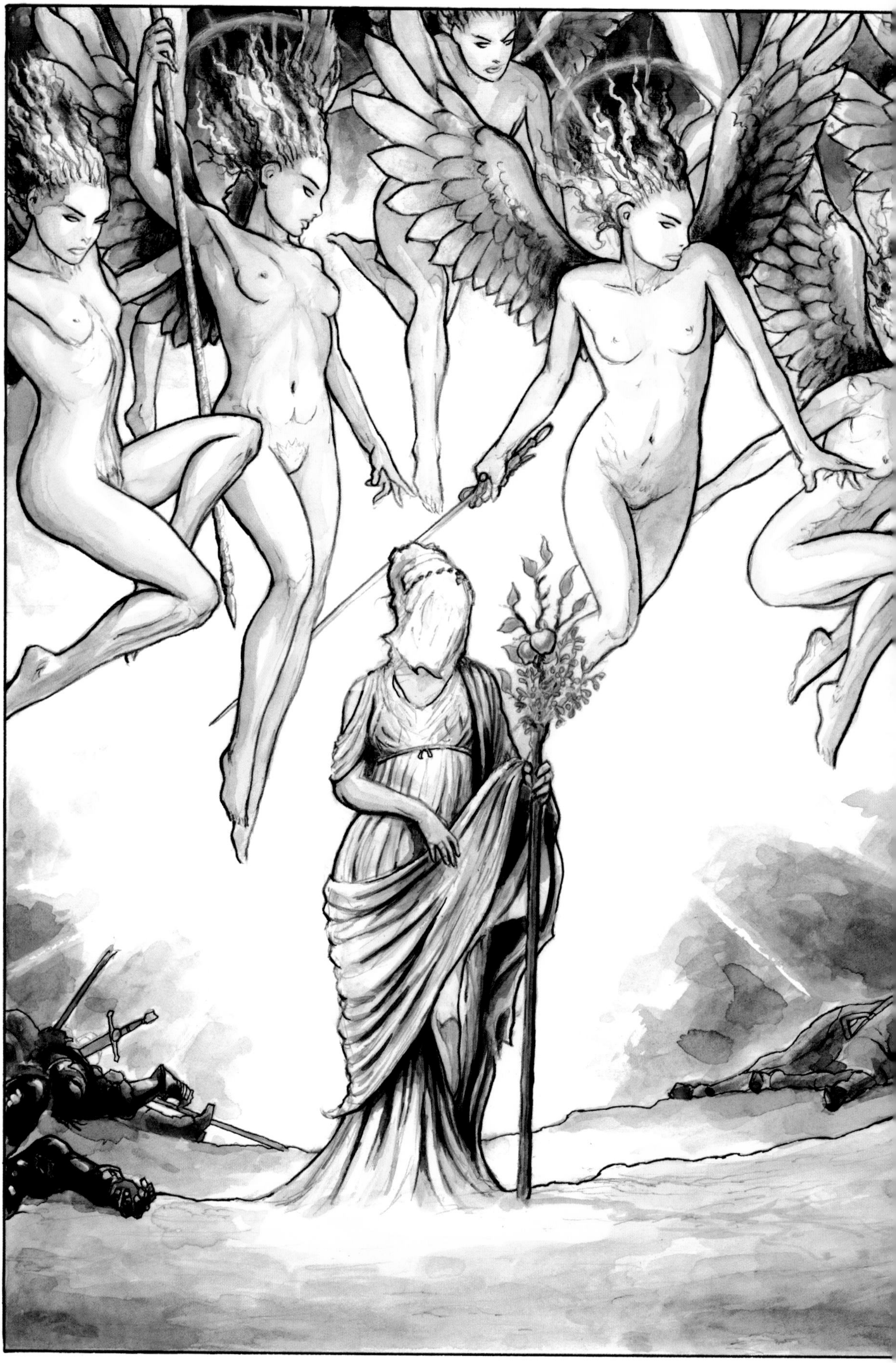

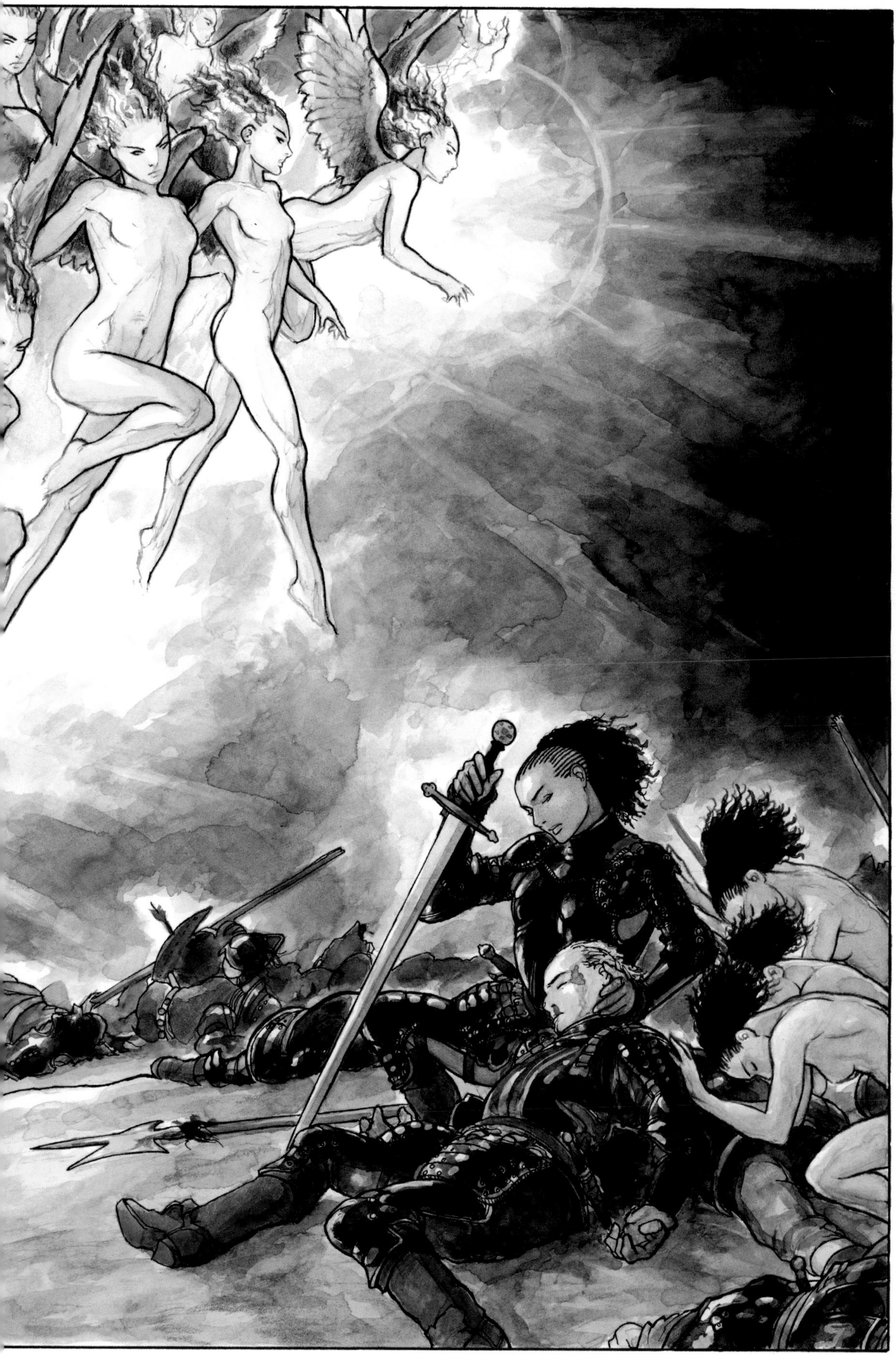

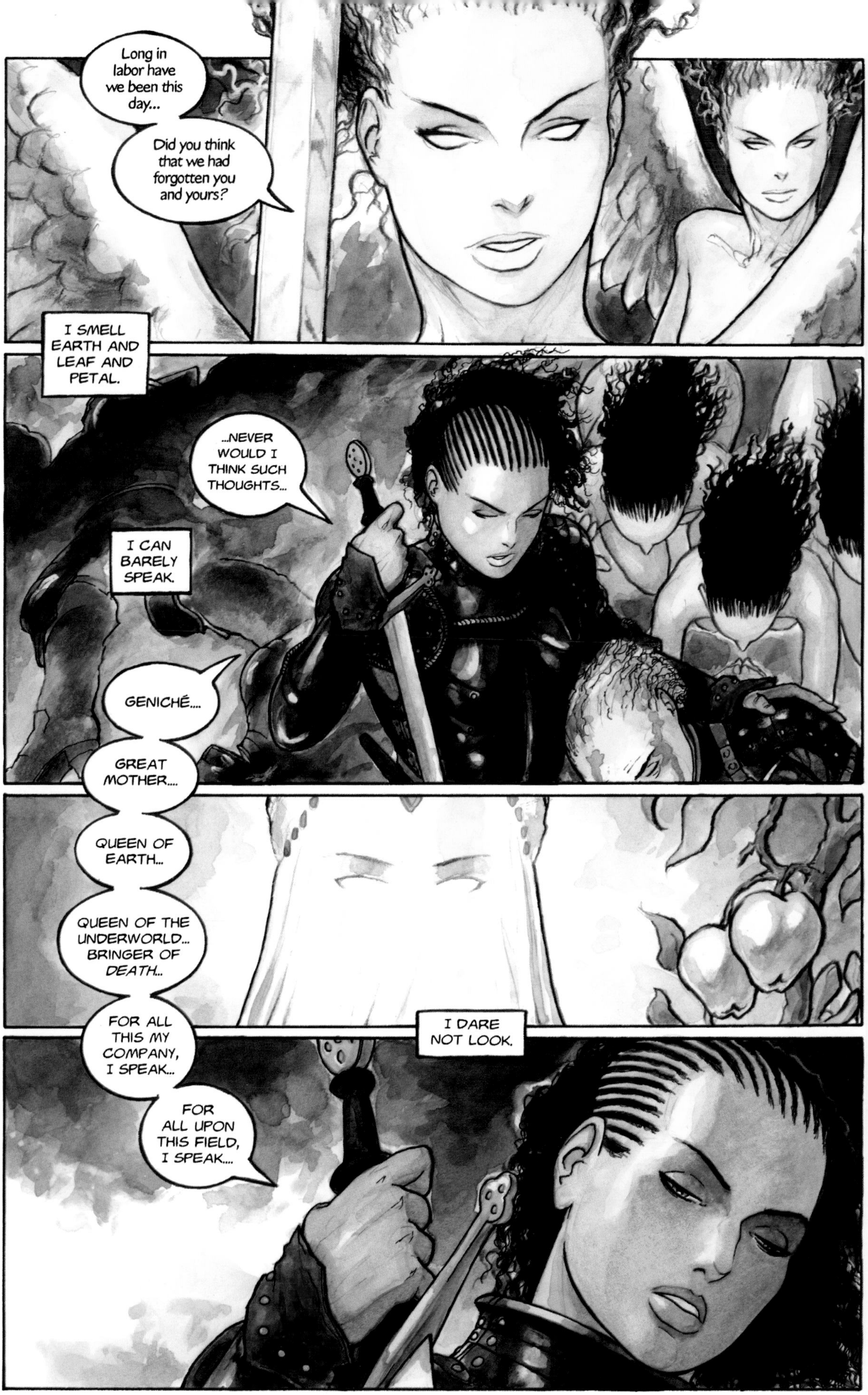
Long in labor have we been this day...
Did you think that we had forgotten you and yours?
I SMELL EARTH AND LEAF AND PETAL.
...NEVER WOULD I THINK SUCH THOUGHTS...
I CAN BARELY SPEAK.
GENICHÉ....
GREAT MOTHER....
QUEEN OF EARTH...
QUEEN OF THE UNDERWORLD... BRINGER OF DEATH...
FOR ALL THIS MY COMPANY, I SPEAK...
I DARE NOT LOOK.
FOR ALL UPON THIS FIELD, I SPEAK....

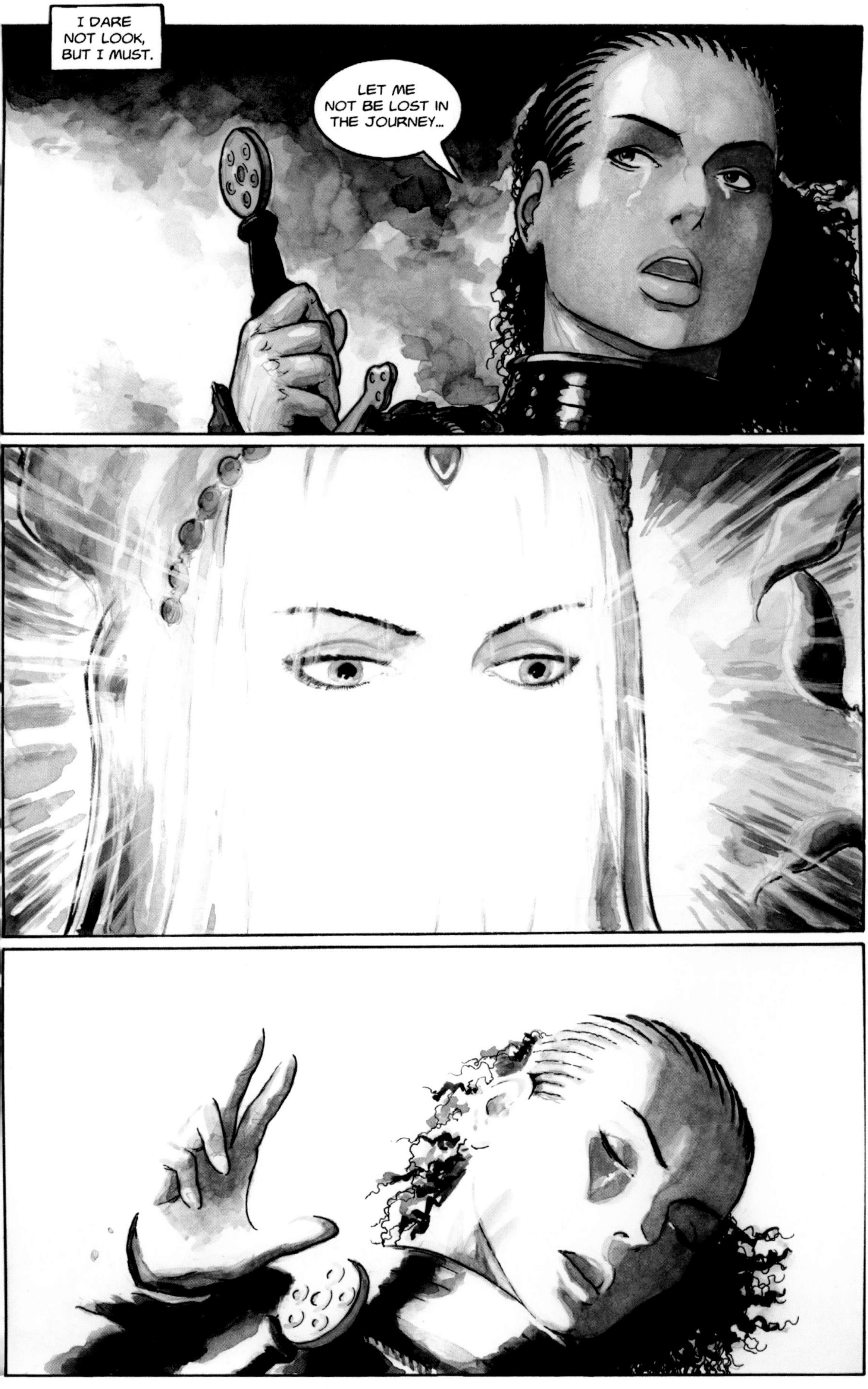
I DARE NOT LOOK, BUT I MUST.
LET ME NOT BE LOST IN THE JOURNEY...

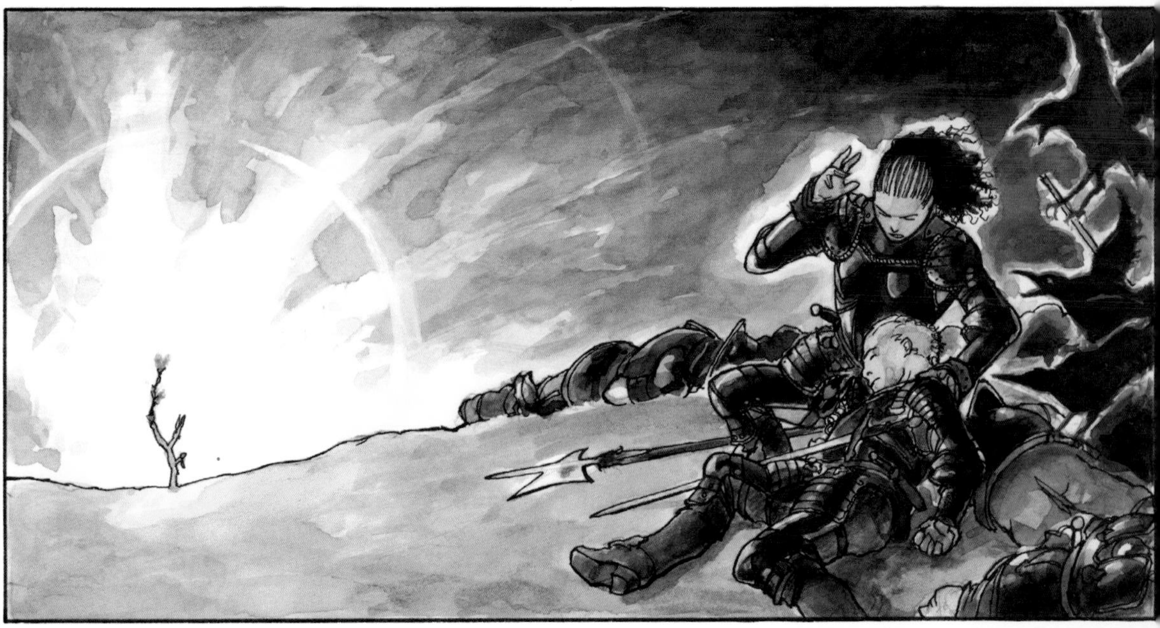

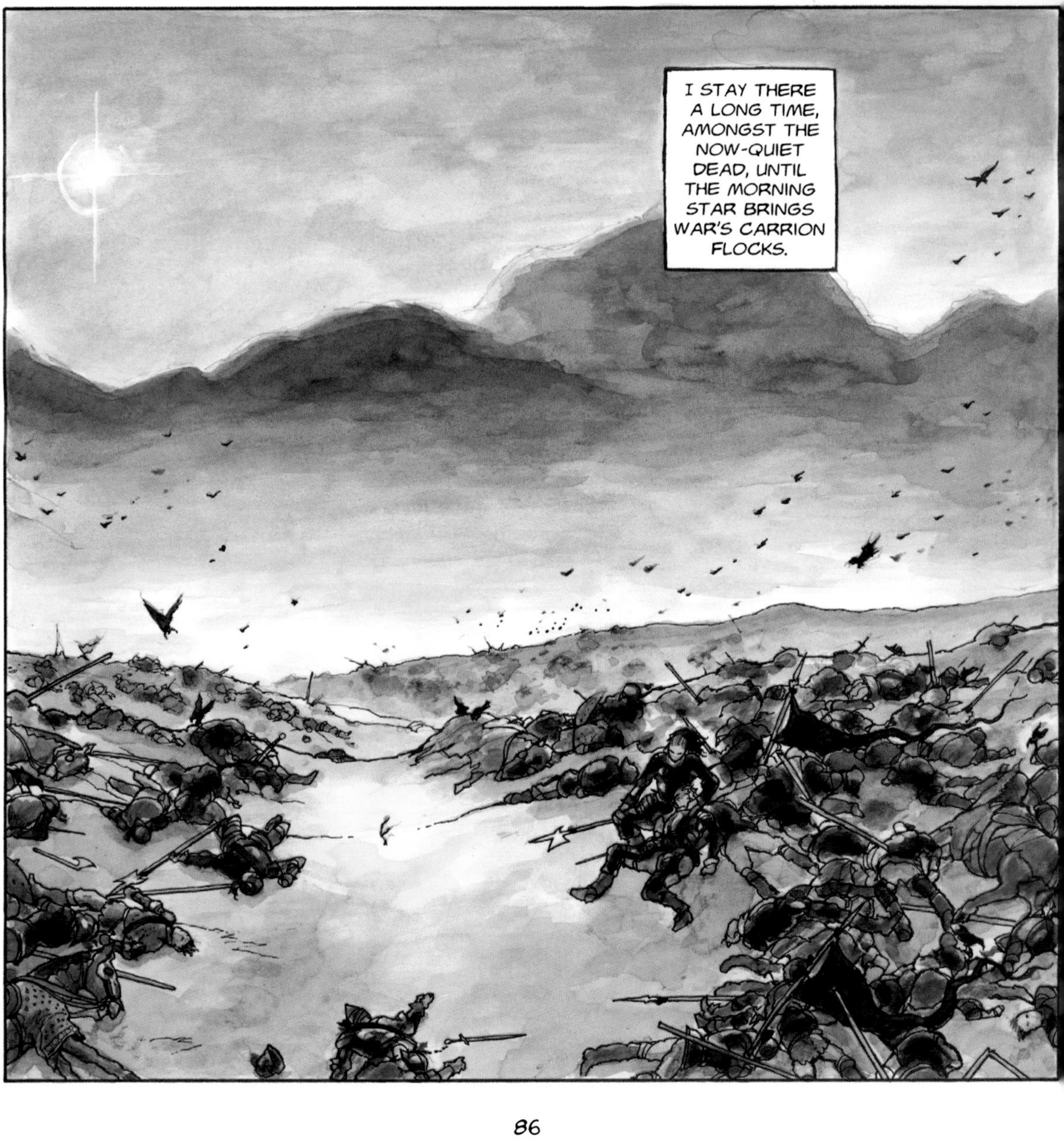
I STAY THERE A LONG TIME, AMONGST THE NOW-QUIET DEAD, UNTIL THE MORNING STAR BRINGS WAR'S CARRION FLOCKS.

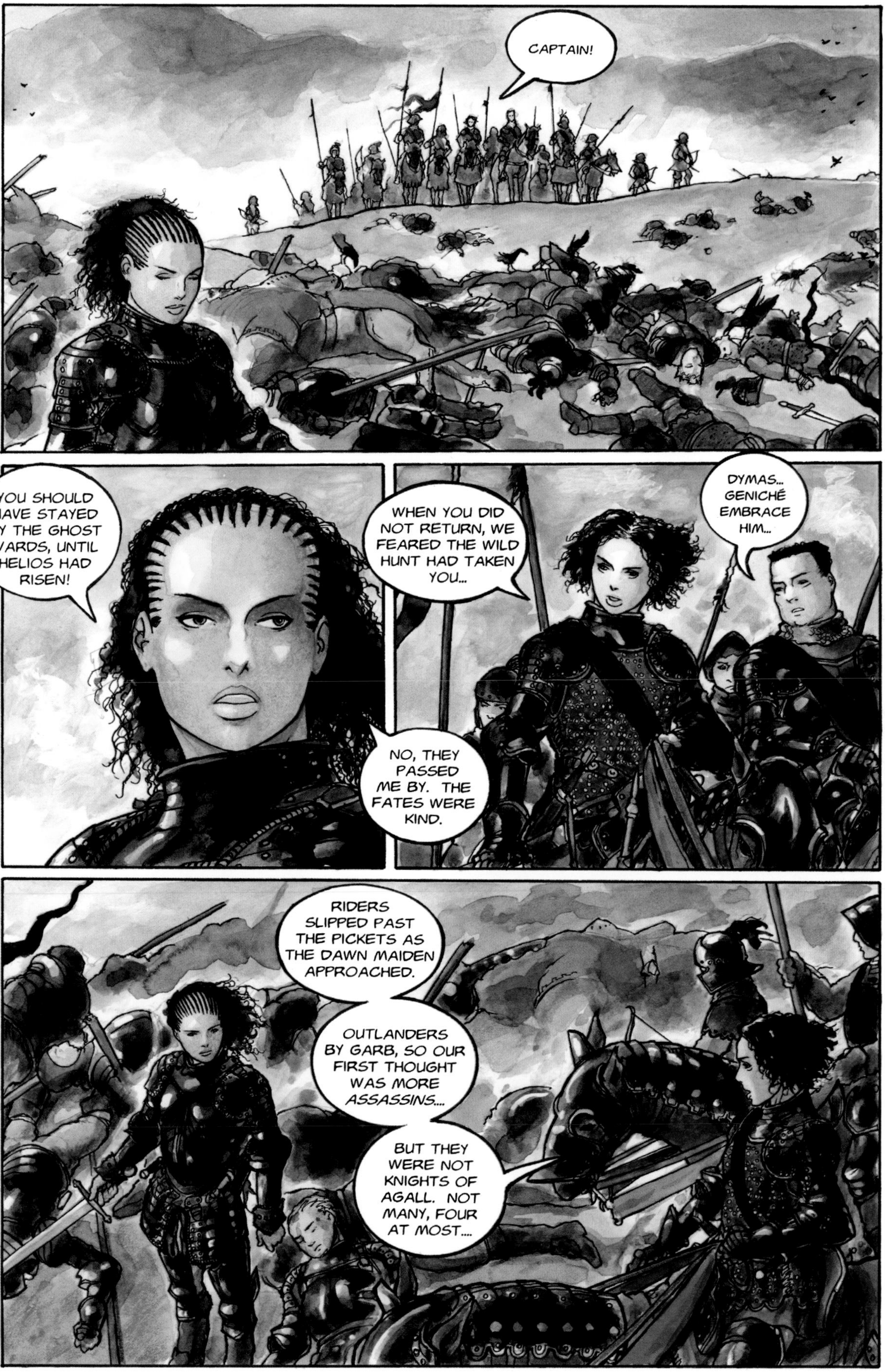
CAPTAIN!
YOU SHOULD HAVE STAYED BY THE GHOST WARDS, UNTIL HELIOS HAD RISEN!
WHEN YOU DID NOT RETURN, WE FEARED THE WILD HUNT HAD TAKEN YOU...
DYMAS... GENICHÉ EMBRACE HIM...
NO, THEY PASSED ME BY. THE FATES WERE KIND.
RIDERS SLIPPED PAST THE PICKETS AS THE DAWN MAIDEN APPROACHED.
OUTLANDERS BY GARB, SO OUR FIRST THOUGHT WAS MORE ASSASSINS....
BUT THEY WERE NOT KNIGHTS OF AGALL. NOT MANY, FOUR AT MOST....

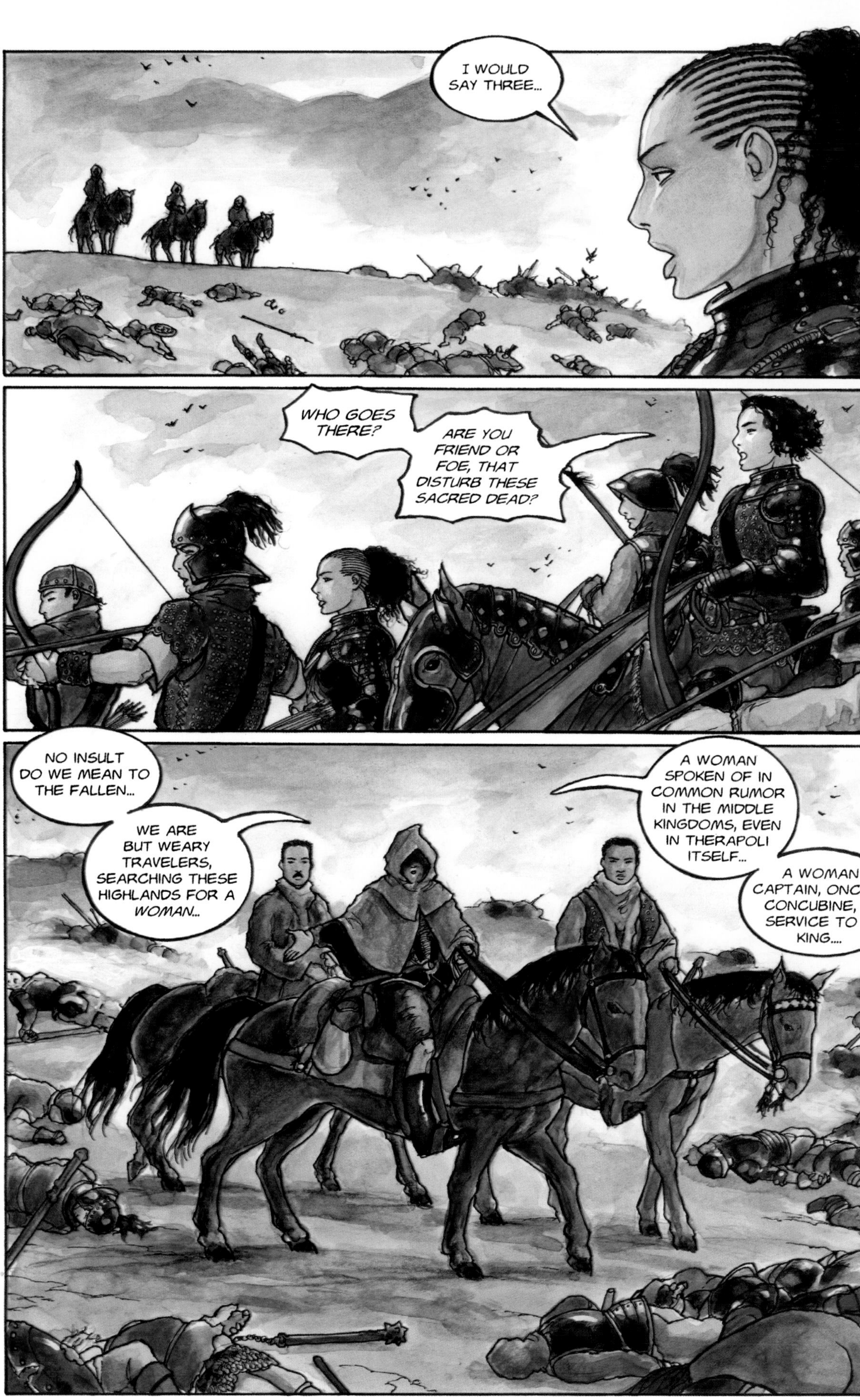
I WOULD SAY THREE...
WHO GOES THERE?
ARE YOU FRIEND OR FOE, THAT DISTURB THESE SACRED DEAD?
NO INSULT DO WE MEAN TO THE FALLEN...
WE ARE BUT WEARY TRAVELERS, SEARCHING THESE HIGHLANDS FOR A WOMAN...
A WOMAN SPOKEN OF IN COMMON RUMOR IN THE MIDDLE KINGDOMS, EVEN IN THERAPOLI ITSELF...
A WOMAN CAPTAIN, ONCE CONCUBINE, IN SERVICE TO A KING....

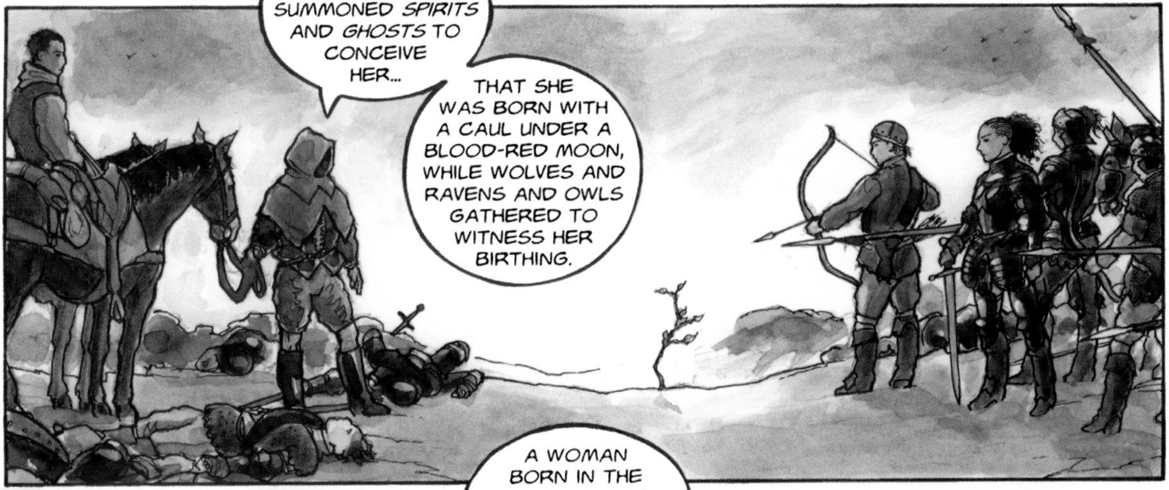
SOME WHISPER THAT HER MOTHER SUMMONED *SPIRITS* AND *GHOSTS* TO CONCEIVE HER...
THAT SHE WAS BORN WITH A CAUL UNDER A BLOOD-RED MOON, WHILE WOLVES AND RAVENS AND OWLS GATHERED TO WITNESS HER BIRTHING.

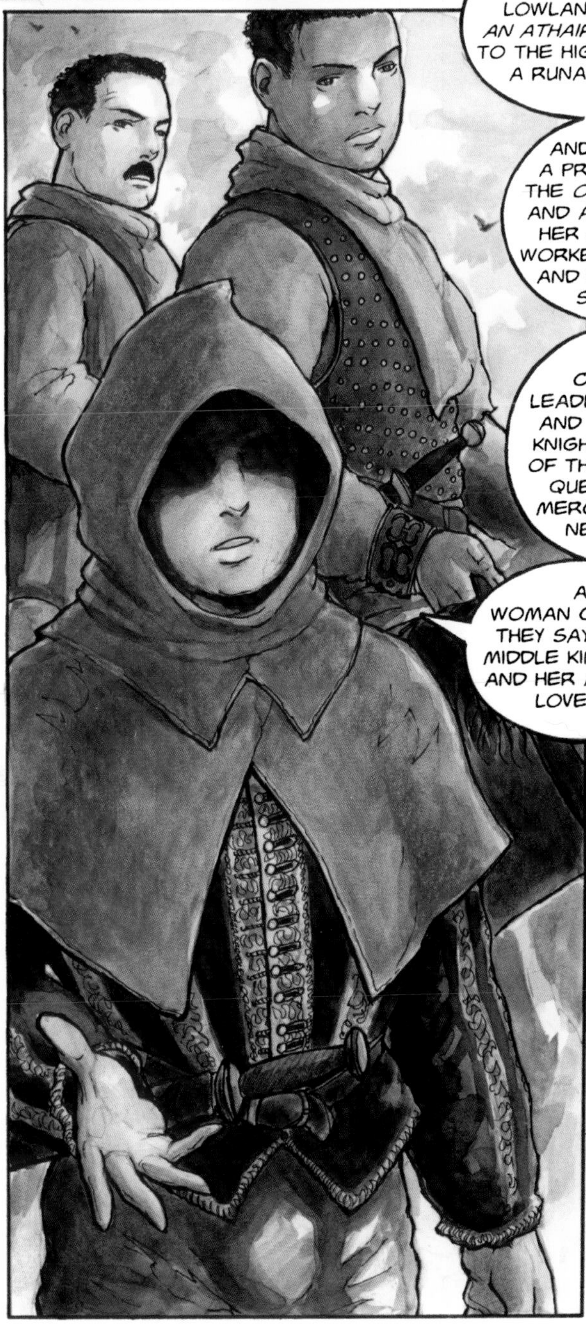

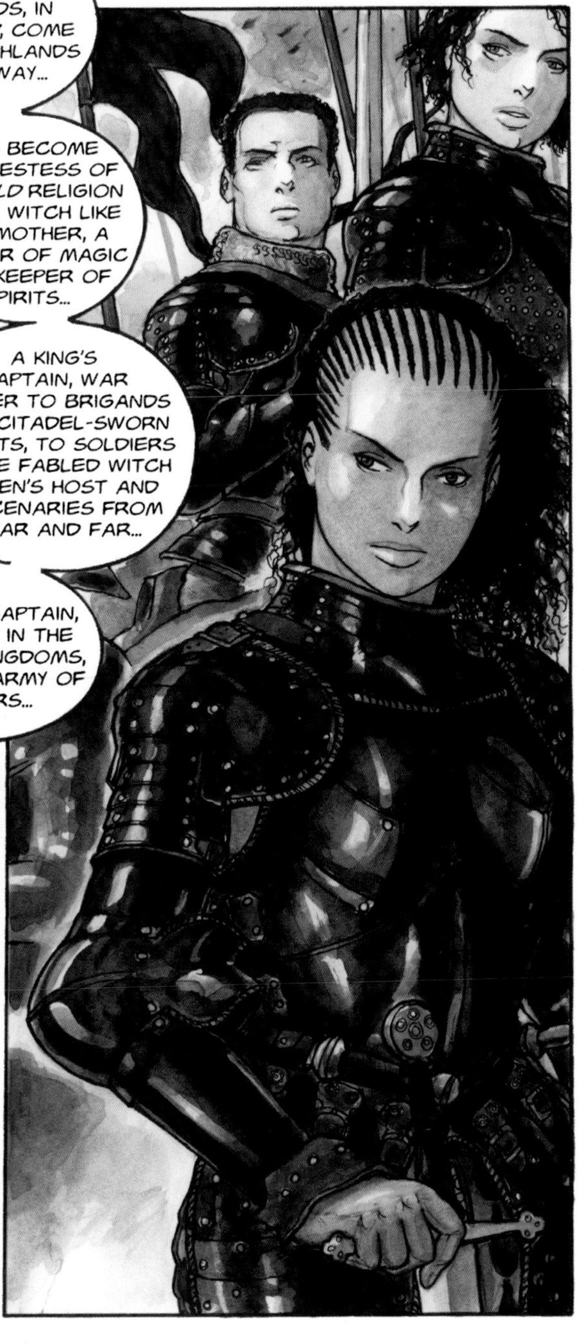
A WOMAN BORN IN THE LOWLANDS, IN *AN ATHAIR*, COME TO THE HIGHLANDS A RUNAWAY...
AND BECOME A PRIESTESS OF THE *OLD* RELIGION AND A WITCH LIKE HER MOTHER, A WORKER OF MAGIC AND KEEPER OF SPIRITS...
A KING'S CAPTAIN, WAR LEADER TO BRIGANDS AND CITADEL-SWORN KNIGHTS, TO SOLDIERS OF THE FABLED WITCH QUEEN'S HOST AND MERCENARIES FROM NEAR AND FAR...
A WOMAN CAPTAIN, THEY SAY IN THE MIDDLE KINGDOMS, AND HER ARMY OF LOVERS...

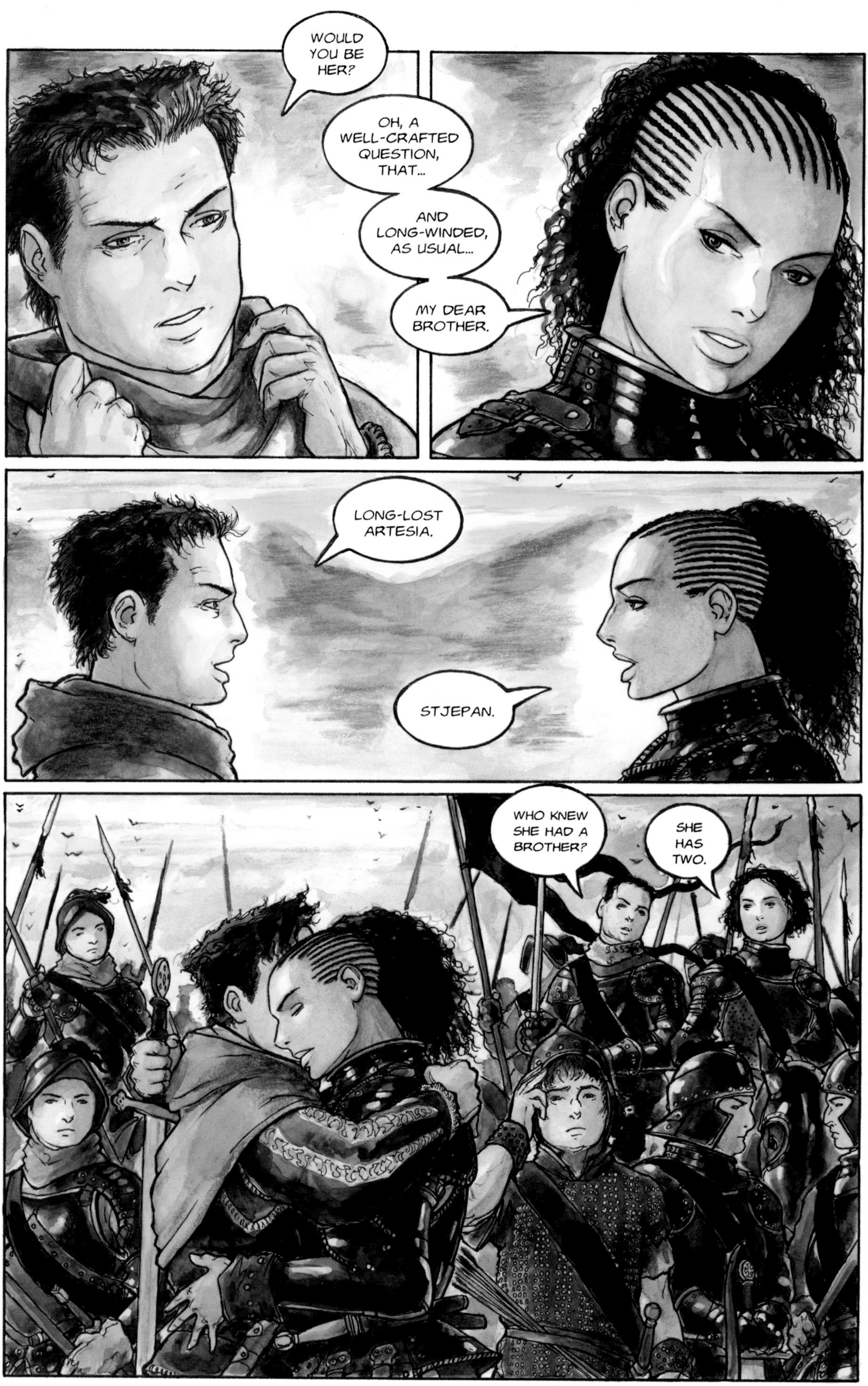
WOULD YOU BE HER?
OH, A WELL-CRAFTED QUESTION, THAT...
AND LONG-WINDED, AS USUAL...
MY DEAR BROTHER.
LONG-LOST ARTESIA.
STJEPAN.
WHO KNEW SHE HAD A BROTHER?
SHE HAS TWO.

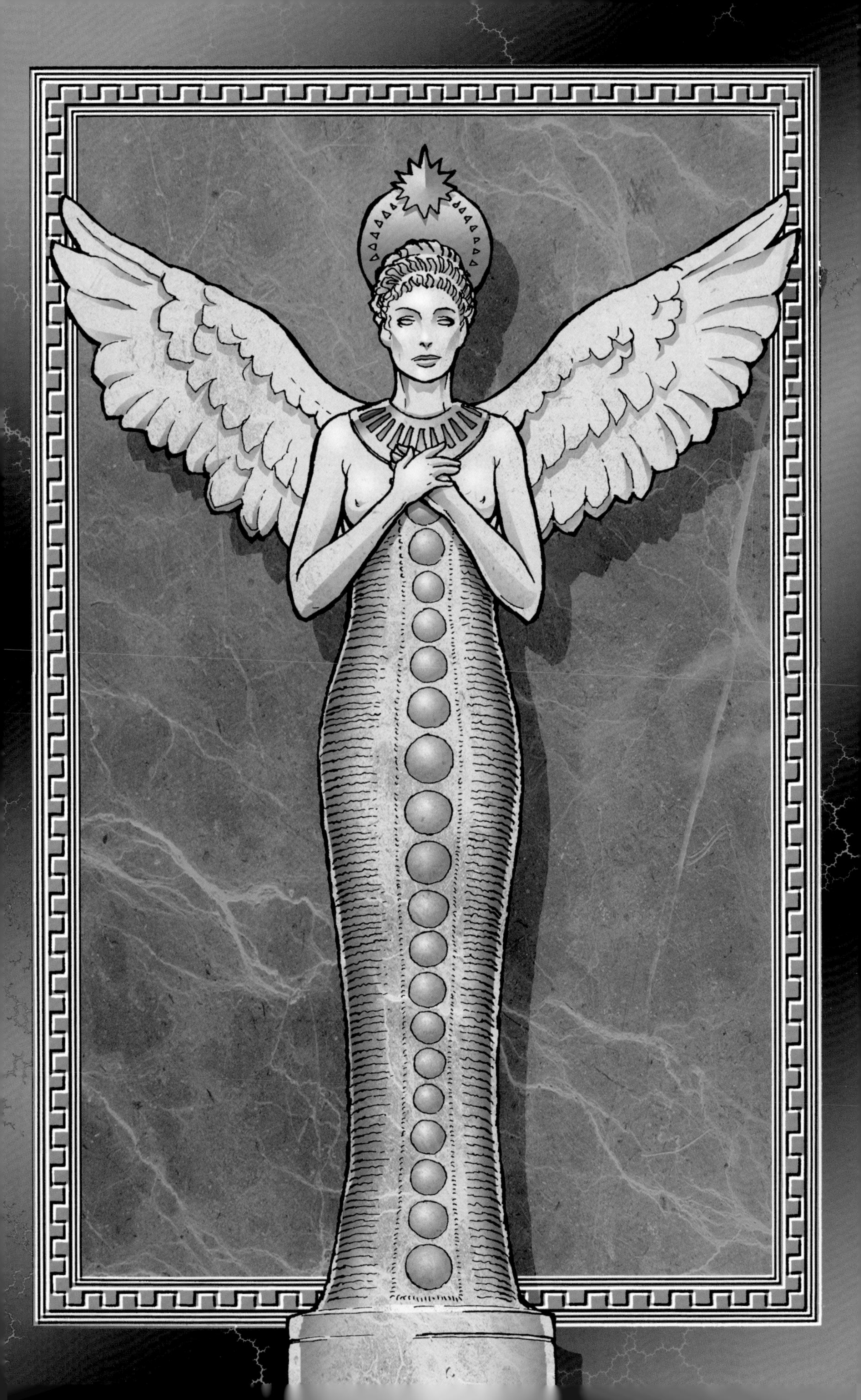

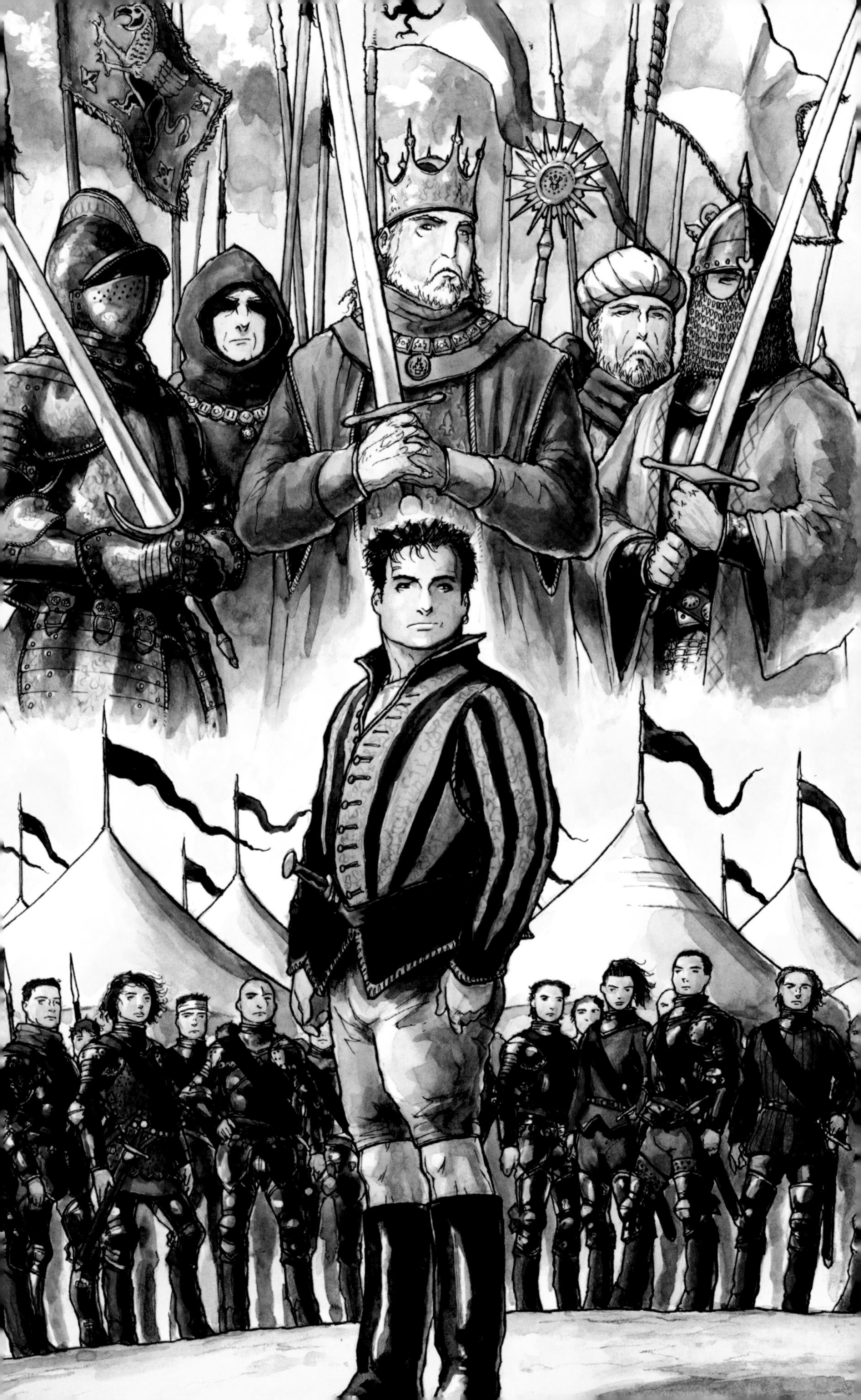

CHAPTER FOUR

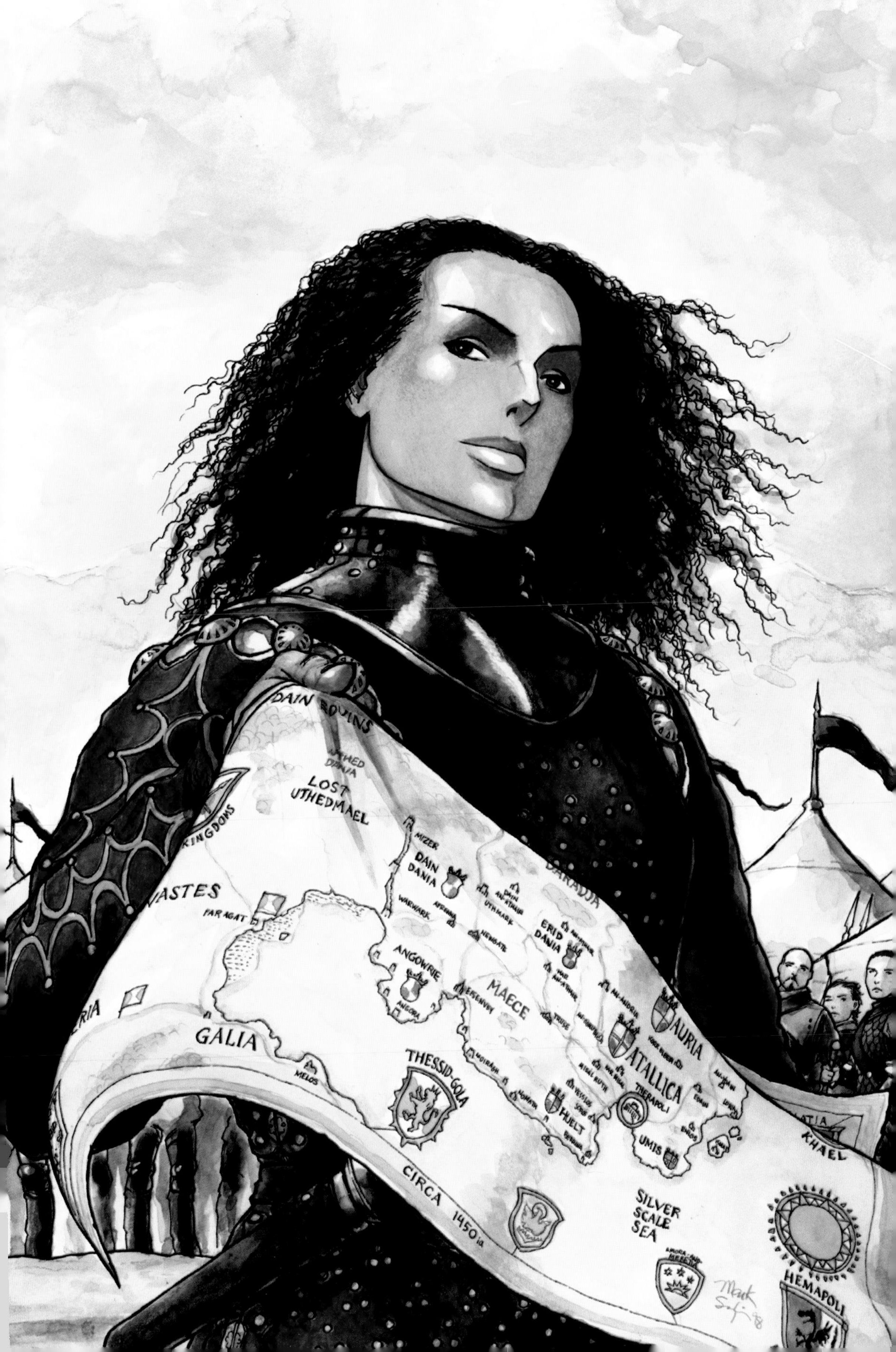
DAIN RUINS
LOST UTHEDMAEL
MIZER
DAIN DANIA
PARAGAT
ANGOWRIE
MAECE
ERID DANIA
NEWGATE
AURIA
ATALLICA
THERAPOLI
GALIA
THESSID-GOLA
MELOS
HUELT
UMIS
KHAEL
CIRCA 1450ia
SILVER SCALE SEA
HEMAPOLI

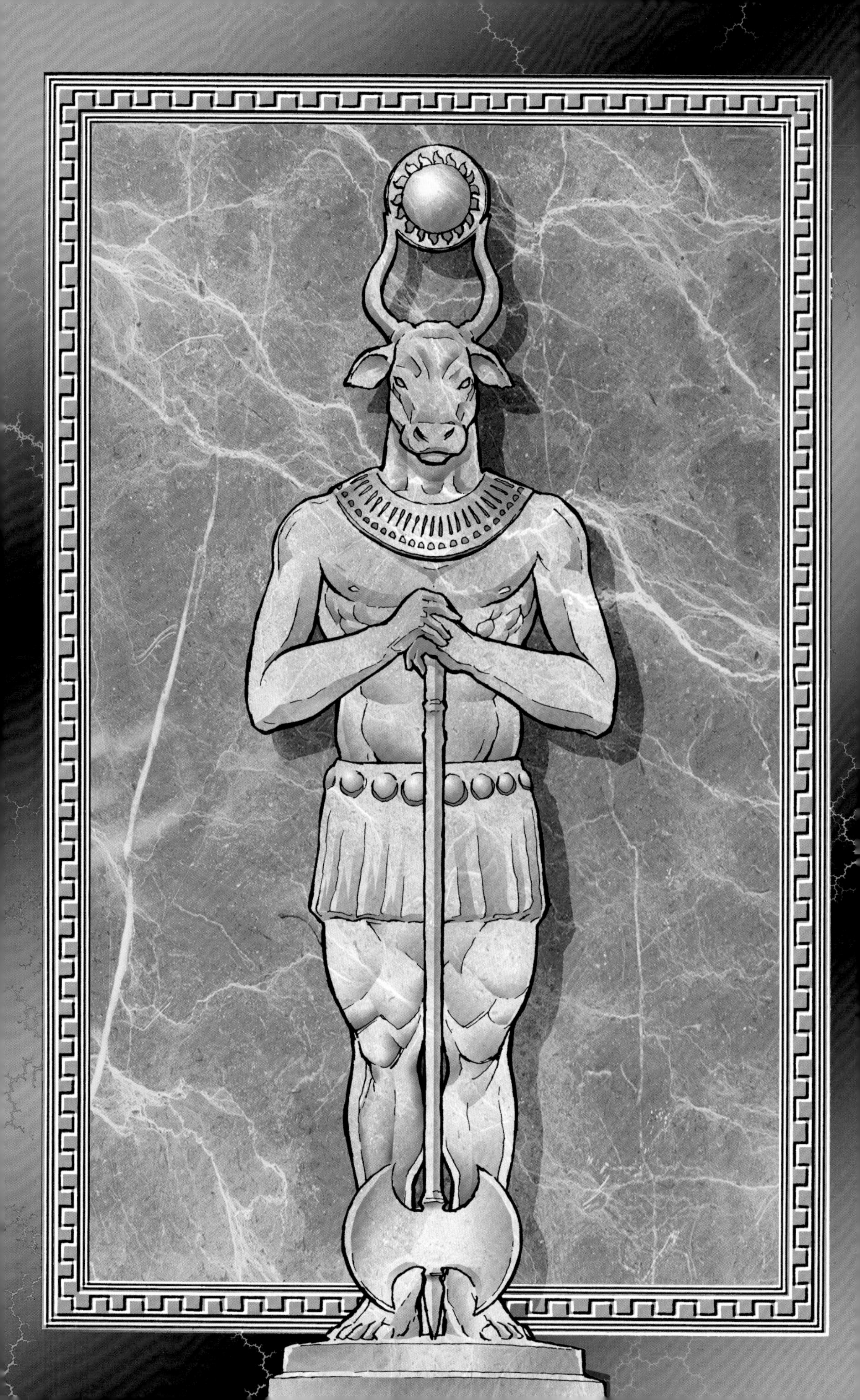

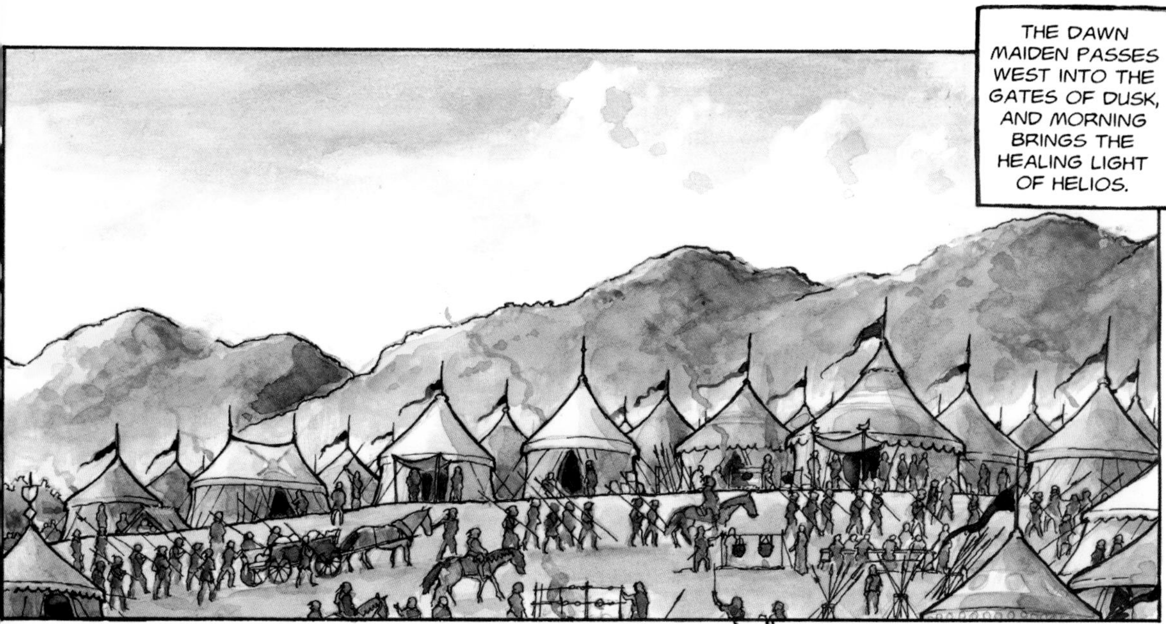
THE DAWN MAIDEN PASSES WEST INTO THE GATES OF DUSK, AND MORNING BRINGS THE HEALING LIGHT OF HELIOS.

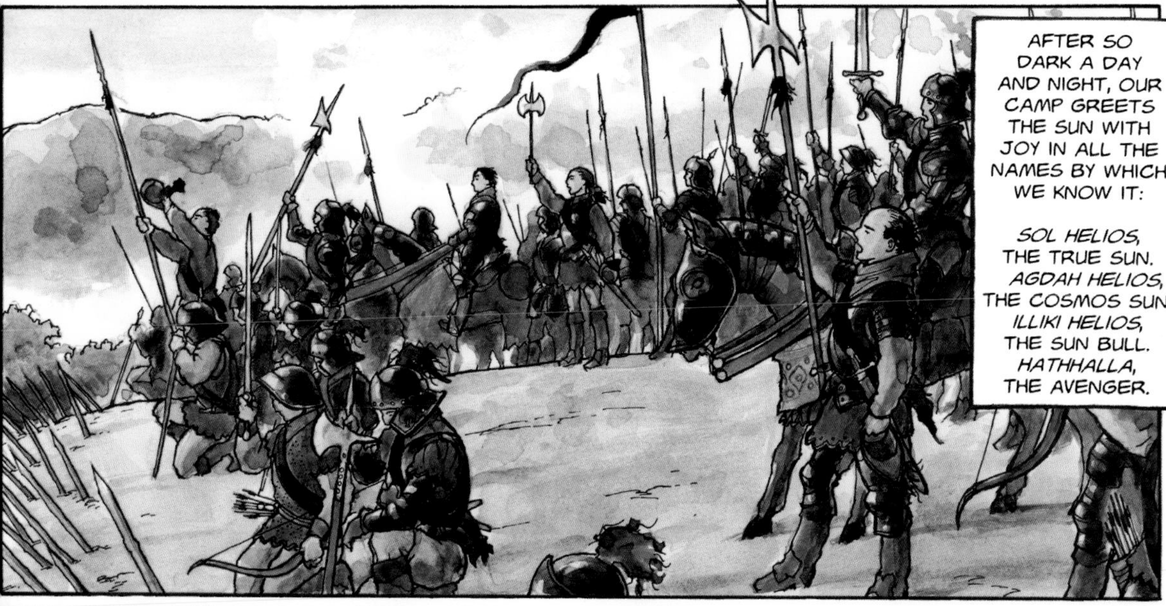
AFTER SO DARK A DAY AND NIGHT, OUR CAMP GREETS THE SUN WITH JOY IN ALL THE NAMES BY WHICH WE KNOW IT:
SOL HELIOS, THE TRUE SUN. *AGDAH HELIOS*, THE COSMOS SUN. *ILLIKI HELIOS*, THE SUN BULL. *HATHHALLA*, THE AVENGER.

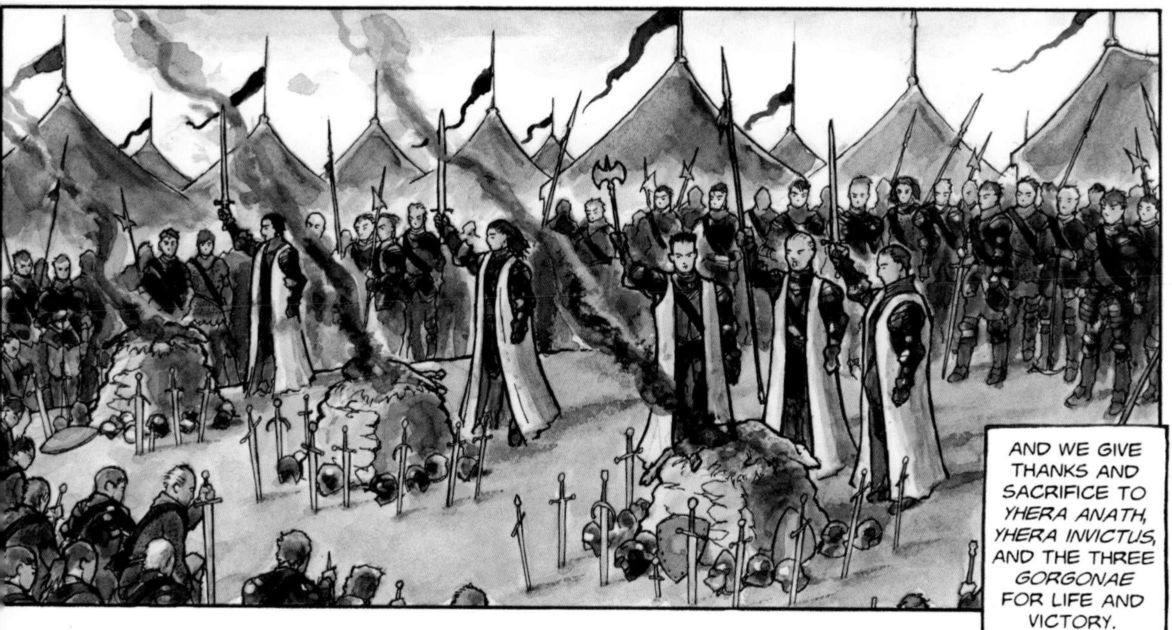
AND WE GIVE THANKS AND SACRIFICE TO *YHERA ANATH*, *YHERA INVICTUS*, AND THE THREE *GORGONAE* FOR LIFE AND VICTORY.

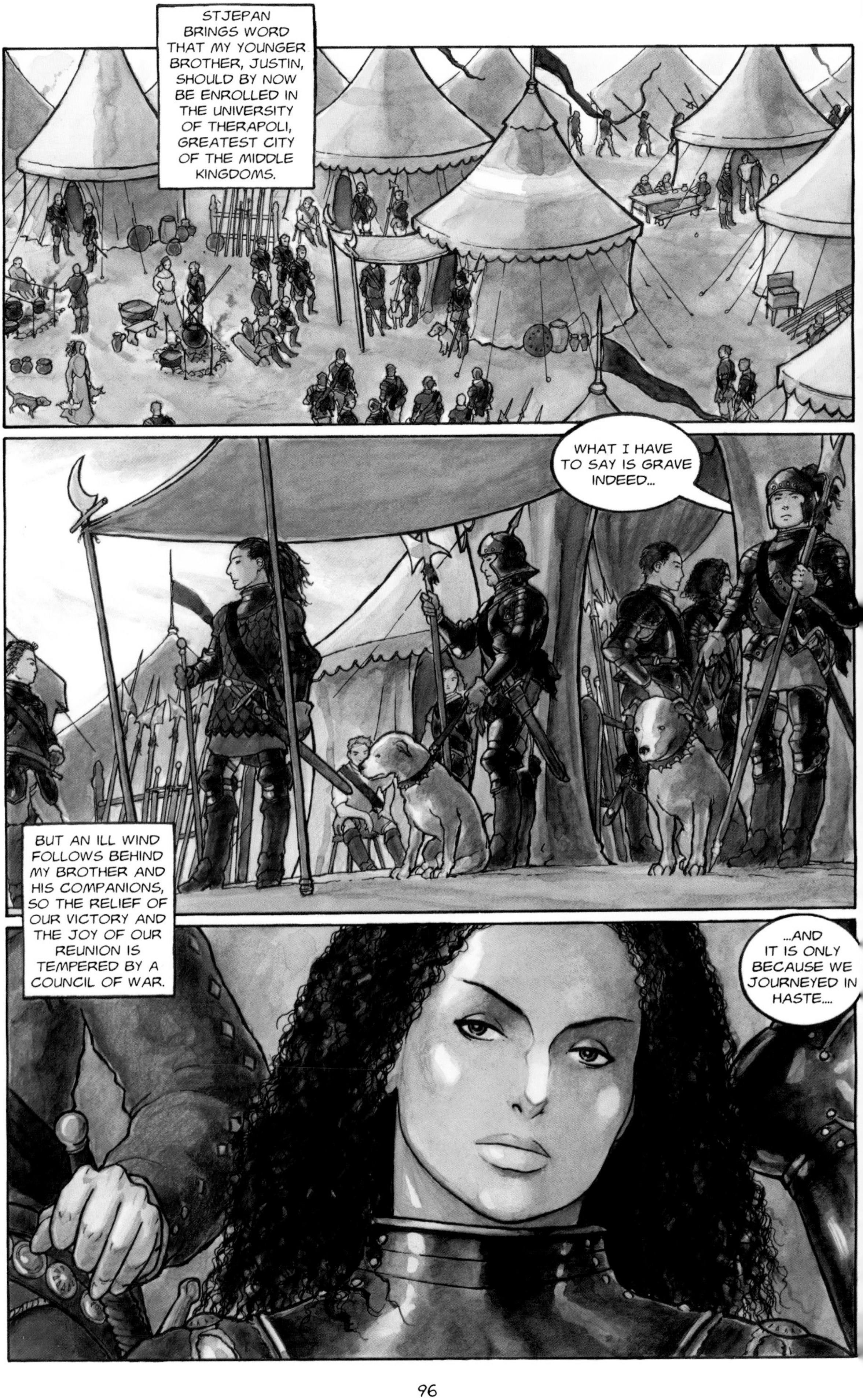
STJEPAN BRINGS WORD THAT MY YOUNGER BROTHER, JUSTIN, SHOULD BY NOW BE ENROLLED IN THE UNIVERSITY OF THERAPOLI, GREATEST CITY OF THE MIDDLE KINGDOMS.
WHAT I HAVE TO SAY IS GRAVE INDEED...
BUT AN ILL WIND FOLLOWS BEHIND MY BROTHER AND HIS COMPANIONS, SO THE RELIEF OF OUR VICTORY AND THE JOY OF OUR REUNION IS TEMPERED BY A COUNCIL OF WAR.
...AND IT IS ONLY BECAUSE WE JOURNEYED IN HASTE....

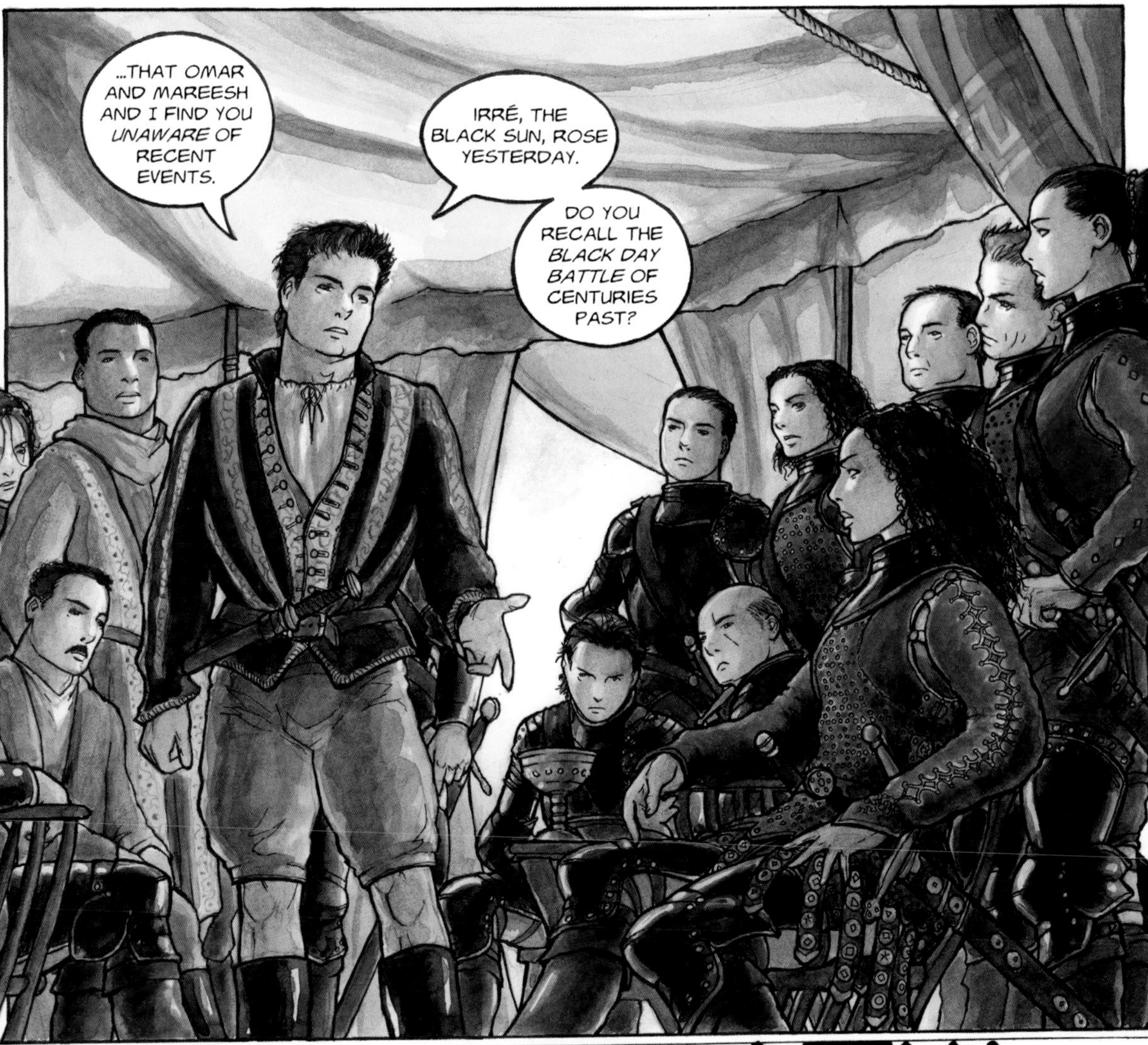
...THAT OMAR AND MAREESH AND I FIND YOU *UNAWARE* OF RECENT EVENTS.
IRRÉ, THE BLACK SUN, ROSE YESTERDAY.
DO YOU RECALL THE *BLACK DAY BATTLE* OF CENTURIES PAST?

The Bearer of Bad Tidings

STORY & ART © 98 MARK SMYLIE

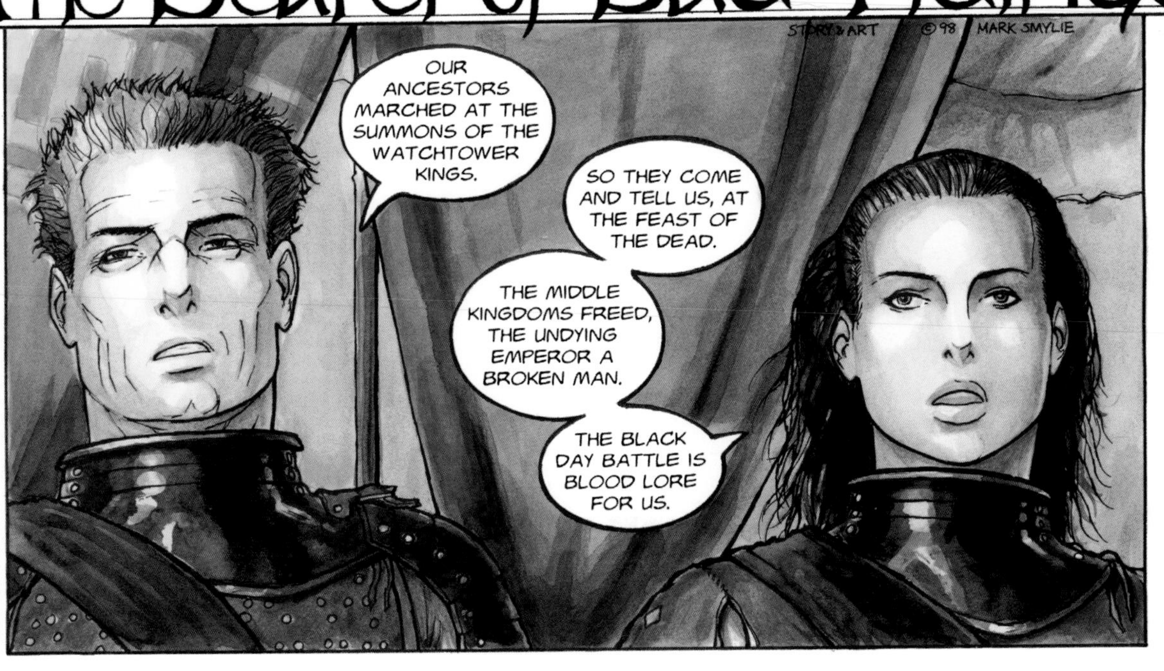
OUR ANCESTORS MARCHED AT THE SUMMONS OF THE WATCHTOWER KINGS.
SO THEY COME AND TELL US, AT THE FEAST OF THE DEAD.
THE MIDDLE KINGDOMS FREED, THE UNDYING EMPEROR A BROKEN MAN.
THE BLACK DAY BATTLE IS BLOOD LORE FOR US.

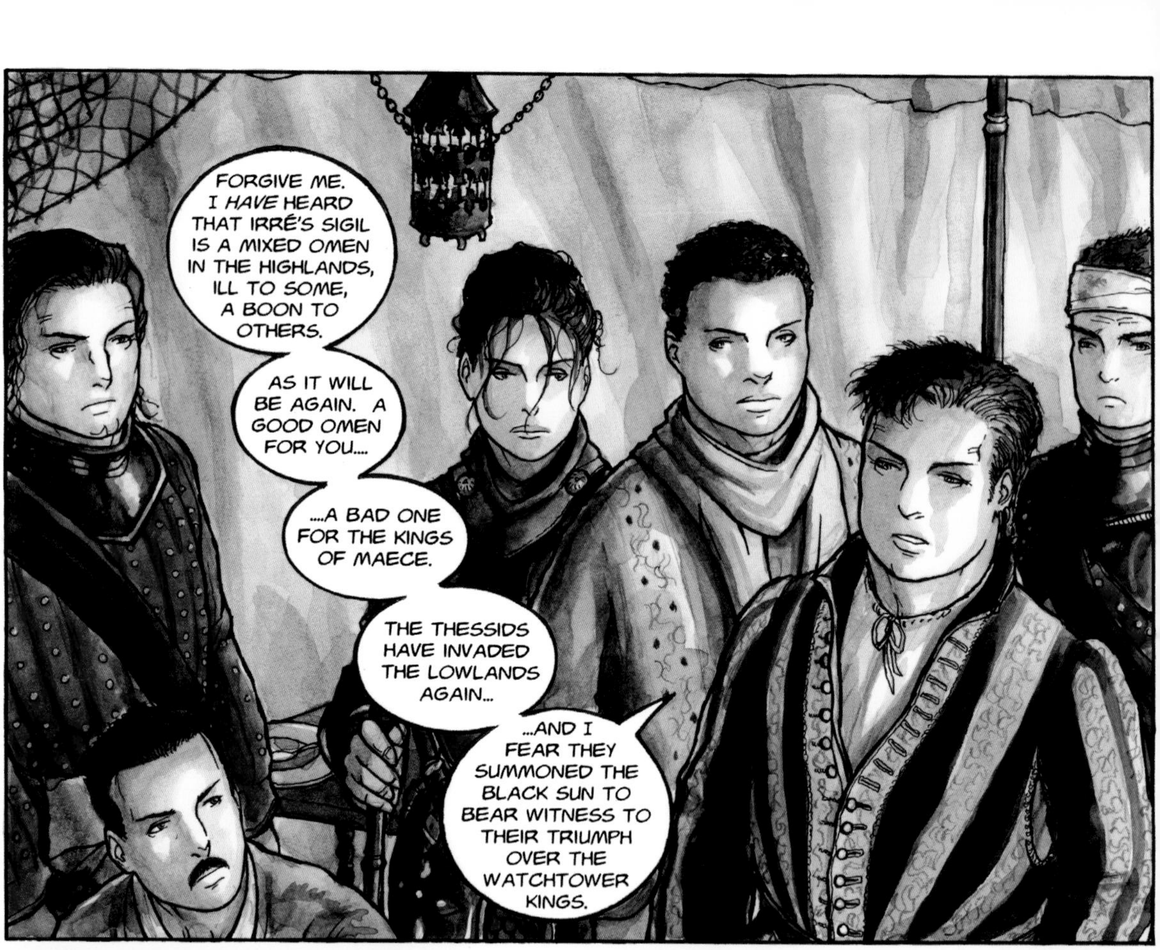
FORGIVE ME. I *HAVE* HEARD THAT IRRÉ'S SIGIL IS A MIXED OMEN IN THE HIGHLANDS, ILL TO SOME, A BOON TO OTHERS.
AS IT WILL BE AGAIN. A GOOD OMEN FOR YOU....
....A BAD ONE FOR THE KINGS OF MAECE.
THE THESSIDS HAVE INVADED THE LOWLANDS AGAIN...
...AND I FEAR THEY SUMMONED THE BLACK SUN TO BEAR WITNESS TO THEIR TRIUMPH OVER THE WATCHTOWER KINGS.

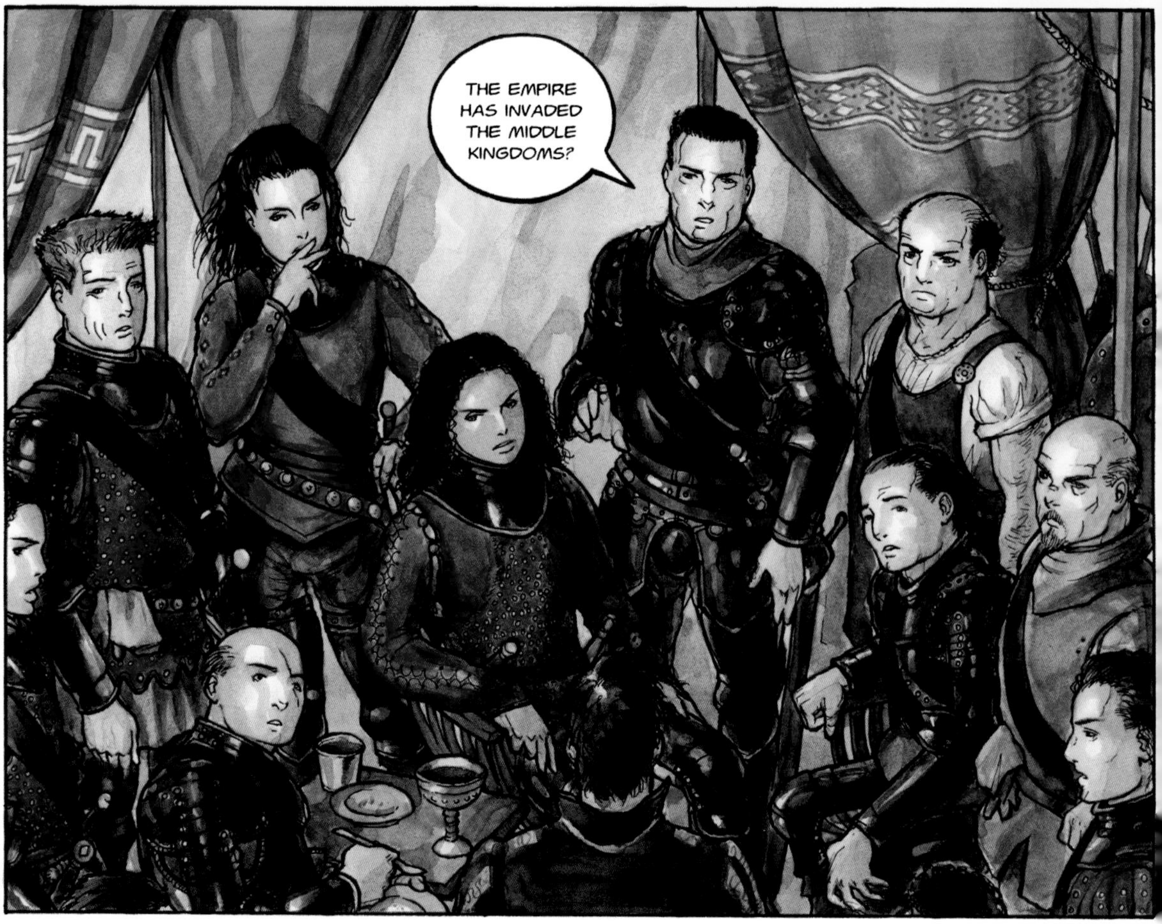
THE EMPIRE HAS INVADED THE MIDDLE KINGDOMS?

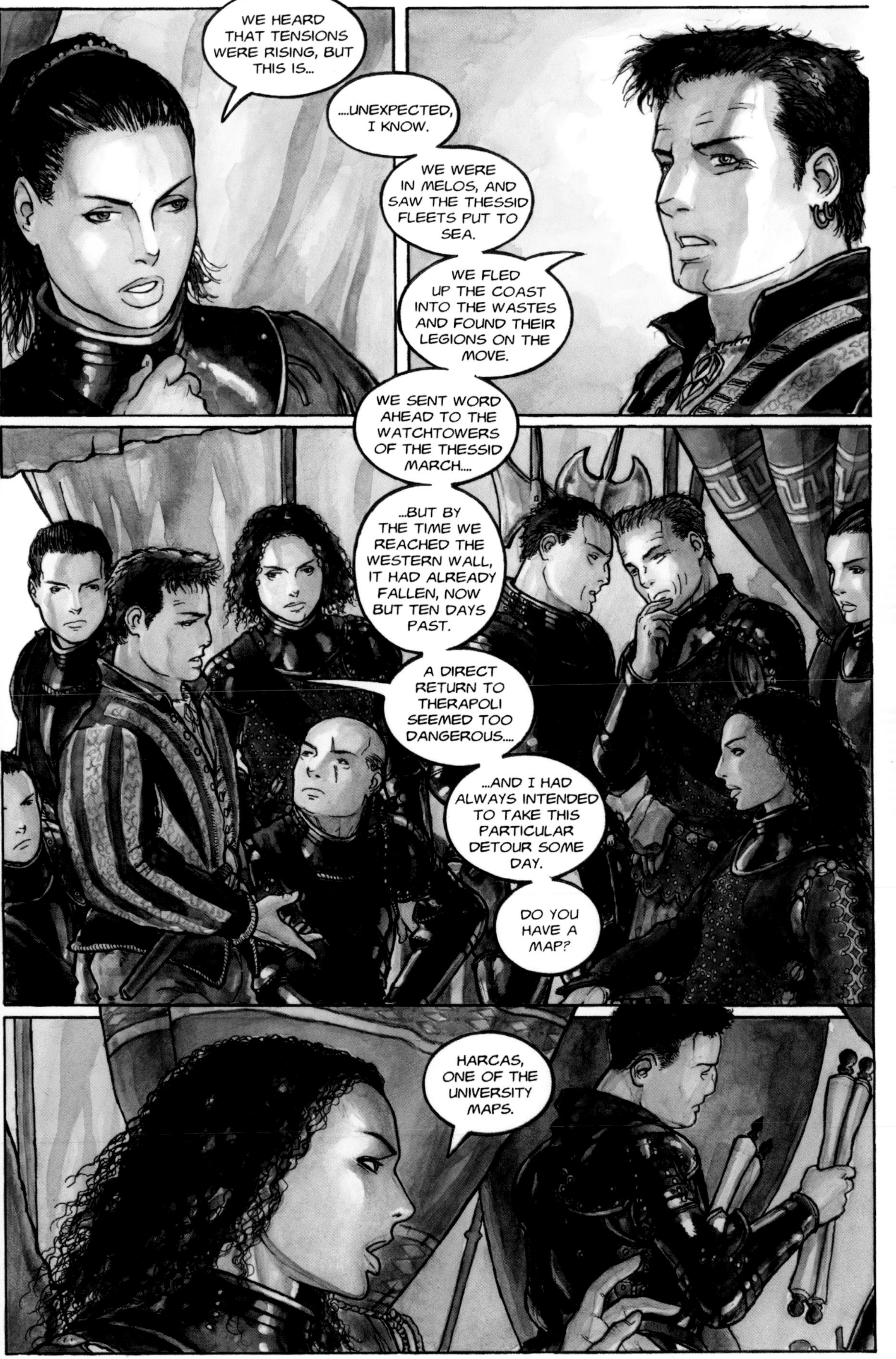
WE HEARD THAT TENSIONS WERE RISING, BUT THIS IS...
....UNEXPECTED, I KNOW.
WE WERE IN MELOS, AND SAW THE THESSID FLEETS PUT TO SEA.
WE FLED UP THE COAST INTO THE WASTES AND FOUND THEIR LEGIONS ON THE MOVE.
WE SENT WORD AHEAD TO THE WATCHTOWERS OF THE THESSID MARCH....
...BUT BY THE TIME WE REACHED THE WESTERN WALL, IT HAD ALREADY FALLEN, NOW BUT TEN DAYS PAST.
A DIRECT RETURN TO THERAPOLI SEEMED TOO DANGEROUS....
...AND I HAD ALWAYS INTENDED TO TAKE THIS PARTICULAR DETOUR SOME DAY.
DO YOU HAVE A MAP?
HARCAS, ONE OF THE UNIVERSITY MAPS.

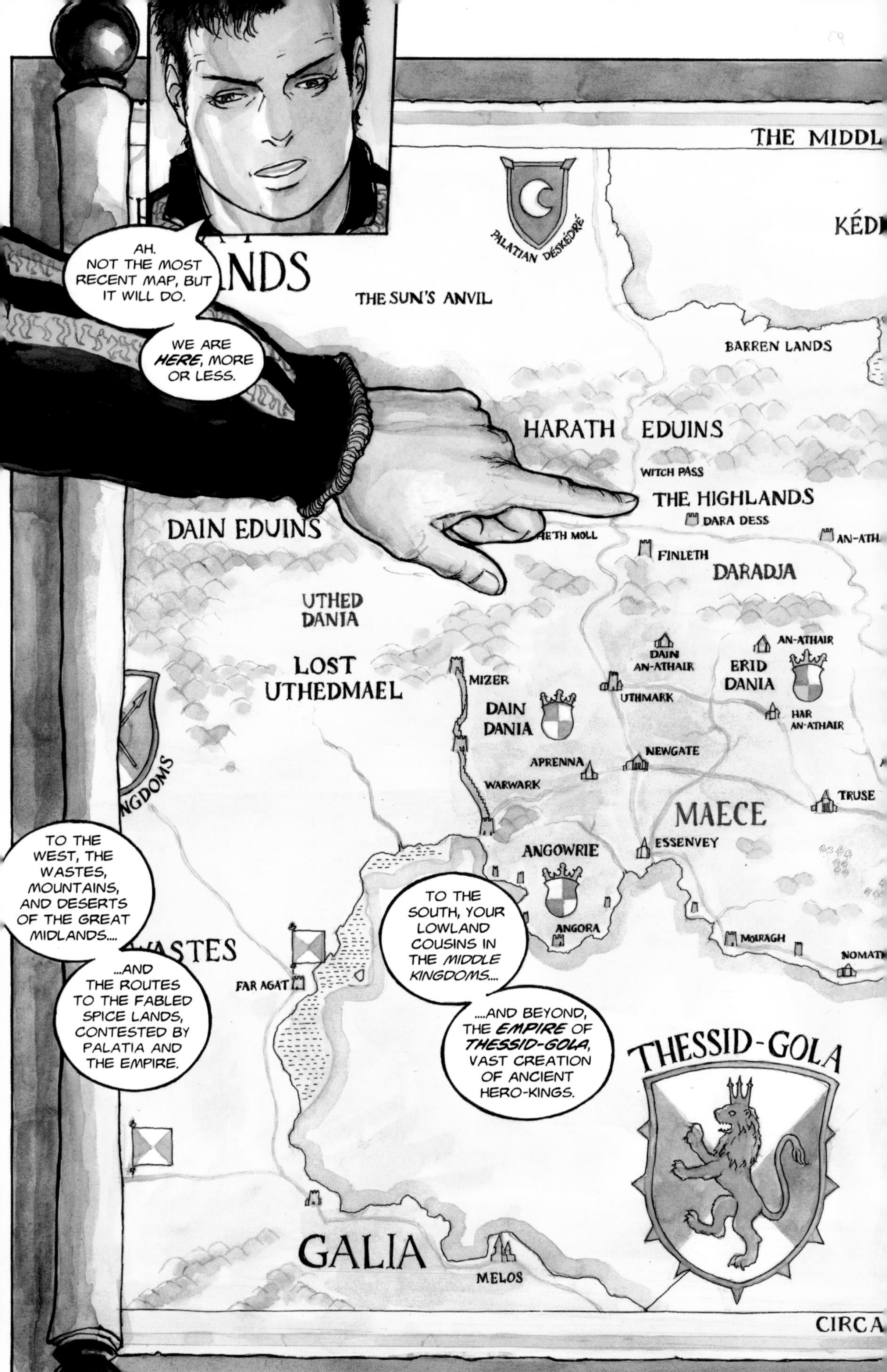
AH. NOT THE MOST RECENT MAP, BUT IT WILL DO.
WE ARE *HERE*, MORE OR LESS.
TO THE WEST, THE WASTES, MOUNTAINS, AND DESERTS OF THE GREAT MIDLANDS....
...AND THE ROUTES TO THE FABLED SPICE LANDS, CONTESTED BY PALATIA AND THE EMPIRE.
TO THE SOUTH, YOUR LOWLAND COUSINS IN THE *MIDDLE KINGDOMS*....
....AND BEYOND, THE *EMPIRE* OF *THESSID-GOLA*, VAST CREATION OF ANCIENT HERO-KINGS.
THE MIDDL
KÉDI
PALATIAN DÉSKÉDRÉ
NDS
THE SUN'S ANVIL
BARREN LANDS
HARATH EDUINS
WITCH PASS
THE HIGHLANDS
DARA DESS
DAIN EDUINS
HETH MOLL
FINLETH
AN-ATHA
DARADJA
UTHED DANIA
LOST UTHEDMAEL
MIZER
DAIN AN-ATHAIR
AN-ATHAIR
ERID DANIA
UTHMARK
DAIN DANIA
HAR AN-ATHAIR
NGDOMS
NEWGATE
APRENNA
WARWARK
TRUSE
MAECE
ANGOWRIE
ESSENVEY
ANGORA
MOIRAGH
NOMATH
WASTES
FAR AGAT
THESSID-GOLA
GALIA
MELOS
CIRCA

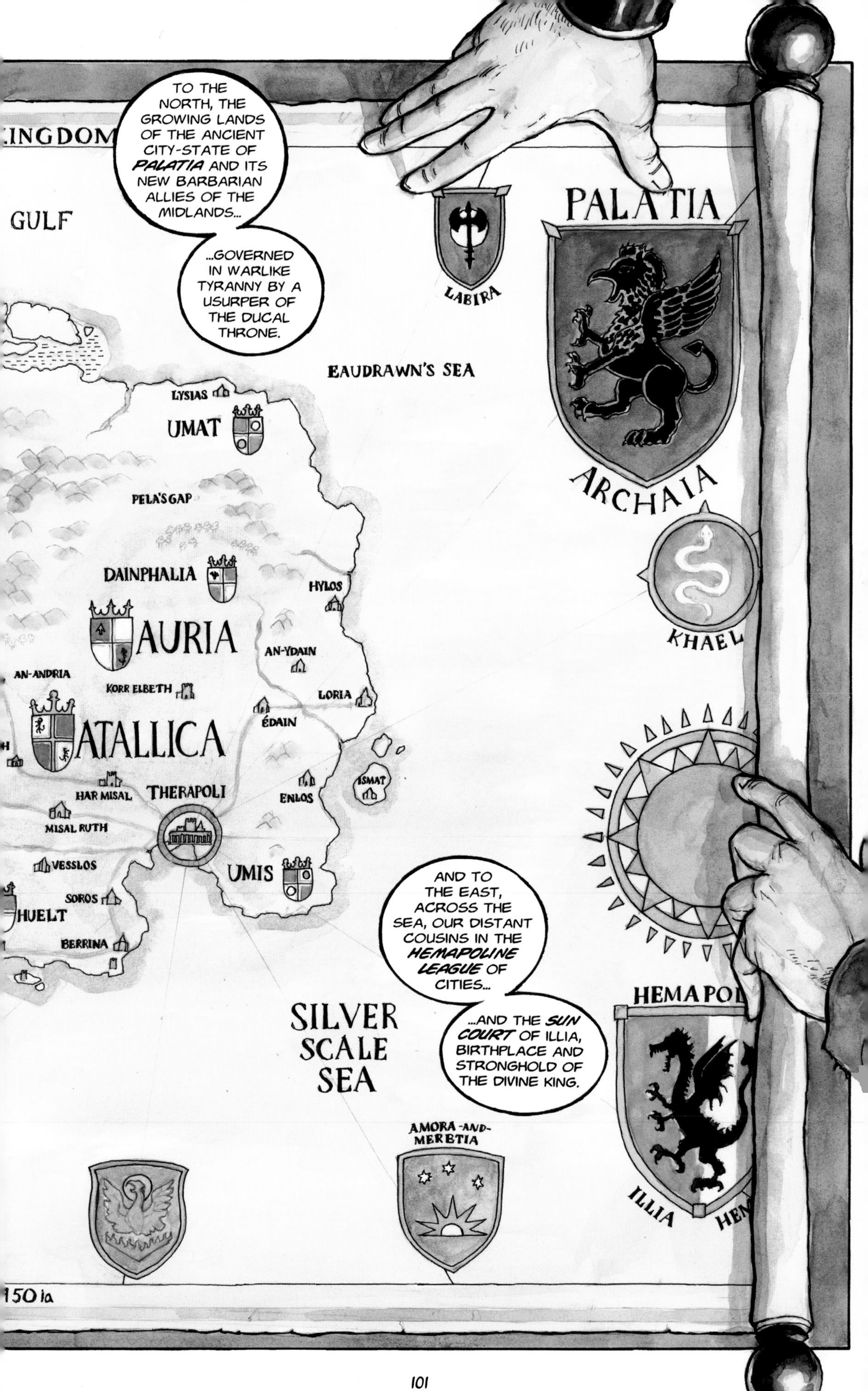
TO THE NORTH, THE GROWING LANDS OF THE ANCIENT CITY-STATE OF *PALATIA* AND ITS NEW BARBARIAN ALLIES OF THE MIDLANDS...
...GOVERNED IN WARLIKE TYRANNY BY A USURPER OF THE DUCAL THRONE.
AND TO THE EAST, ACROSS THE SEA, OUR DISTANT COUSINS IN THE *HEMAPOLINE LEAGUE* OF CITIES...
...AND THE *SUN COURT* OF ILLIA, BIRTHPLACE AND STRONGHOLD OF THE DIVINE KING.
KINGDOM
GULF
LABIRA
PALATIA
ARCHAIA
KHAEL
EAUDRAWN'S SEA
LYSIAS
UMAT
PELA'S GAP
DAINPHALIA
HYLOS
AURIA
AN-YDAIN
AN-ANDRIA
KORR ELBETH
LORIA
ATALLICA
ÉDAIN
ISMAT
HAR MISAL
THERAPOLI
ENLOS
MISAL RUTH
VESSLOS
UMIS
SOROS
HUELT
BERRINA
SILVER SCALE SEA
HEMAPOL
AMORA-AND-MERETIA
ILLIA
150 ia

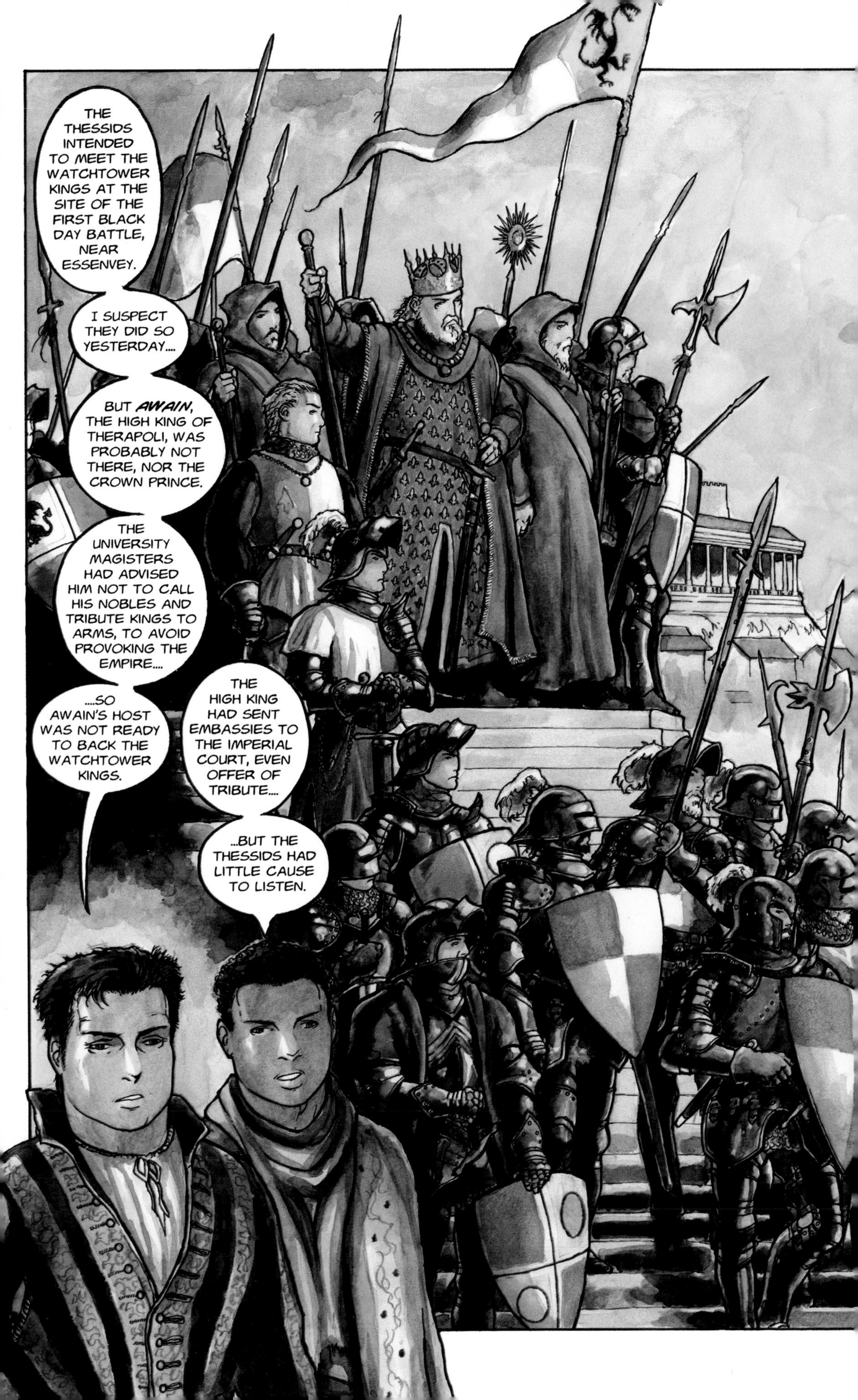
THE THESSIDS INTENDED TO MEET THE WATCHTOWER KINGS AT THE SITE OF THE FIRST BLACK DAY BATTLE, NEAR ESSENVEY.
I SUSPECT THEY DID SO YESTERDAY....
BUT *AWAIN*, THE HIGH KING OF THERAPOLI, WAS PROBABLY NOT THERE, NOR THE CROWN PRINCE.
THE UNIVERSITY MAGISTERS HAD ADVISED HIM NOT TO CALL HIS NOBLES AND TRIBUTE KINGS TO ARMS, TO AVOID PROVOKING THE EMPIRE....
....SO AWAIN'S HOST WAS NOT READY TO BACK THE WATCHTOWER KINGS.
THE HIGH KING HAD SENT EMBASSIES TO THE IMPERIAL COURT, EVEN OFFER OF TRIBUTE....
...BUT THE THESSIDS HAD LITTLE CAUSE TO LISTEN.

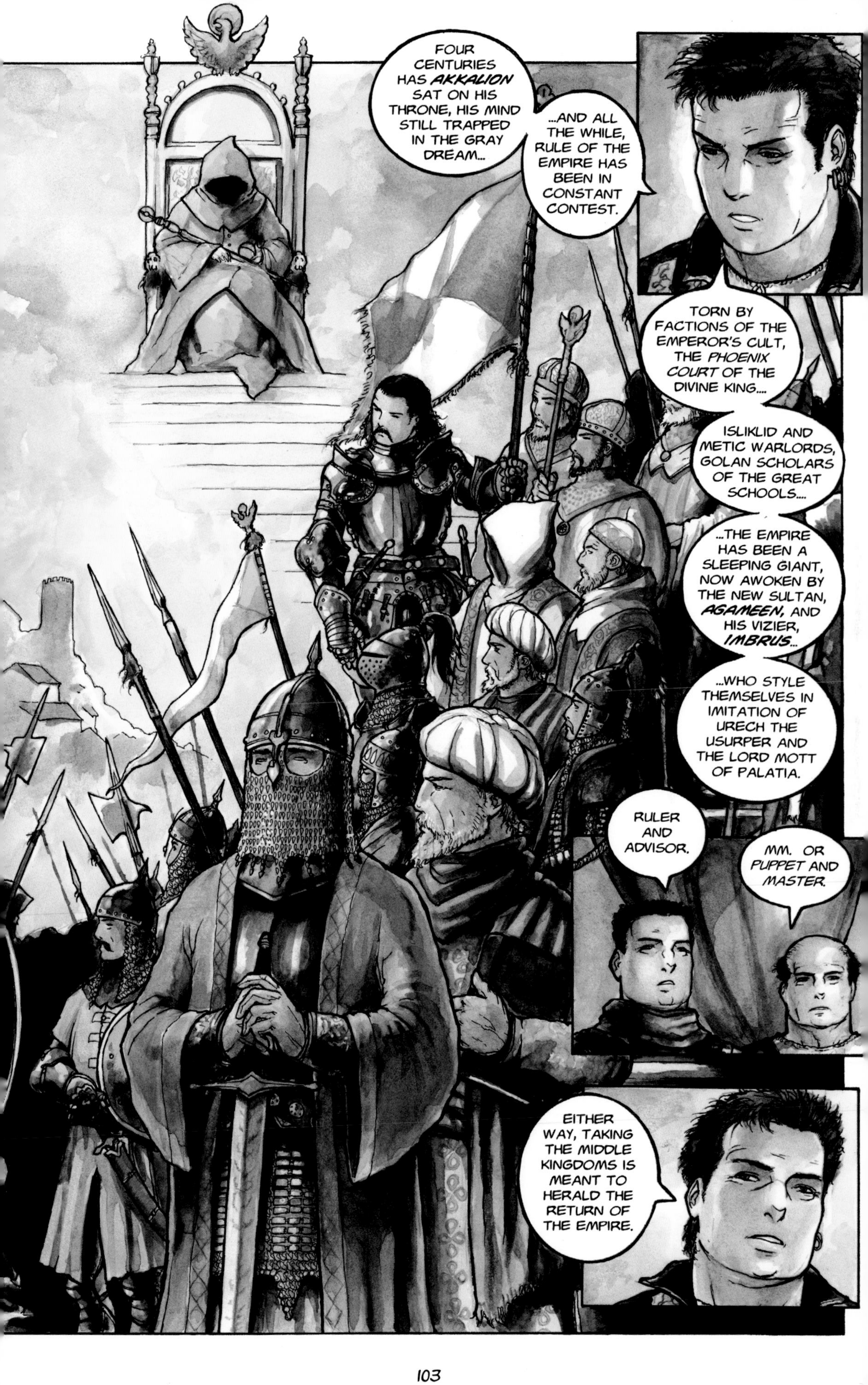
FOUR CENTURIES HAS AKKALION SAT ON HIS THRONE, HIS MIND STILL TRAPPED IN THE GRAY DREAM...
...AND ALL THE WHILE, RULE OF THE EMPIRE HAS BEEN IN CONSTANT CONTEST.
TORN BY FACTIONS OF THE EMPEROR'S CULT, THE PHOENIX COURT OF THE DIVINE KING....
ISLIKLID AND METIC WARLORDS, GOLAN SCHOLARS OF THE GREAT SCHOOLS....
...THE EMPIRE HAS BEEN A SLEEPING GIANT, NOW AWOKEN BY THE NEW SULTAN, AGAMEEN, AND HIS VIZIER, IMBRUS...
...WHO STYLE THEMSELVES IN IMITATION OF URECH THE USURPER AND THE LORD MOTT OF PALATIA.
RULER AND ADVISOR.
MM. OR PUPPET AND MASTER.
EITHER WAY, TAKING THE MIDDLE KINGDOMS IS MEANT TO HERALD THE RETURN OF THE EMPIRE.

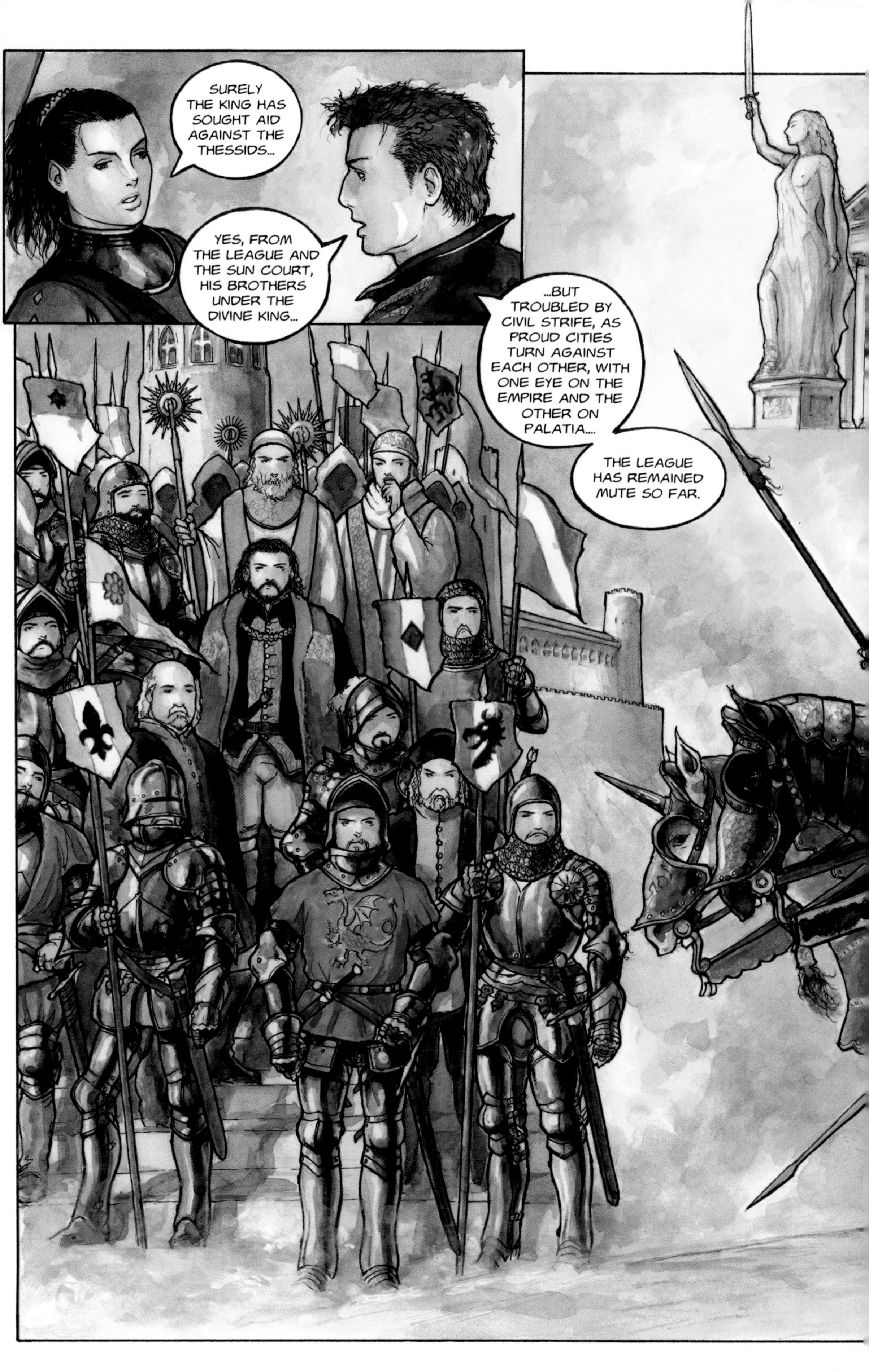
SURELY THE KING HAS SOUGHT AID AGAINST THE THESSIDS...
YES, FROM THE LEAGUE AND THE SUN COURT, HIS BROTHERS UNDER THE DIVINE KING...
...BUT TROUBLED BY CIVIL STRIFE, AS PROUD CITIES TURN AGAINST EACH OTHER, WITH ONE EYE ON THE EMPIRE AND THE OTHER ON PALATIA....
THE LEAGUE HAS REMAINED MUTE SO FAR.

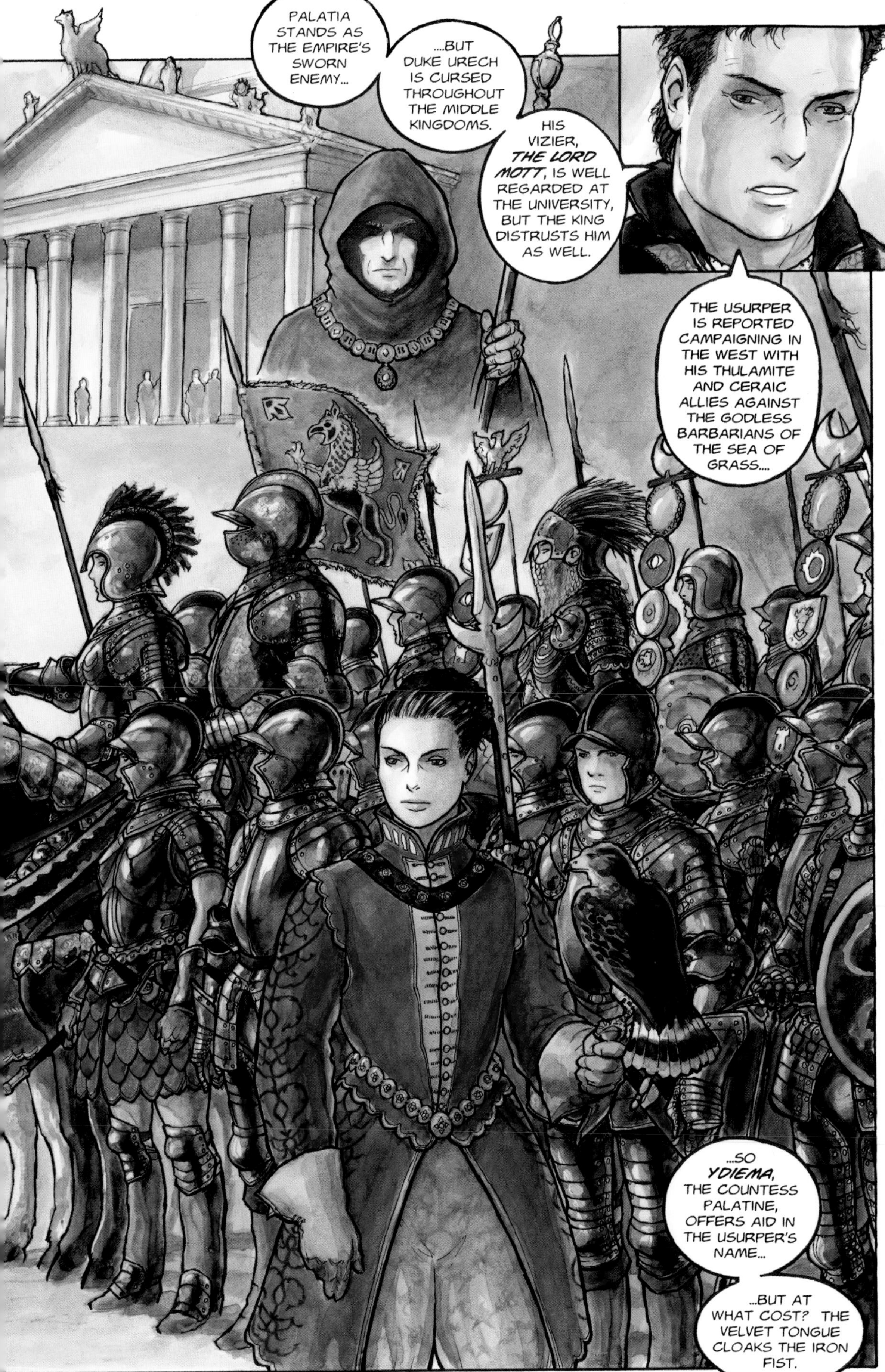
PALATIA STANDS AS THE EMPIRE'S SWORN ENEMY...
....BUT DUKE URECH IS CURSED THROUGHOUT THE MIDDLE KINGDOMS.
HIS VIZIER, ***THE LORD MOTT***, IS WELL REGARDED AT THE UNIVERSITY, BUT THE KING DISTRUSTS HIM AS WELL.
THE USURPER IS REPORTED CAMPAIGNING IN THE WEST WITH HIS THULAMITE AND CERAIC ALLIES AGAINST THE GODLESS BARBARIANS OF THE SEA OF GRASS....
...SO ***YDIEMA***, THE COUNTESS PALATINE, OFFERS AID IN THE USURPER'S NAME...
...BUT AT WHAT COST? THE VELVET TONGUE CLOAKS THE IRON FIST.

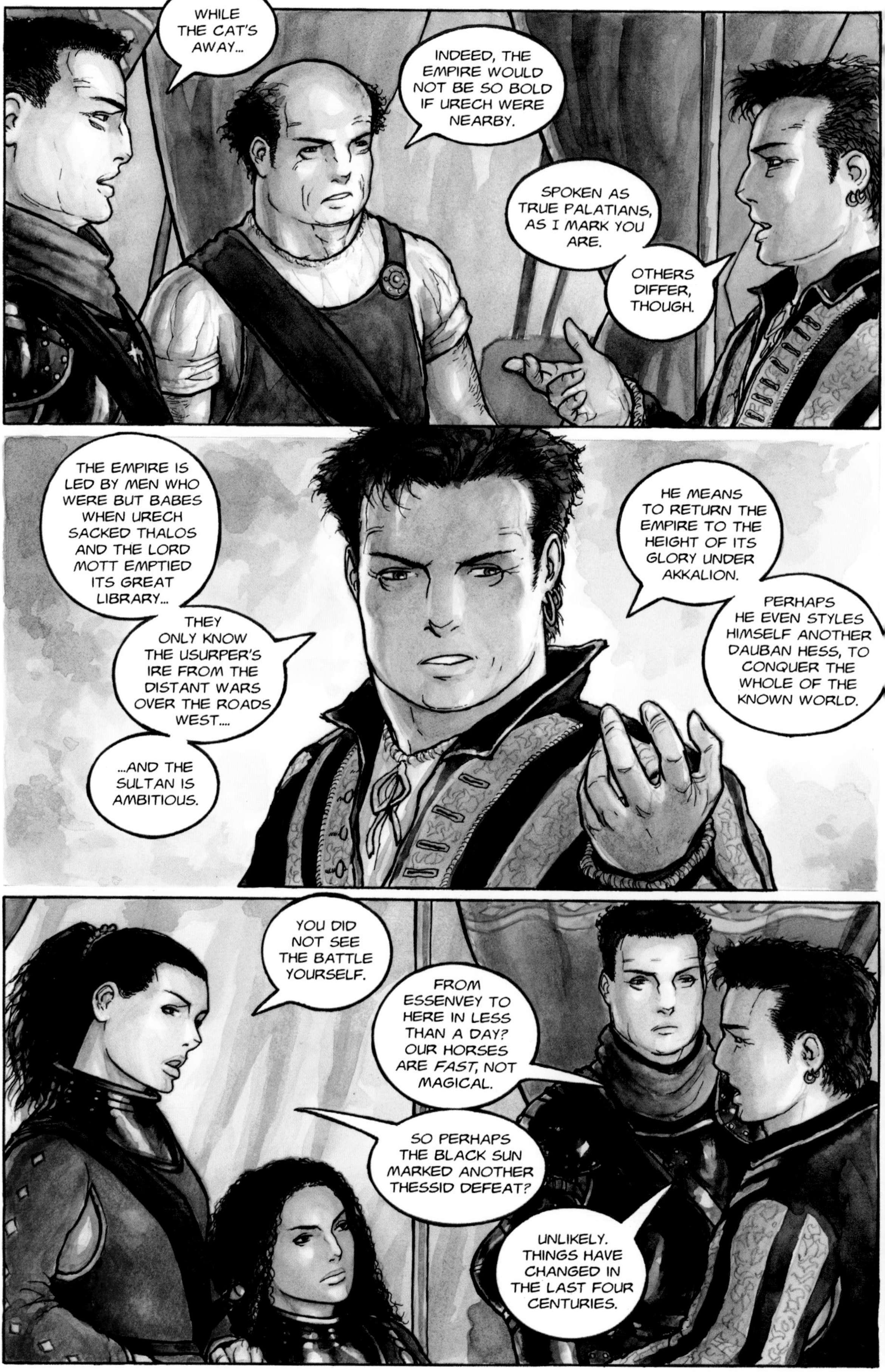
WHILE THE CAT'S AWAY...
INDEED, THE EMPIRE WOULD NOT BE SO BOLD IF URECH WERE NEARBY.
SPOKEN AS TRUE PALATIANS, AS I MARK YOU ARE.
OTHERS DIFFER, THOUGH.
THE EMPIRE IS LED BY MEN WHO WERE BUT BABES WHEN URECH SACKED THALOS AND THE LORD MOTT EMPTIED ITS GREAT LIBRARY...
THEY ONLY KNOW THE USURPER'S IRE FROM THE DISTANT WARS OVER THE ROADS WEST....
...AND THE SULTAN IS AMBITIOUS.
HE MEANS TO RETURN THE EMPIRE TO THE HEIGHT OF ITS GLORY UNDER AKKALION.
PERHAPS HE EVEN STYLES HIMSELF ANOTHER DAUBAN HESS, TO CONQUER THE WHOLE OF THE KNOWN WORLD.
YOU DID NOT SEE THE BATTLE YOURSELF.
FROM ESSENVEY TO HERE IN LESS THAN A DAY? OUR HORSES ARE *FAST*, NOT MAGICAL.
SO PERHAPS THE BLACK SUN MARKED ANOTHER THESSID DEFEAT?
UNLIKELY. THINGS HAVE CHANGED IN THE LAST FOUR CENTURIES.

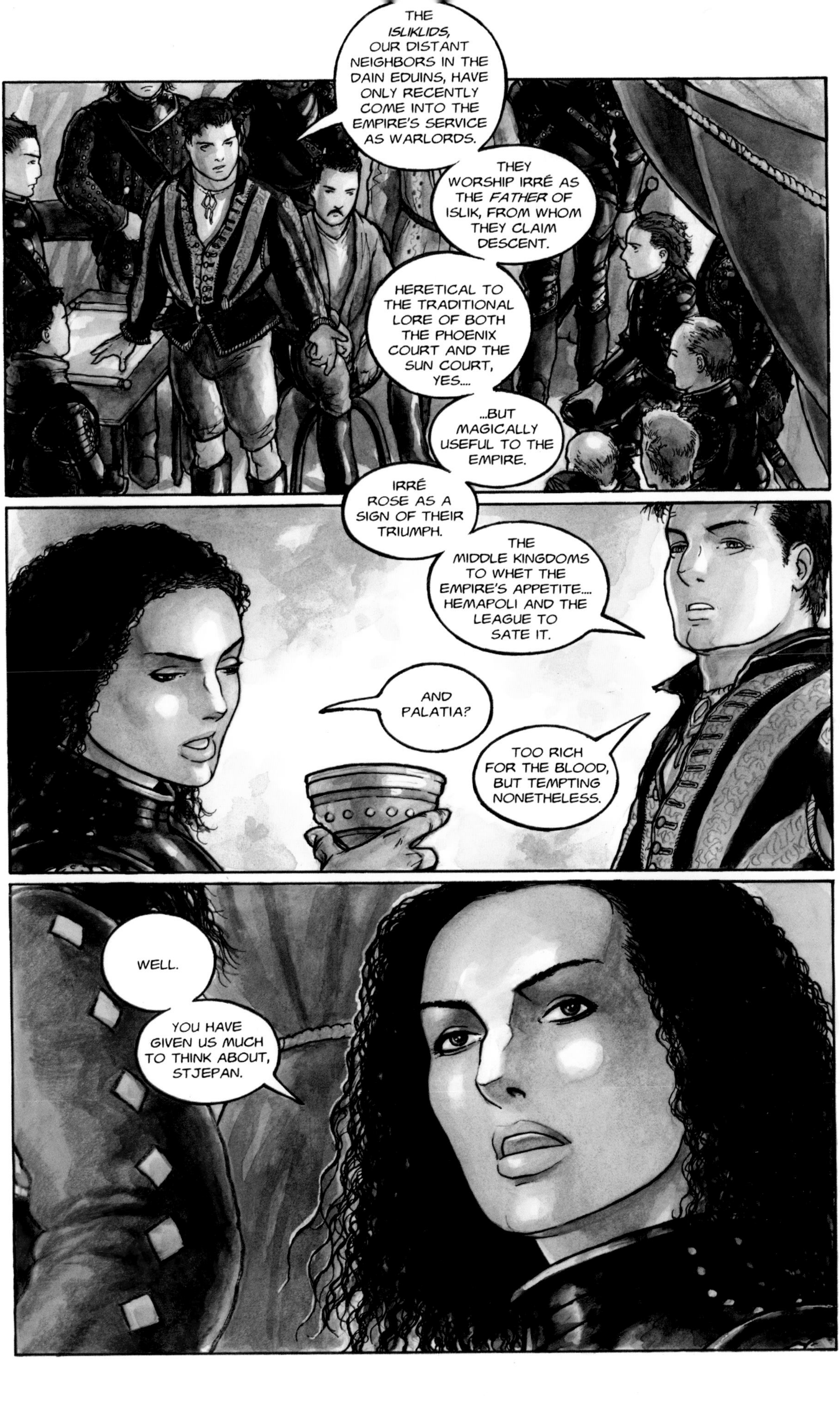
THE *ISLIKLIDS*, OUR DISTANT NEIGHBORS IN THE DAIN EDUINS, HAVE ONLY RECENTLY COME INTO THE EMPIRE'S SERVICE AS WARLORDS.
THEY WORSHIP IRRÉ AS THE *FATHER* OF ISLIK, FROM WHOM THEY CLAIM DESCENT.
HERETICAL TO THE TRADITIONAL LORE OF BOTH THE PHOENIX COURT AND THE SUN COURT, YES....
...BUT MAGICALLY USEFUL TO THE EMPIRE.
IRRÉ ROSE AS A SIGN OF THEIR TRIUMPH.
THE MIDDLE KINGDOMS TO WHET THE EMPIRE'S APPETITE.... HEMAPOLI AND THE LEAGUE TO SATE IT.
AND PALATIA?
TOO RICH FOR THE BLOOD, BUT TEMPTING NONETHELESS.
WELL.
YOU HAVE GIVEN US MUCH TO THINK ABOUT, STJEPAN.

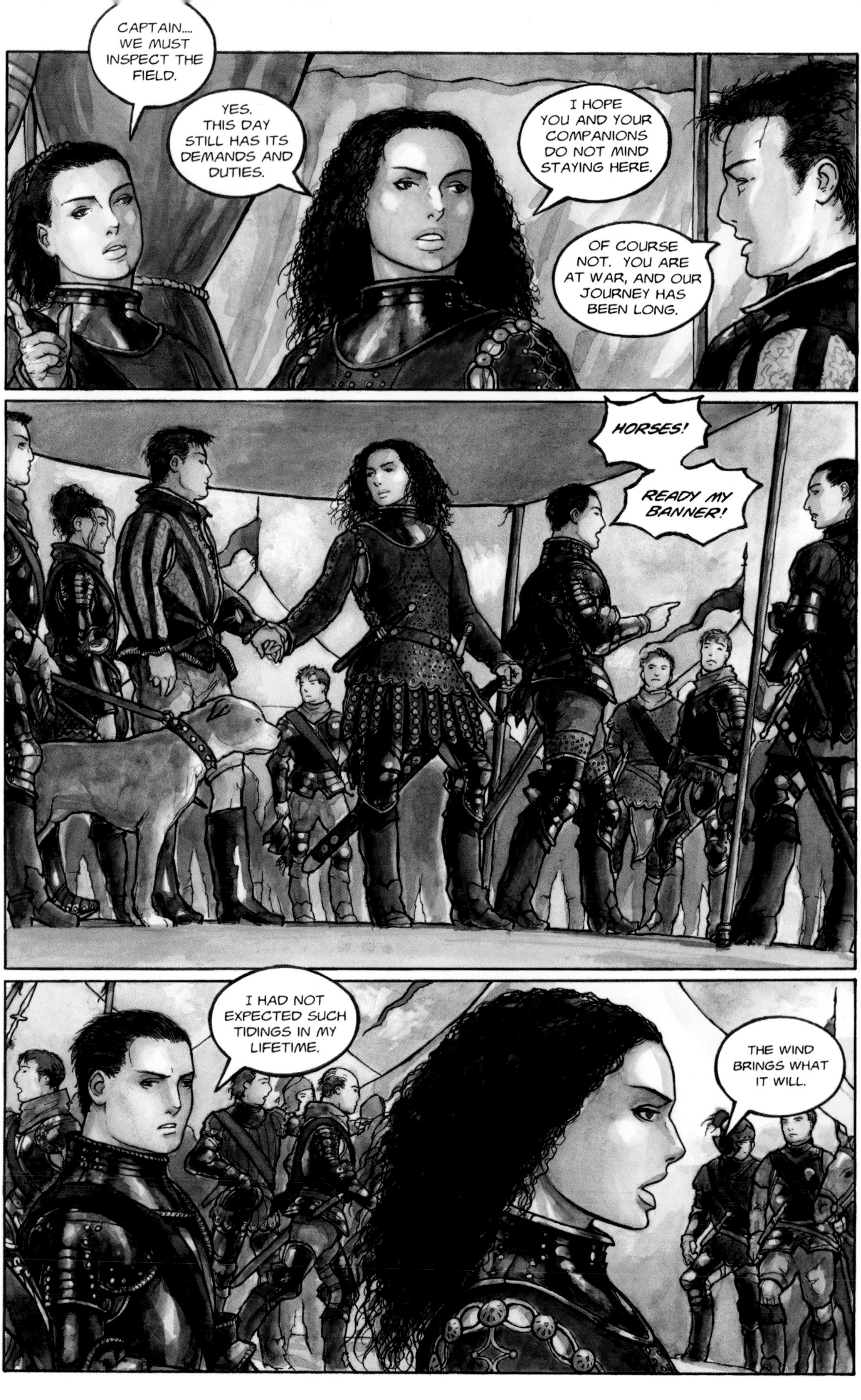
CAPTAIN.... WE MUST INSPECT THE FIELD.
YES. THIS DAY STILL HAS ITS DEMANDS AND DUTIES.
I HOPE YOU AND YOUR COMPANIONS DO NOT MIND STAYING HERE.
OF COURSE NOT. YOU ARE AT WAR, AND OUR JOURNEY HAS BEEN LONG.
HORSES!
READY MY BANNER!
I HAD NOT EXPECTED SUCH TIDINGS IN MY LIFETIME.
THE WIND BRINGS WHAT IT WILL.

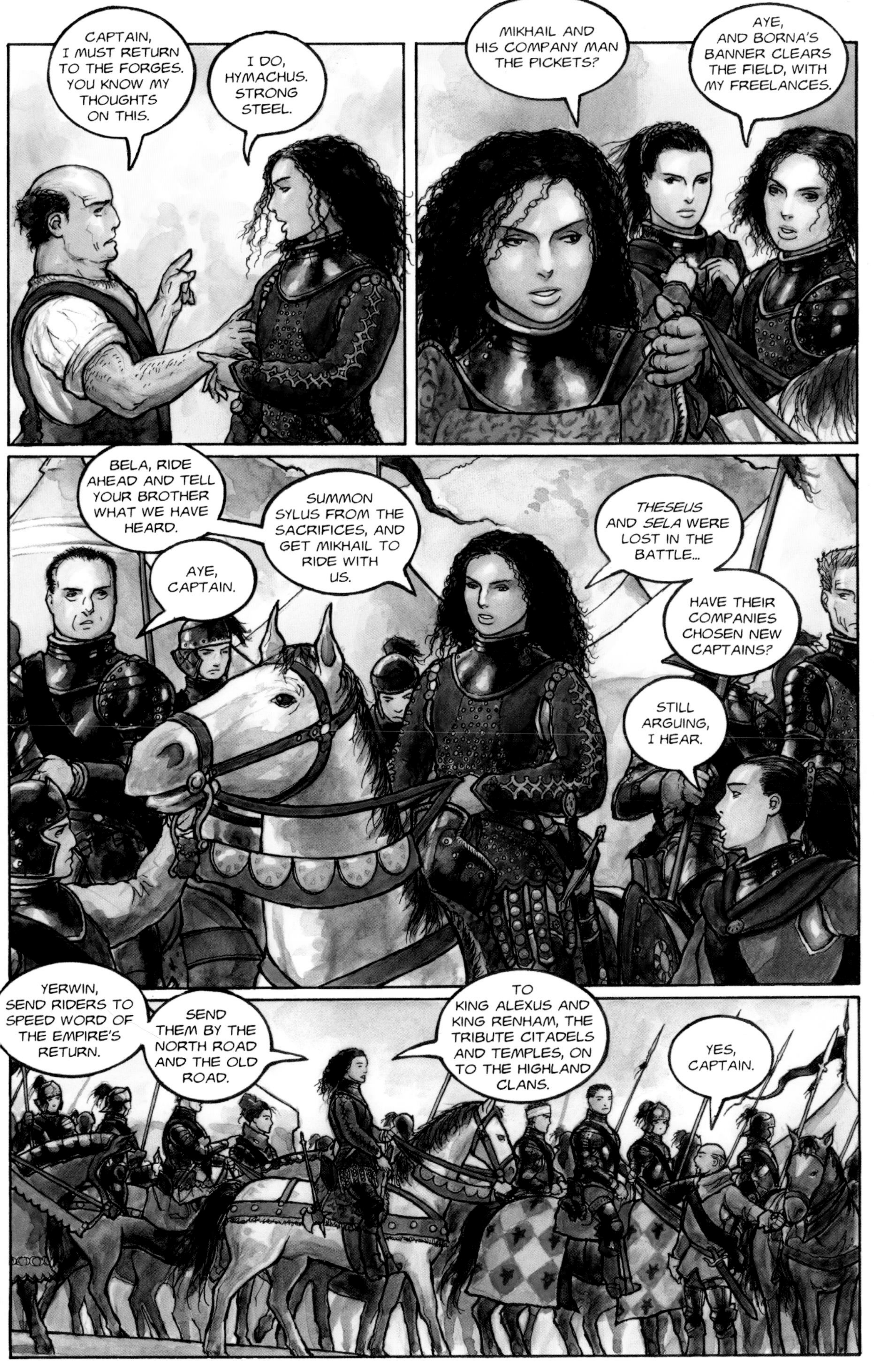
CAPTAIN, I MUST RETURN TO THE FORGES. YOU KNOW MY THOUGHTS ON THIS.
I DO, HYMACHUS. STRONG STEEL.
MIKHAIL AND HIS COMPANY MAN THE PICKETS?
AYE, AND BORNA'S BANNER CLEARS THE FIELD, WITH MY FREELANCES.
BELA, RIDE AHEAD AND TELL YOUR BROTHER WHAT WE HAVE HEARD.
AYE, CAPTAIN.
SUMMON SYLUS FROM THE SACRIFICES, AND GET MIKHAIL TO RIDE WITH US.
THESEUS AND *SELA* WERE LOST IN THE BATTLE...
HAVE THEIR COMPANIES CHOSEN NEW CAPTAINS?
STILL ARGUING, I HEAR.
YERWIN, SEND RIDERS TO SPEED WORD OF THE EMPIRE'S RETURN.
SEND THEM BY THE NORTH ROAD AND THE OLD ROAD.
TO KING ALEXUS AND KING RENHAM, THE TRIBUTE CITADELS AND TEMPLES, ON TO THE HIGHLAND CLANS.
YES, CAPTAIN.

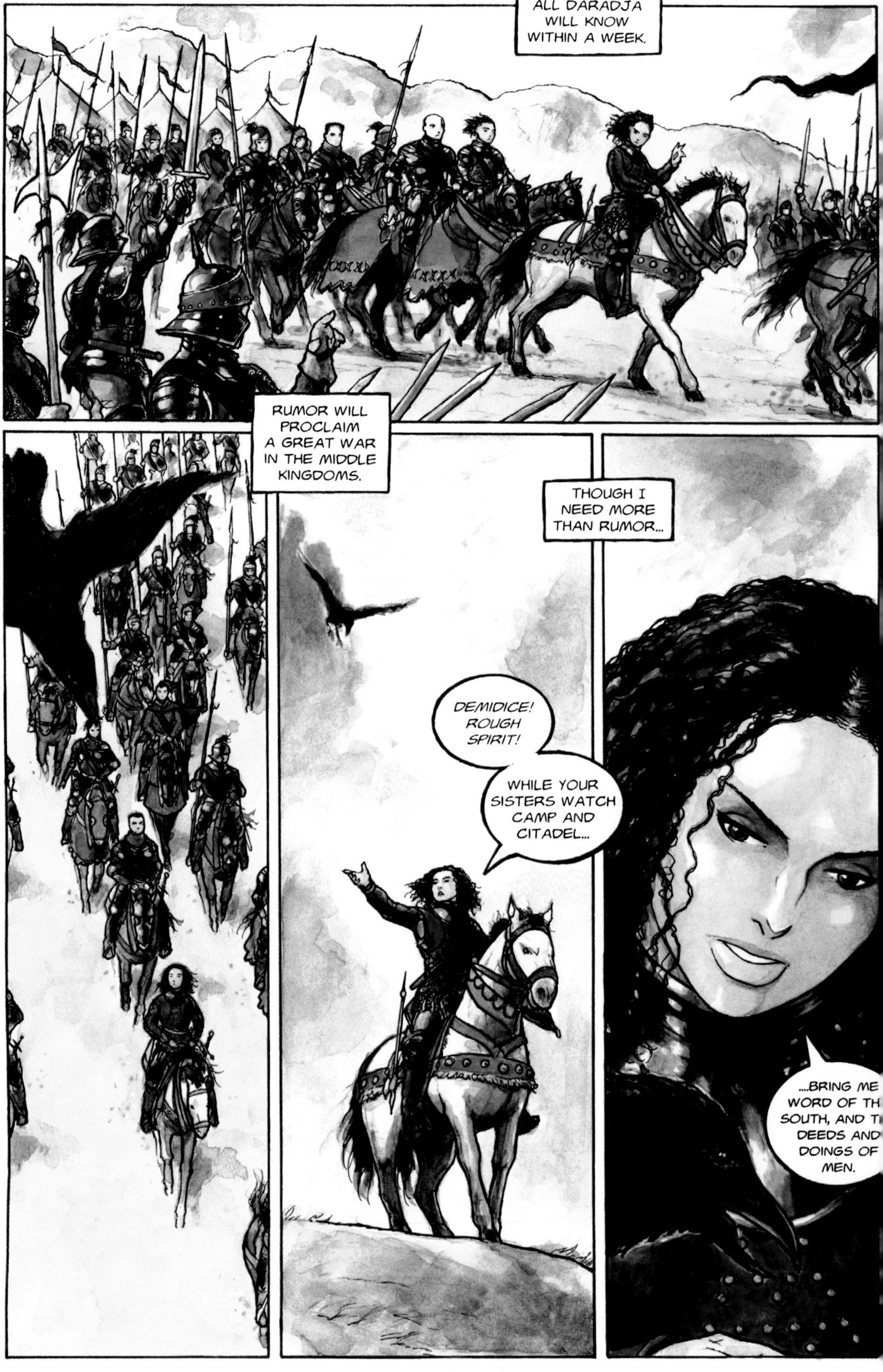
ALL DARADJA WILL KNOW WITHIN A WEEK.
RUMOR WILL PROCLAIM A GREAT WAR IN THE MIDDLE KINGDOMS.
THOUGH I NEED MORE THAN RUMOR...
DEMIDICE! ROUGH SPIRIT!
WHILE YOUR SISTERS WATCH CAMP AND CITADEL...
...BRING ME WORD OF TH SOUTH, AND T DEEDS AND DOINGS OF MEN.

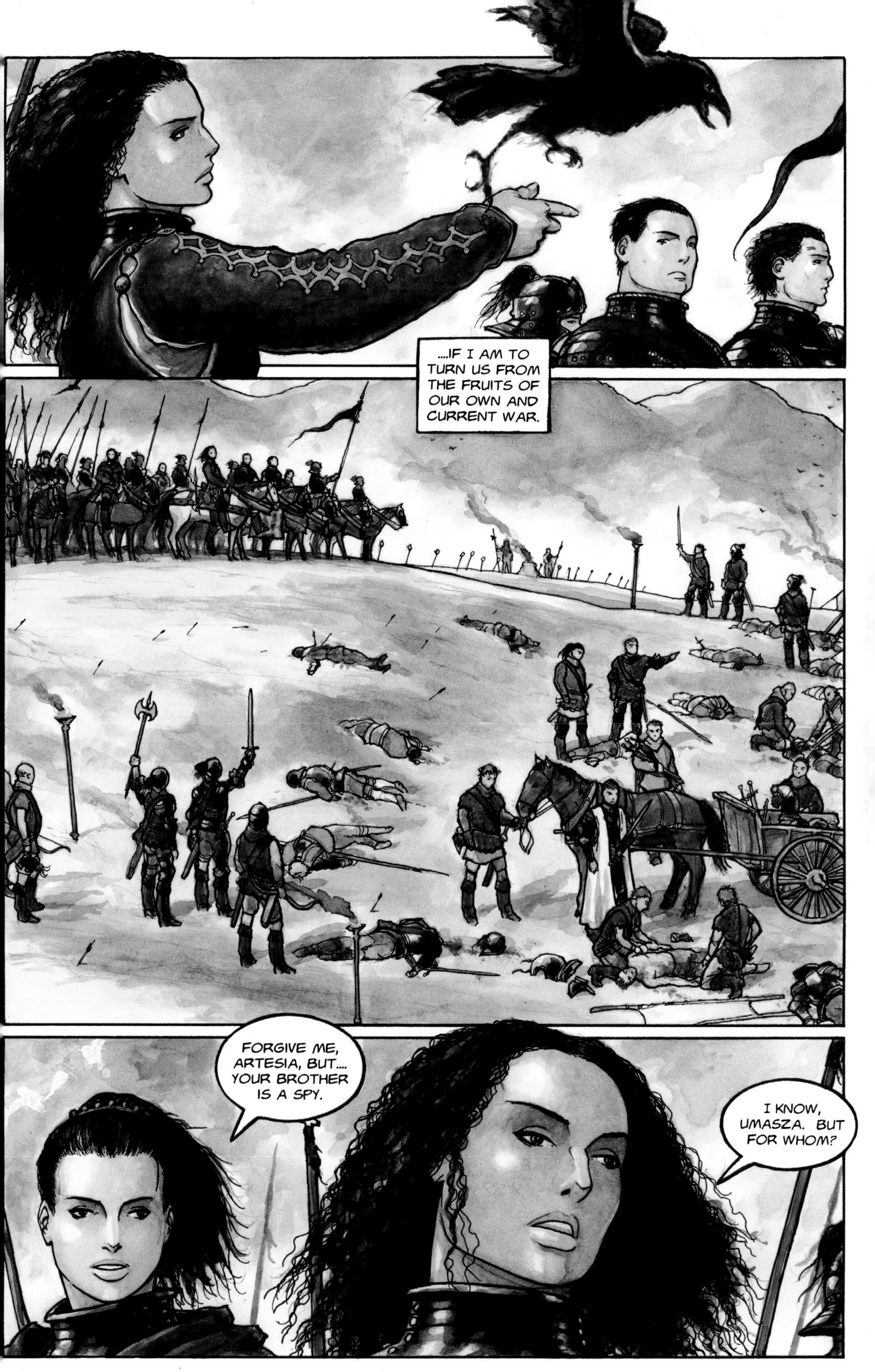
....IF I AM TO TURN US FROM THE FRUITS OF OUR OWN AND CURRENT WAR.
FORGIVE ME, ARTESIA, BUT.... YOUR BROTHER IS A SPY.
I KNOW, UMASZA. BUT FOR WHOM?

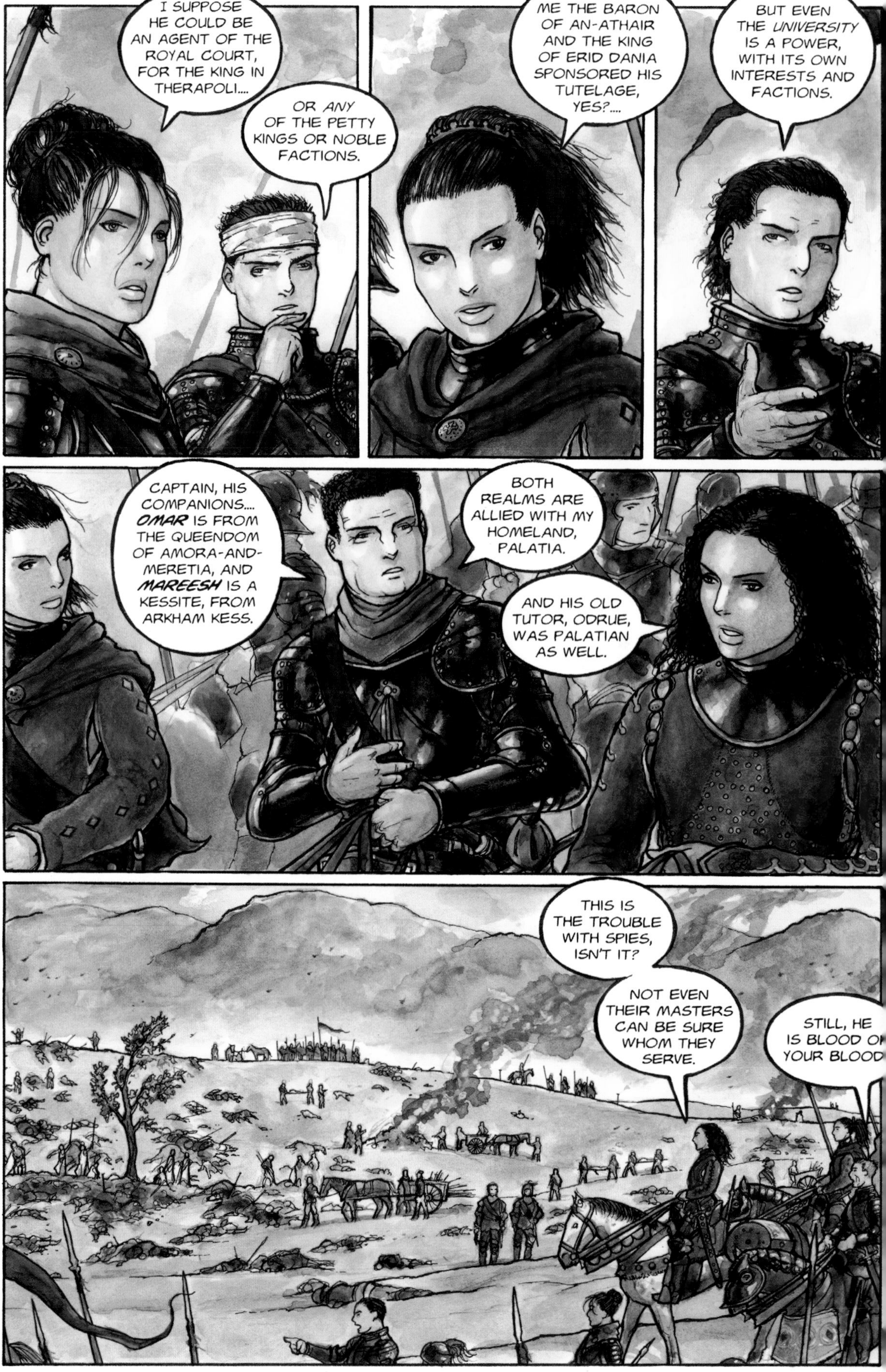
I SUPPOSE HE COULD BE AN AGENT OF THE ROYAL COURT, FOR THE KING IN THERAPOLI....
OR *ANY* OF THE PETTY KINGS OR NOBLE FACTIONS.
YOU TOLD ME THE BARON OF AN-ATHAIR AND THE KING OF ERID DANIA SPONSORED HIS TUTELAGE, YES?....
BUT EVEN THE *UNIVERSITY* IS A POWER, WITH ITS OWN INTERESTS AND FACTIONS.
CAPTAIN, HIS COMPANIONS.... ***OMAR*** IS FROM THE QUEENDOM OF AMORA-AND-MERETIA, AND ***MAREESH*** IS A KESSITE, FROM ARKHAM KESS.
BOTH REALMS ARE ALLIED WITH MY HOMELAND, PALATIA.
AND HIS OLD TUTOR, ODRUE, WAS PALATIAN AS WELL.
THIS IS THE TROUBLE WITH SPIES, ISN'T IT?
NOT EVEN THEIR MASTERS CAN BE SURE WHOM THEY SERVE.
STILL, HE IS BLOOD OF YOUR BLOOD

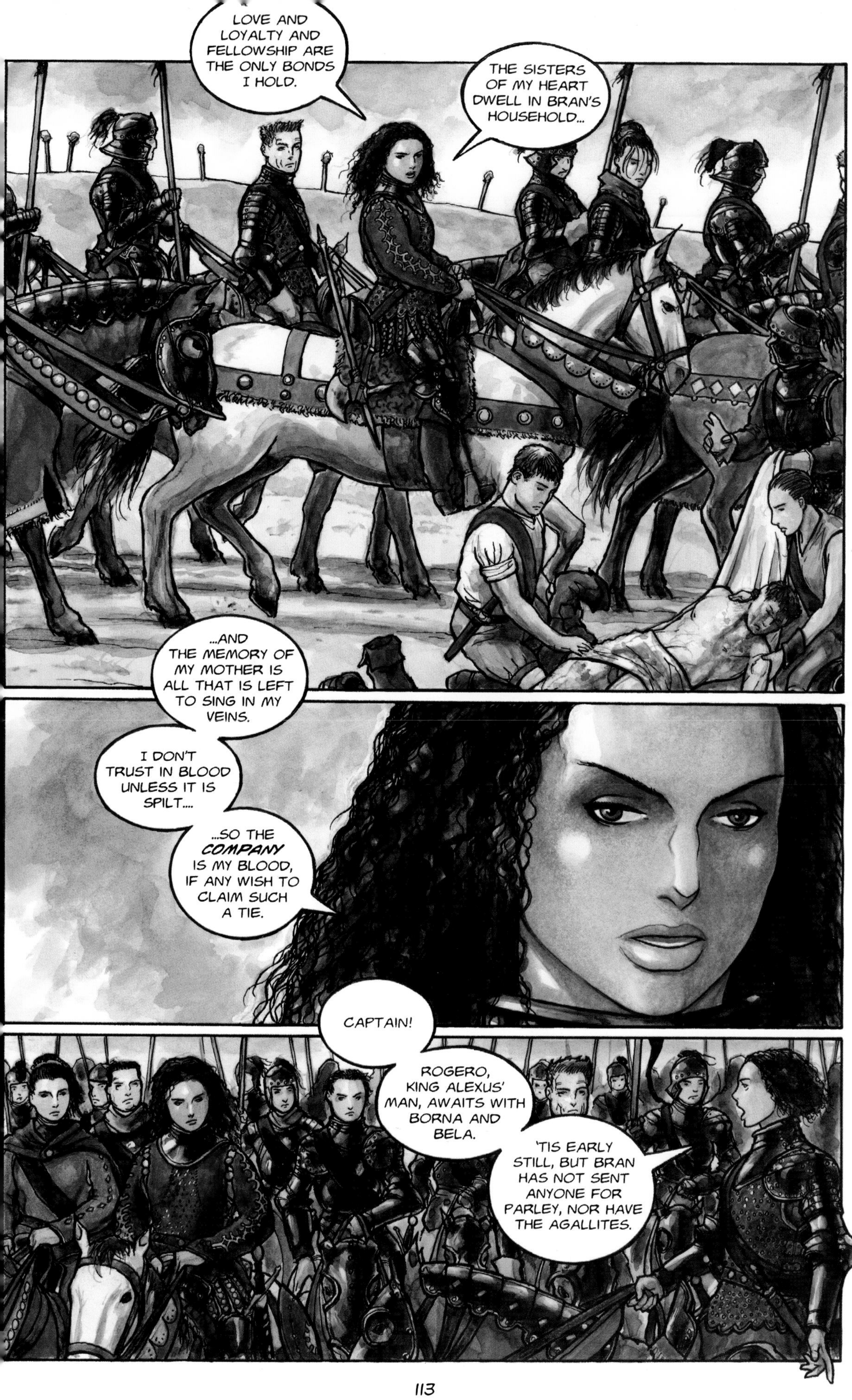
LOVE AND LOYALTY AND FELLOWSHIP ARE THE ONLY BONDS I HOLD.
THE SISTERS OF MY HEART DWELL IN BRAN'S HOUSEHOLD...
...AND THE MEMORY OF MY MOTHER IS ALL THAT IS LEFT TO SING IN MY VEINS.
I DON'T TRUST IN BLOOD UNLESS IT IS SPILT....
...SO THE *COMPANY* IS MY BLOOD, IF ANY WISH TO CLAIM SUCH A TIE.
CAPTAIN!
ROGERO, KING ALEXUS' MAN, AWAITS WITH BORNA AND BELA.
'TIS EARLY STILL, BUT BRAN HAS NOT SENT ANYONE FOR PARLEY, NOR HAVE THE AGALLITES.

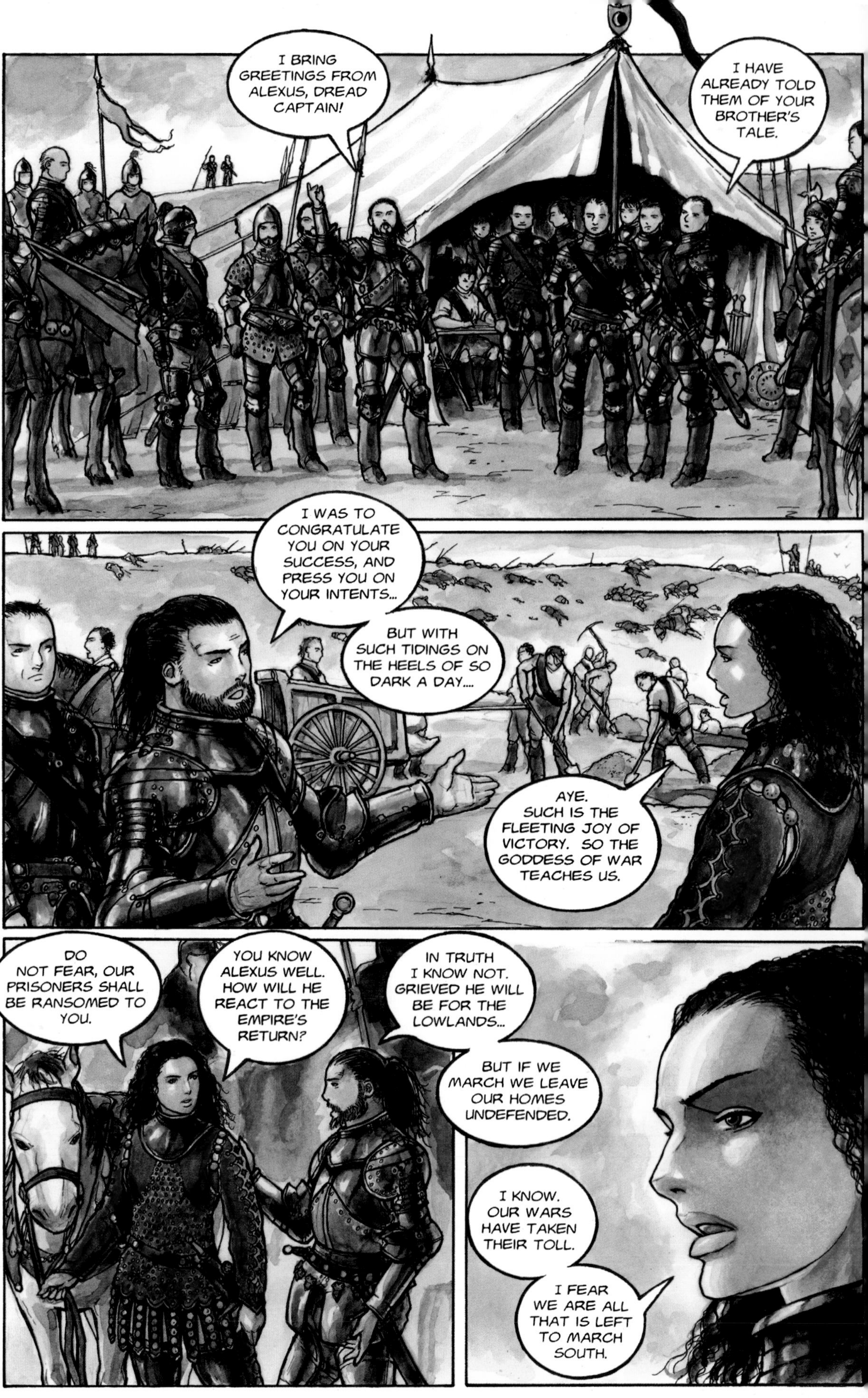
I BRING GREETINGS FROM ALEXUS, DREAD CAPTAIN!
I HAVE ALREADY TOLD THEM OF YOUR BROTHER'S TALE.
I WAS TO CONGRATULATE YOU ON YOUR SUCCESS, AND PRESS YOU ON YOUR INTENTS...
BUT WITH SUCH TIDINGS ON THE HEELS OF SO DARK A DAY....
AYE. SUCH IS THE FLEETING JOY OF VICTORY. SO THE GODDESS OF WAR TEACHES US.
DO NOT FEAR, OUR PRISONERS SHALL BE RANSOMED TO YOU.
YOU KNOW ALEXUS WELL. HOW WILL HE REACT TO THE EMPIRE'S RETURN?
IN TRUTH I KNOW NOT. GRIEVED HE WILL BE FOR THE LOWLANDS...
BUT IF WE MARCH WE LEAVE OUR HOMES UNDEFENDED.
I KNOW. OUR WARS HAVE TAKEN THEIR TOLL.
I FEAR WE ARE ALL THAT IS LEFT TO MARCH SOUTH.

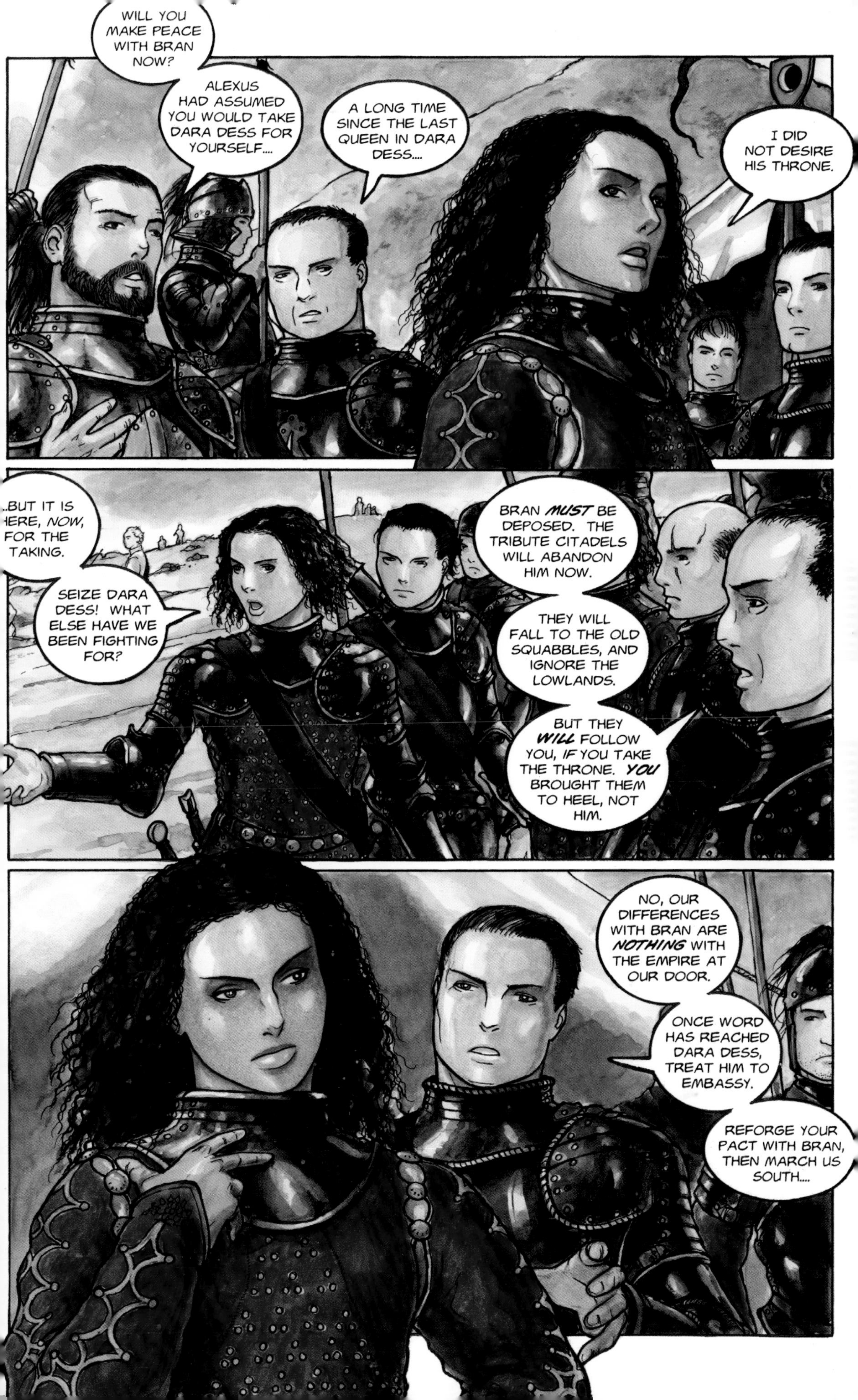
WILL YOU MAKE PEACE WITH BRAN NOW?
ALEXUS HAD ASSUMED YOU WOULD TAKE DARA DESS FOR YOURSELF....
A LONG TIME SINCE THE LAST QUEEN IN DARA DESS....
I DID NOT DESIRE HIS THRONE.
..BUT IT IS HERE, NOW, FOR THE TAKING.
SEIZE DARA DESS! WHAT ELSE HAVE WE BEEN FIGHTING FOR?
BRAN MUST BE DEPOSED. THE TRIBUTE CITADELS WILL ABANDON HIM NOW.
THEY WILL FALL TO THE OLD SQUABBLES, AND IGNORE THE LOWLANDS.
BUT THEY WILL FOLLOW YOU, IF YOU TAKE THE THRONE. YOU BROUGHT THEM TO HEEL, NOT HIM.
NO, OUR DIFFERENCES WITH BRAN ARE NOTHING WITH THE EMPIRE AT OUR DOOR.
ONCE WORD HAS REACHED DARA DESS, TREAT HIM TO EMBASSY.
REFORGE YOUR PACT WITH BRAN, THEN MARCH US SOUTH....

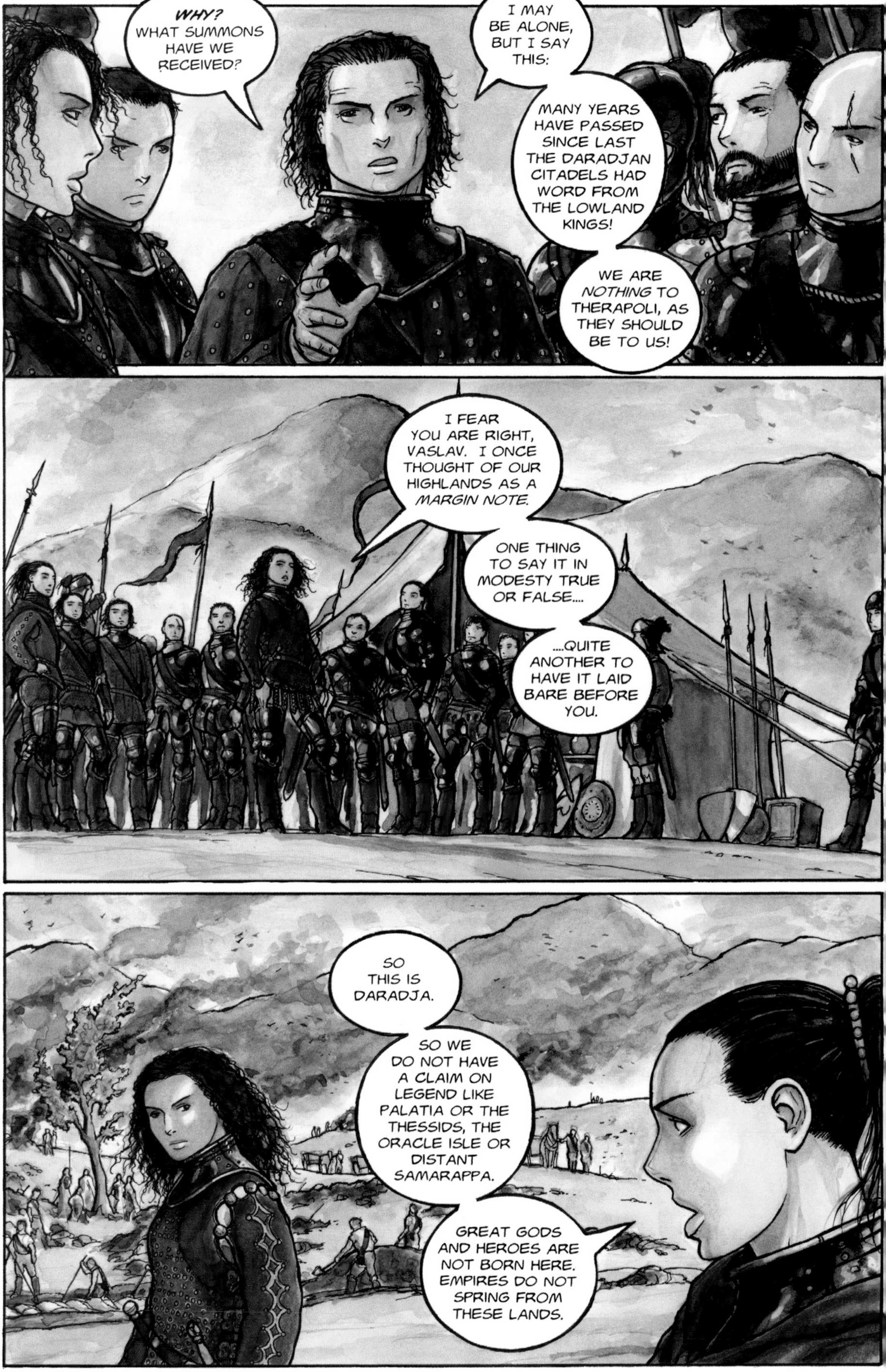
WHY? WHAT SUMMONS HAVE WE RECEIVED?
I MAY BE ALONE, BUT I SAY THIS:
MANY YEARS HAVE PASSED SINCE LAST THE DARADJAN CITADELS HAD WORD FROM THE LOWLAND KINGS!
WE ARE NOTHING TO THERAPOLI, AS THEY SHOULD BE TO US!
I FEAR YOU ARE RIGHT, VASLAV. I ONCE THOUGHT OF OUR HIGHLANDS AS A MARGIN NOTE.
ONE THING TO SAY IT IN MODESTY TRUE OR FALSE....
....QUITE ANOTHER TO HAVE IT LAID BARE BEFORE YOU.
SO THIS IS DARADJA.
SO WE DO NOT HAVE A CLAIM ON LEGEND LIKE PALATIA OR THE THESSIDS, THE ORACLE ISLE OR DISTANT SAMARAPPA.
GREAT GODS AND HEROES ARE NOT BORN HERE. EMPIRES DO NOT SPRING FROM THESE LANDS.

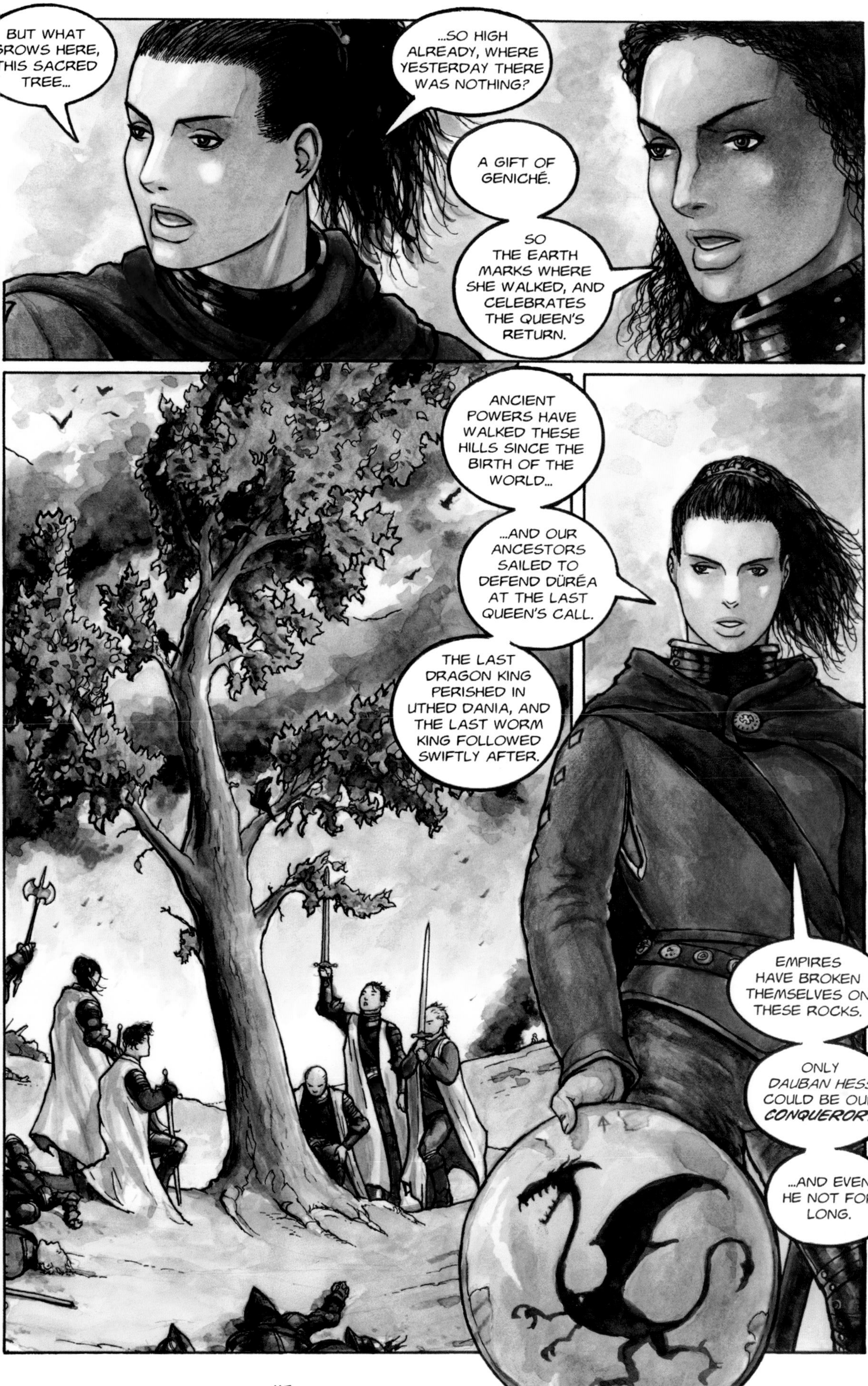
BUT WHAT GROWS HERE, THIS SACRED TREE...
...SO HIGH ALREADY, WHERE YESTERDAY THERE WAS NOTHING?
A GIFT OF GENICHÉ.
SO THE EARTH MARKS WHERE SHE WALKED, AND CELEBRATES THE QUEEN'S RETURN.
ANCIENT POWERS HAVE WALKED THESE HILLS SINCE THE BIRTH OF THE WORLD...
...AND OUR ANCESTORS SAILED TO DEFEND DÜRÉA AT THE LAST QUEEN'S CALL.
THE LAST DRAGON KING PERISHED IN UTHED DANIA, AND THE LAST WORM KING FOLLOWED SWIFTLY AFTER.
EMPIRES HAVE BROKEN THEMSELVES ON THESE ROCKS.
ONLY *DAUBAN HESS* COULD BE OUR ***CONQUEROR***...
...AND EVEN HE NOT FOR LONG.

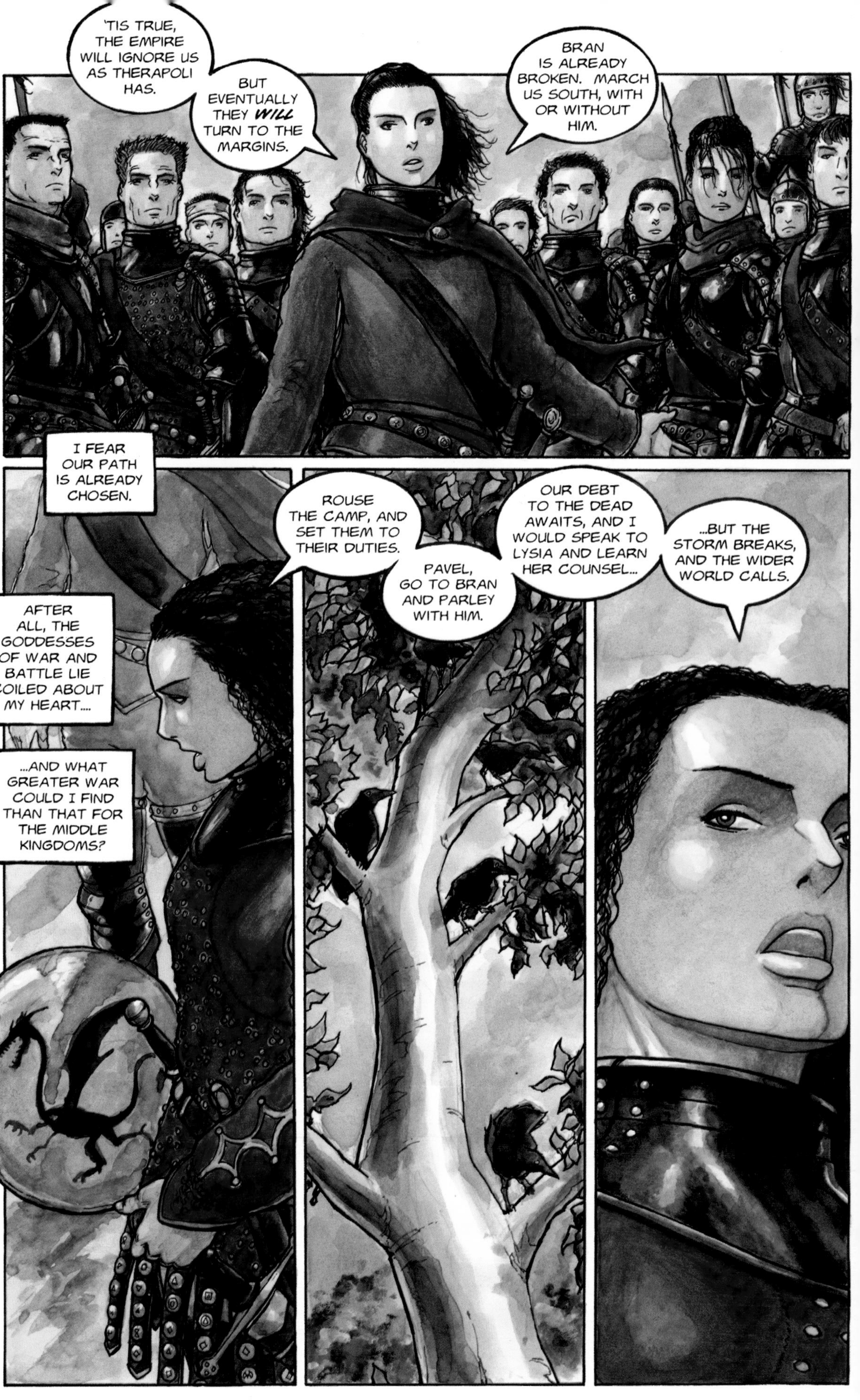
'TIS TRUE, THE EMPIRE WILL IGNORE US AS THERAPOLI HAS.
BUT EVENTUALLY THEY WILL TURN TO THE MARGINS.
BRAN IS ALREADY BROKEN. MARCH US SOUTH, WITH OR WITHOUT HIM.
I FEAR OUR PATH IS ALREADY CHOSEN.
AFTER ALL, THE GODDESSES OF WAR AND BATTLE LIE COILED ABOUT MY HEART....
...AND WHAT GREATER WAR COULD I FIND THAN THAT FOR THE MIDDLE KINGDOMS?
ROUSE THE CAMP, AND SET THEM TO THEIR DUTIES.
PAVEL, GO TO BRAN AND PARLEY WITH HIM.
OUR DEBT TO THE DEAD AWAITS, AND I WOULD SPEAK TO LYSIA AND LEARN HER COUNSEL...
...BUT THE STORM BREAKS, AND THE WIDER WORLD CALLS.

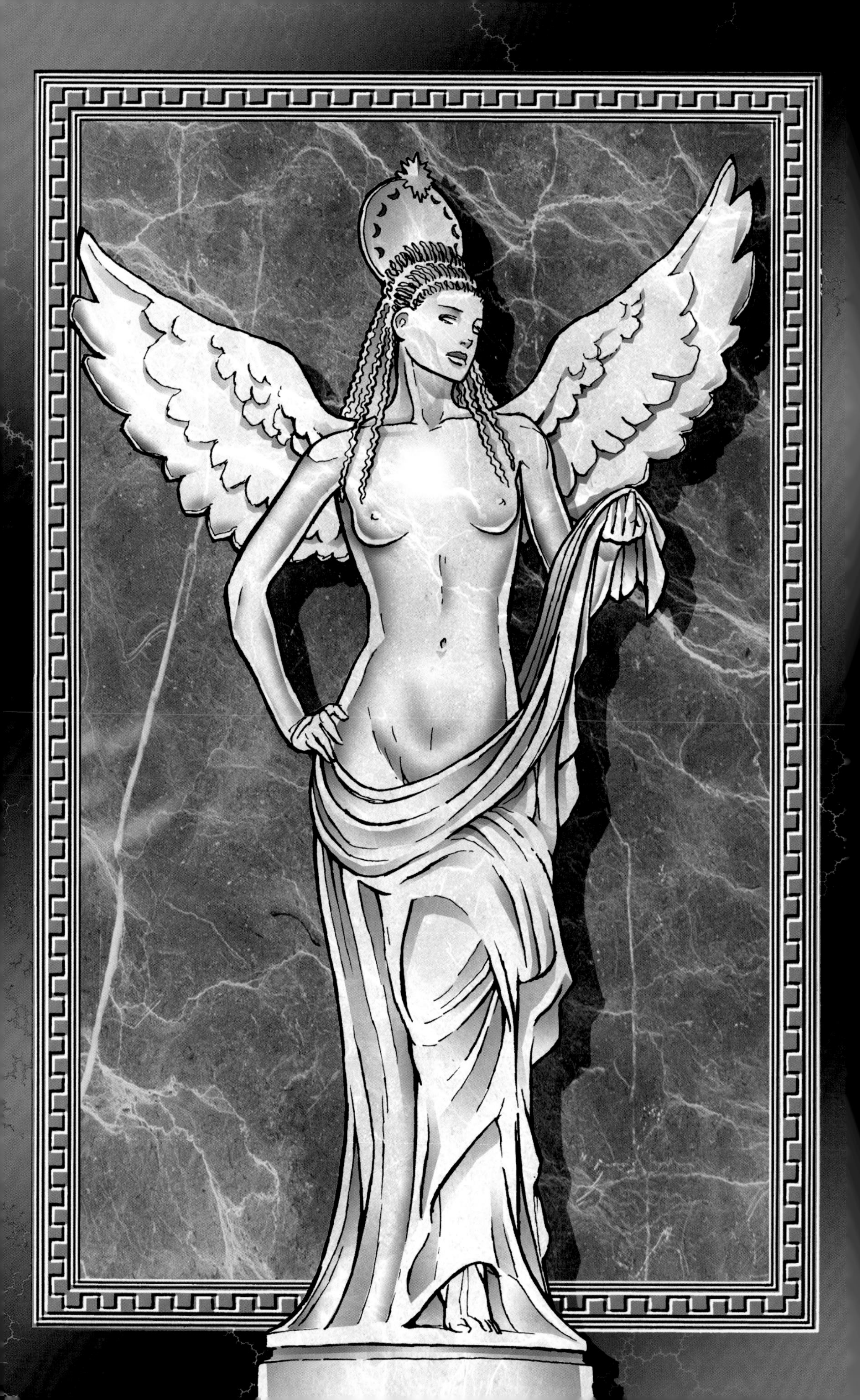

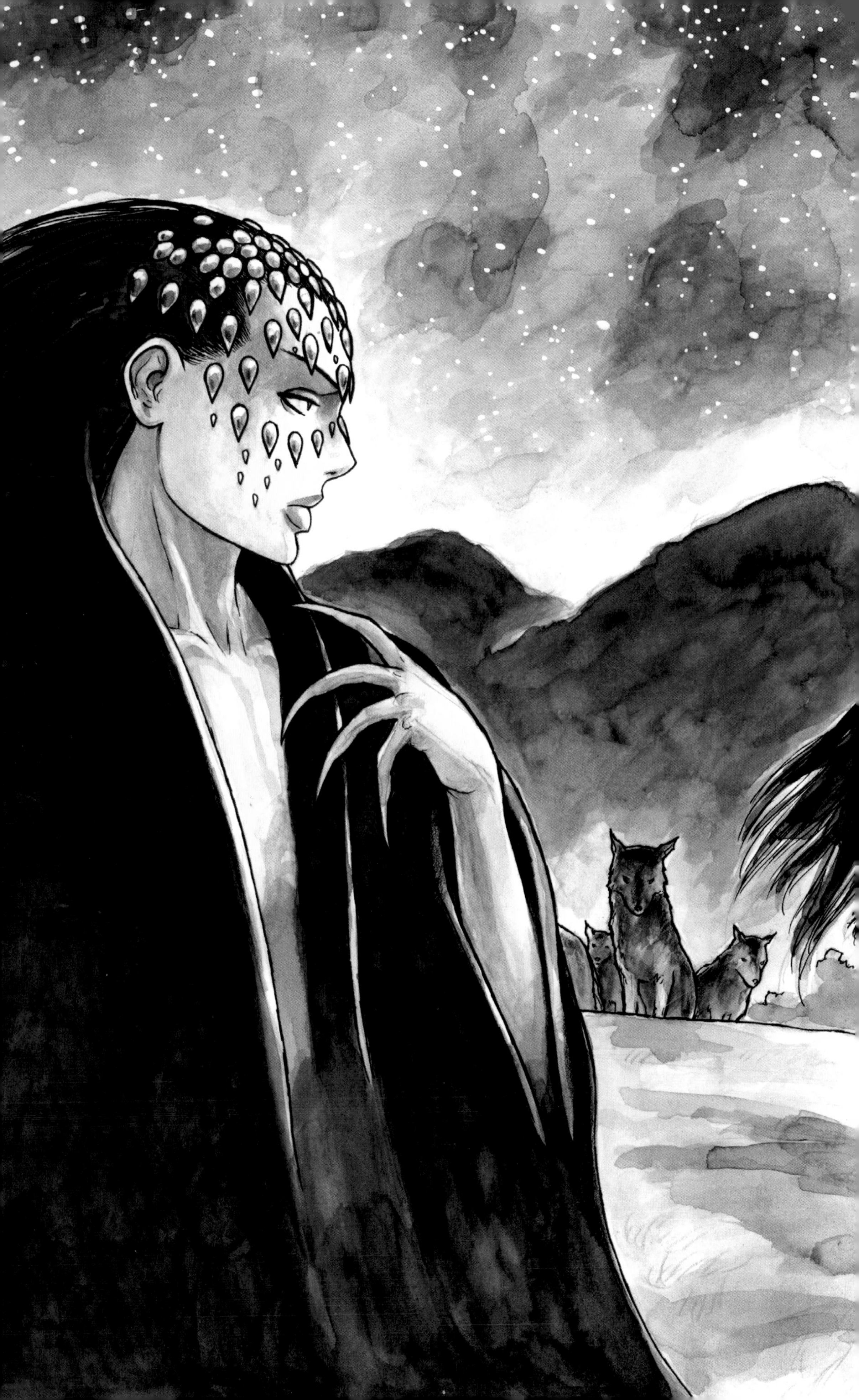

CHAPTER FIVE

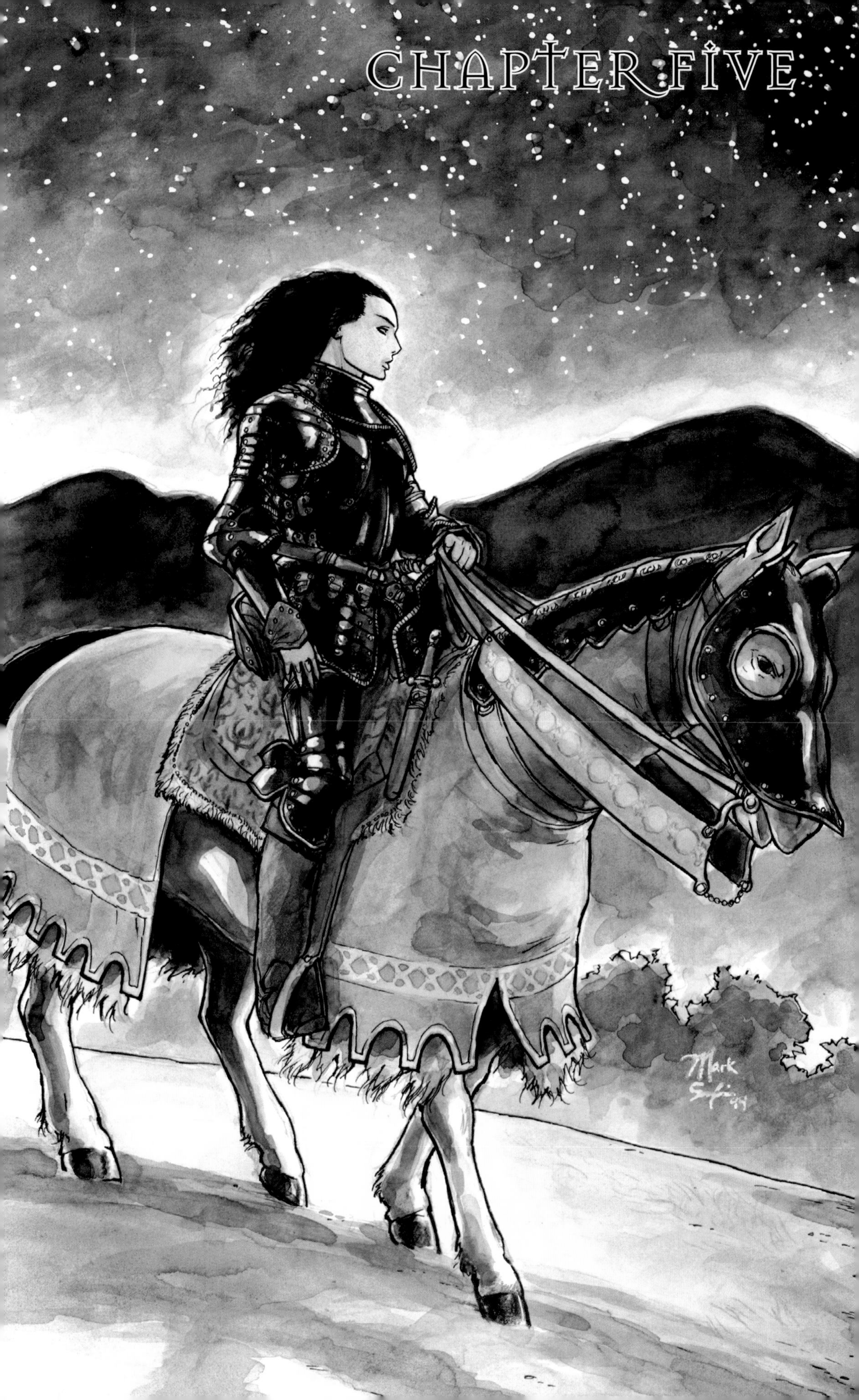

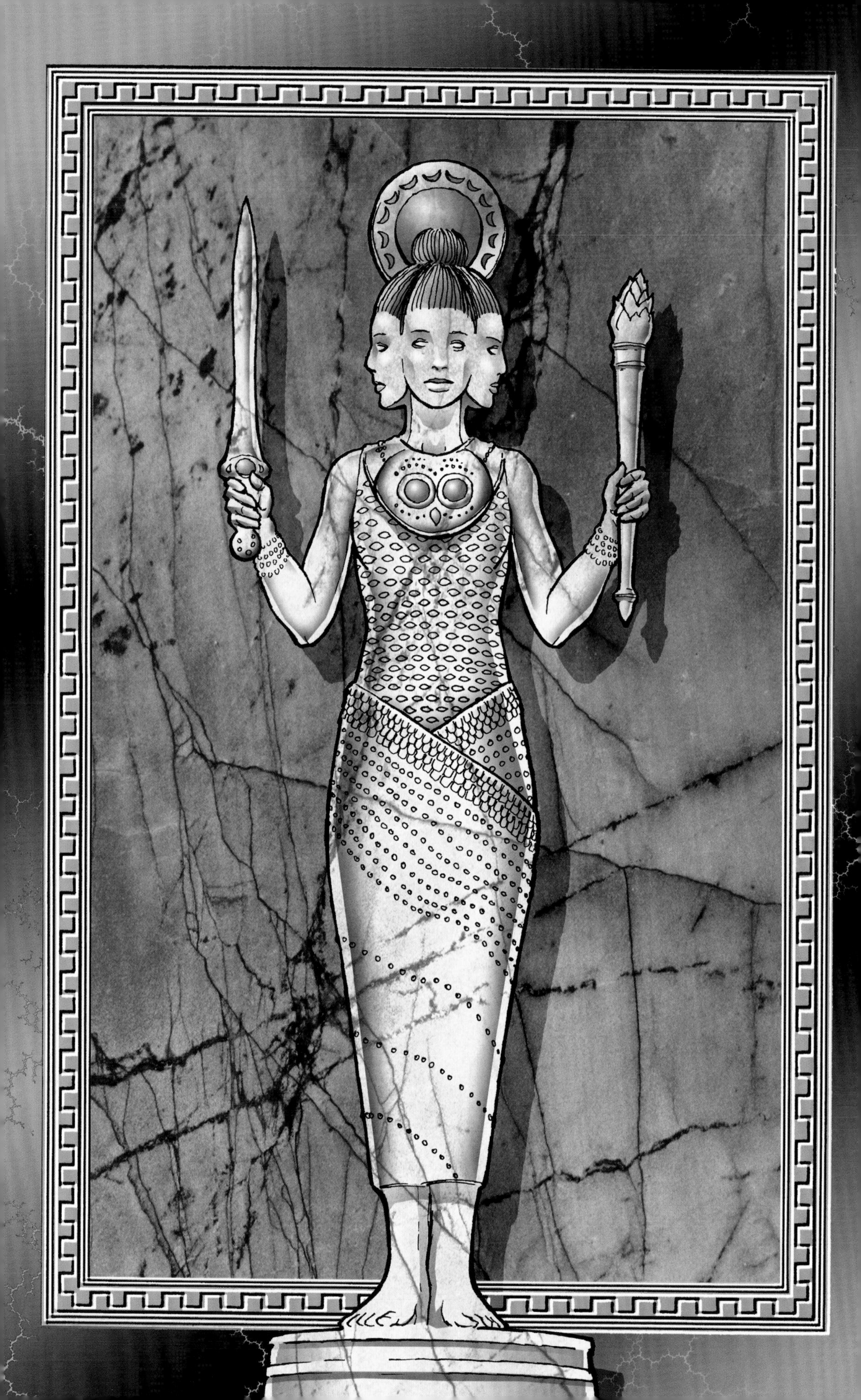

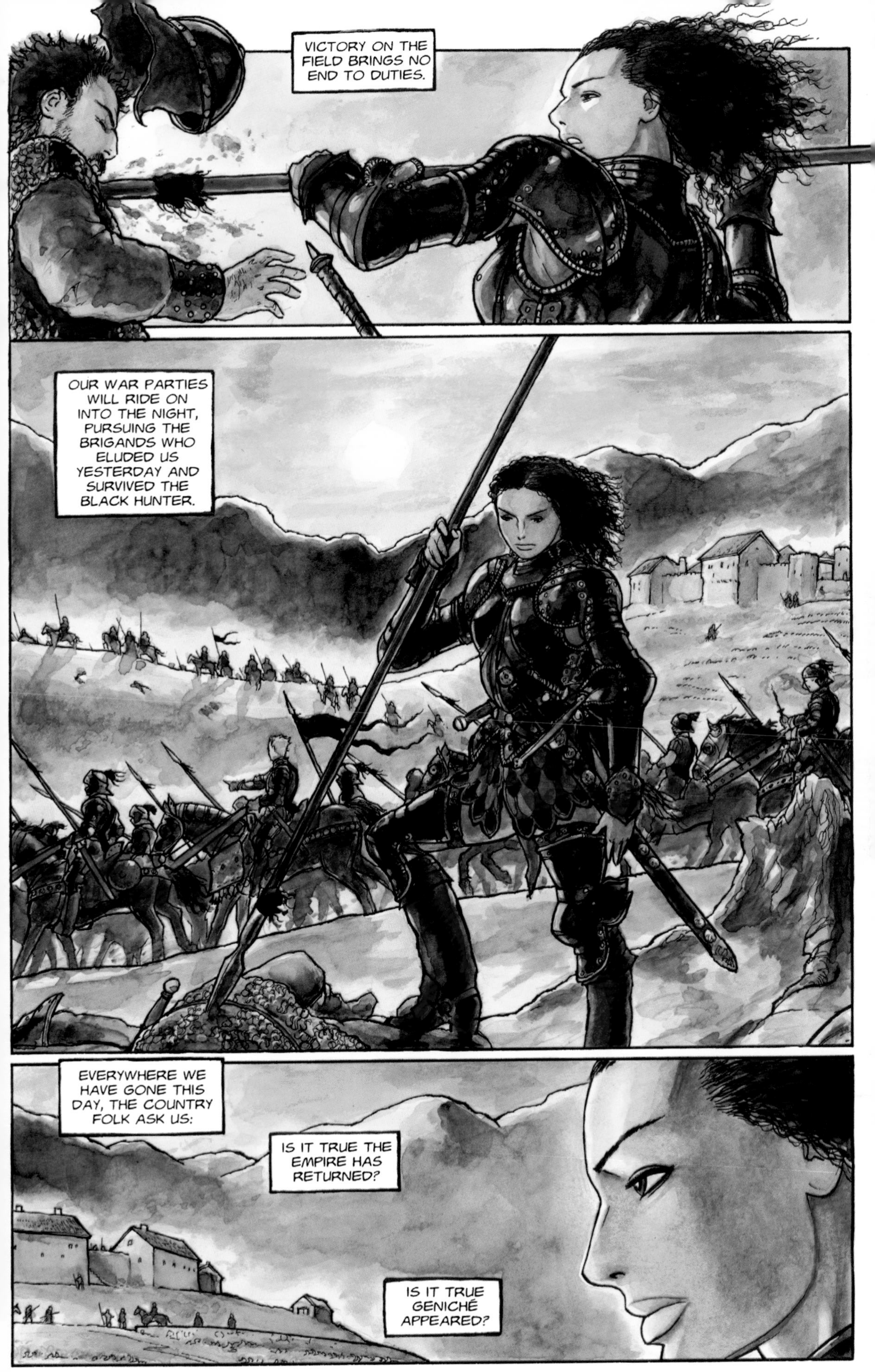
VICTORY ON THE FIELD BRINGS NO END TO DUTIES.
OUR WAR PARTIES WILL RIDE ON INTO THE NIGHT, PURSUING THE BRIGANDS WHO ELUDED US YESTERDAY AND SURVIVED THE BLACK HUNTER.
EVERYWHERE WE HAVE GONE THIS DAY, THE COUNTRY FOLK ASK US:
IS IT TRUE THE EMPIRE HAS RETURNED?
IS IT TRUE GENICHÉ APPEARED?

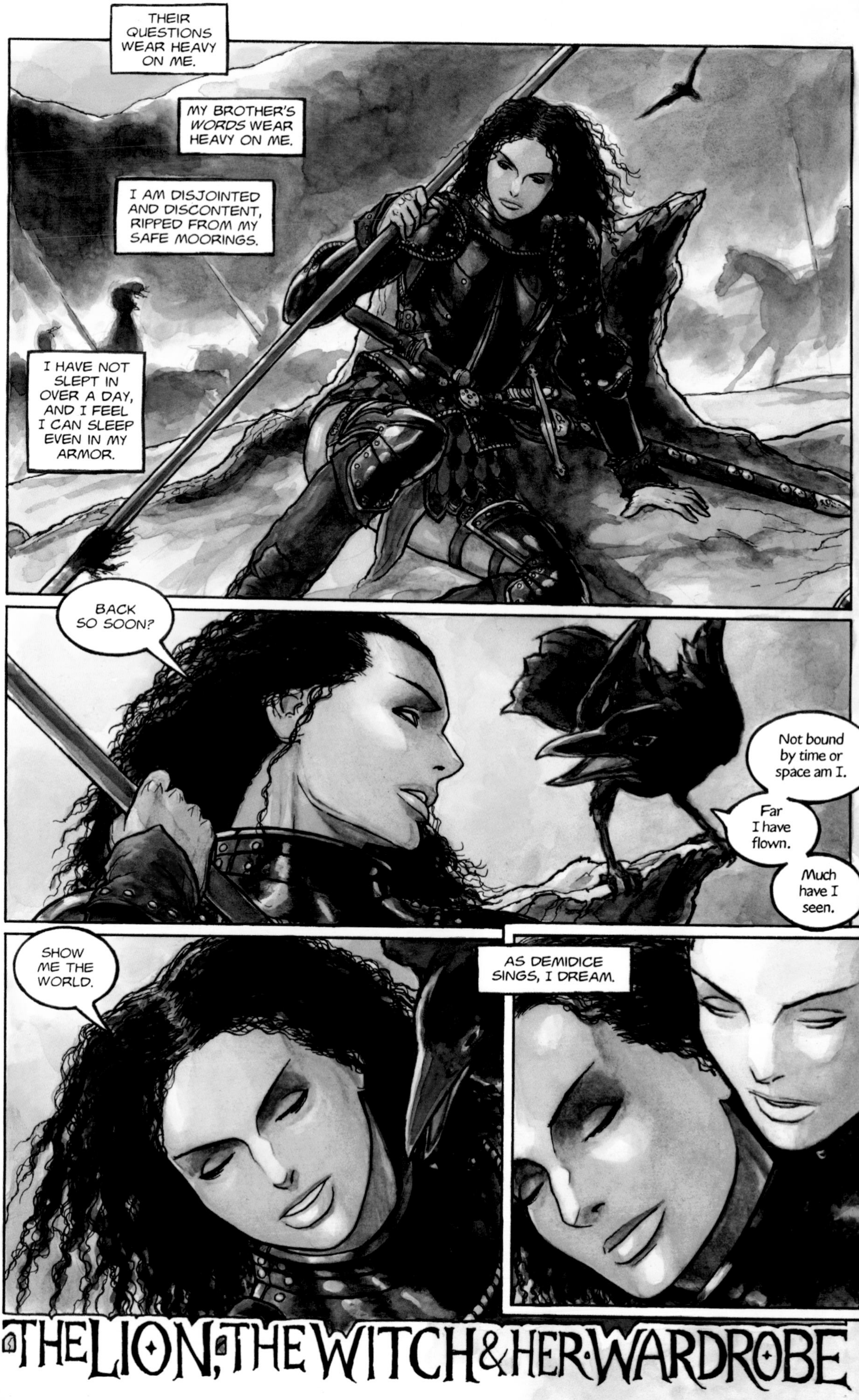
THEIR QUESTIONS WEAR HEAVY ON ME.
MY BROTHER'S *WORDS* WEAR HEAVY ON ME.
I AM DISJOINTED AND DISCONTENT, RIPPED FROM MY SAFE MOORINGS.
I HAVE NOT SLEPT IN OVER A DAY, AND I FEEL I CAN SLEEP EVEN IN MY ARMOR.
BACK SO SOON?
Not bound by time or space am I.
Far I have flown.
Much have I seen.
SHOW ME THE WORLD.
AS DEMIDICE SINGS, I DREAM.

THE LION, THE WITCH & HER WARDROBE

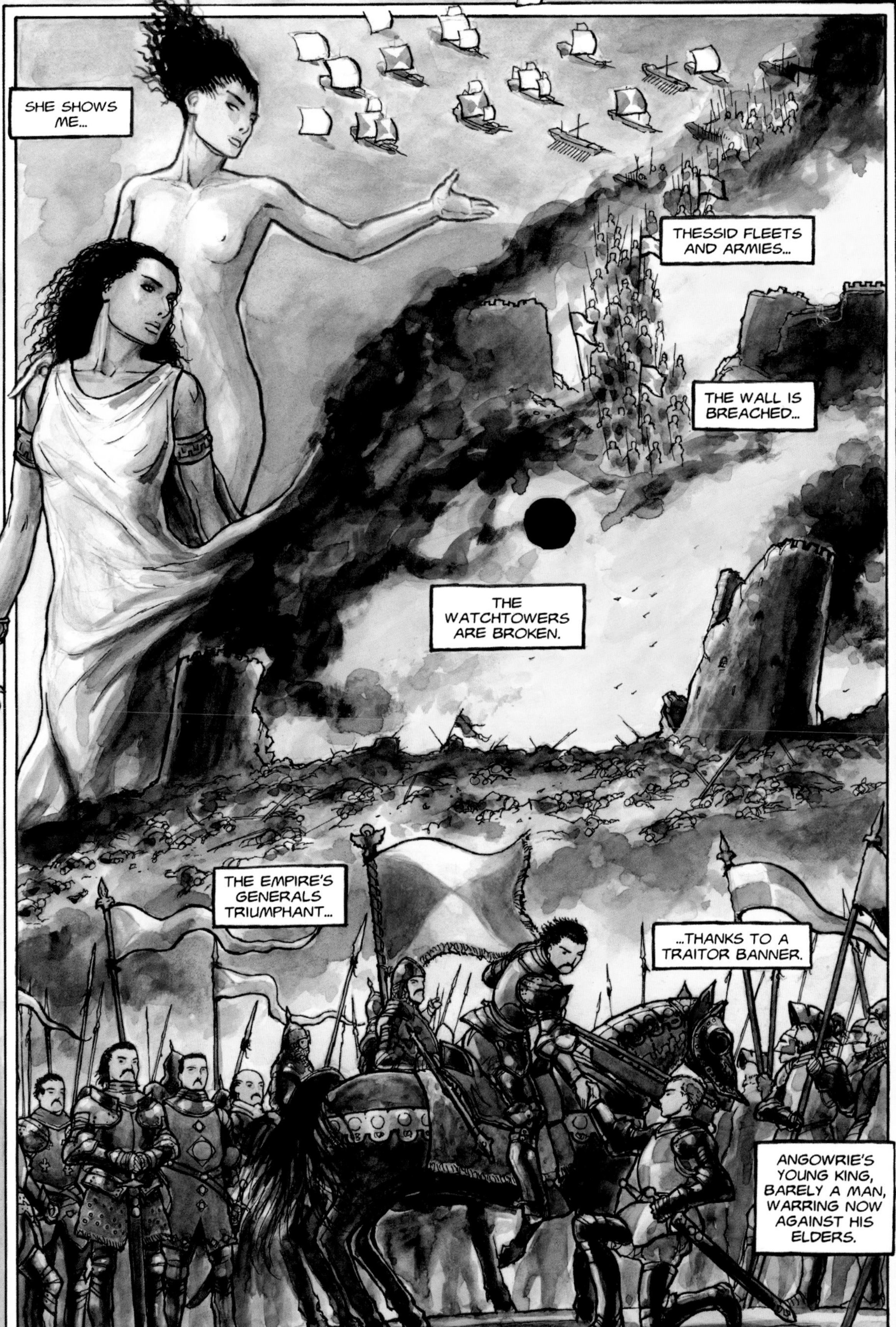
SHE SHOWS ME...
THESSID FLEETS AND ARMIES...
THE WALL IS BREACHED...
THE WATCHTOWERS ARE BROKEN.
THE EMPIRE'S GENERALS TRIUMPHANT...
...THANKS TO A TRAITOR BANNER.
ANGOWRIE'S YOUNG KING, BARELY A MAN, WARRING NOW AGAINST HIS ELDERS.

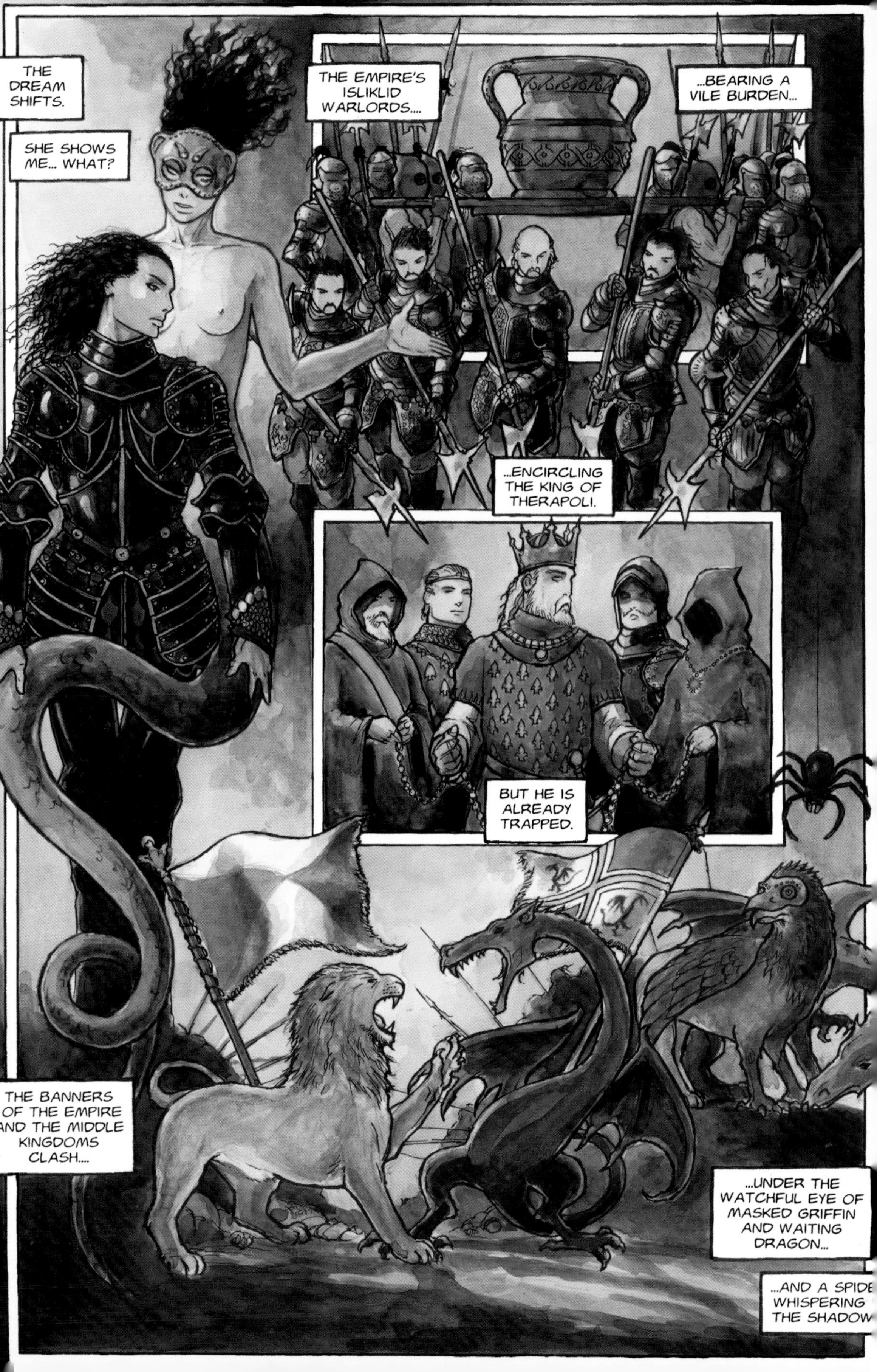

THE DREAM SHIFTS.
SHE SHOWS ME... WHAT?
THE EMPIRE'S ISLIKLID WARLORDS....
...BEARING A VILE BURDEN...
...ENCIRCLING THE KING OF THERAPOLI.
BUT HE IS ALREADY TRAPPED.
THE BANNERS OF THE EMPIRE AND THE MIDDLE KINGDOMS CLASH....
...UNDER THE WATCHFUL EYE OF MASKED GRIFFIN AND WAITING DRAGON...
...AND A SPIDE
WHISPERING
THE SHADOW

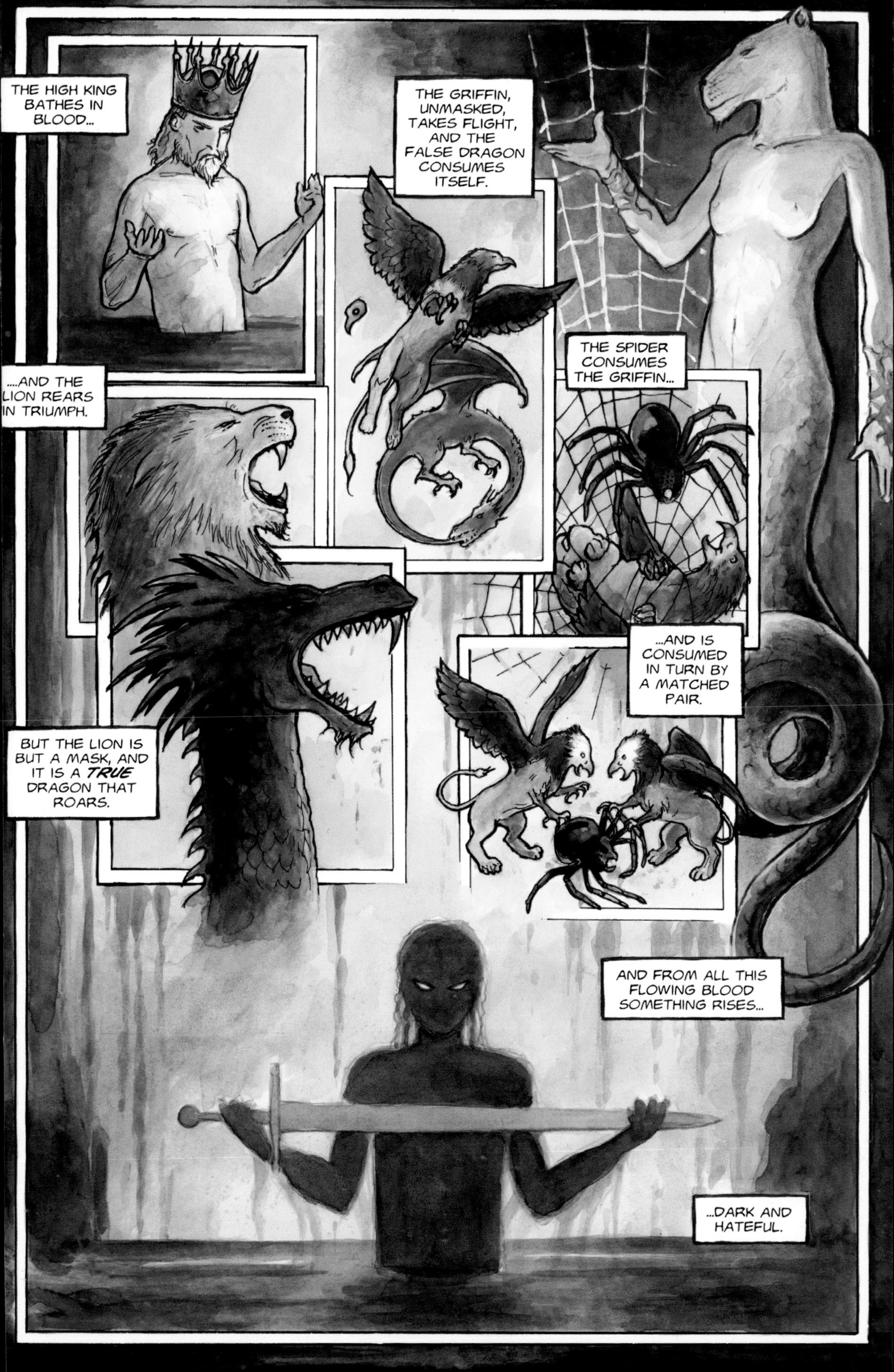
THE HIGH KING BATHES IN BLOOD...
....AND THE LION REARS IN TRIUMPH.
THE GRIFFIN, UNMASKED, TAKES FLIGHT, AND THE FALSE DRAGON CONSUMES ITSELF.
BUT THE LION IS BUT A MASK, AND IT IS A *TRUE* DRAGON THAT ROARS.
THE SPIDER CONSUMES THE GRIFFIN...
...AND IS CONSUMED IN TURN BY A MATCHED PAIR.
AND FROM ALL THIS FLOWING BLOOD SOMETHING RISES...
...DARK AND HATEFUL.

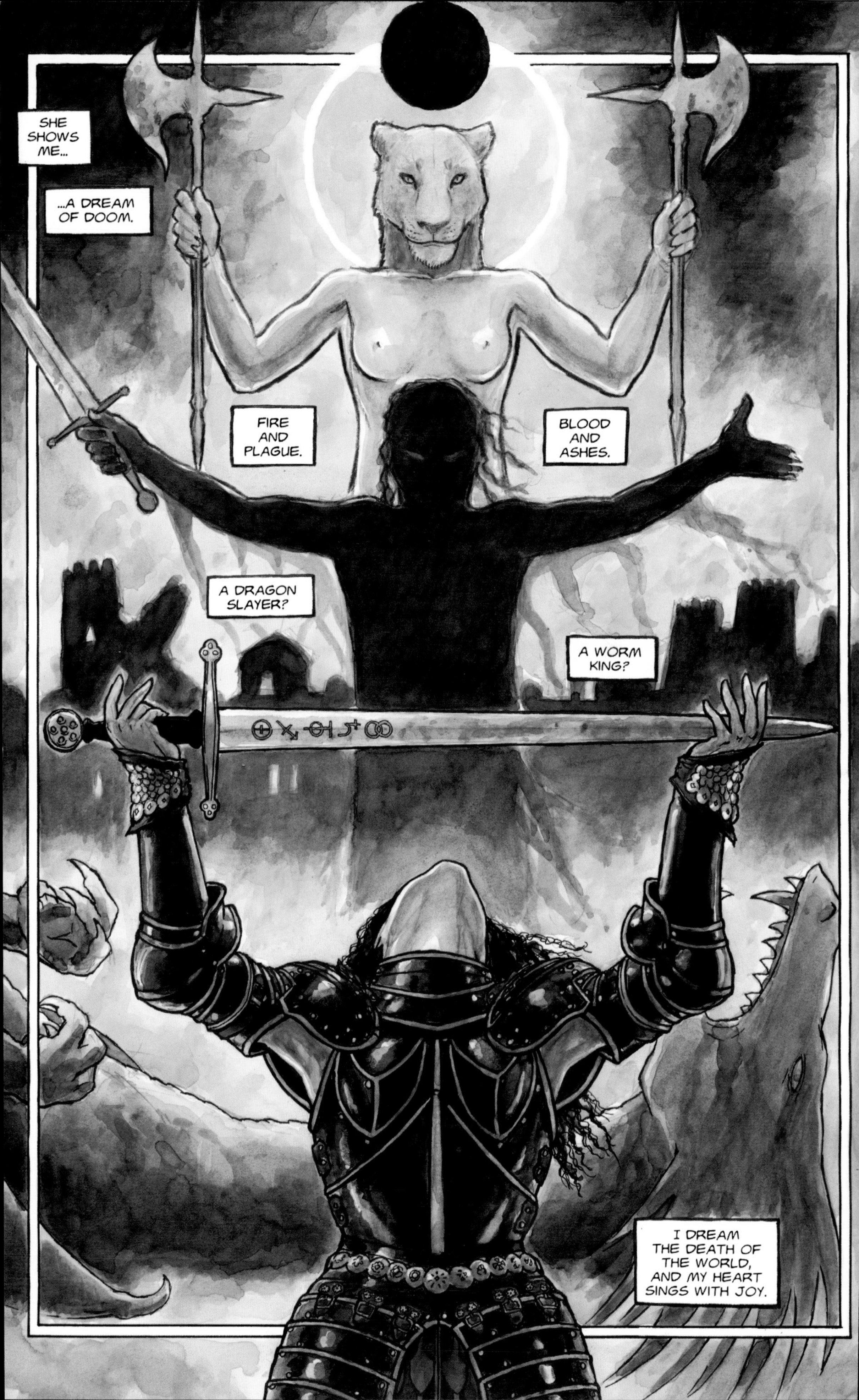
SHE SHOWS ME...
...A DREAM OF DOOM.
FIRE AND PLAGUE.
BLOOD AND ASHES.
A DRAGON SLAYER?
A WORM KING?
I DREAM THE DEATH OF THE WORLD, AND MY HEART SINGS WITH JOY.

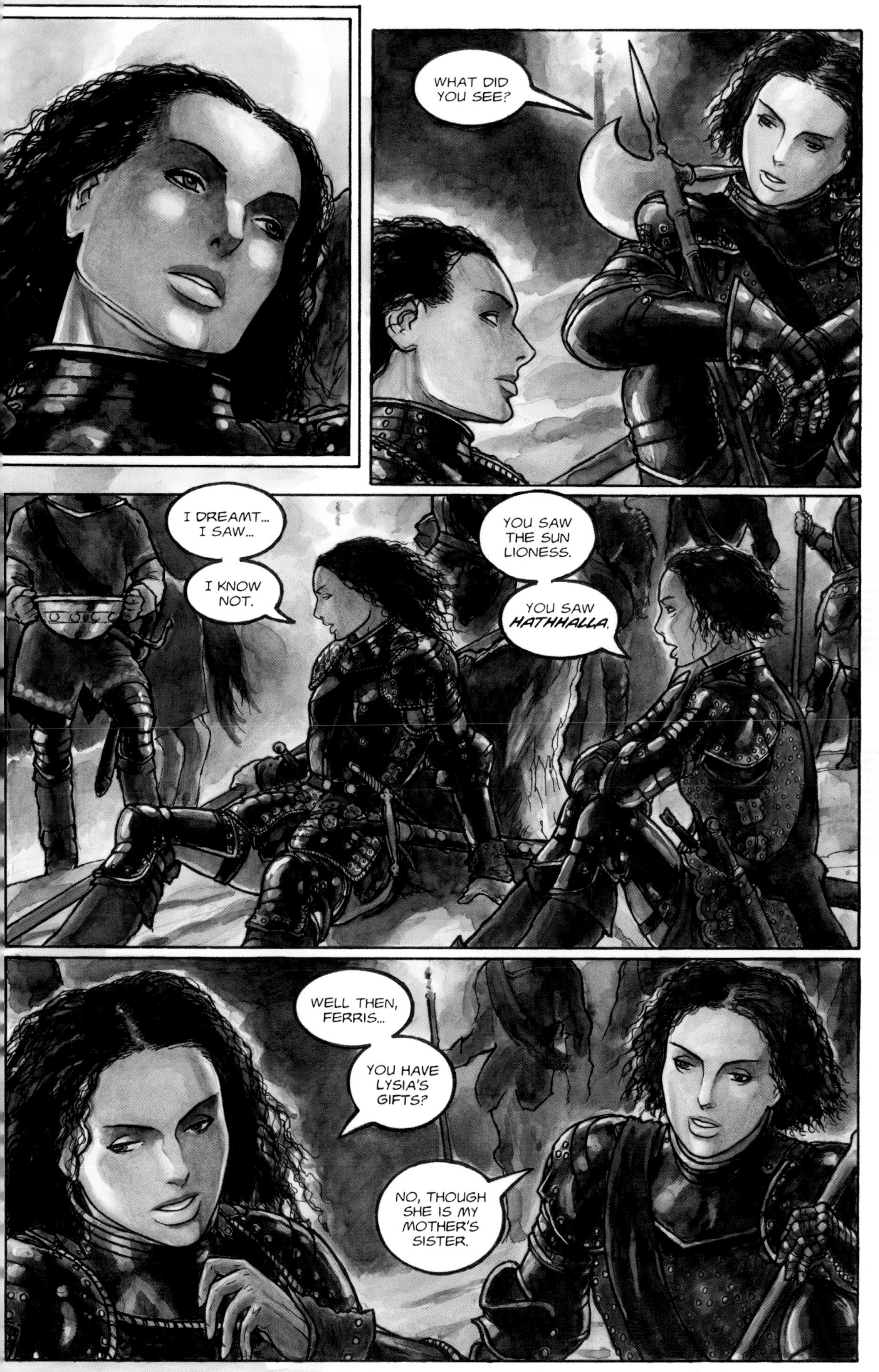
WHAT DID YOU SEE?
I DREAMT... I SAW...
I KNOW NOT.
YOU SAW THE SUN LIONESS.
YOU SAW *HATHHALLA*.
WELL THEN, FERRIS...
YOU HAVE LYSIA'S GIFTS?
NO, THOUGH SHE IS MY MOTHER'S SISTER.

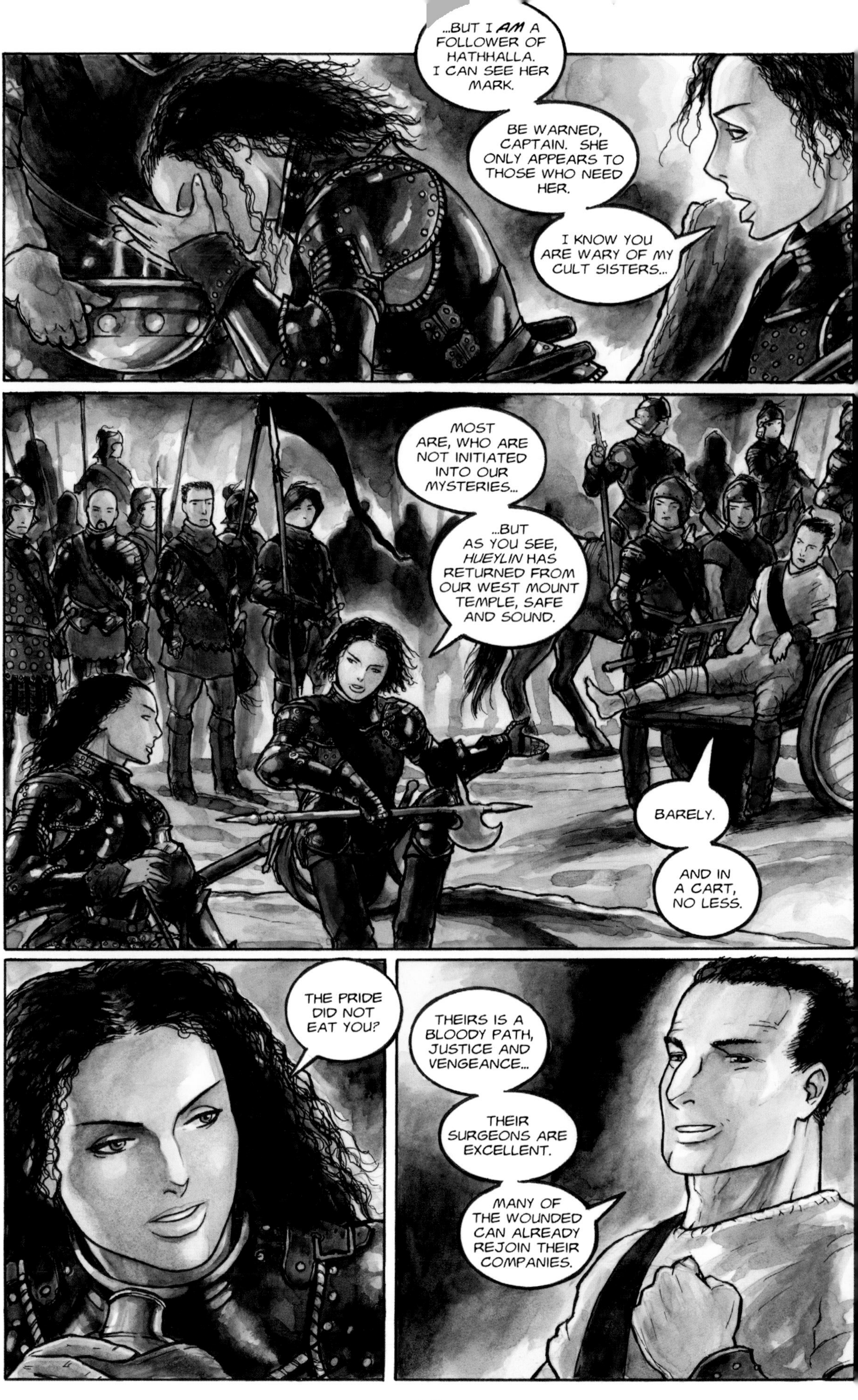

...BUT I *AM* A FOLLOWER OF HATHHALLA. I CAN SEE HER MARK.
BE WARNED, CAPTAIN. SHE ONLY APPEARS TO THOSE WHO NEED HER.
I KNOW YOU ARE WARY OF MY CULT SISTERS...
MOST ARE, WHO ARE NOT INITIATED INTO OUR MYSTERIES...
...BUT AS YOU SEE, *HUEYLIN* HAS RETURNED FROM OUR WEST MOUNT TEMPLE, SAFE AND SOUND.
BARELY.
AND IN A CART, NO LESS.
THE PRIDE DID NOT EAT YOU?
THEIRS IS A BLOODY PATH, JUSTICE AND VENGEANCE...
THEIR SURGEONS ARE EXCELLENT.
MANY OF THE WOUNDED CAN ALREADY REJOIN THEIR COMPANIES.

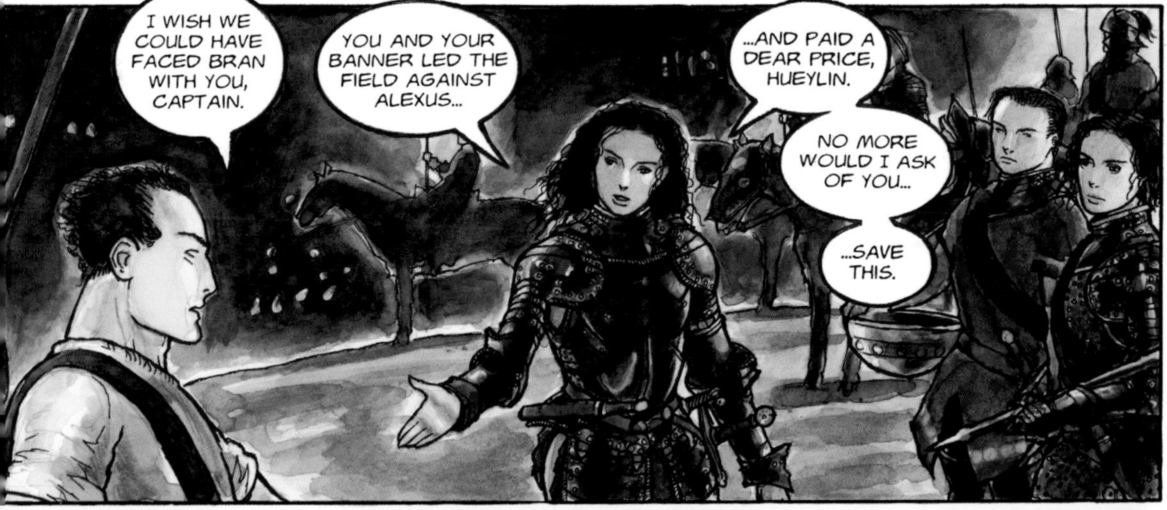
I WISH WE COULD HAVE FACED BRAN WITH YOU, CAPTAIN.
YOU AND YOUR BANNER LED THE FIELD AGAINST ALEXUS...
...AND PAID A DEAR PRICE, HUEYLIN.
NO MORE WOULD I ASK OF YOU...
...SAVE THIS.

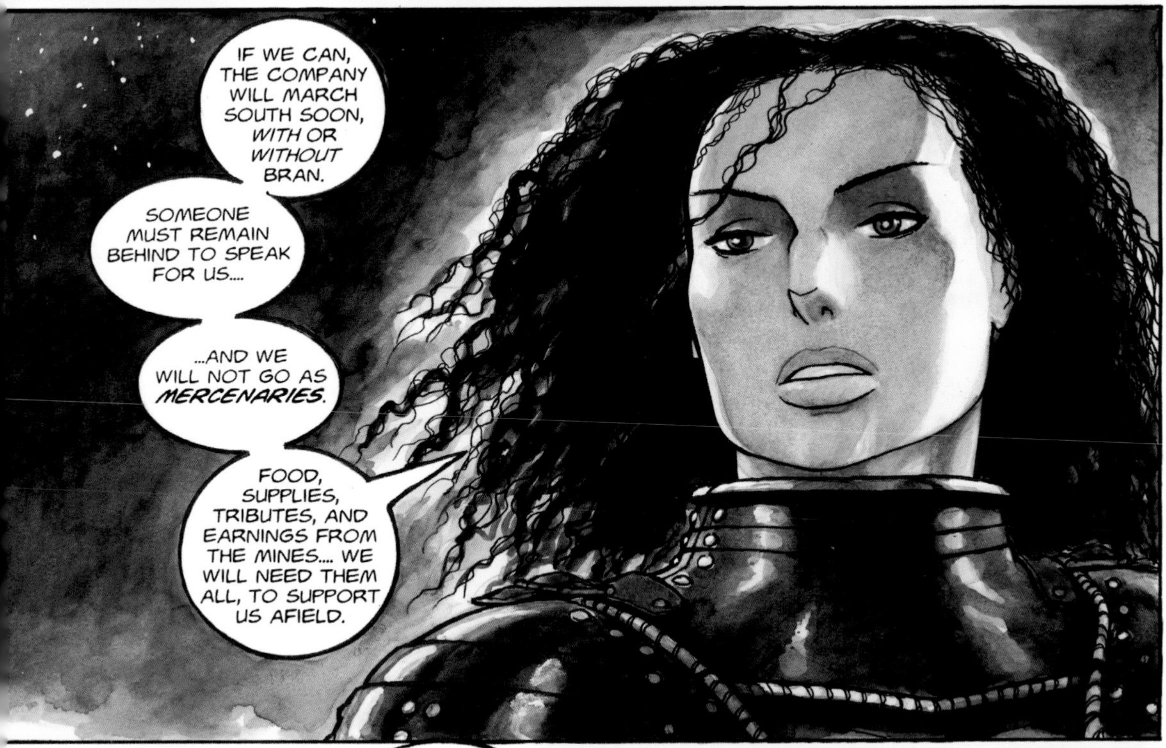
IF WE CAN, THE COMPANY WILL MARCH SOUTH SOON, *WITH* OR *WITHOUT* BRAN.
SOMEONE MUST REMAIN BEHIND TO SPEAK FOR US....
...AND WE WILL NOT GO AS ***MERCENARIES***.
FOOD, SUPPLIES, TRIBUTES, AND EARNINGS FROM THE MINES.... WE WILL NEED THEM ALL, TO SUPPORT US AFIELD.

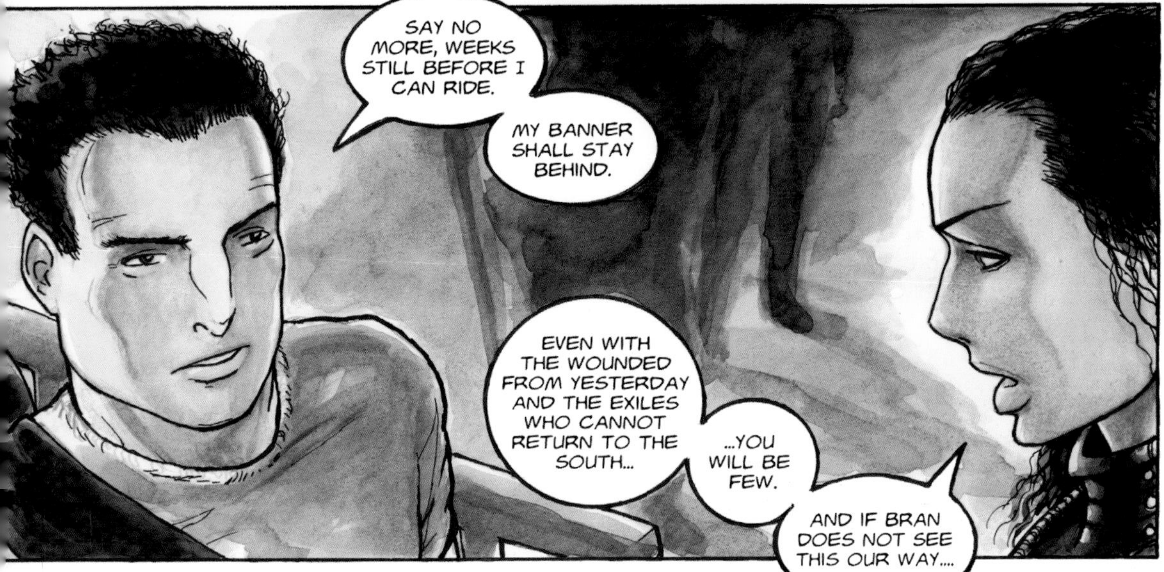
SAY NO MORE, WEEKS STILL BEFORE I CAN RIDE.
MY BANNER SHALL STAY BEHIND.
EVEN WITH THE WOUNDED FROM YESTERDAY AND THE EXILES WHO CANNOT RETURN TO THE SOUTH...
...YOU WILL BE FEW.
AND IF BRAN DOES NOT SEE THIS OUR WAY....

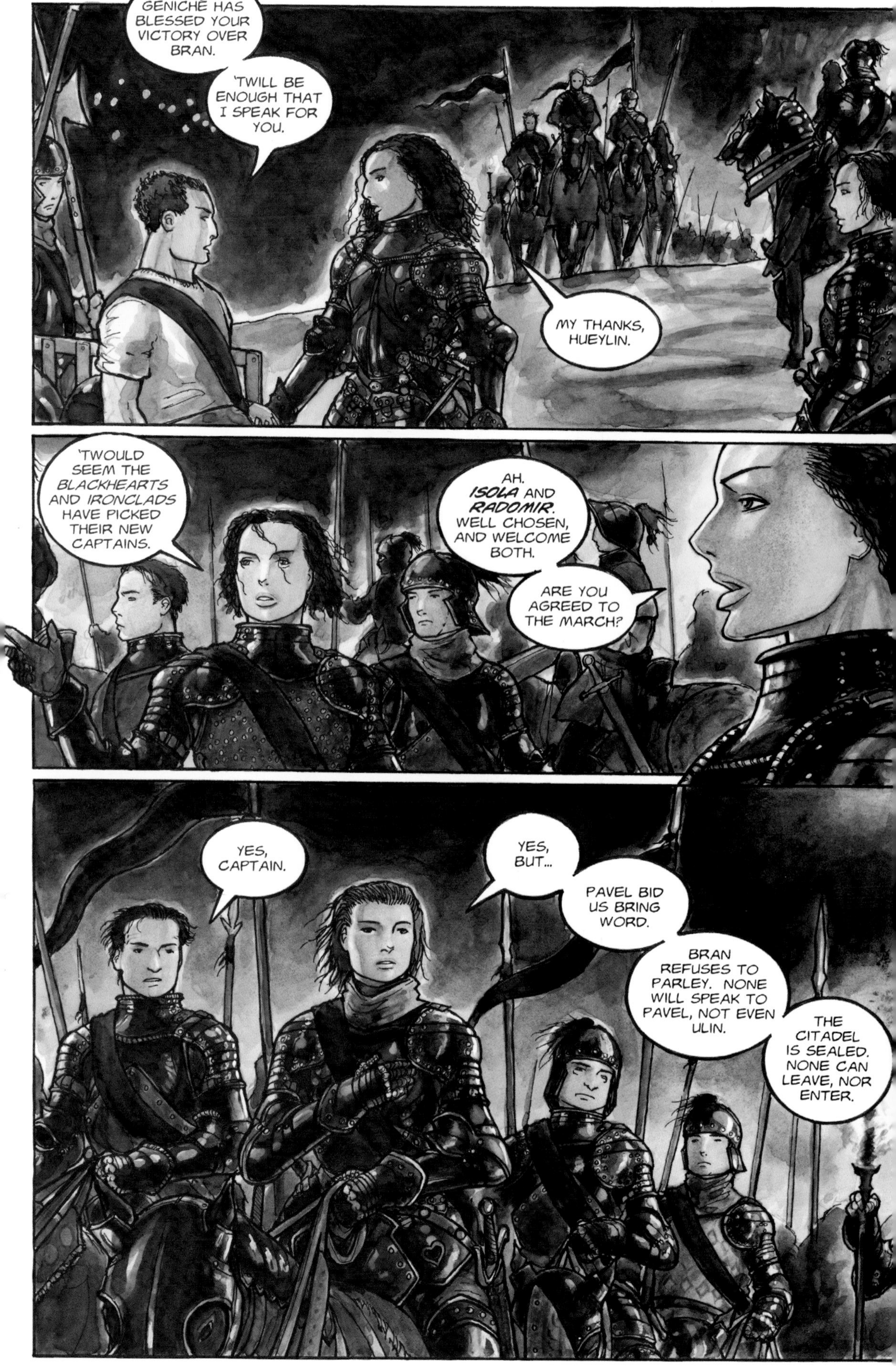
GENICHÉ HAS BLESSED YOUR VICTORY OVER BRAN.
'TWILL BE ENOUGH THAT I SPEAK FOR YOU.
MY THANKS, HUEYLIN.
'TWOULD SEEM THE *BLACKHEARTS* AND *IRONCLADS* HAVE PICKED THEIR NEW CAPTAINS.
AH. ***ISOLA*** AND ***RADOMIR***. WELL CHOSEN, AND WELCOME BOTH.
ARE YOU AGREED TO THE MARCH?
YES, CAPTAIN.
YES, BUT...
PAVEL BID US BRING WORD.
BRAN REFUSES TO PARLEY. NONE WILL SPEAK TO PAVEL, NOT EVEN ULIN.
THE CITADEL IS SEALED. NONE CAN LEAVE, NOR ENTER.

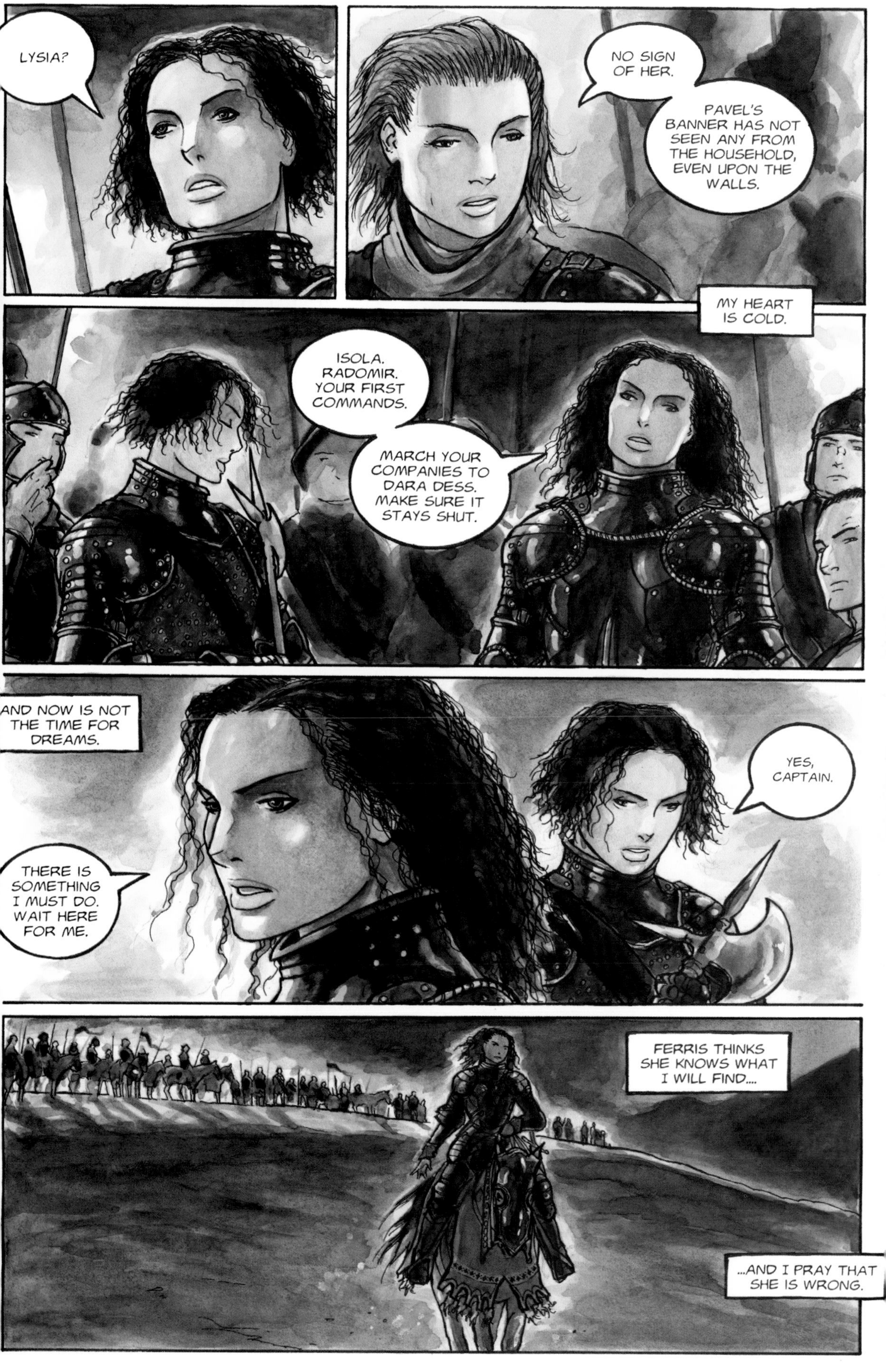

LYSIA?
NO SIGN OF HER.
PAVEL'S BANNER HAS NOT SEEN ANY FROM THE HOUSEHOLD, EVEN UPON THE WALLS.
MY HEART IS COLD.
ISOLA. RADOMIR. YOUR FIRST COMMANDS.
MARCH YOUR COMPANIES TO DARA DESS. MAKE SURE IT STAYS SHUT.
AND NOW IS NOT THE TIME FOR DREAMS.
YES, CAPTAIN.
THERE IS SOMETHING I MUST DO. WAIT HERE FOR ME.
FERRIS THINKS SHE KNOWS WHAT I WILL FIND....
...AND I PRAY THAT SHE IS WRONG.

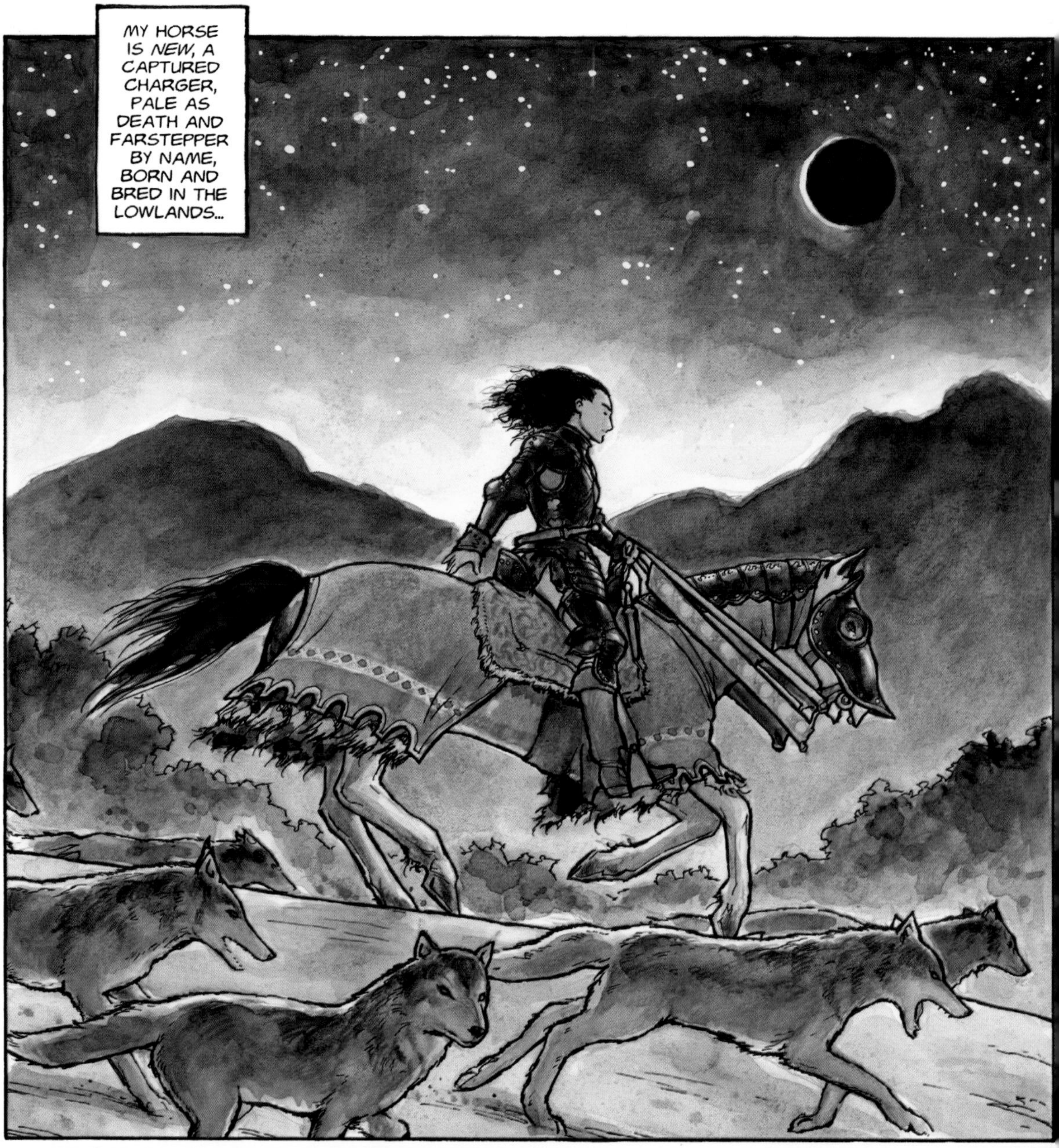
MY HORSE IS NEW, A CAPTURED CHARGER, PALE AS DEATH AND FARSTEPPER BY NAME, BORN AND BRED IN THE LOWLANDS...

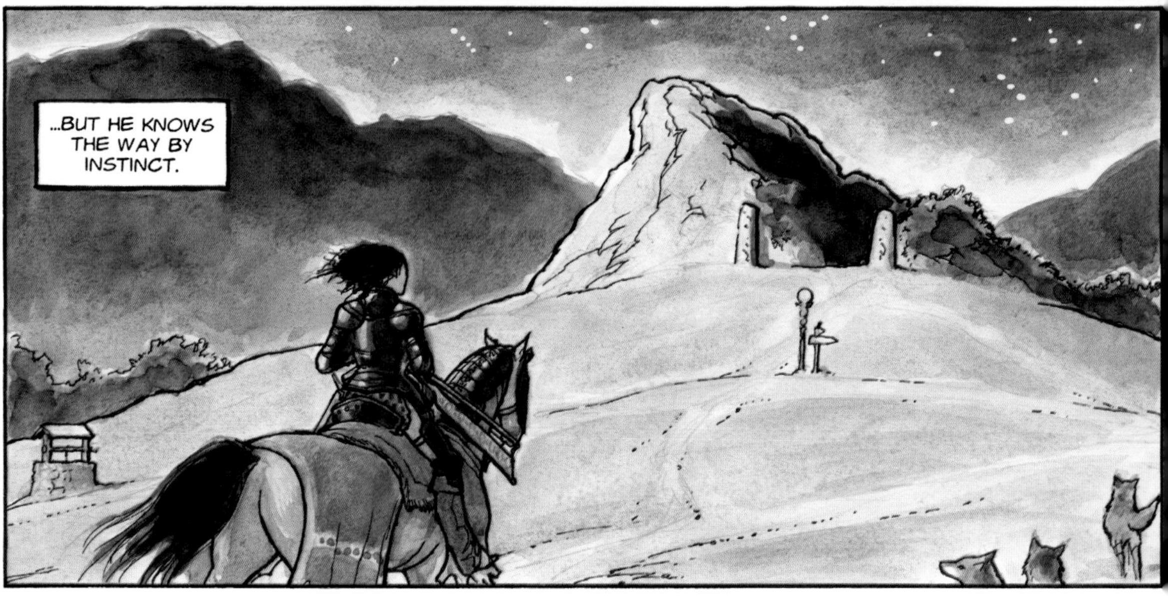
...BUT HE KNOWS THE WAY BY INSTINCT.

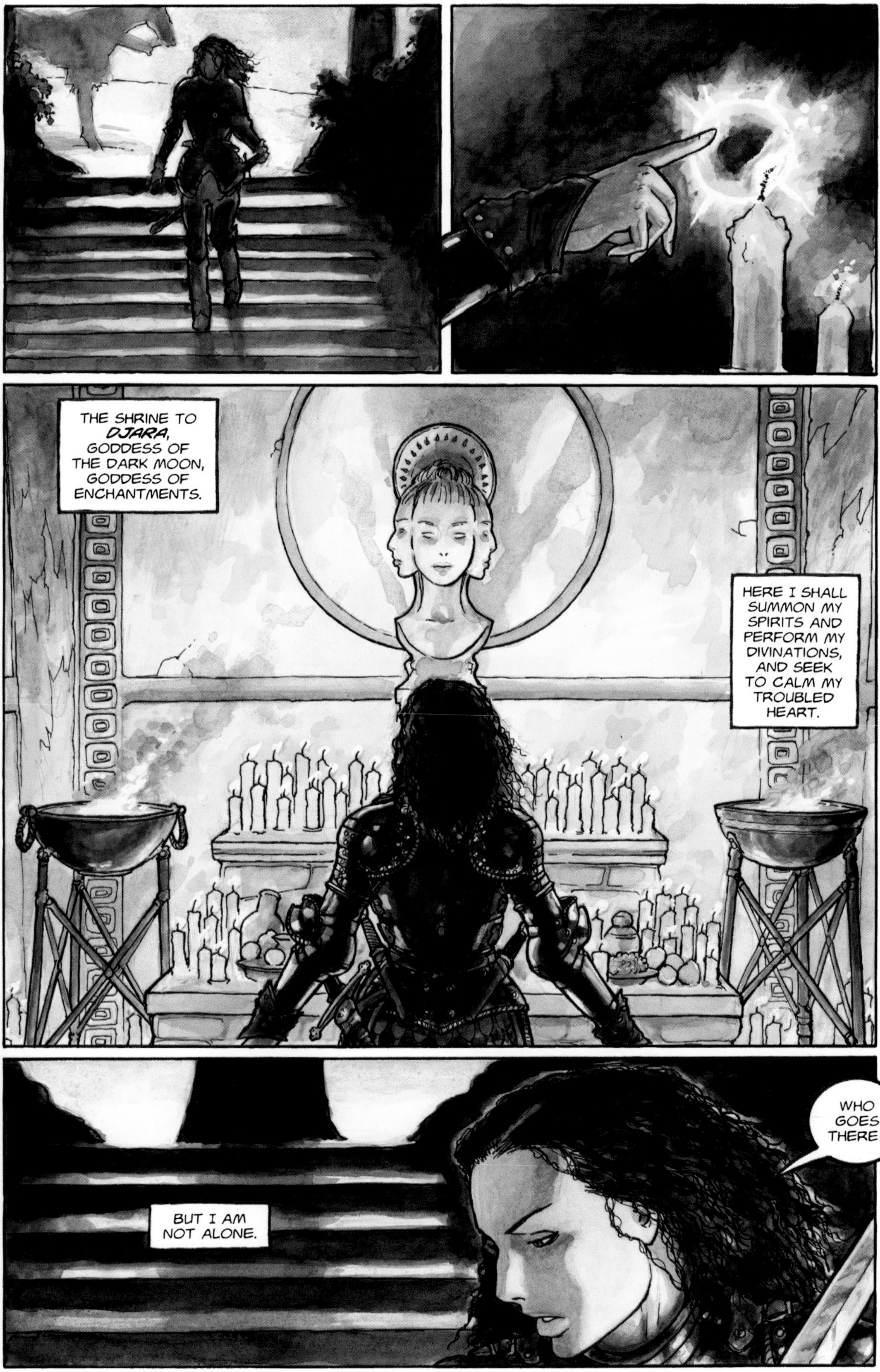
THE SHRINE TO DJARA, GODDESS OF THE DARK MOON, GODDESS OF ENCHANTMENTS.
HERE I SHALL SUMMON MY SPIRITS AND PERFORM MY DIVINATIONS, AND SEEK TO CALM MY TROUBLED HEART.
BUT I AM NOT ALONE.
WHO GOES THERE?

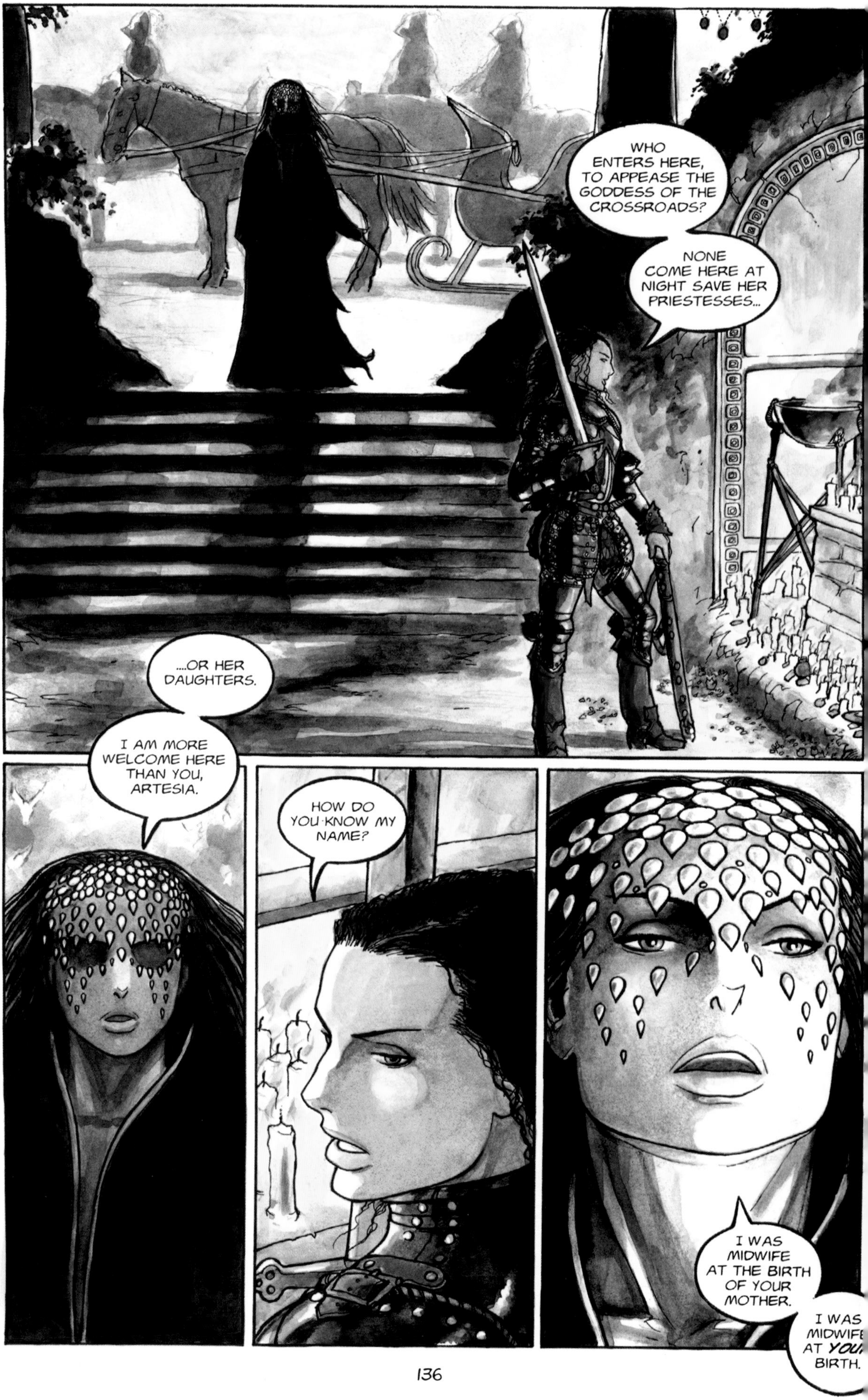
WHO ENTERS HERE, TO APPEASE THE GODDESS OF THE CROSSROADS?
NONE COME HERE AT NIGHT SAVE HER PRIESTESSES...
....OR HER DAUGHTERS.
I AM MORE WELCOME HERE THAN YOU, ARTESIA.
HOW DO YOU KNOW MY NAME?
I WAS MIDWIFE AT THE BIRTH OF YOUR MOTHER.
I WAS MIDWIFE AT YOUR BIRTH.

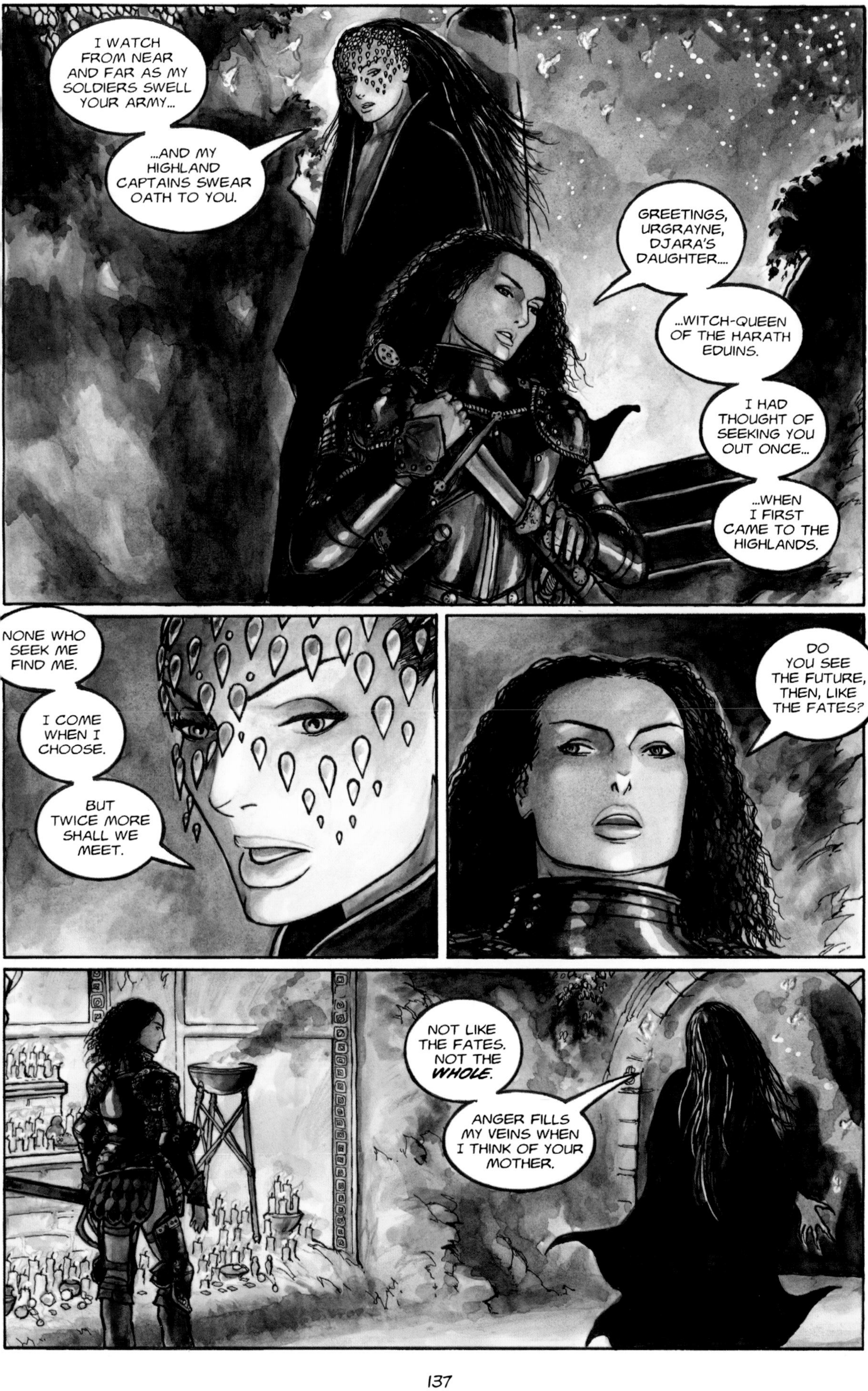
I WATCH FROM NEAR AND FAR AS MY SOLDIERS SWELL YOUR ARMY...
...AND MY HIGHLAND CAPTAINS SWEAR OATH TO YOU.
GREETINGS, URGRAYNE, DJARA'S DAUGHTER....
...WITCH-QUEEN OF THE HARATH EDUINS.
I HAD THOUGHT OF SEEKING YOU OUT ONCE...
...WHEN I FIRST CAME TO THE HIGHLANDS.
NONE WHO SEEK ME FIND ME.
I COME WHEN I CHOOSE.
BUT TWICE MORE SHALL WE MEET.
DO YOU SEE THE FUTURE, THEN, LIKE THE FATES?
NOT LIKE THE FATES. NOT THE *WHOLE*.
ANGER FILLS MY VEINS WHEN I THINK OF YOUR MOTHER.

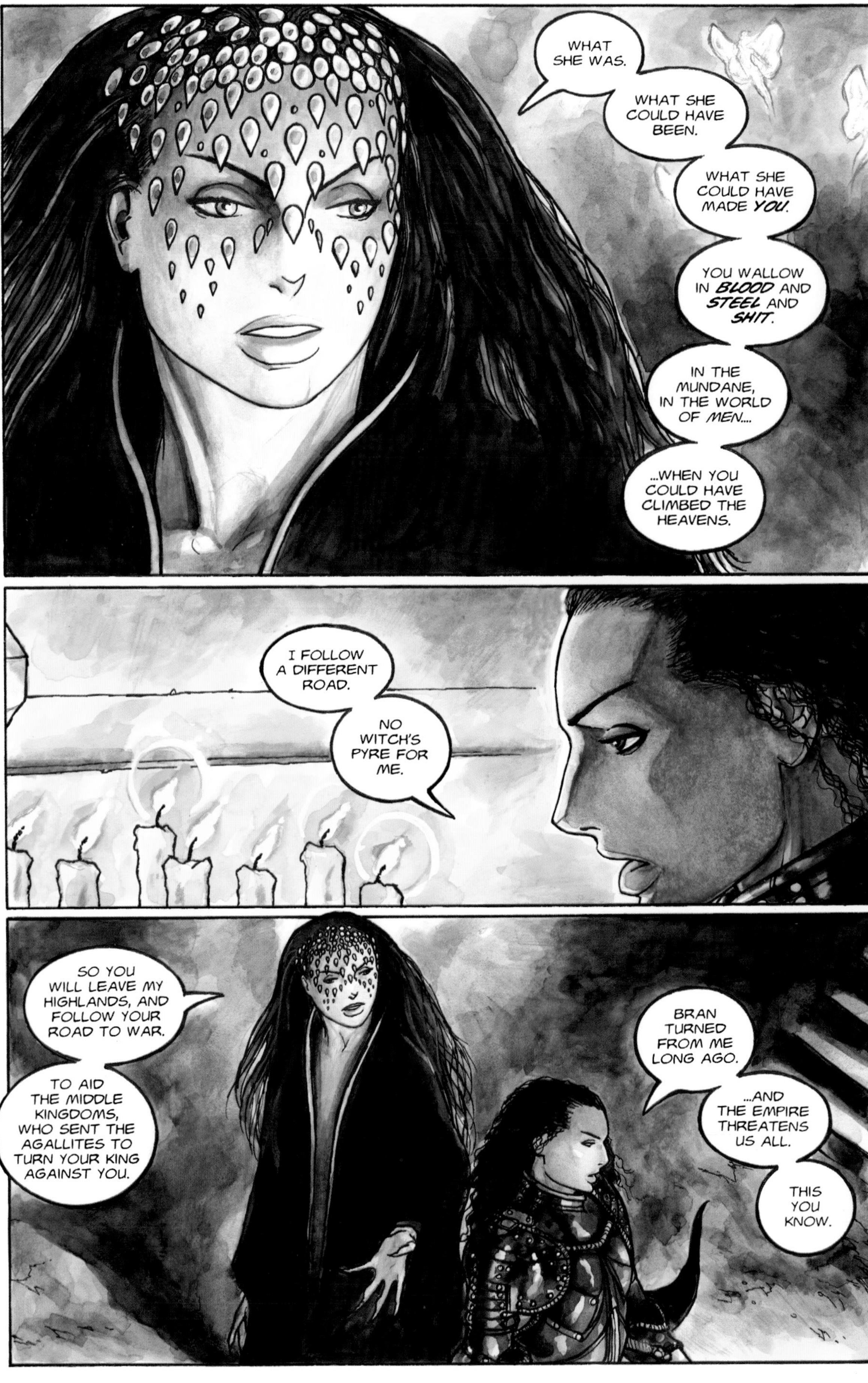
WHAT SHE WAS.
WHAT SHE COULD HAVE BEEN.
WHAT SHE COULD HAVE MADE YOU.
YOU WALLOW IN BLOOD AND STEEL AND SHIT.
IN THE MUNDANE, IN THE WORLD OF MEN....
...WHEN YOU COULD HAVE CLIMBED THE HEAVENS.
I FOLLOW A DIFFERENT ROAD.
NO WITCH'S PYRE FOR ME.
SO YOU WILL LEAVE MY HIGHLANDS, AND FOLLOW YOUR ROAD TO WAR.
TO AID THE MIDDLE KINGDOMS, WHO SENT THE AGALLITES TO TURN YOUR KING AGAINST YOU.
BRAN TURNED FROM ME LONG AGO.
...AND THE EMPIRE THREATENS US ALL.
THIS YOU KNOW.

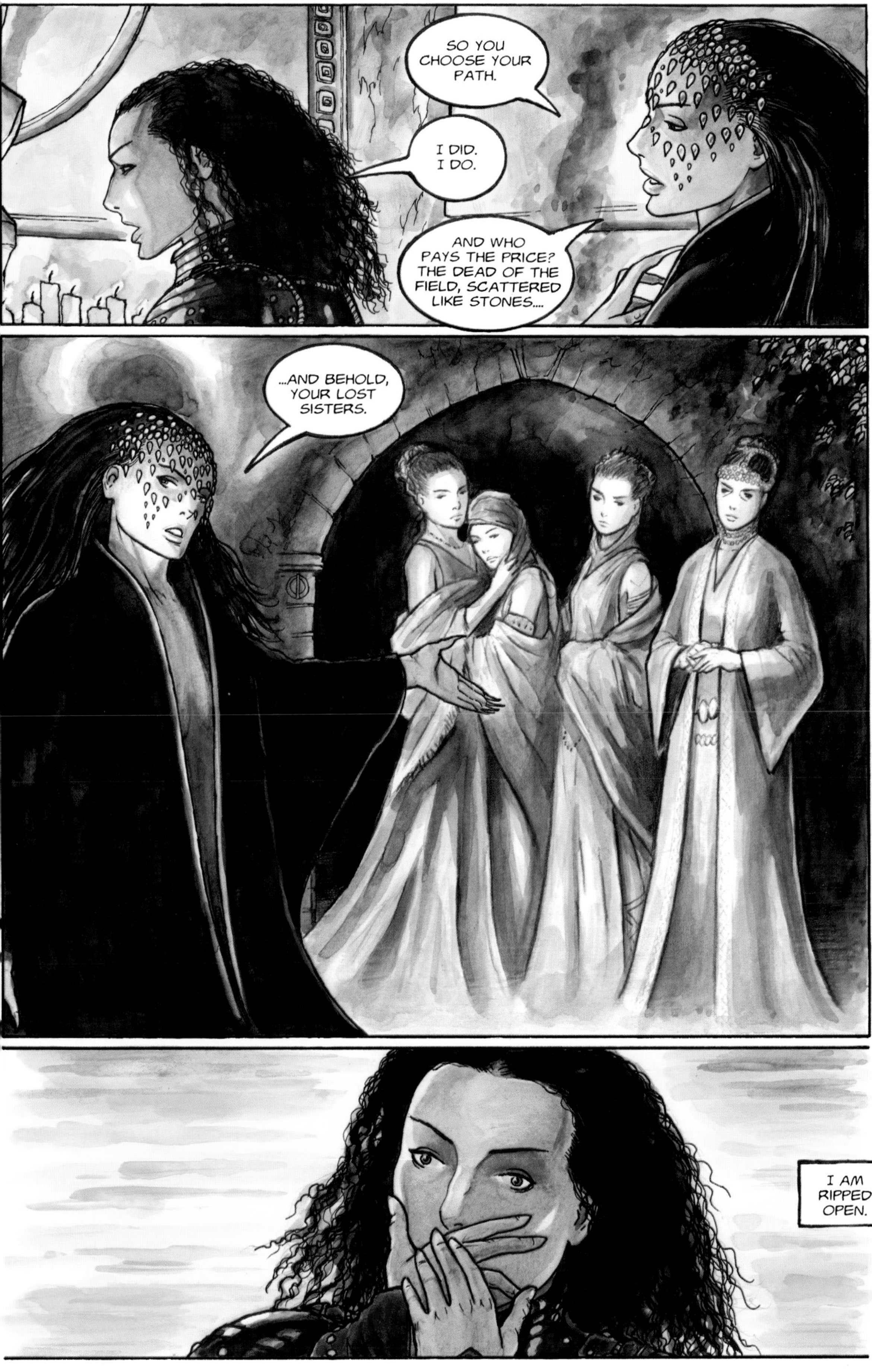
SO YOU CHOOSE YOUR PATH.
I DID. I DO.
AND WHO PAYS THE PRICE? THE DEAD OF THE FIELD, SCATTERED LIKE STONES....
...AND BEHOLD, YOUR LOST SISTERS.
I AM RIPPED OPEN.

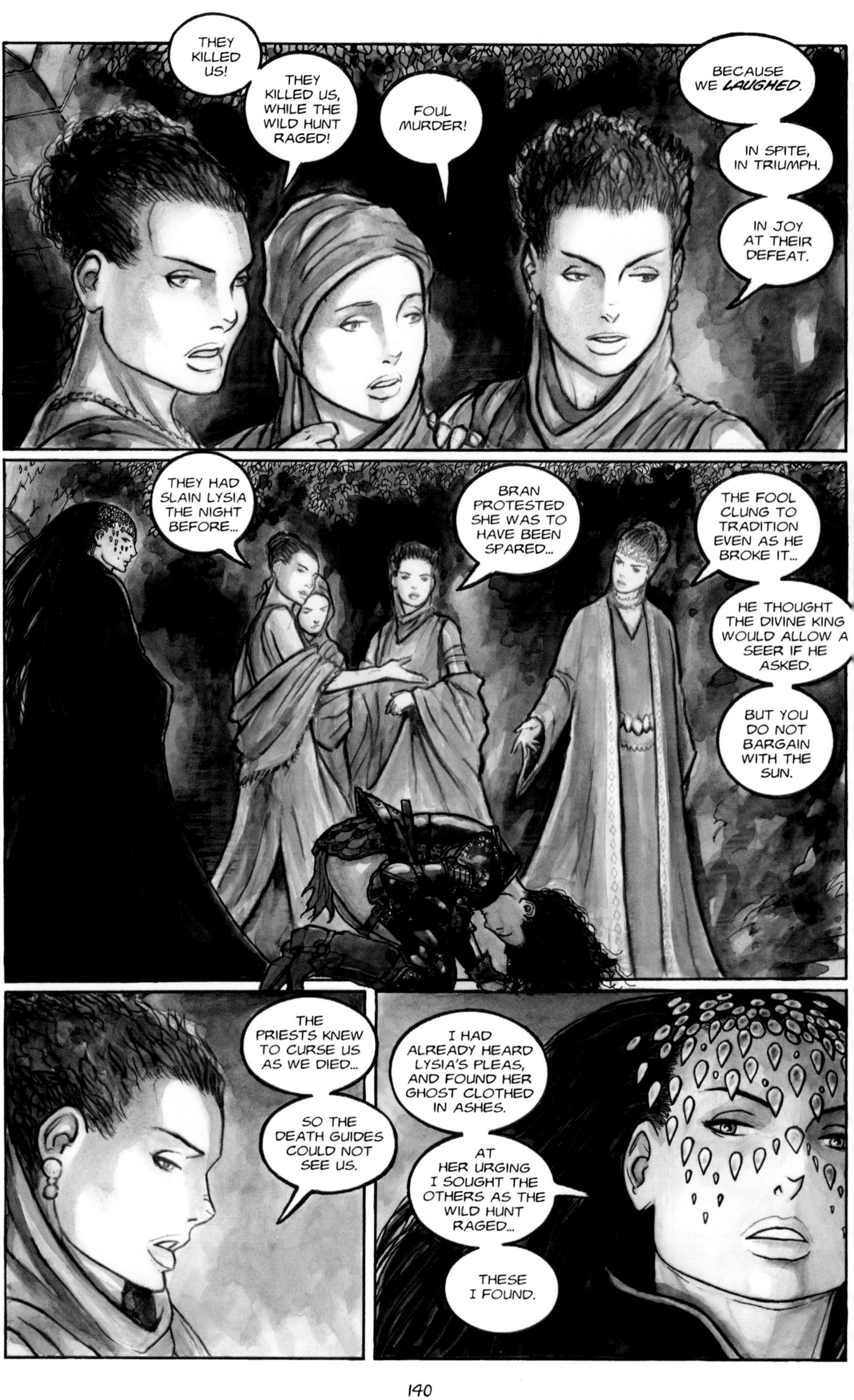
THEY KILLED US!
THEY KILLED US, WHILE THE WILD HUNT RAGED!
FOUL MURDER!
BECAUSE WE *LAUGHED*.
IN SPITE, IN TRIUMPH.
IN JOY AT THEIR DEFEAT.
THEY HAD SLAIN LYSIA THE NIGHT BEFORE...
BRAN PROTESTED SHE WAS TO HAVE BEEN SPARED...
THE FOOL CLUNG TO TRADITION EVEN AS HE BROKE IT...
HE THOUGHT THE DIVINE KING WOULD ALLOW A SEER IF HE ASKED.
BUT YOU DO NOT BARGAIN WITH THE SUN.
THE PRIESTS KNEW TO CURSE US AS WE DIED...
SO THE DEATH GUIDES COULD NOT SEE US.
I HAD ALREADY HEARD LYSIA'S PLEAS, AND FOUND HER GHOST CLOTHED IN ASHES.
AT HER URGING I SOUGHT THE OTHERS AS THE WILD HUNT RAGED...
THESE I FOUND.

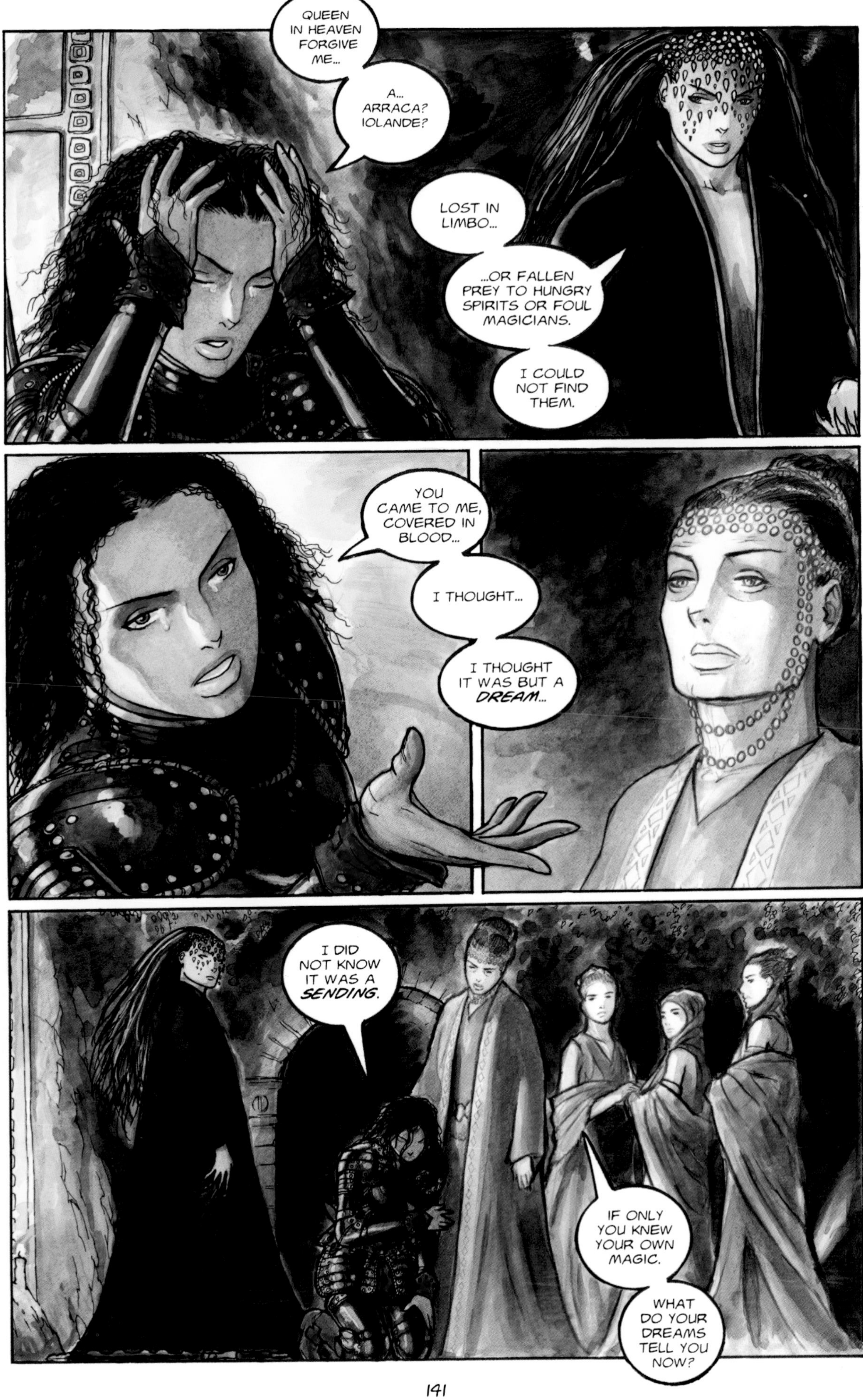
QUEEN IN HEAVEN FORGIVE ME...
A... ARRACA? IOLANDE?
LOST IN LIMBO...
...OR FALLEN PREY TO HUNGRY SPIRITS OR FOUL MAGICIANS.
I COULD NOT FIND THEM.
YOU CAME TO ME, COVERED IN BLOOD...
I THOUGHT...
I THOUGHT IT WAS BUT A *DREAM*...
I DID NOT KNOW IT WAS A *SENDING*.
IF ONLY YOU KNEW YOUR OWN MAGIC.
WHAT DO YOUR DREAMS TELL YOU NOW?

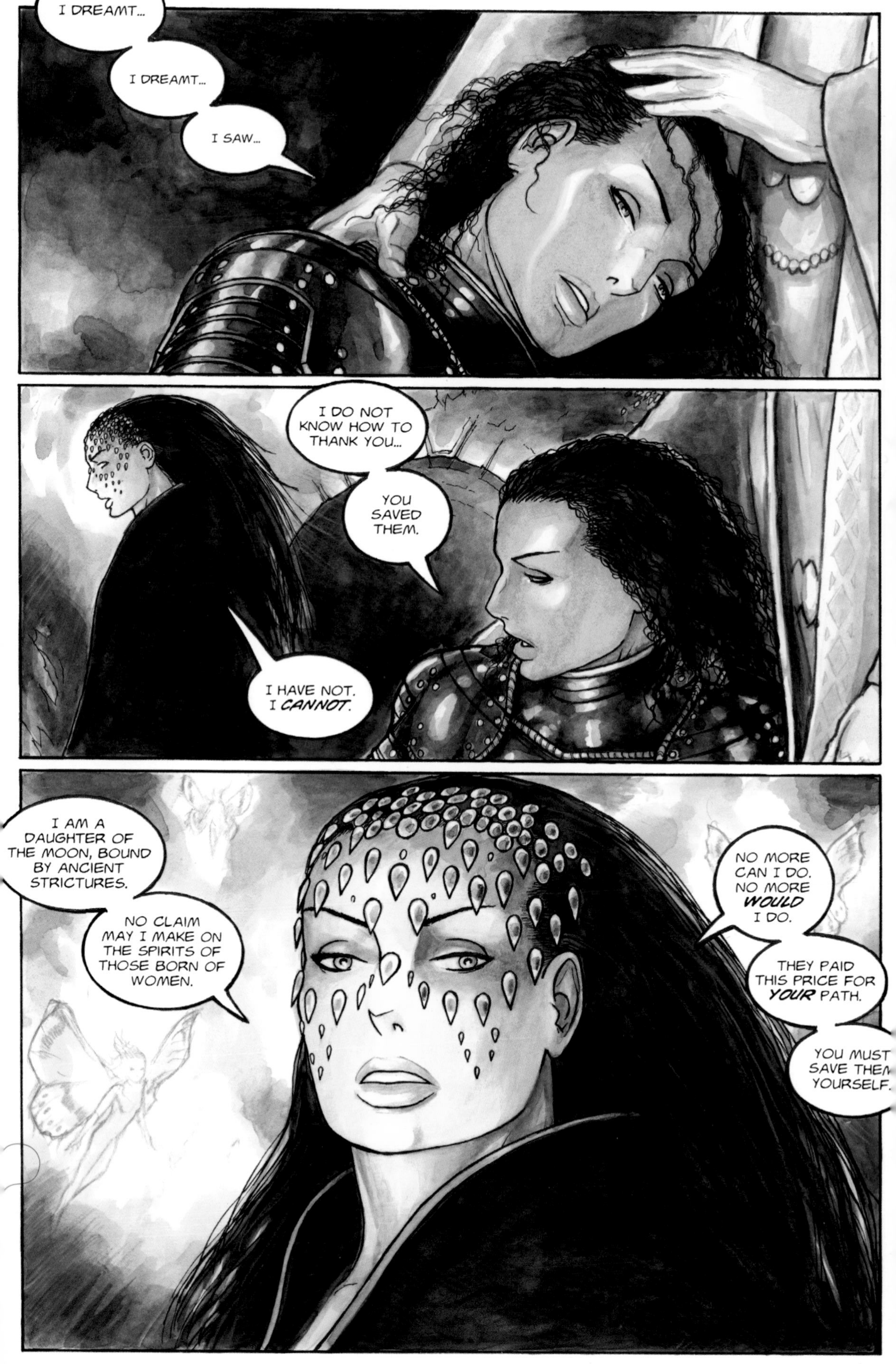
I DREAMT...
I DREAMT...
I SAW...
I DO NOT KNOW HOW TO THANK YOU...
YOU SAVED THEM.
I HAVE NOT. I *CANNOT*.
I AM A DAUGHTER OF THE MOON, BOUND BY ANCIENT STRICTURES.
NO CLAIM MAY I MAKE ON THE SPIRITS OF THOSE BORN OF WOMEN.
NO MORE CAN I DO. NO MORE *WOULD* I DO.
THEY PAID THIS PRICE FOR *YOUR* PATH.
YOU MUST SAVE THEM YOURSELF.

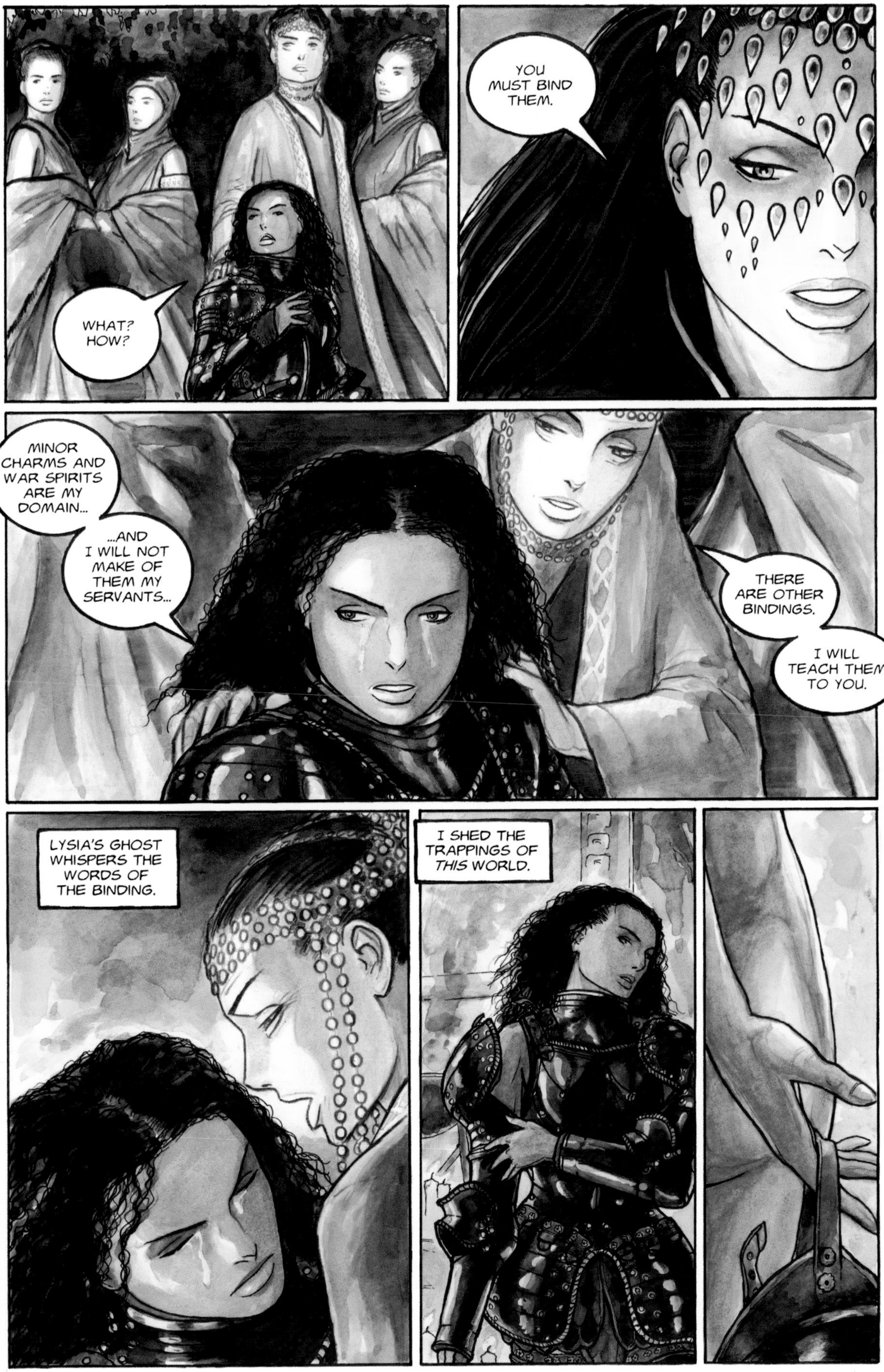

WHAT? HOW?
YOU MUST BIND THEM.
MINOR CHARMS AND WAR SPIRITS ARE MY DOMAIN...
...AND I WILL NOT MAKE OF THEM MY SERVANTS...
THERE ARE OTHER BINDINGS.
I WILL TEACH THEM TO YOU.
LYSIA'S GHOST WHISPERS THE WORDS OF THE BINDING.
I SHED THE TRAPPINGS OF *THIS* WORLD.

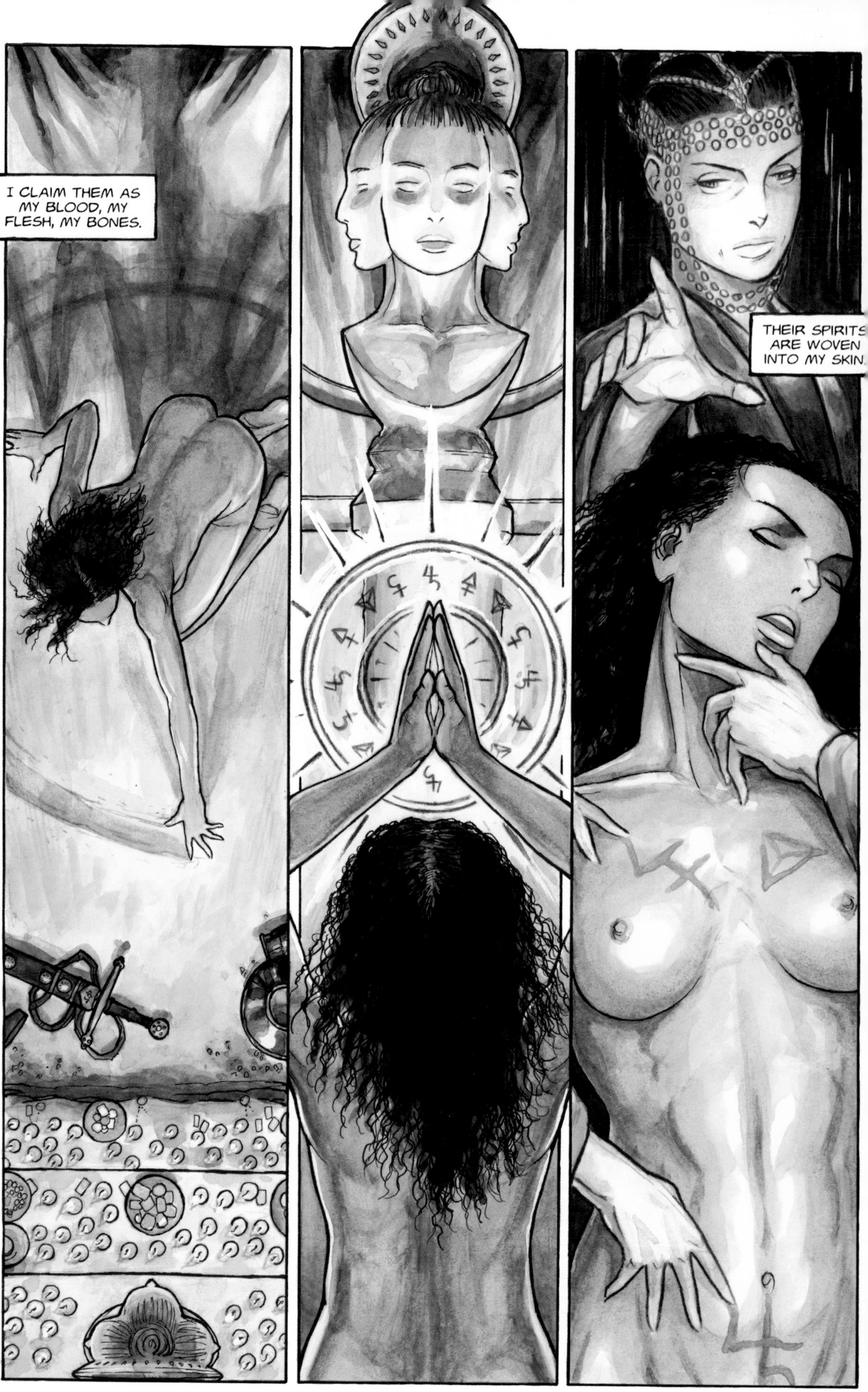
I CLAIM THEM AS MY BLOOD, MY FLESH, MY BONES.
THEIR SPIRITS ARE WOVEN INTO MY SKIN.

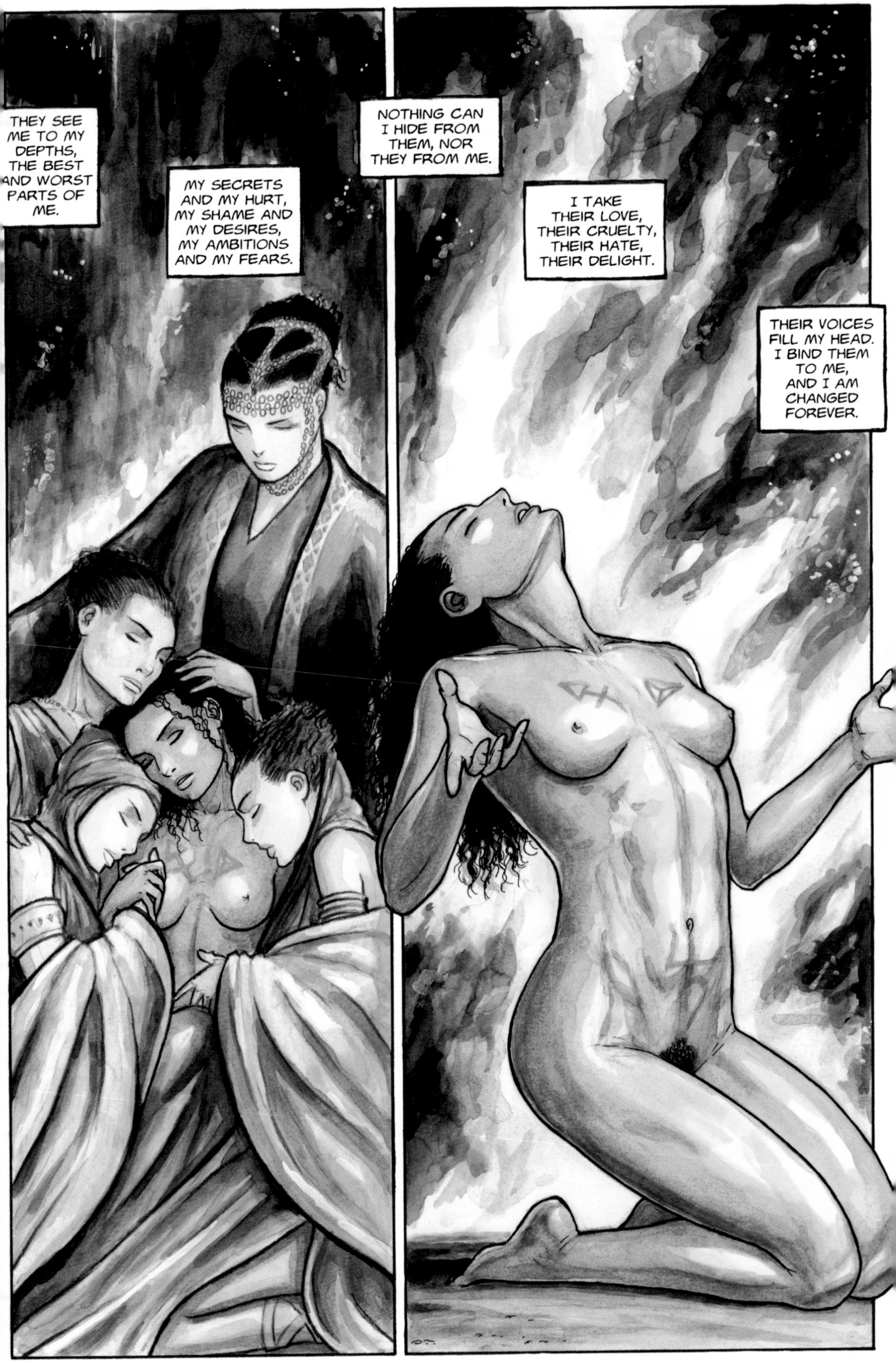
THEY SEE ME TO MY DEPTHS, THE BEST AND WORST PARTS OF ME.
MY SECRETS AND MY HURT, MY SHAME AND MY DESIRES, MY AMBITIONS AND MY FEARS.
NOTHING CAN I HIDE FROM THEM, NOR THEY FROM ME.
I TAKE THEIR LOVE, THEIR CRUELTY, THEIR HATE, THEIR DELIGHT.
THEIR VOICES FILL MY HEAD. I BIND THEM TO ME, AND I AM CHANGED FOREVER.

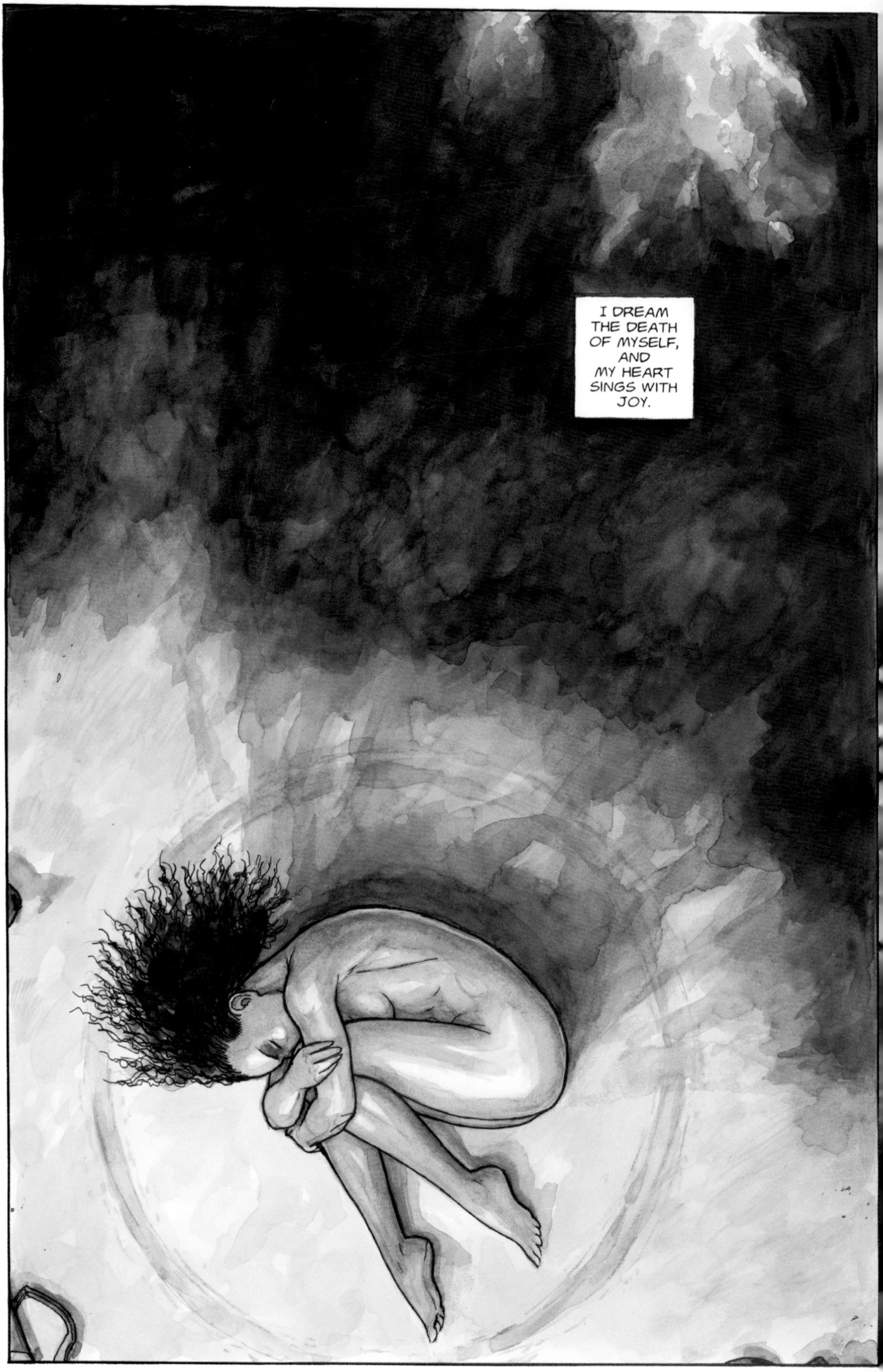
I DREAM THE DEATH OF MYSELF, AND MY HEART SINGS WITH JOY.

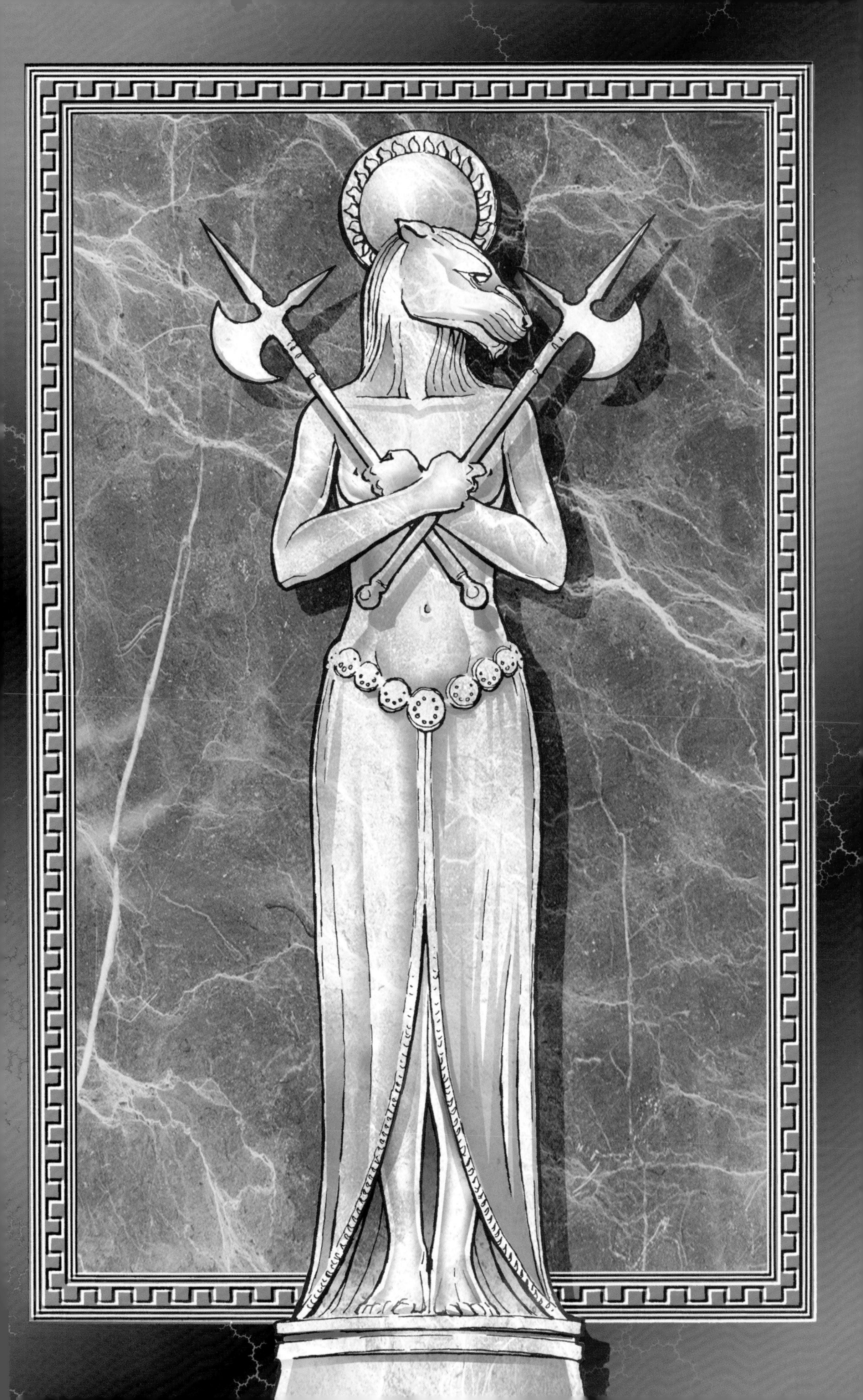

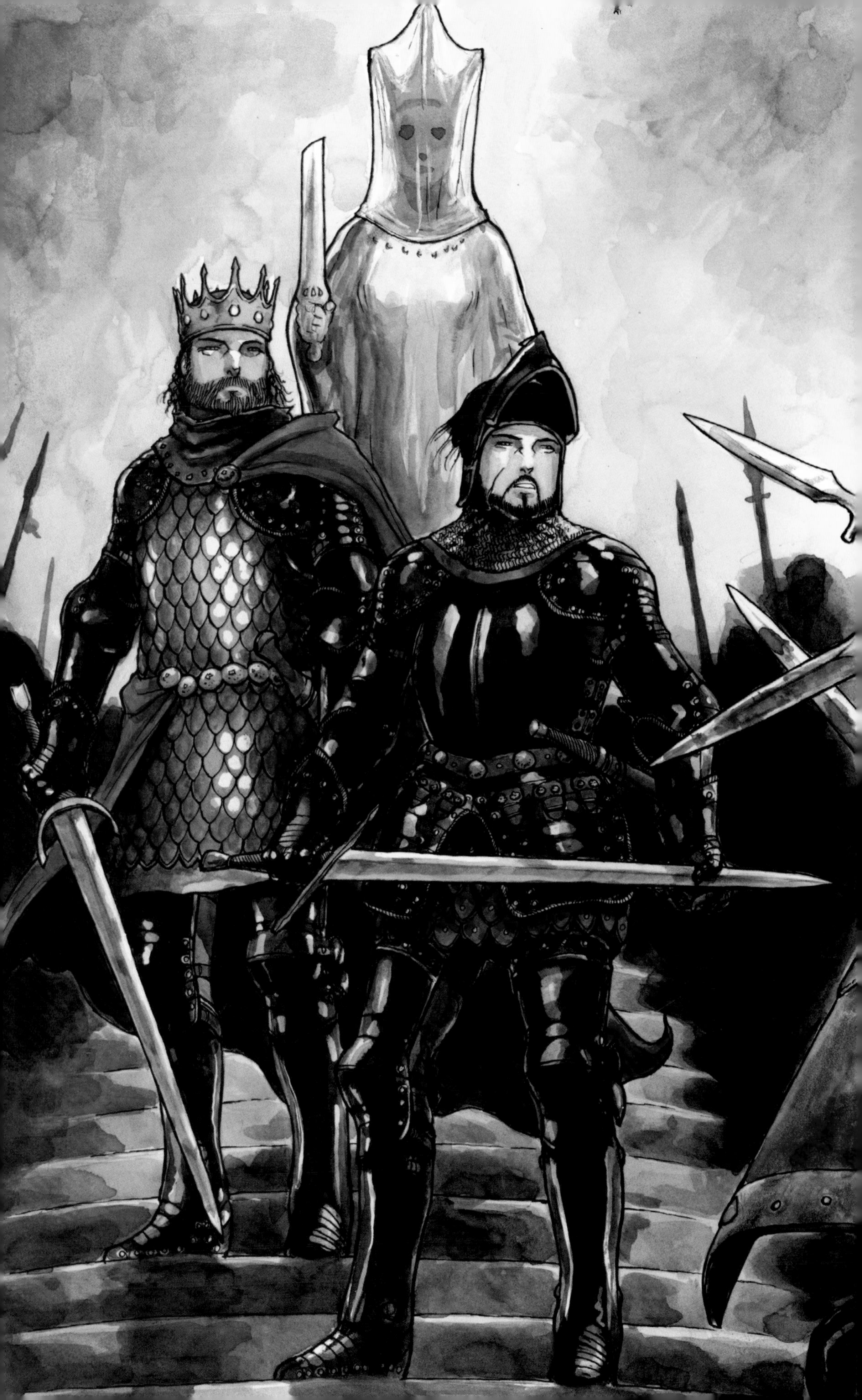

CHAPTER SIX

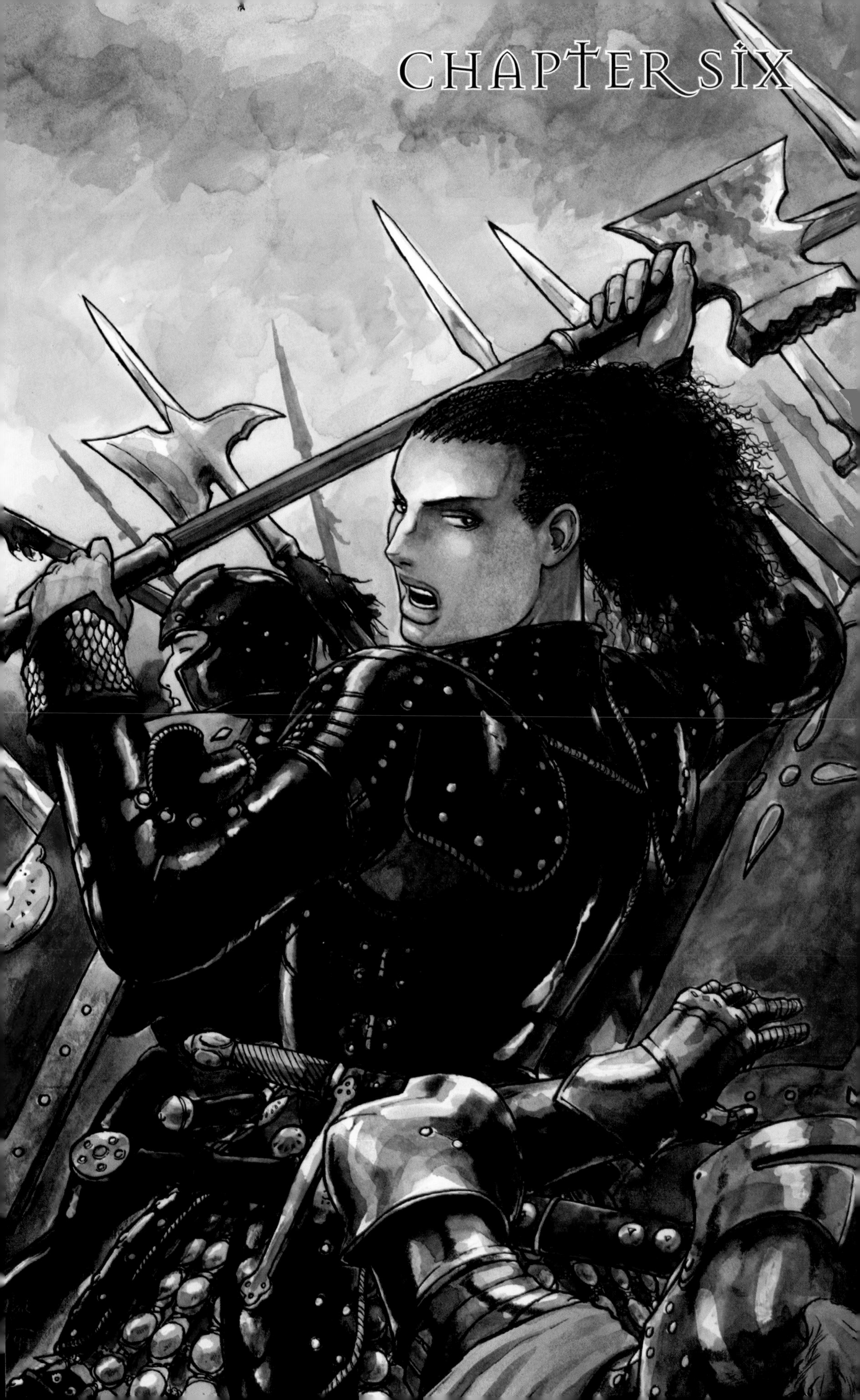

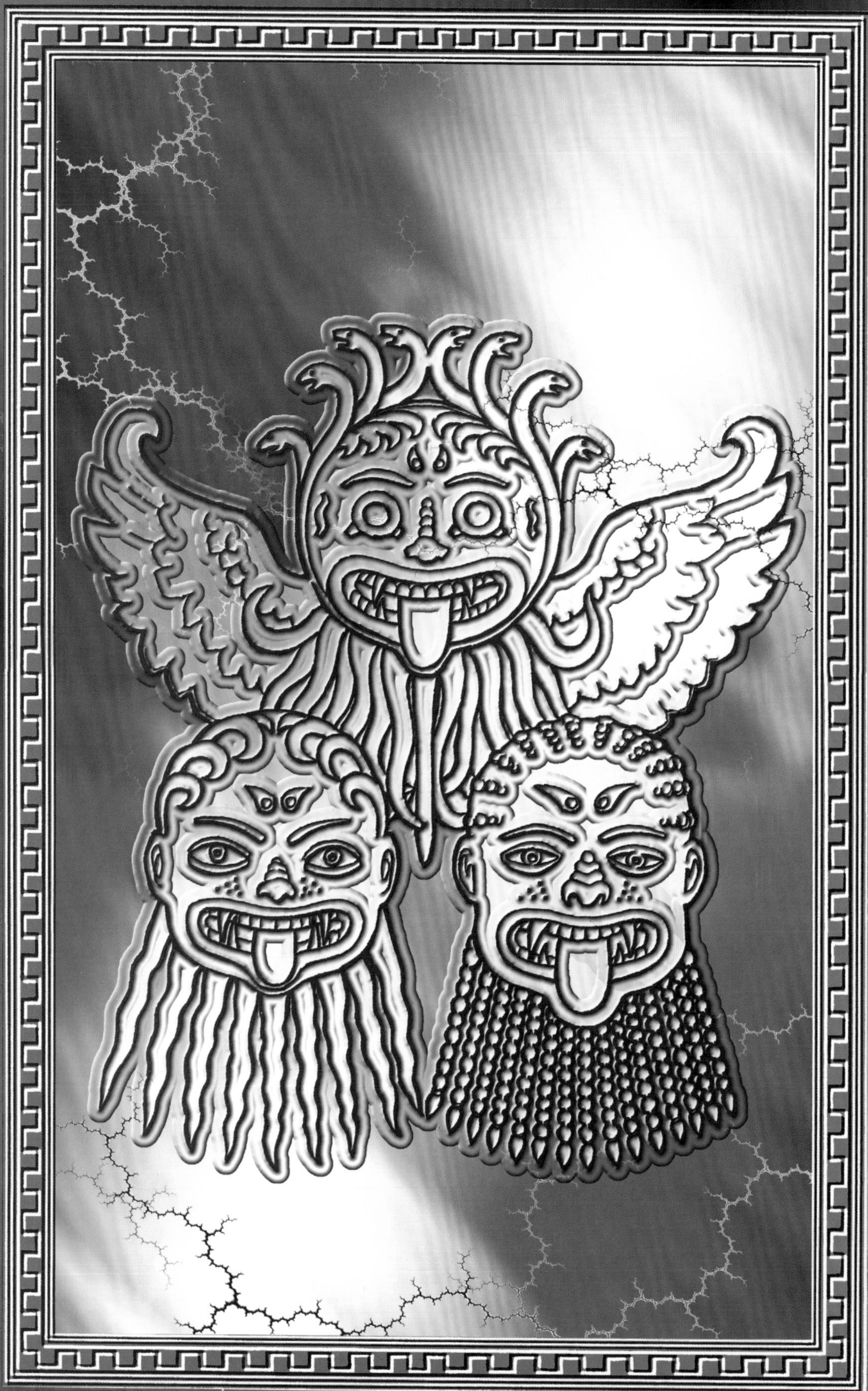

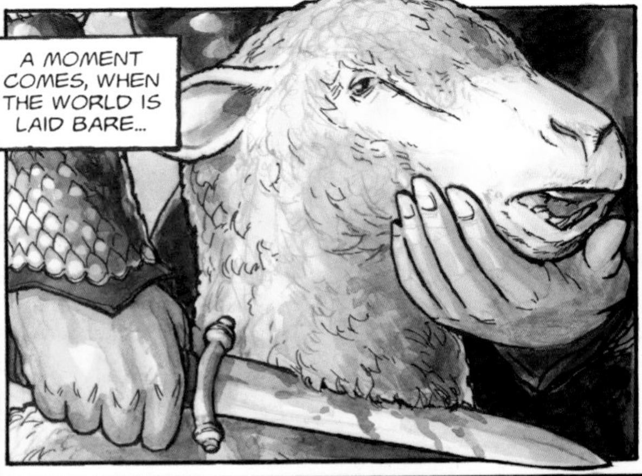
A MOMENT COMES, WHEN THE WORLD IS LAID BARE...
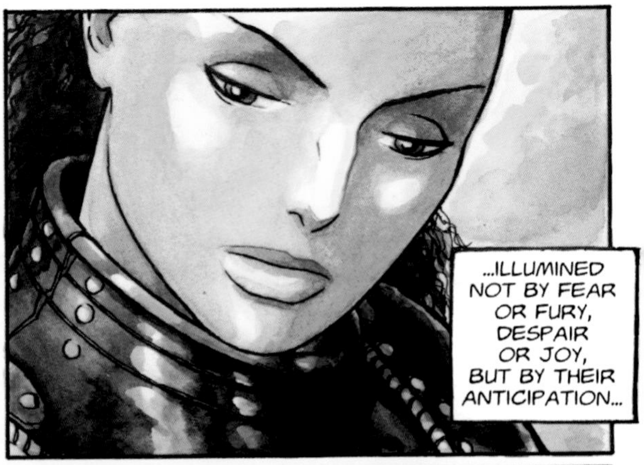
...ILLUMINED NOT BY FEAR OR FURY, DESPAIR OR JOY, BUT BY THEIR ANTICIPATION...
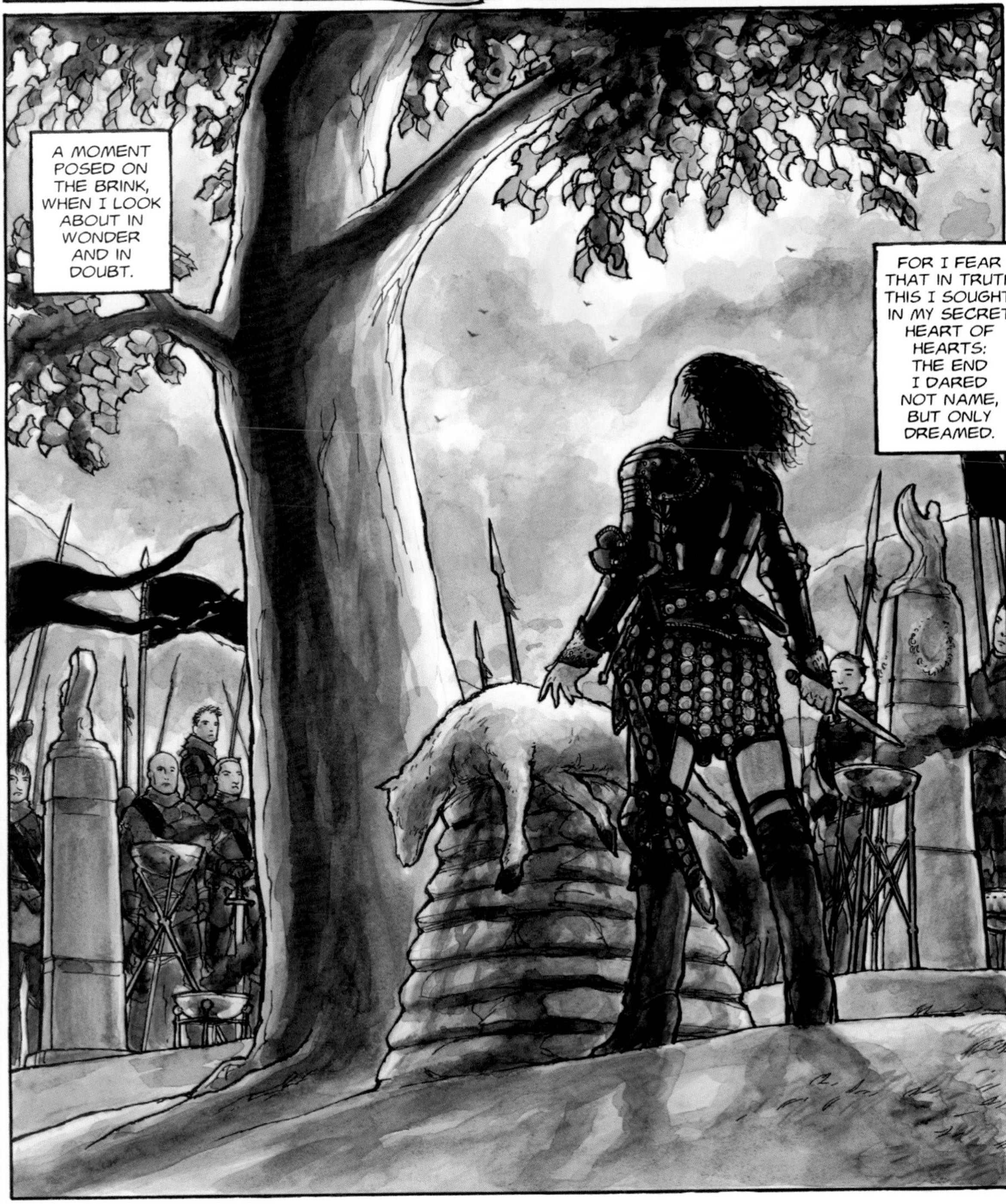
A MOMENT POSED ON THE BRINK, WHEN I LOOK ABOUT IN WONDER AND IN DOUBT.
FOR I FEAR THAT IN TRUTH THIS I SOUGHT, IN MY SECRET HEART OF HEARTS: THE END I DARED NOT NAME, BUT ONLY DREAMED.

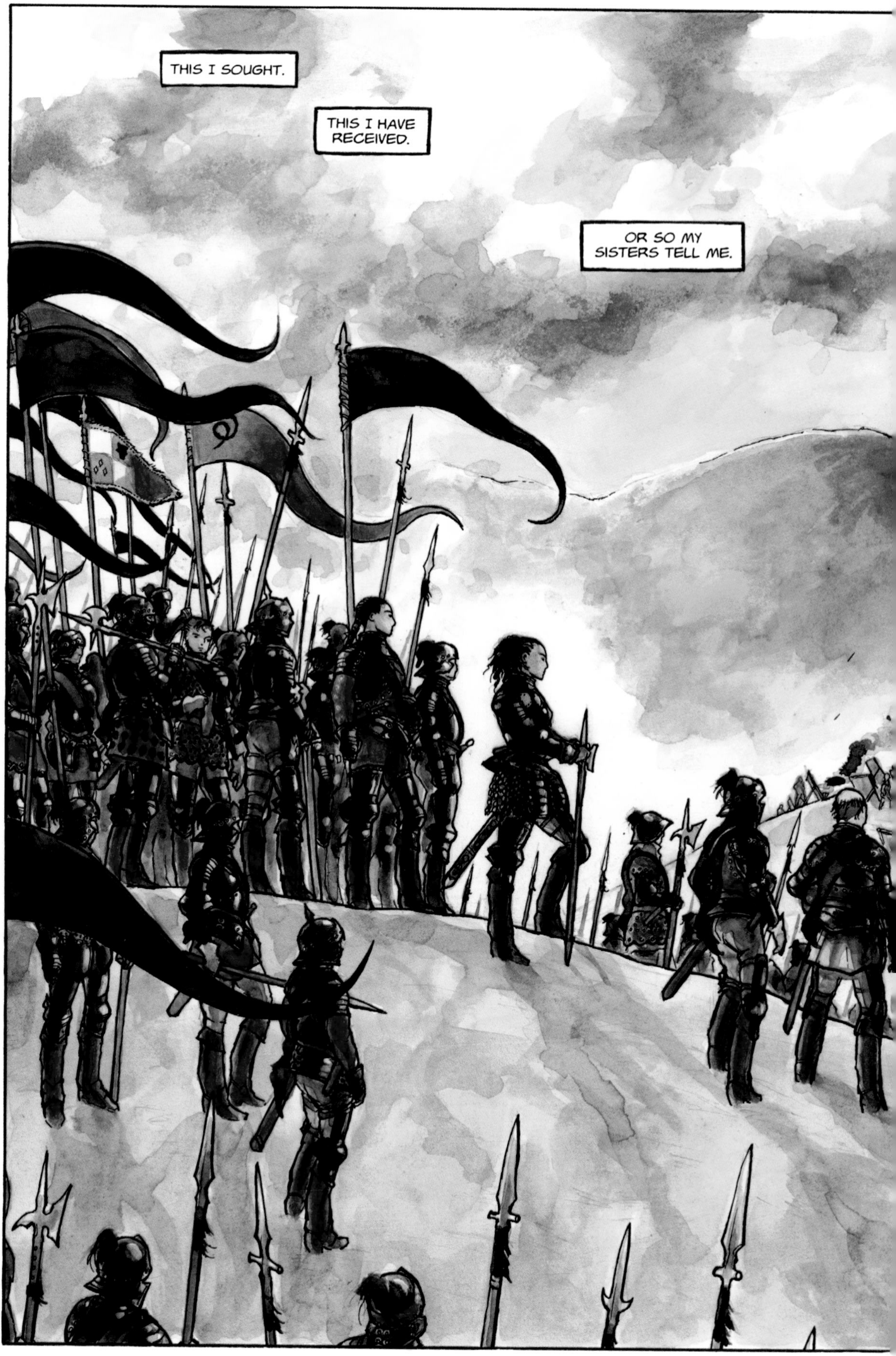
THIS I SOUGHT.
THIS I HAVE RECEIVED.
OR SO MY SISTERS TELL ME.

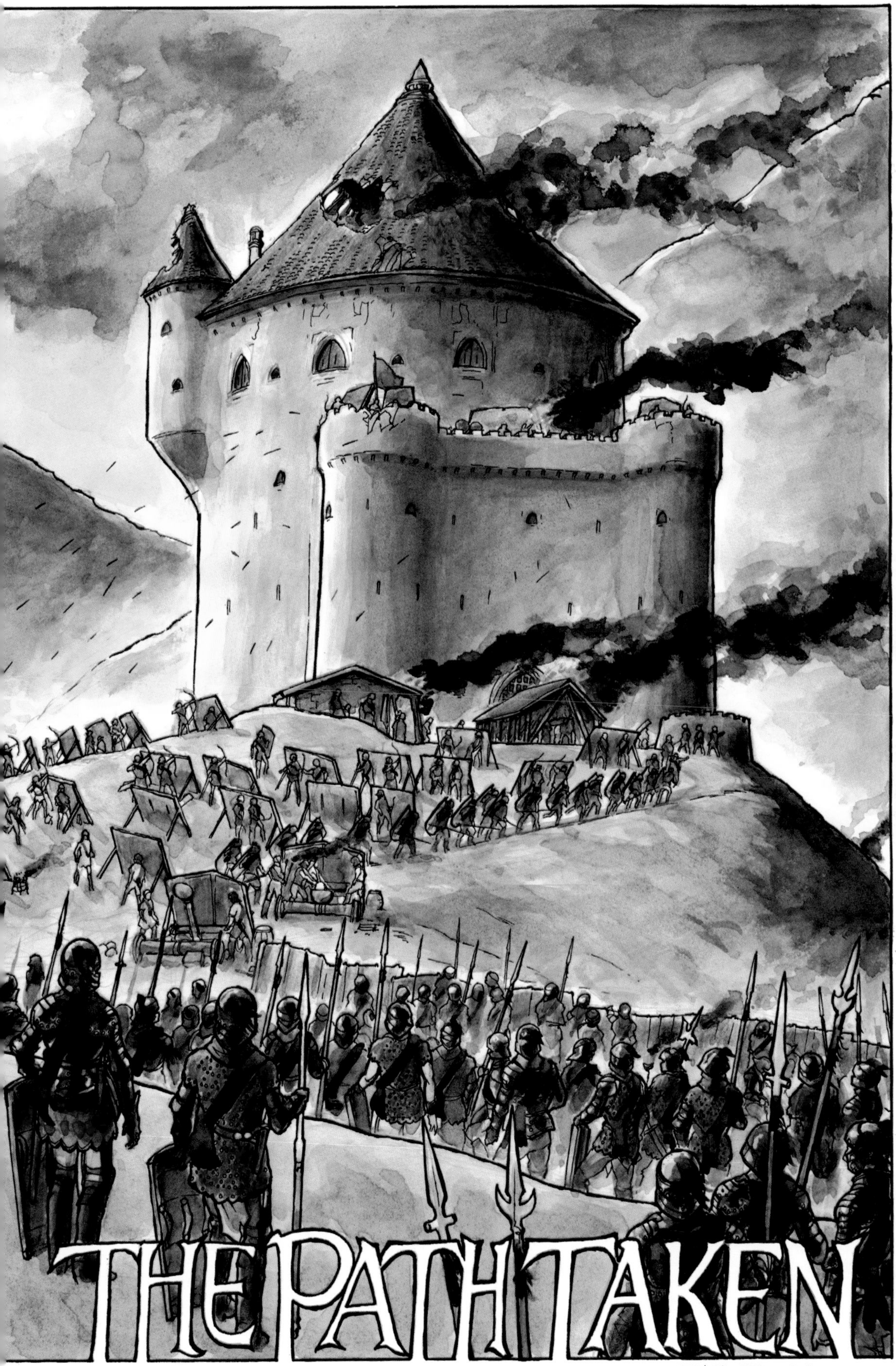
THE PATH TAKEN

STORY & ART © 99 MARK SMYLIE

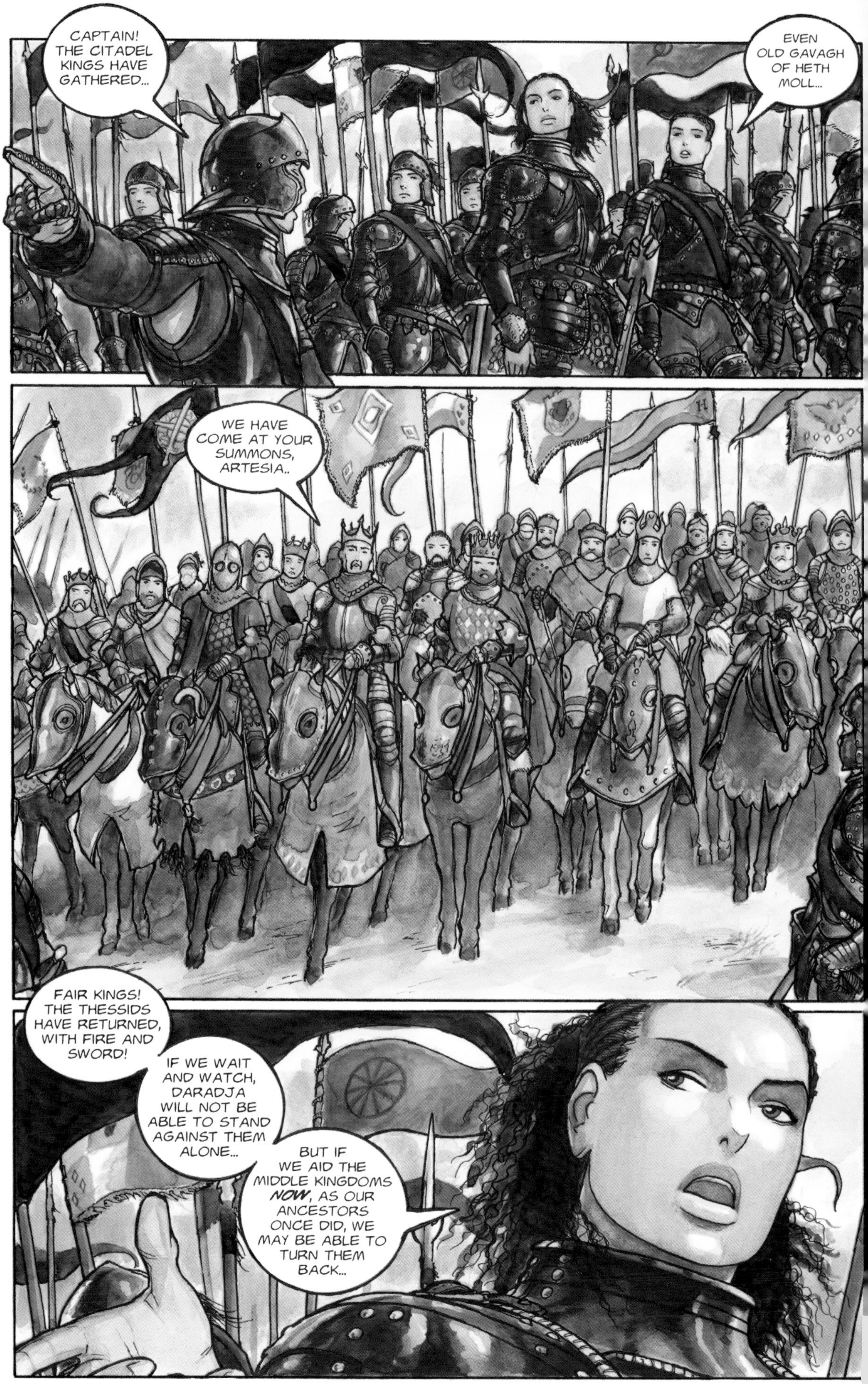
CAPTAIN! THE CITADEL KINGS HAVE GATHERED...
EVEN OLD GAVAGH OF HETH MOLL...
WE HAVE COME AT YOUR SUMMONS, ARTESIA..
FAIR KINGS! THE THESSIDS HAVE RETURNED, WITH FIRE AND SWORD!
IF WE WAIT AND WATCH, DARADJA WILL NOT BE ABLE TO STAND AGAINST THEM ALONE...
BUT IF WE AID THE MIDDLE KINGDOMS *NOW*, AS OUR ANCESTORS ONCE DID, WE MAY BE ABLE TO TURN THEM BACK...

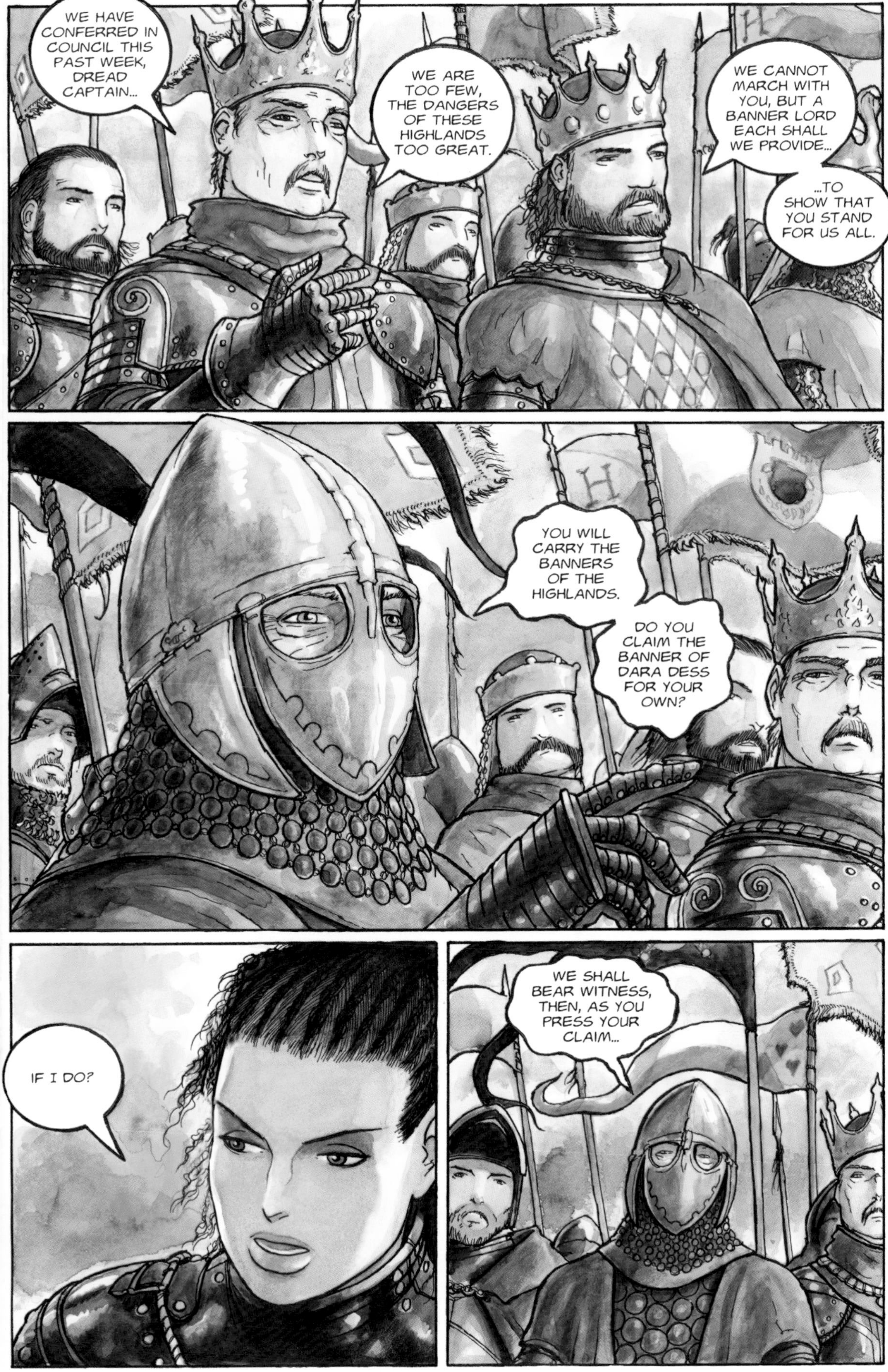
WE HAVE CONFERRED IN COUNCIL THIS PAST WEEK, DREAD CAPTAIN...
WE ARE TOO FEW, THE DANGERS OF THESE HIGHLANDS TOO GREAT.
WE CANNOT MARCH WITH YOU, BUT A BANNER LORD EACH SHALL WE PROVIDE...
...TO SHOW THAT YOU STAND FOR US ALL.
YOU WILL CARRY THE BANNERS OF THE HIGHLANDS.
DO YOU CLAIM THE BANNER OF DARA DESS FOR YOUR OWN?
IF I DO?
WE SHALL BEAR WITNESS, THEN, AS YOU PRESS YOUR CLAIM...

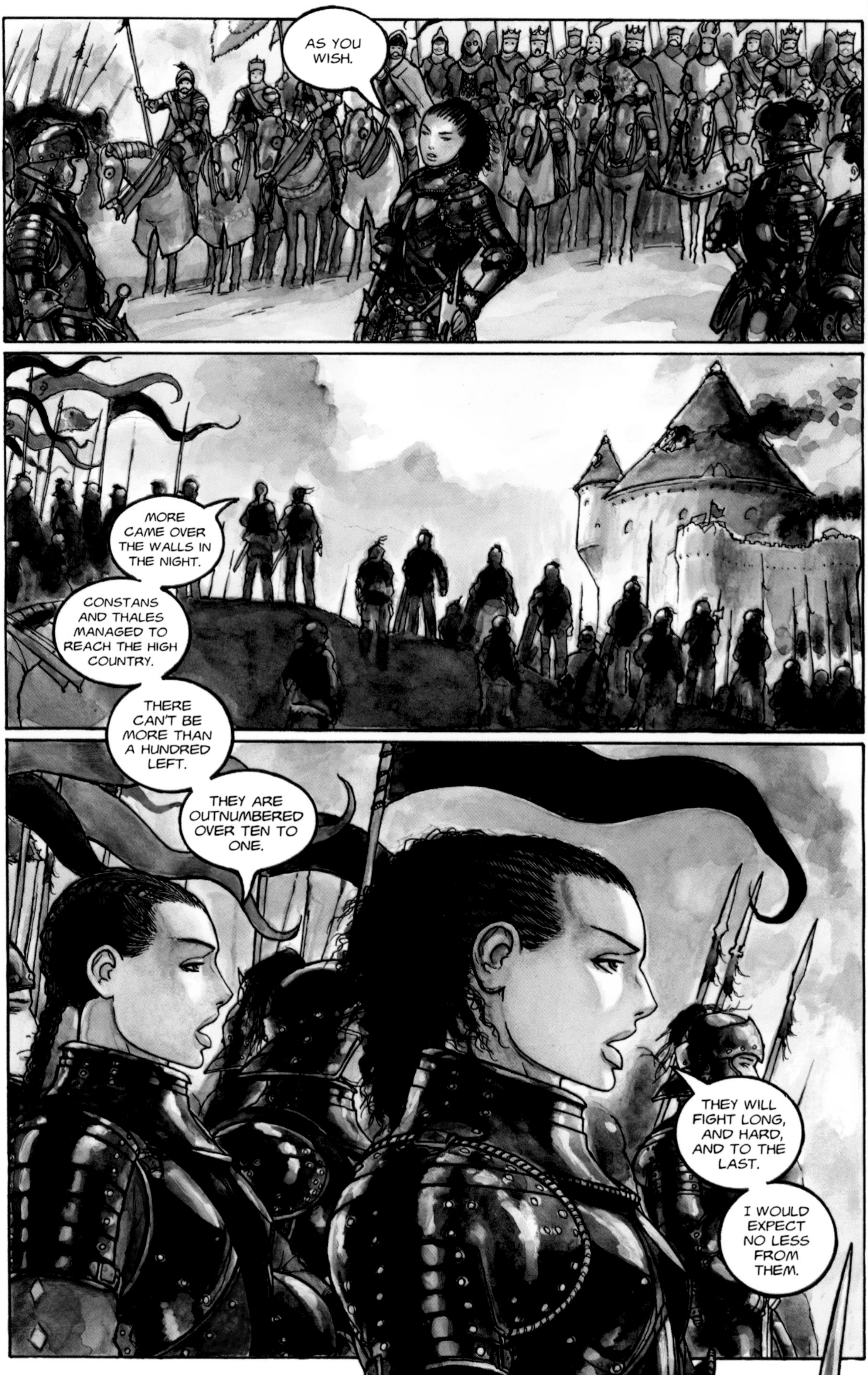
AS YOU WISH.
MORE CAME OVER THE WALLS IN THE NIGHT.
CONSTANS AND THALES MANAGED TO REACH THE HIGH COUNTRY.
THERE CAN'T BE MORE THAN A HUNDRED LEFT.
THEY ARE OUTNUMBERED OVER TEN TO ONE.
THEY WILL FIGHT LONG, AND HARD, AND TO THE LAST.
I WOULD EXPECT NO LESS FROM THEM.

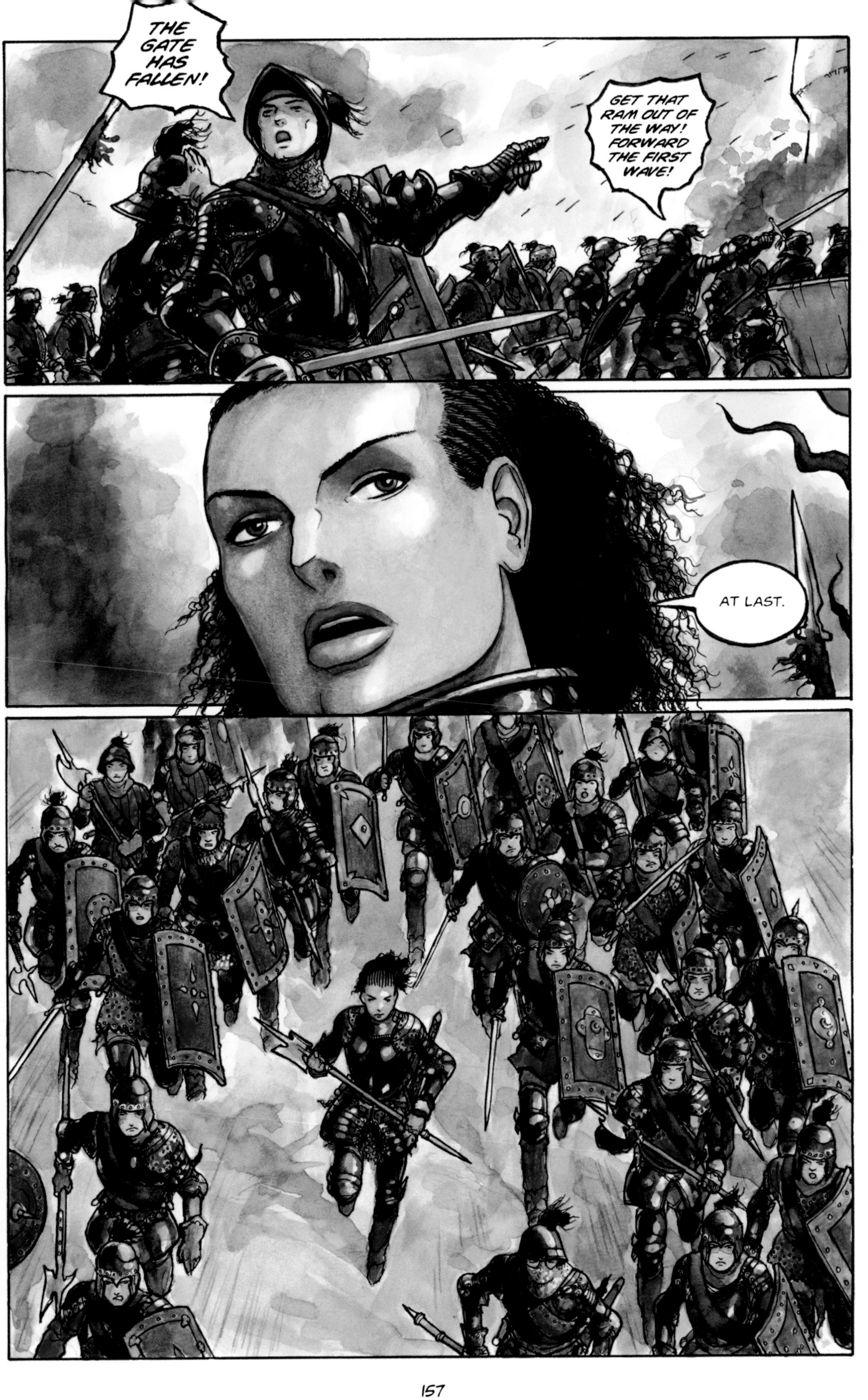
THE GATE HAS FALLEN!
GET THAT RAM OUT OF THE WAY! FORWARD THE FIRST WAVE!
AT LAST.

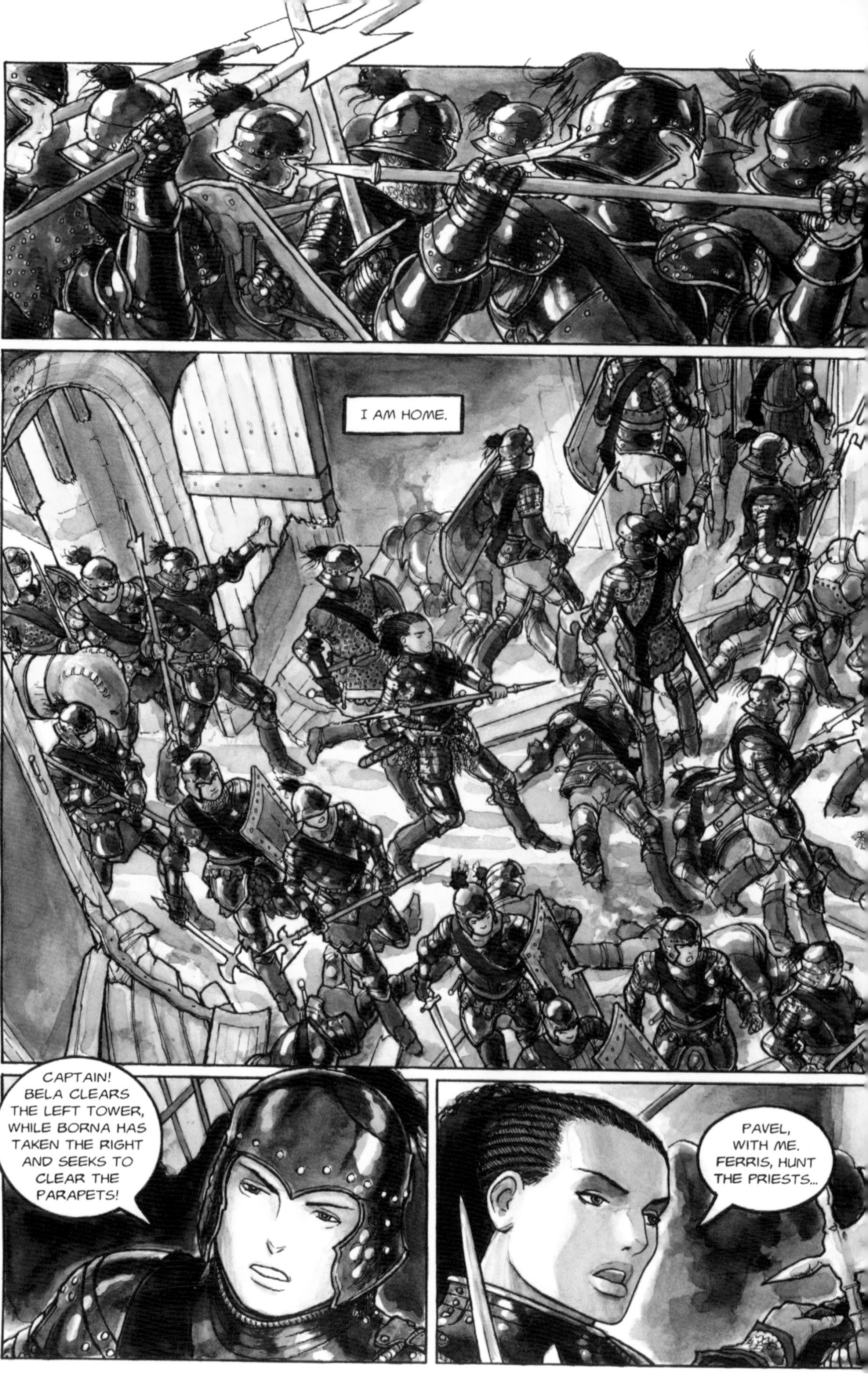
I AM HOME.
CAPTAIN! BELA CLEARS THE LEFT TOWER, WHILE BORNA HAS TAKEN THE RIGHT AND SEEKS TO CLEAR THE PARAPETS!
PAVEL, WITH ME. FERRIS, HUNT THE PRIESTS...

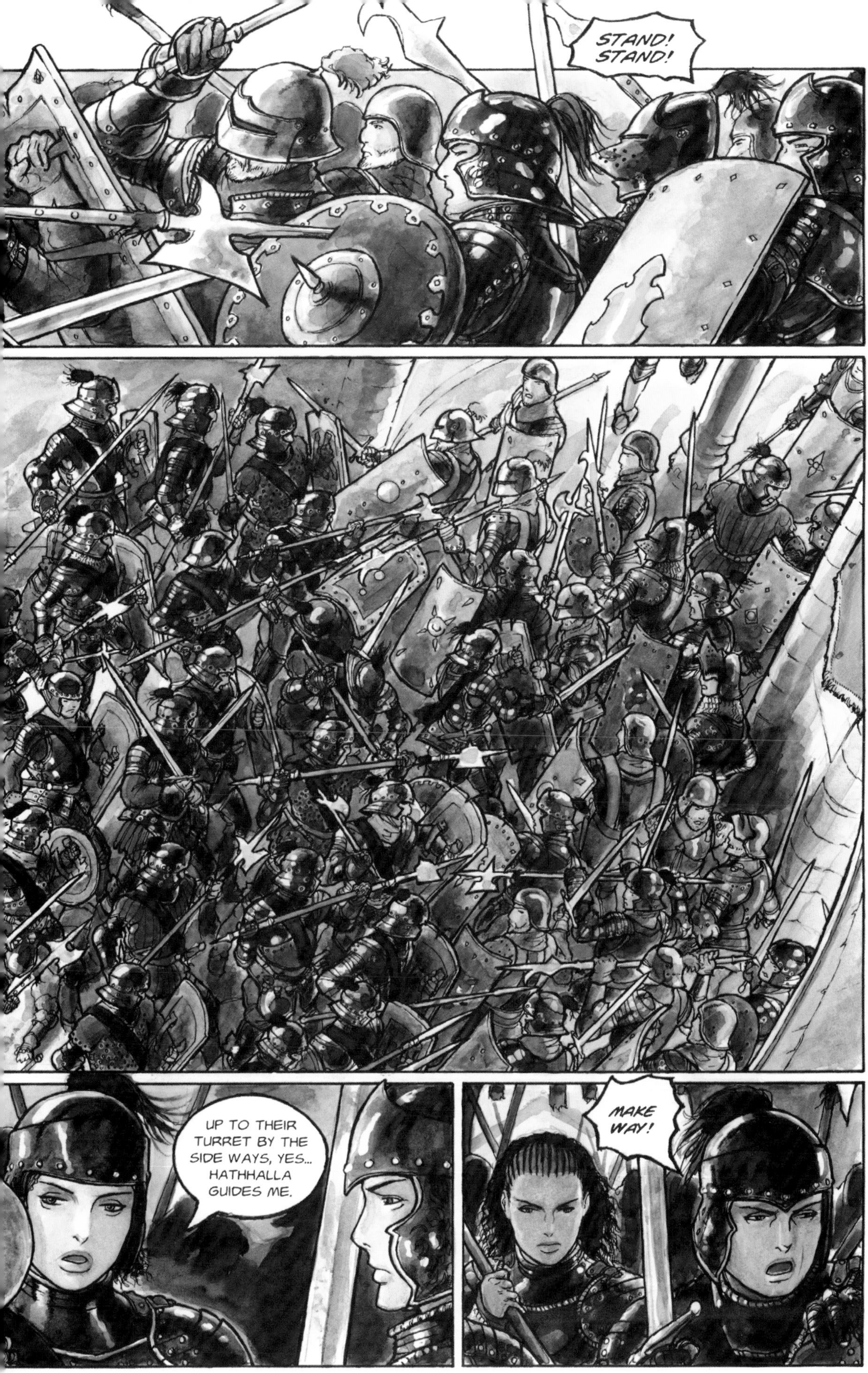
STAND! STAND!
UP TO THEIR TURRET BY THE SIDE WAYS, YES... HATHHALLA GUIDES ME.
MAKE WAY!

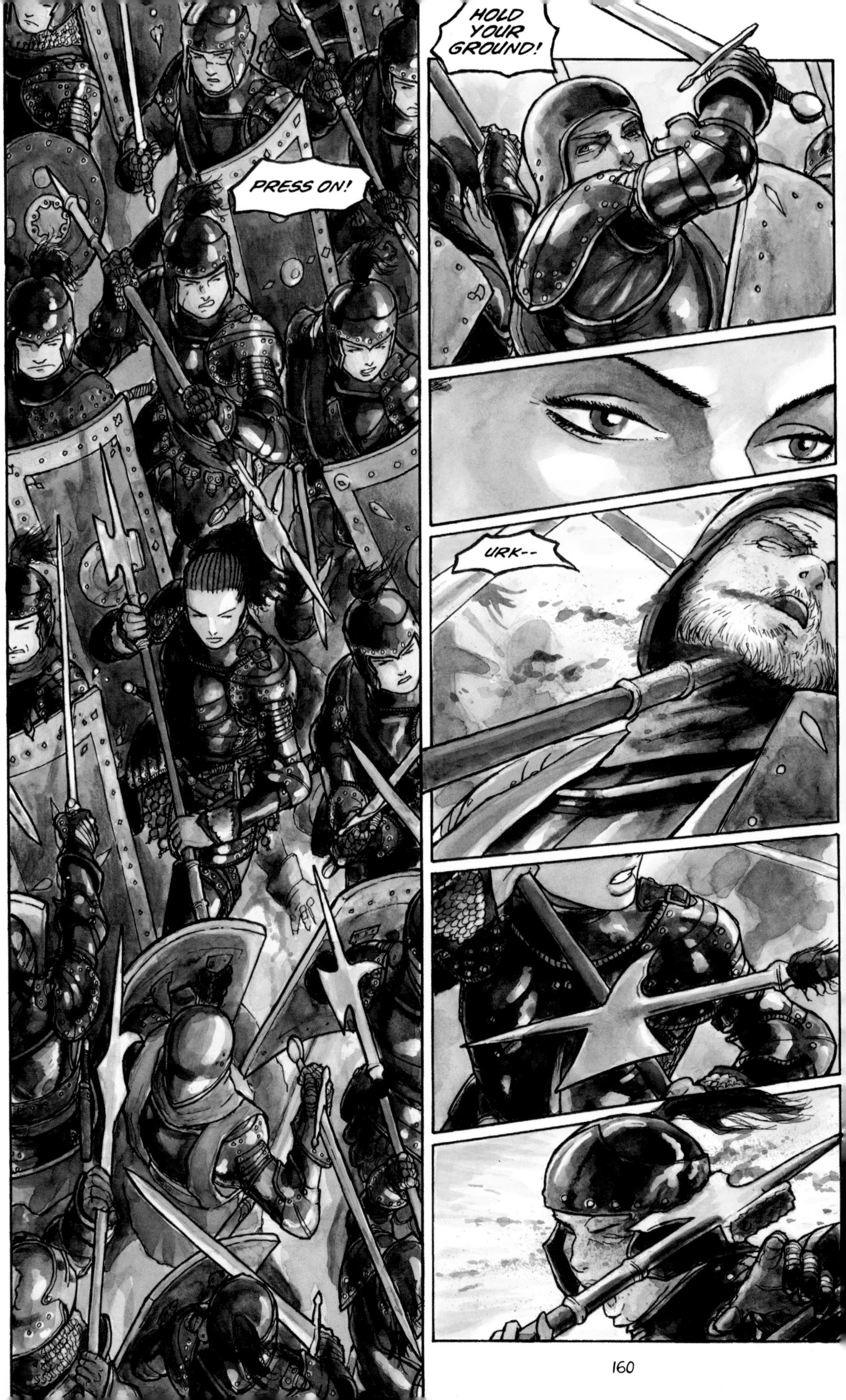
PRESS ON!
HOLD YOUR GROUND!
URK--

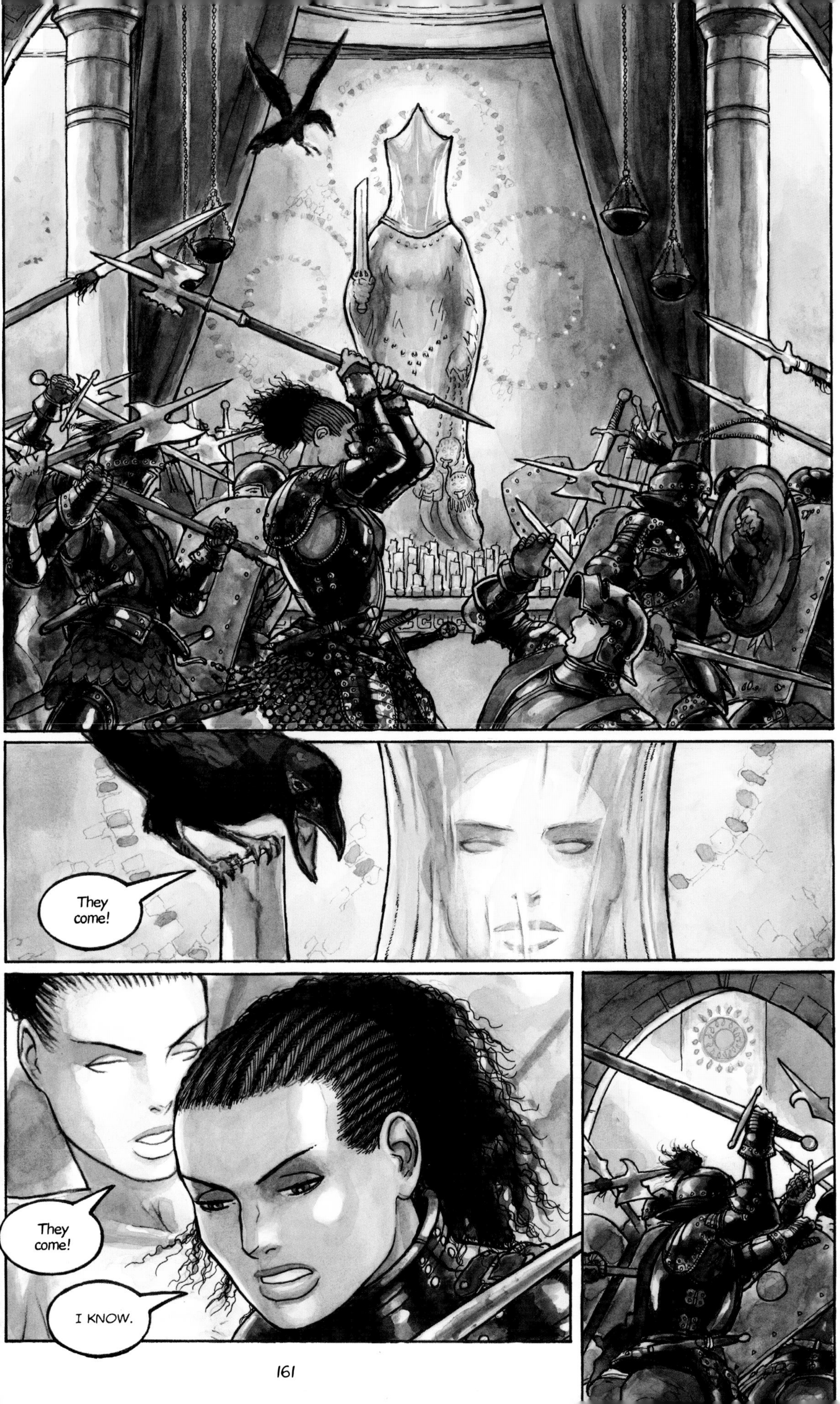
They come!
They come!
I KNOW.

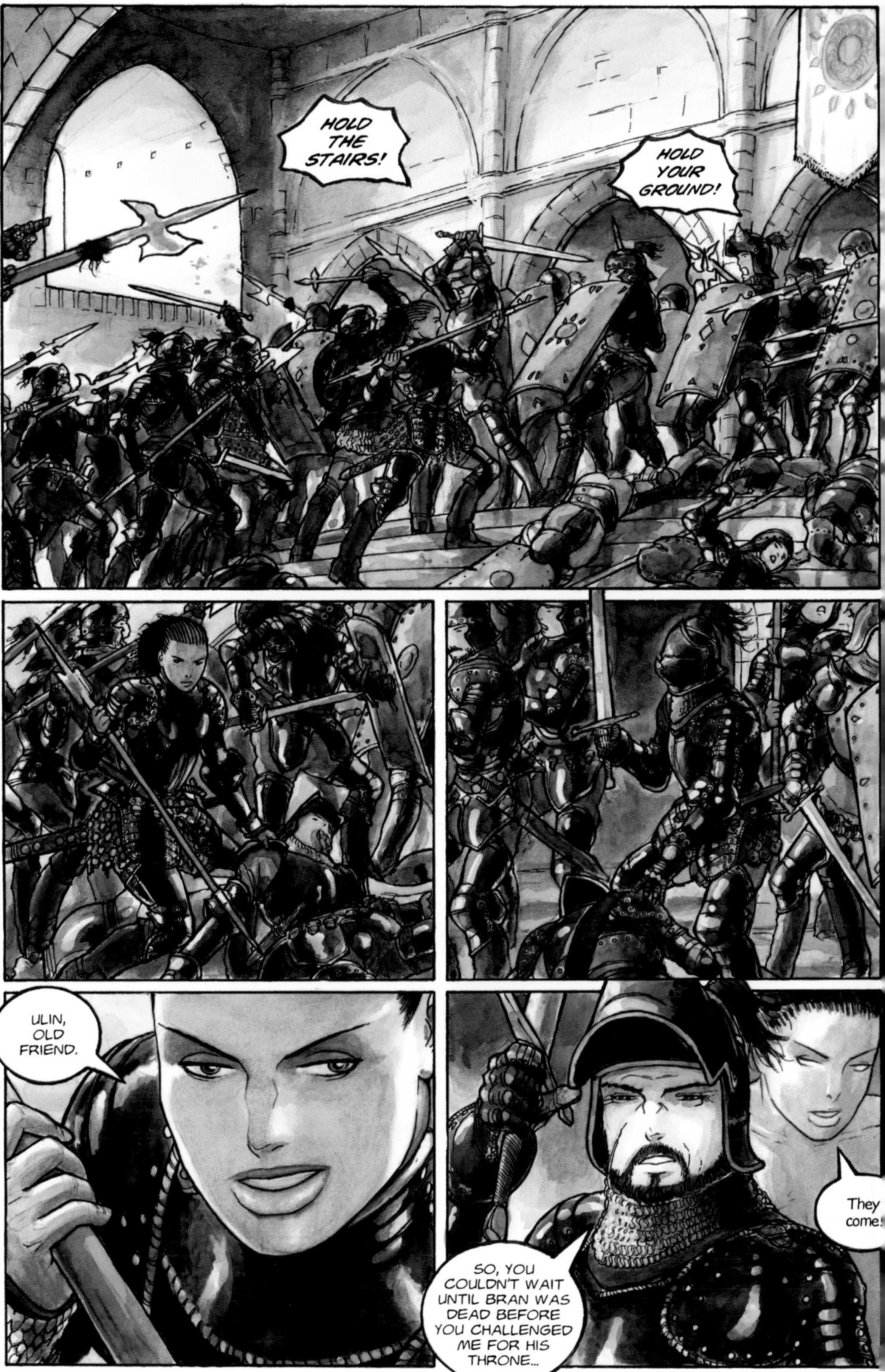
HOLD THE STAIRS!
HOLD YOUR GROUND!
ULIN, OLD FRIEND.
They come!
SO, YOU COULDN'T WAIT UNTIL BRAN WAS DEAD BEFORE YOU CHALLENGED ME FOR HIS THRONE...

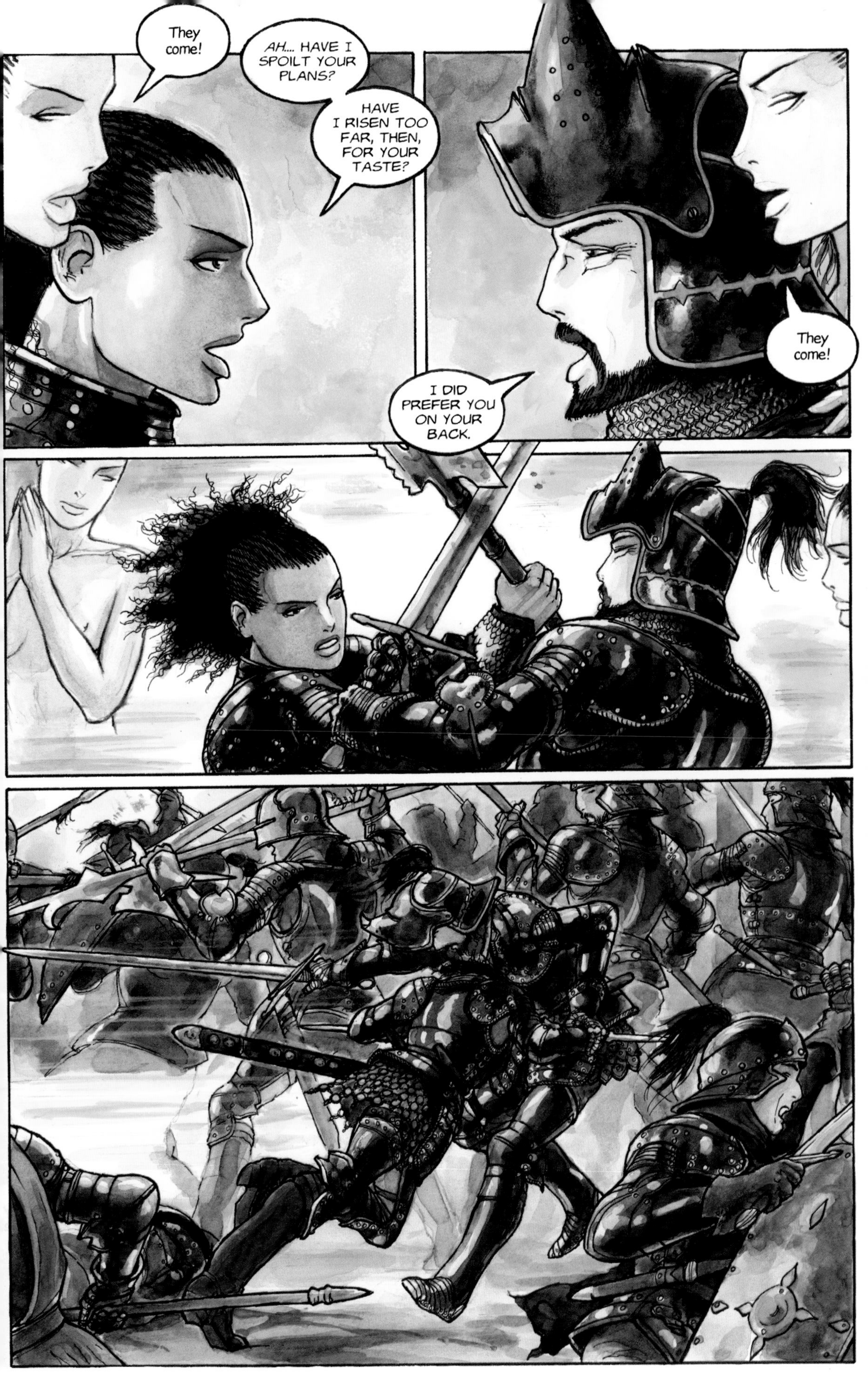
They come!
AH.... HAVE I SPOILT YOUR PLANS?
HAVE I RISEN TOO FAR, THEN, FOR YOUR TASTE?
They come!
I DID PREFER YOU ON YOUR BACK.

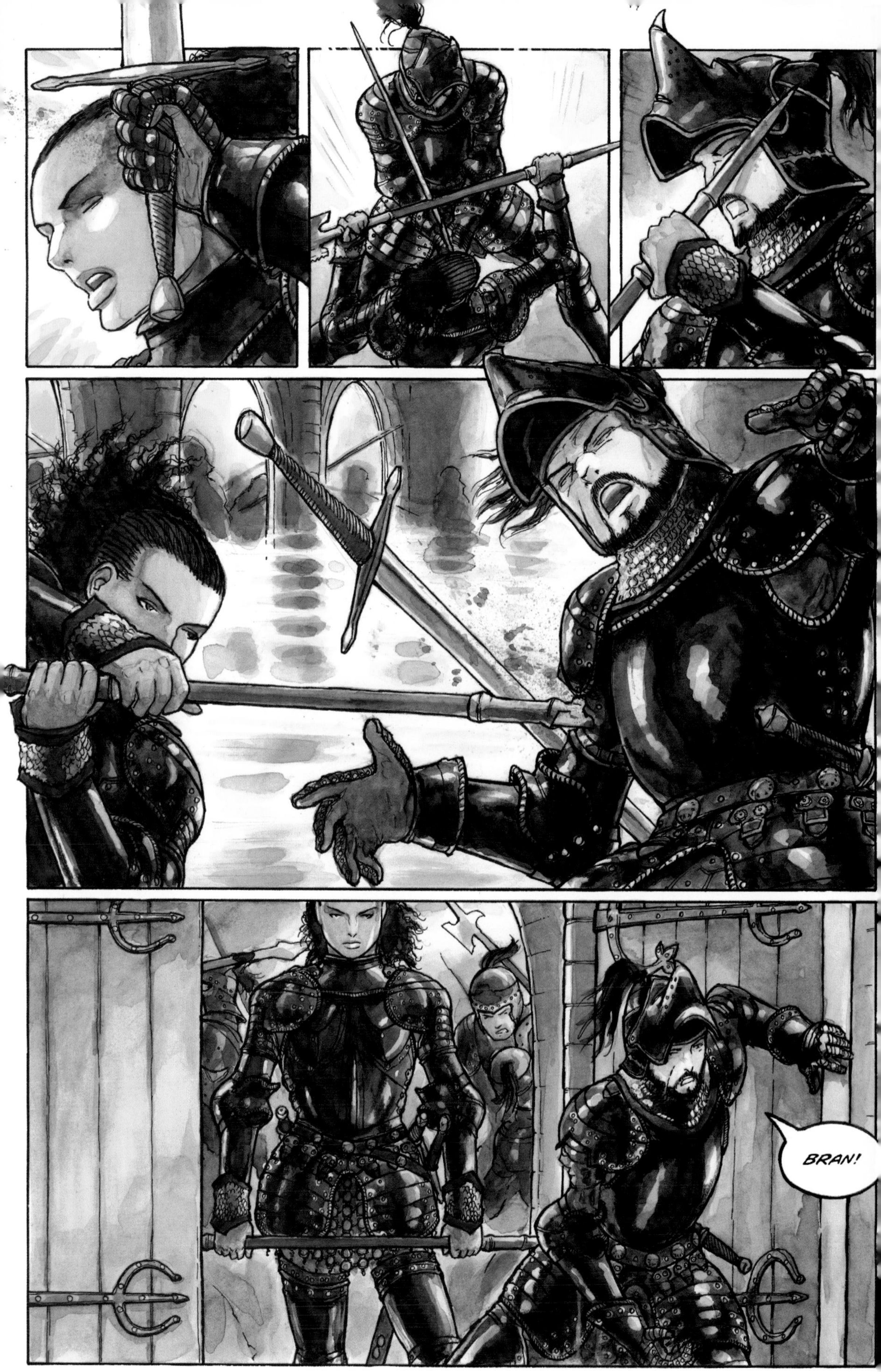
BRAN!

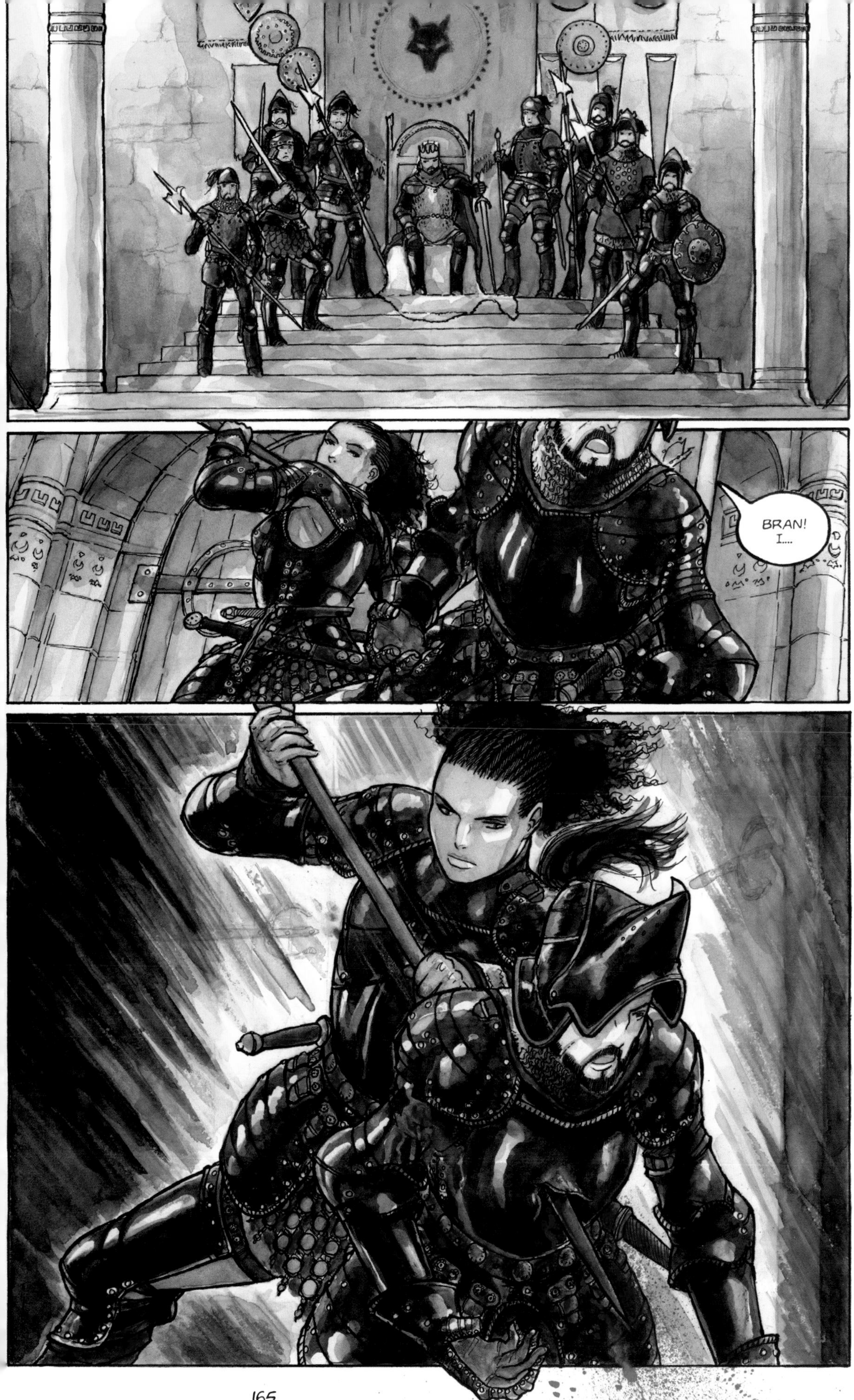
BRAN!
I....

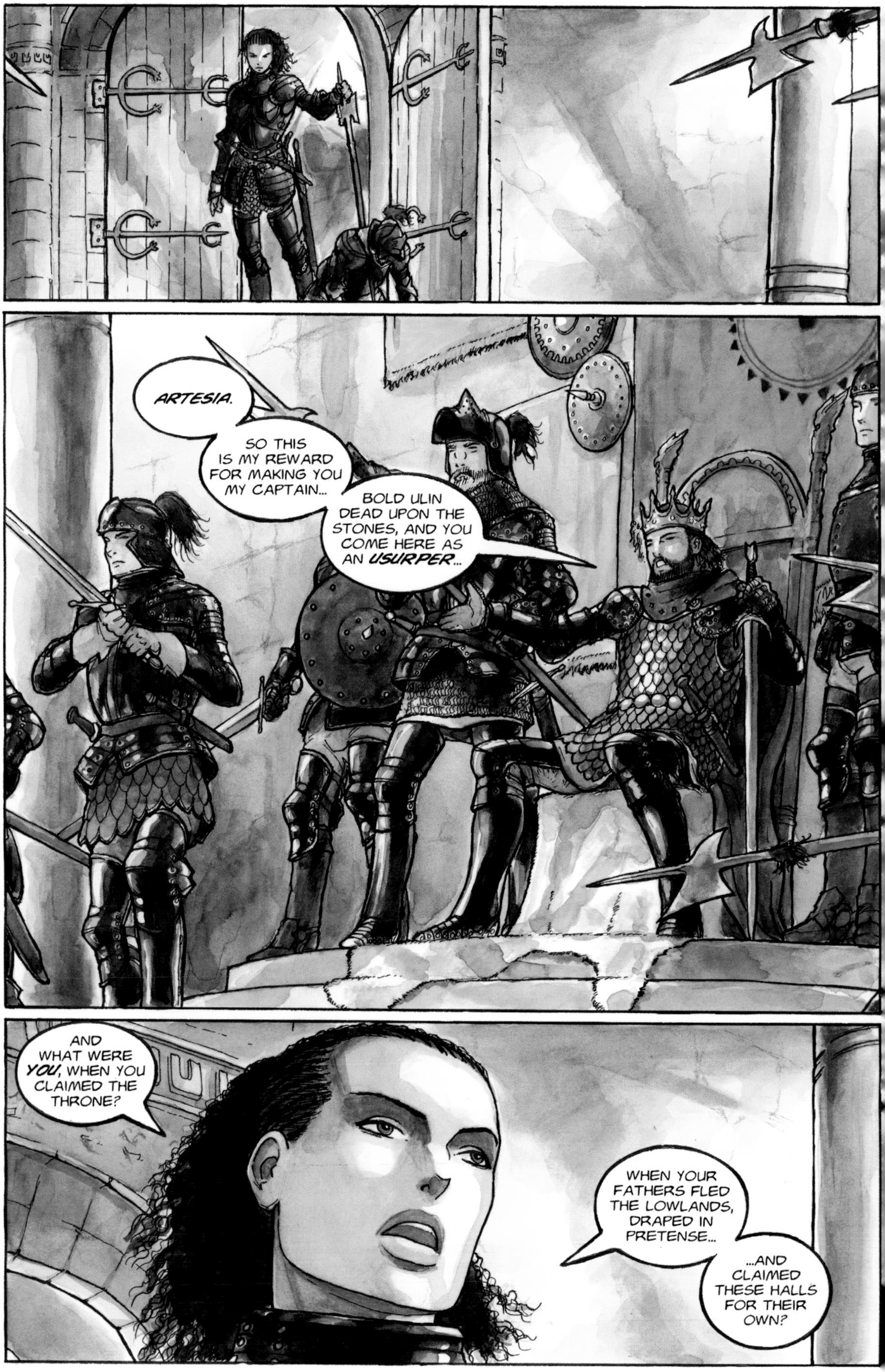
ARTESIA.
SO THIS IS MY REWARD FOR MAKING YOU MY CAPTAIN...
BOLD ULIN DEAD UPON THE STONES, AND YOU COME HERE AS AN USURPER...
AND WHAT WERE YOU, WHEN YOU CLAIMED THE THRONE?
WHEN YOUR FATHERS FLED THE LOWLANDS, DRAPED IN PRETENSE...
...AND CLAIMED THESE HALLS FOR THEIR OWN?

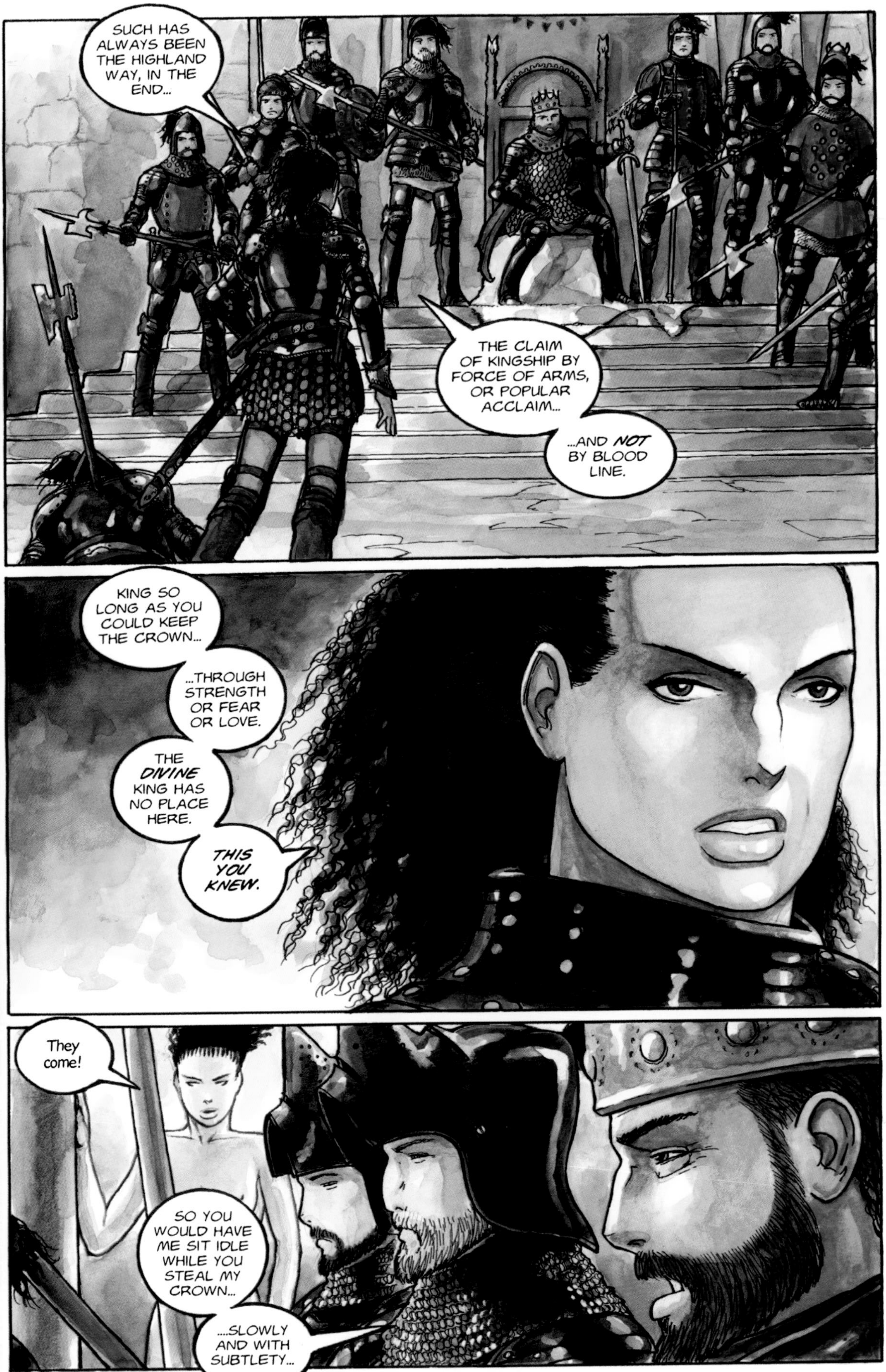
SUCH HAS ALWAYS BEEN THE HIGHLAND WAY, IN THE END...
THE CLAIM OF KINGSHIP BY FORCE OF ARMS, OR POPULAR ACCLAIM...
...AND NOT BY BLOOD LINE.
KING SO LONG AS YOU COULD KEEP THE CROWN...
...THROUGH STRENGTH OR FEAR OR LOVE.
THE DIVINE KING HAS NO PLACE HERE.
THIS YOU KNEW.
They come!
SO YOU WOULD HAVE ME SIT IDLE WHILE YOU STEAL MY CROWN...
....SLOWLY AND WITH SUBTLETY...

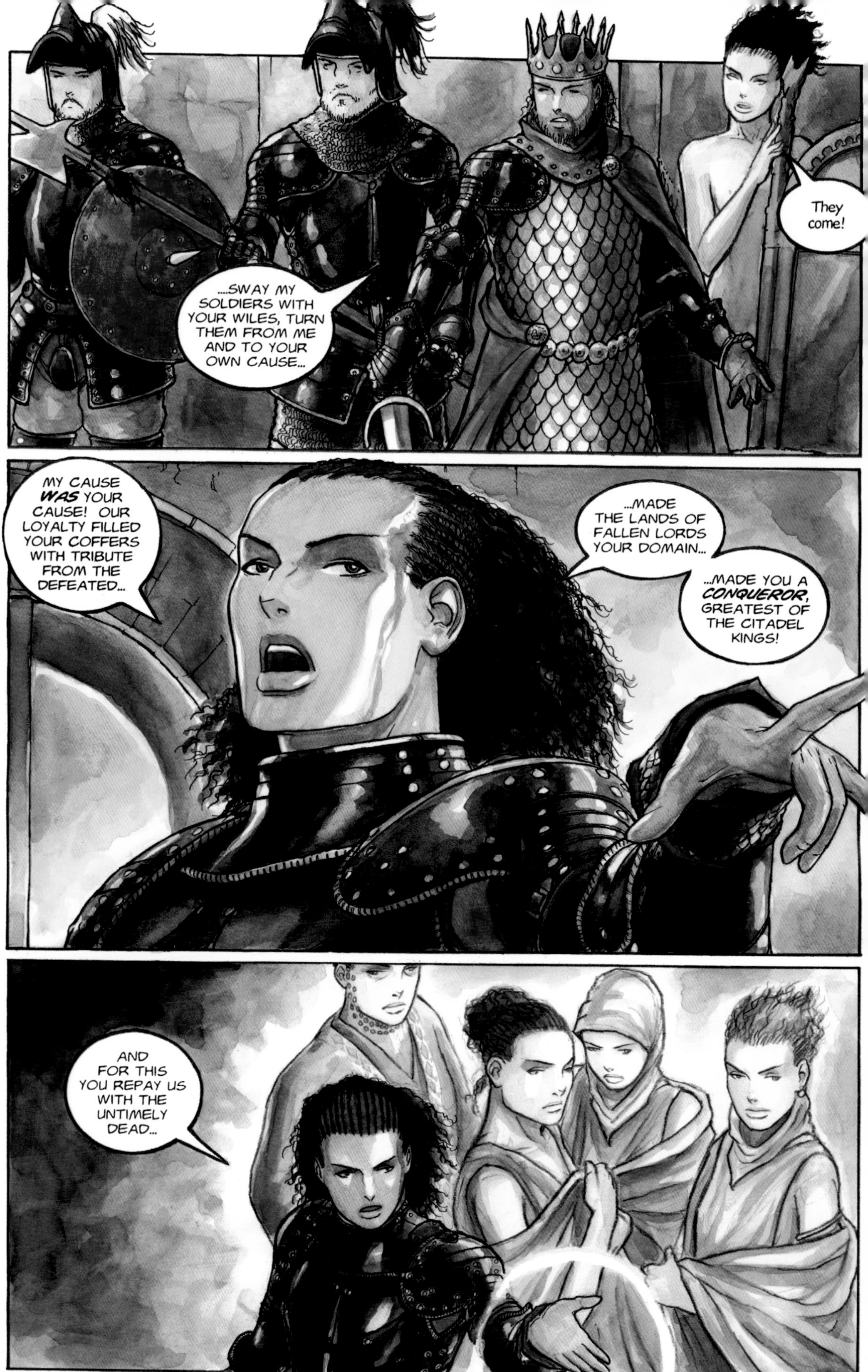
They come!
...SWAY MY SOLDIERS WITH YOUR WILES, TURN THEM FROM ME AND TO YOUR OWN CAUSE...
MY CAUSE **WAS** YOUR CAUSE! OUR LOYALTY FILLED YOUR COFFERS WITH TRIBUTE FROM THE DEFEATED...
...MADE THE LANDS OF FALLEN LORDS YOUR DOMAIN...
...MADE YOU A ***CONQUEROR***, GREATEST OF THE CITADEL KINGS!
AND FOR THIS YOU REPAY US WITH THE UNTIMELY DEAD...

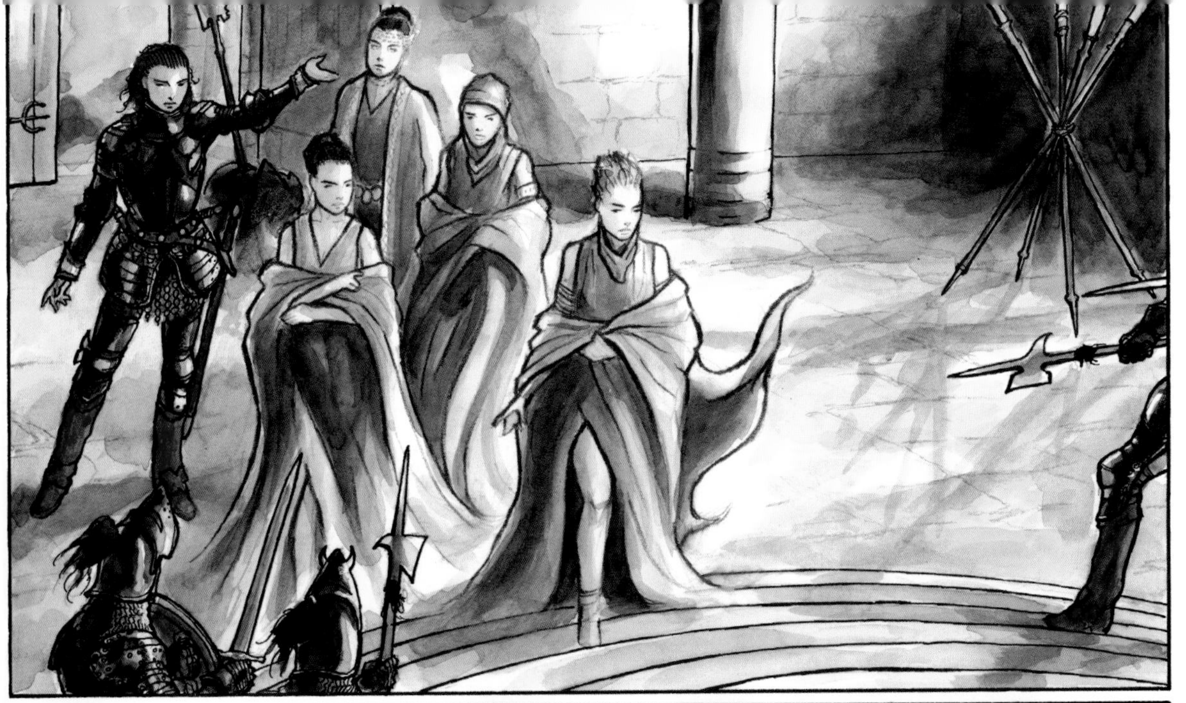

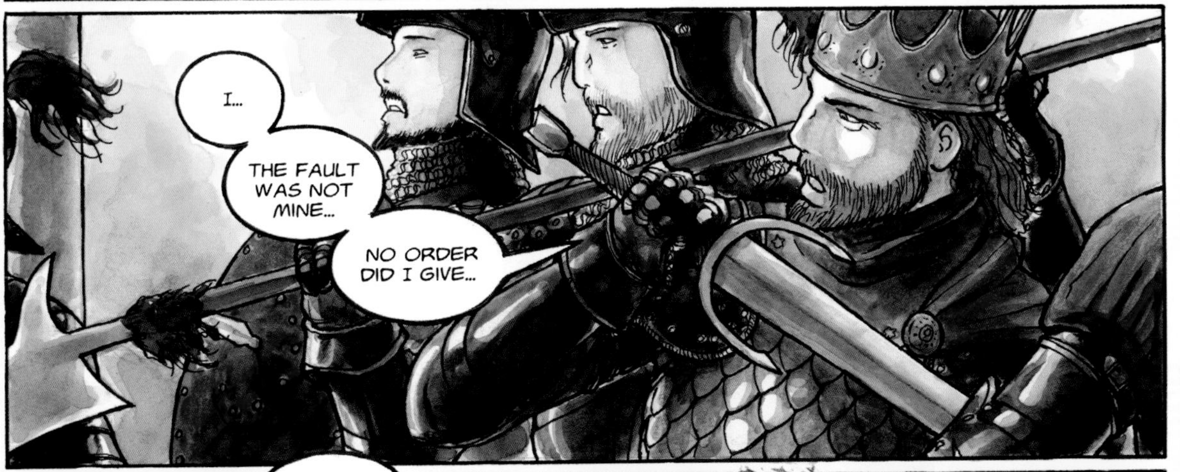

I...
THE FAULT WAS NOT MINE...
NO ORDER DID I GIVE...

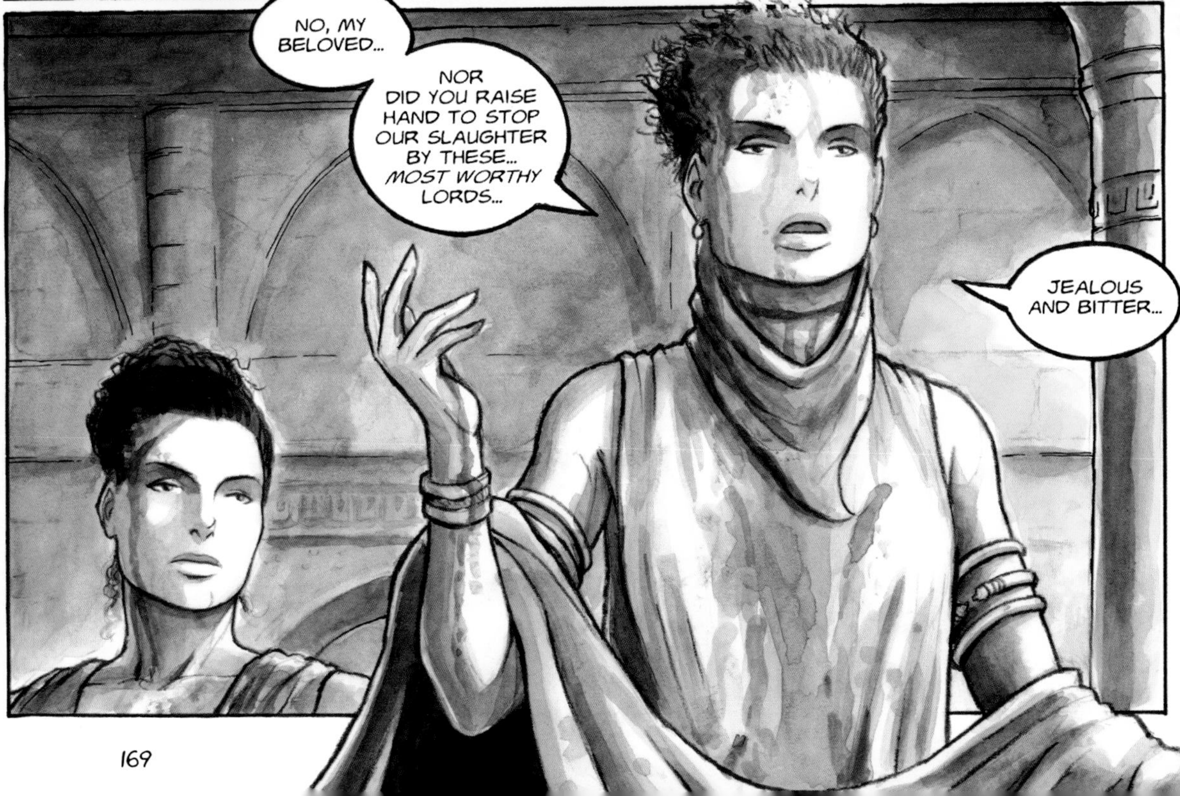

NO, MY BELOVED...
NOR DID YOU RAISE HAND TO STOP OUR SLAUGHTER BY THESE... *MOST WORTHY* LORDS...
JEALOUS AND BITTER...

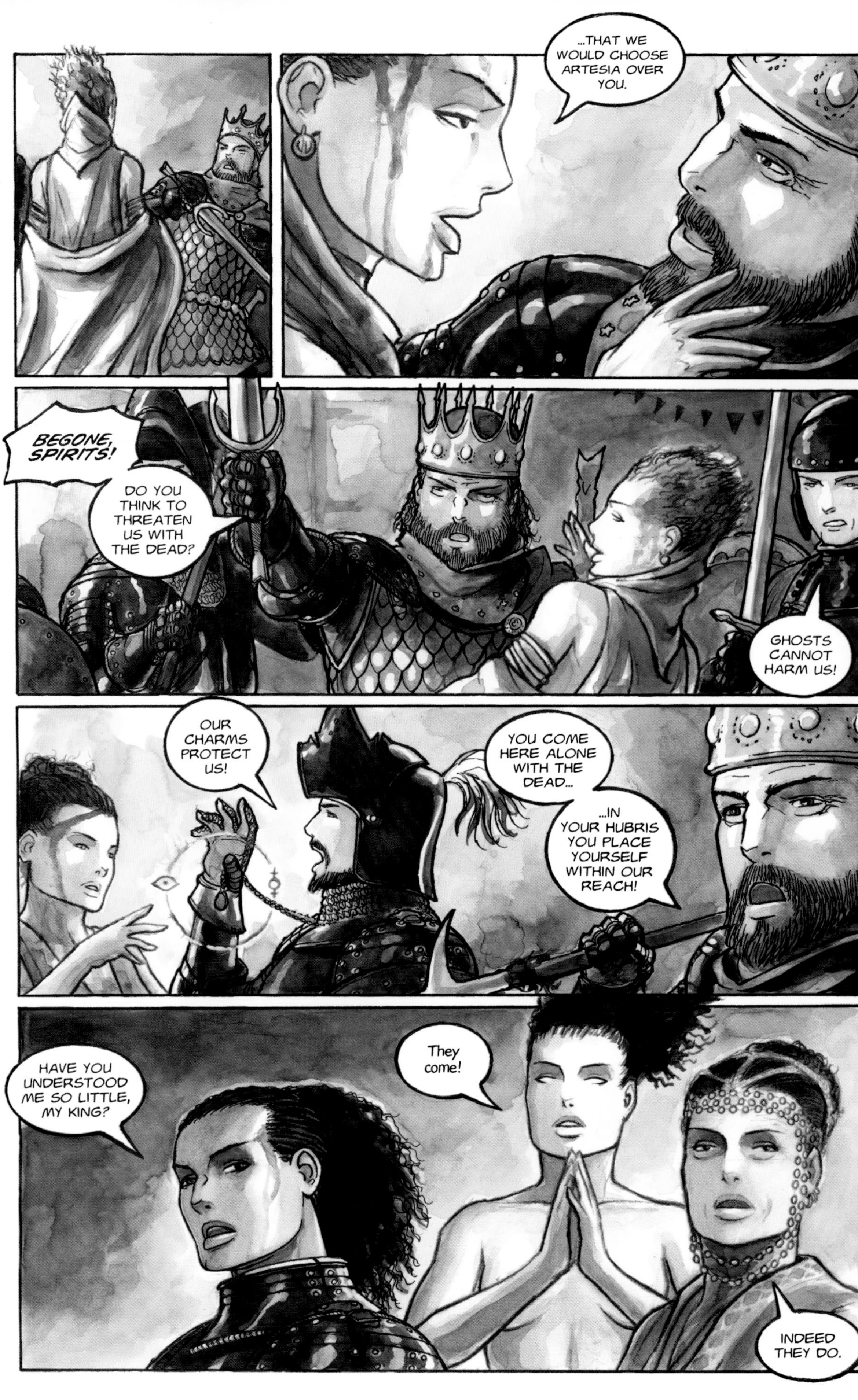

...THAT WE WOULD CHOOSE ARTESIA OVER YOU.
BEGONE, SPIRITS!
DO YOU THINK TO THREATEN US WITH THE DEAD?
GHOSTS CANNOT HARM US!
OUR CHARMS PROTECT US!
YOU COME HERE ALONE WITH THE DEAD...
...IN YOUR HUBRIS YOU PLACE YOURSELF WITHIN OUR REACH!
HAVE YOU UNDERSTOOD ME SO LITTLE, MY KING?
They come!
INDEED THEY DO.

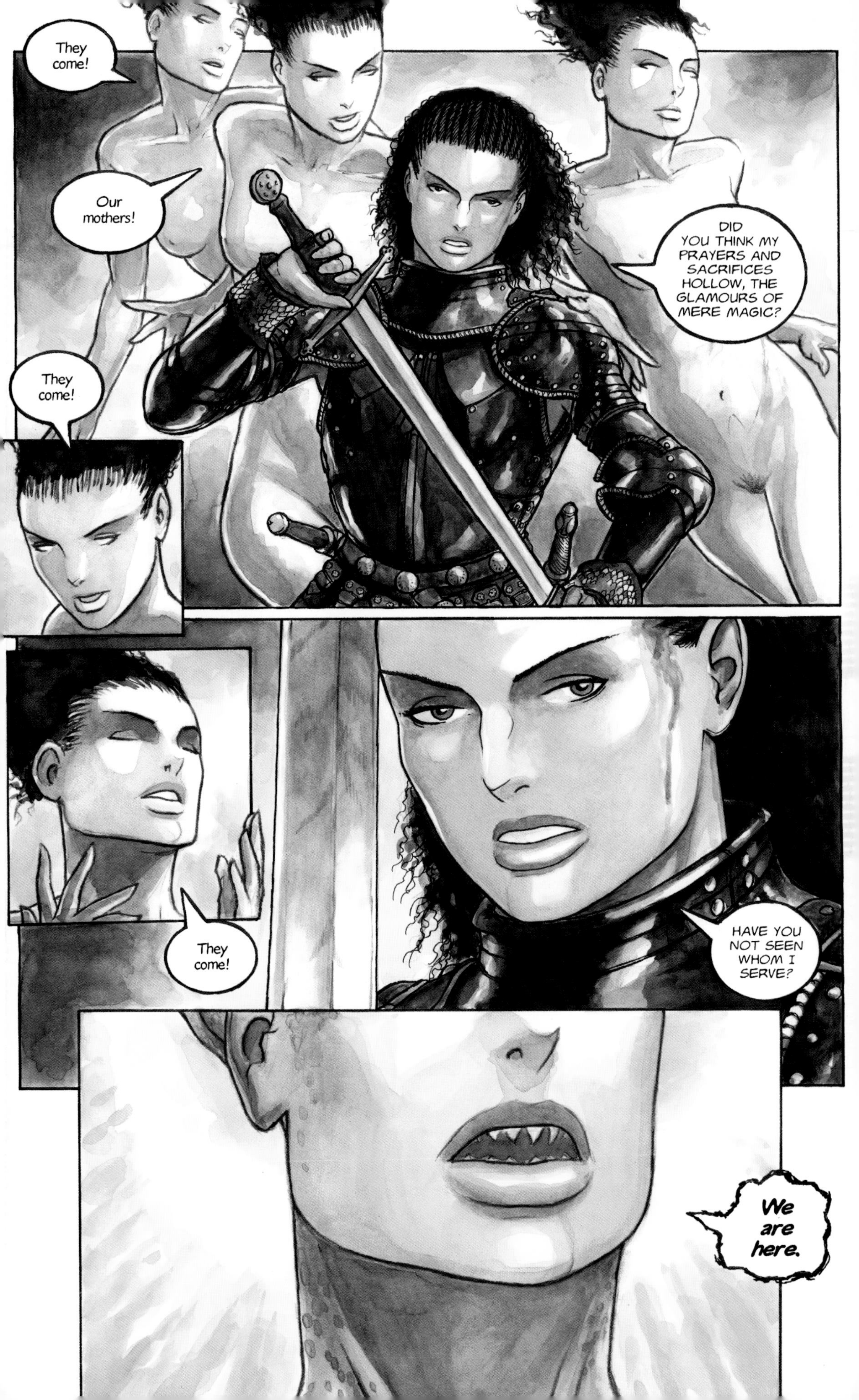
They come!
Our mothers!
DID YOU THINK MY PRAYERS AND SACRIFICES HOLLOW, THE GLAMOURS OF MERE MAGIC?
They come!
They come!
HAVE YOU NOT SEEN WHOM I SERVE?
We are here.

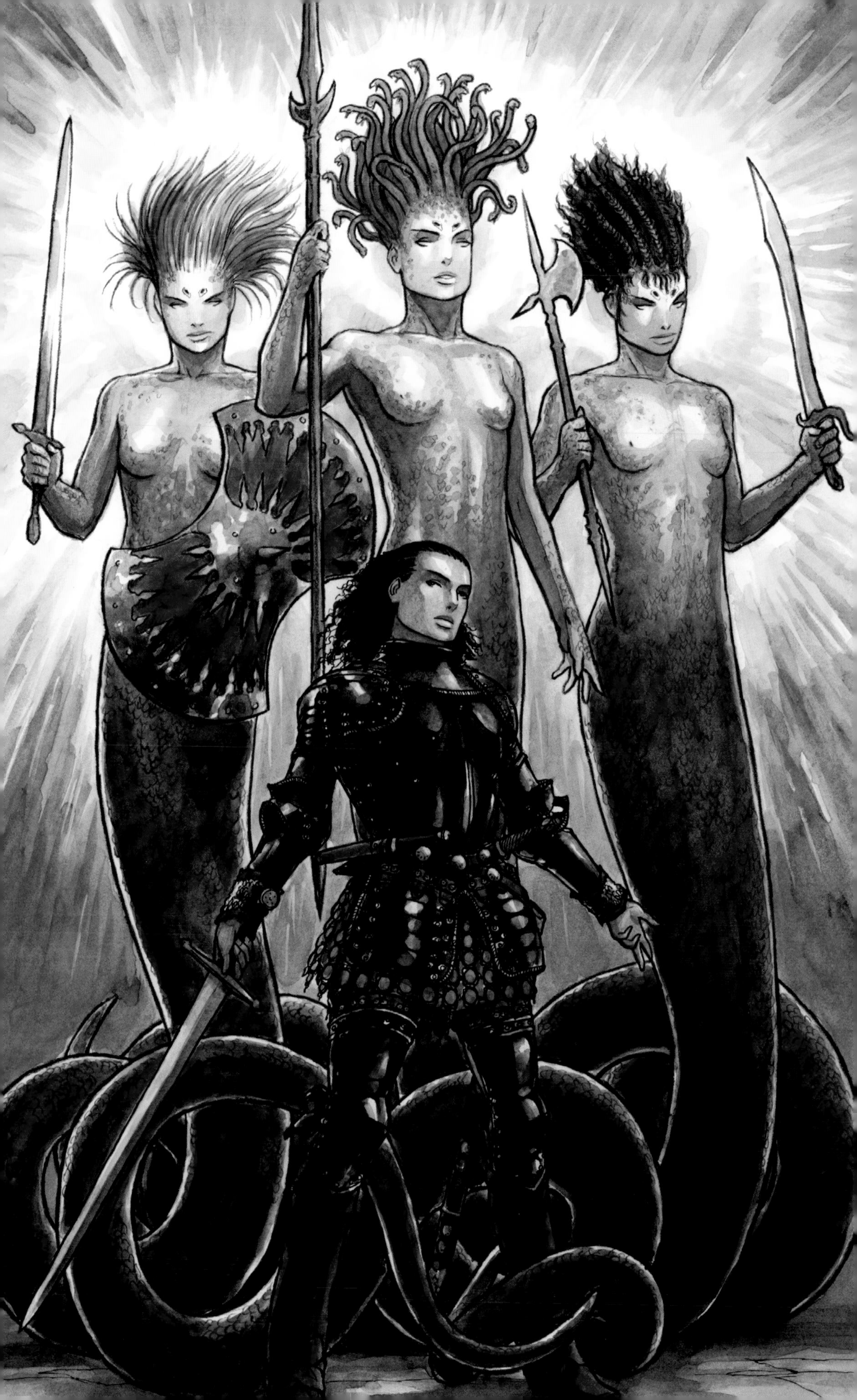

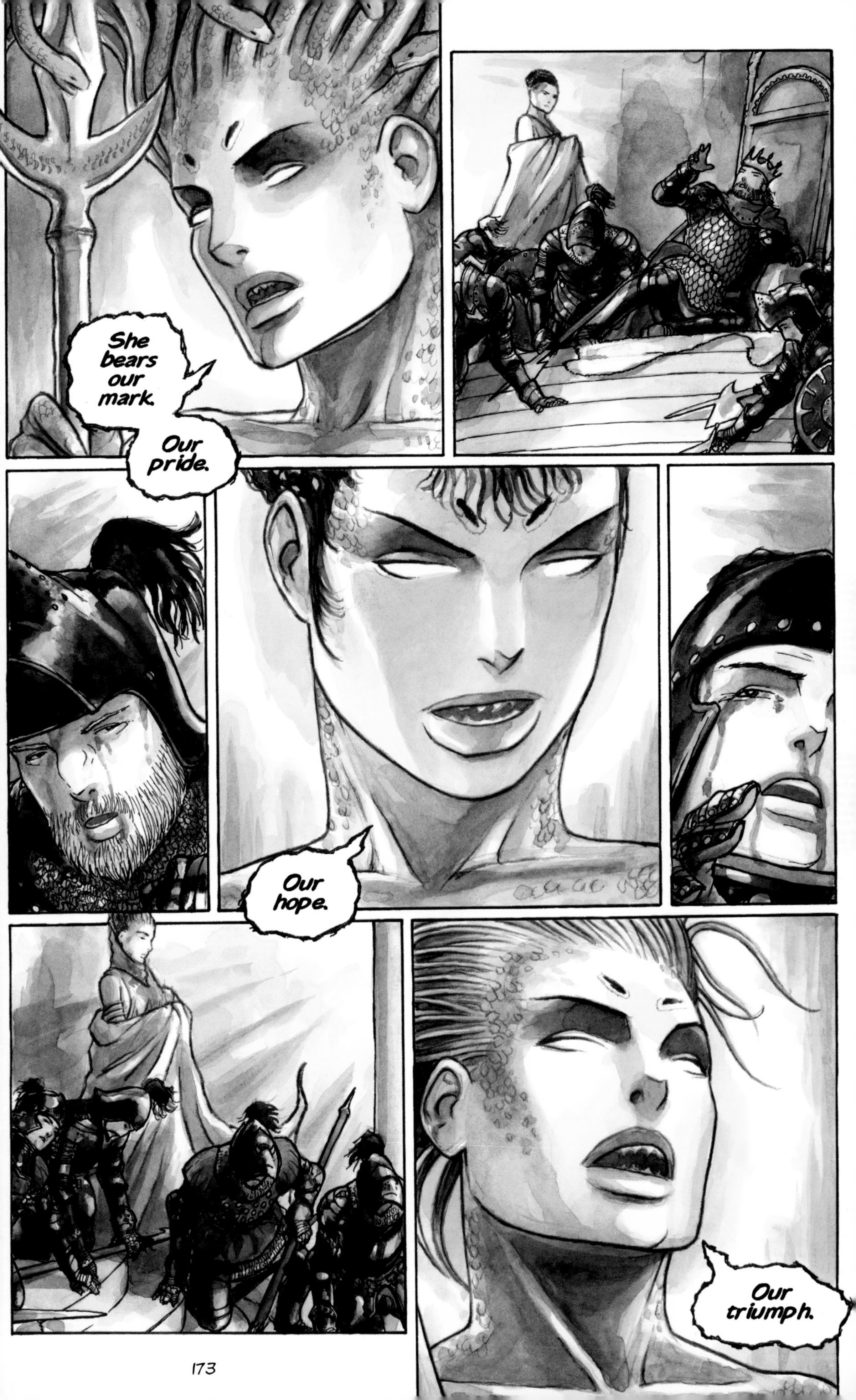
She bears our mark.
Our pride.
Our hope.
Our triumph.

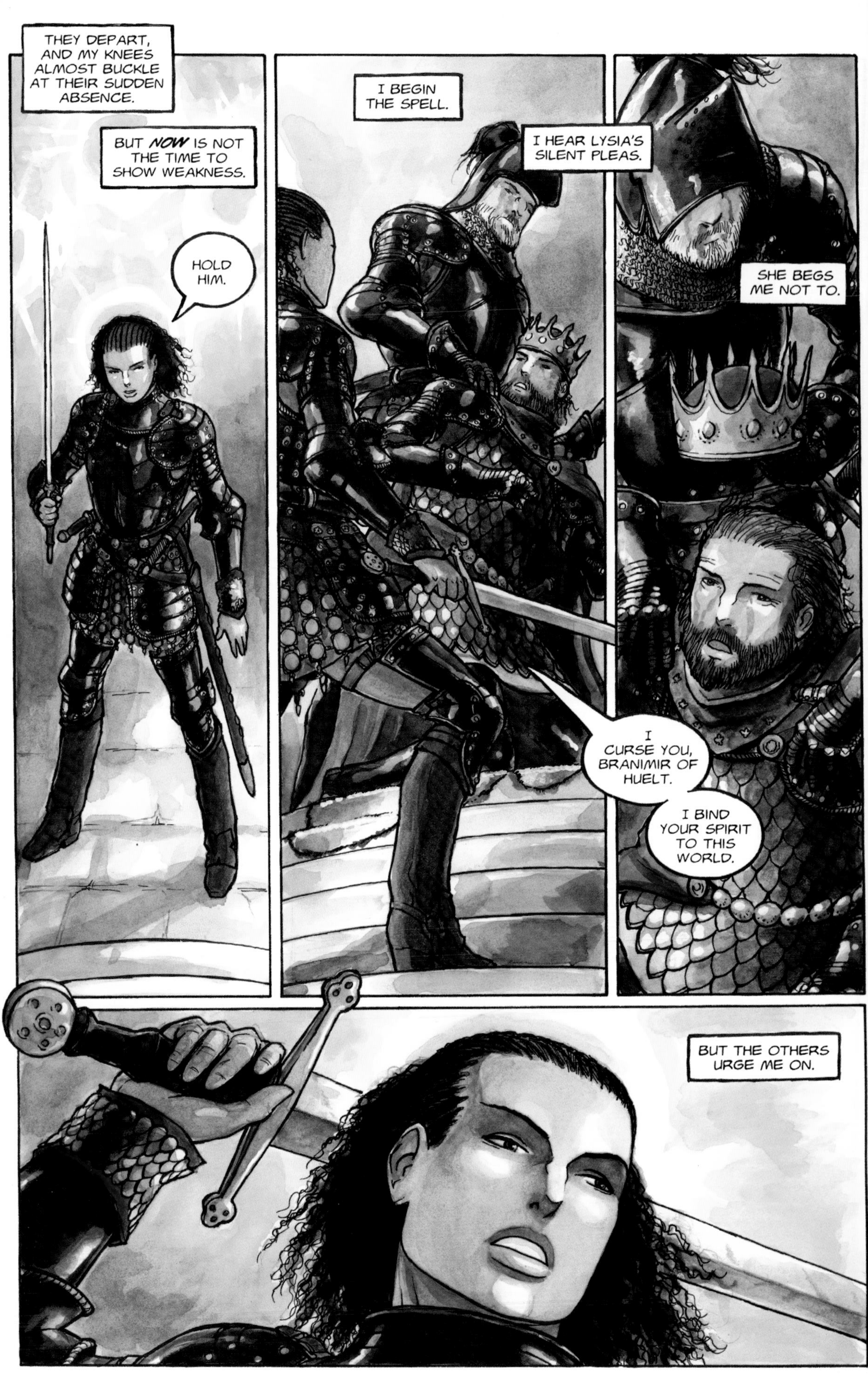
THEY DEPART, AND MY KNEES ALMOST BUCKLE AT THEIR SUDDEN ABSENCE.
BUT NOW IS NOT THE TIME TO SHOW WEAKNESS.
HOLD HIM.
I BEGIN THE SPELL.
I HEAR LYSIA'S SILENT PLEAS.
SHE BEGS ME NOT TO.
I CURSE YOU, BRANIMIR OF HUELT.
I BIND YOUR SPIRIT TO THIS WORLD.
BUT THE OTHERS URGE ME ON.

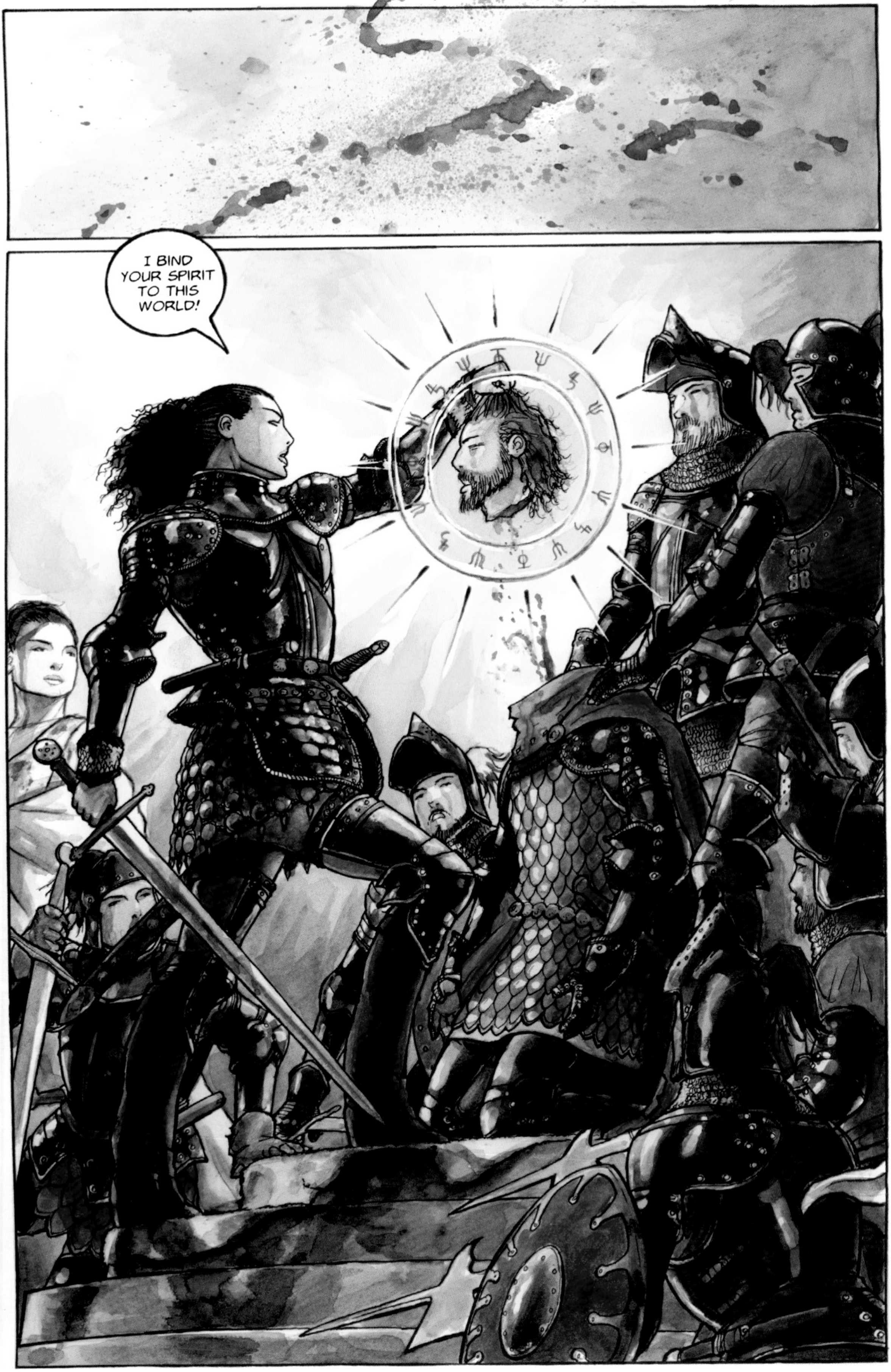
I BIND YOUR SPIRIT TO THIS WORLD!

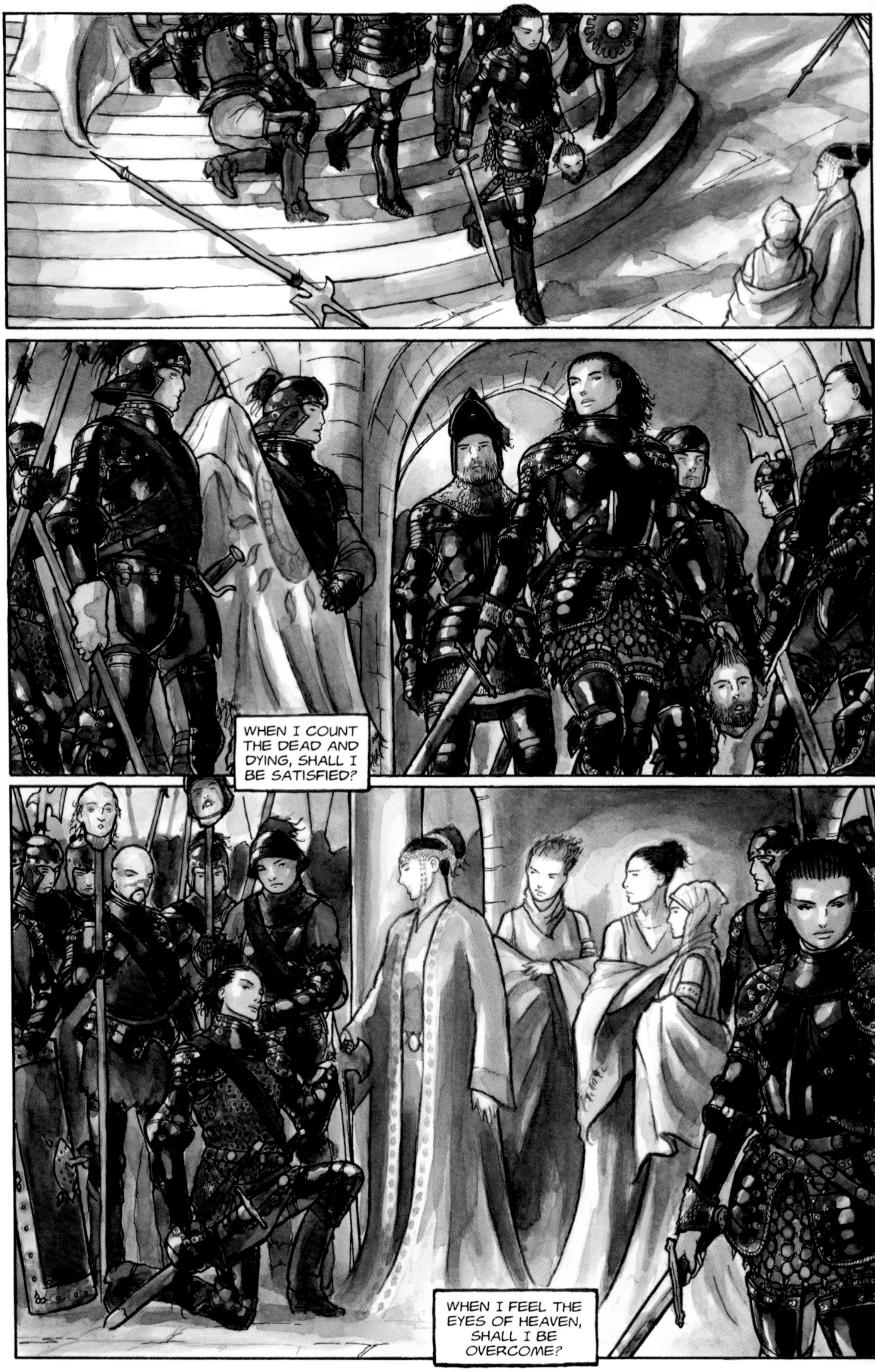
WHEN I COUNT THE DEAD AND DYING, SHALL I BE SATISFIED?
WHEN I FEEL THE EYES OF HEAVEN, SHALL I BE OVERCOME?

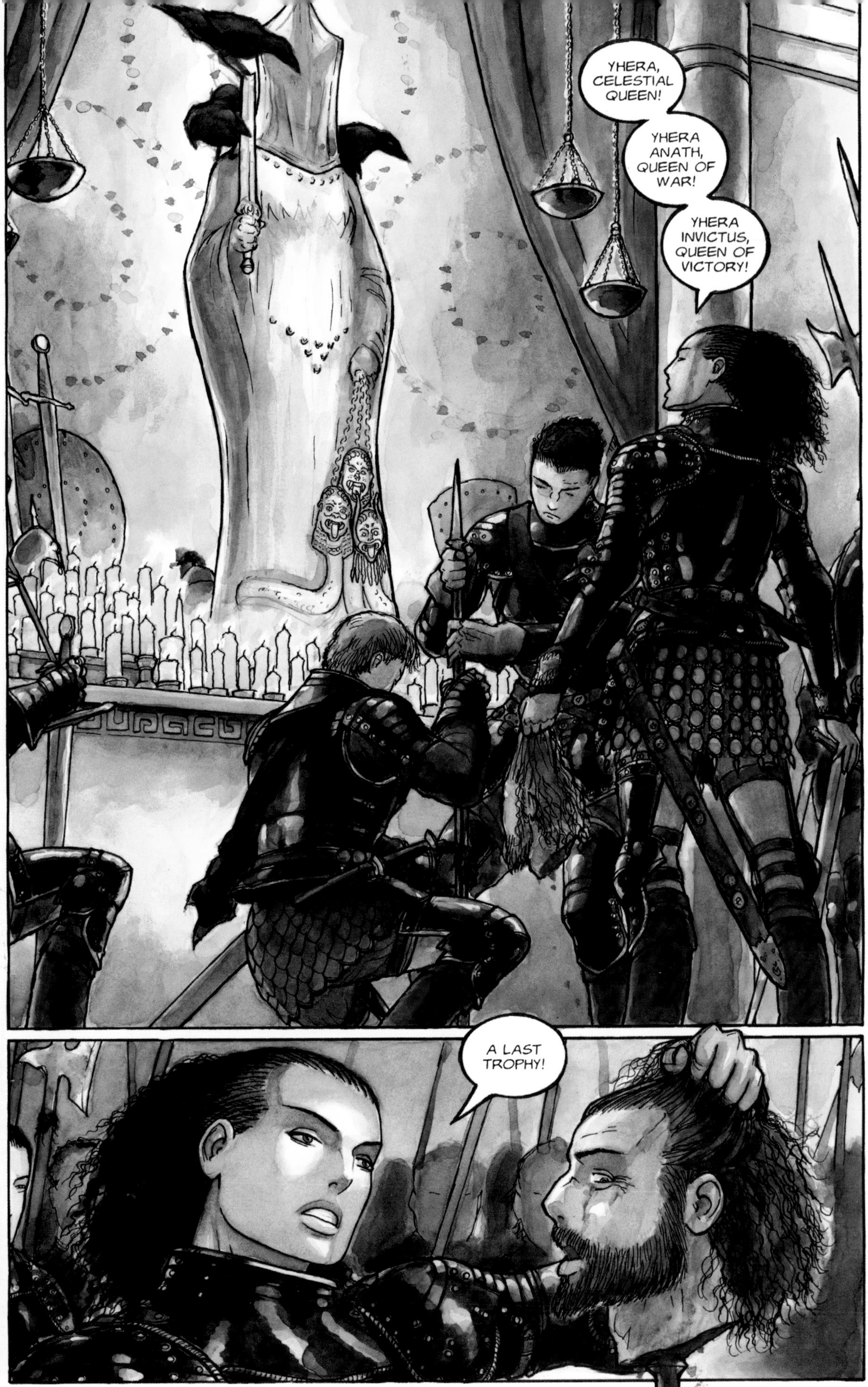
YHERA, CELESTIAL QUEEN!
YHERA ANATH, QUEEN OF WAR!
YHERA INVICTUS, QUEEN OF VICTORY!
A LAST TROPHY!

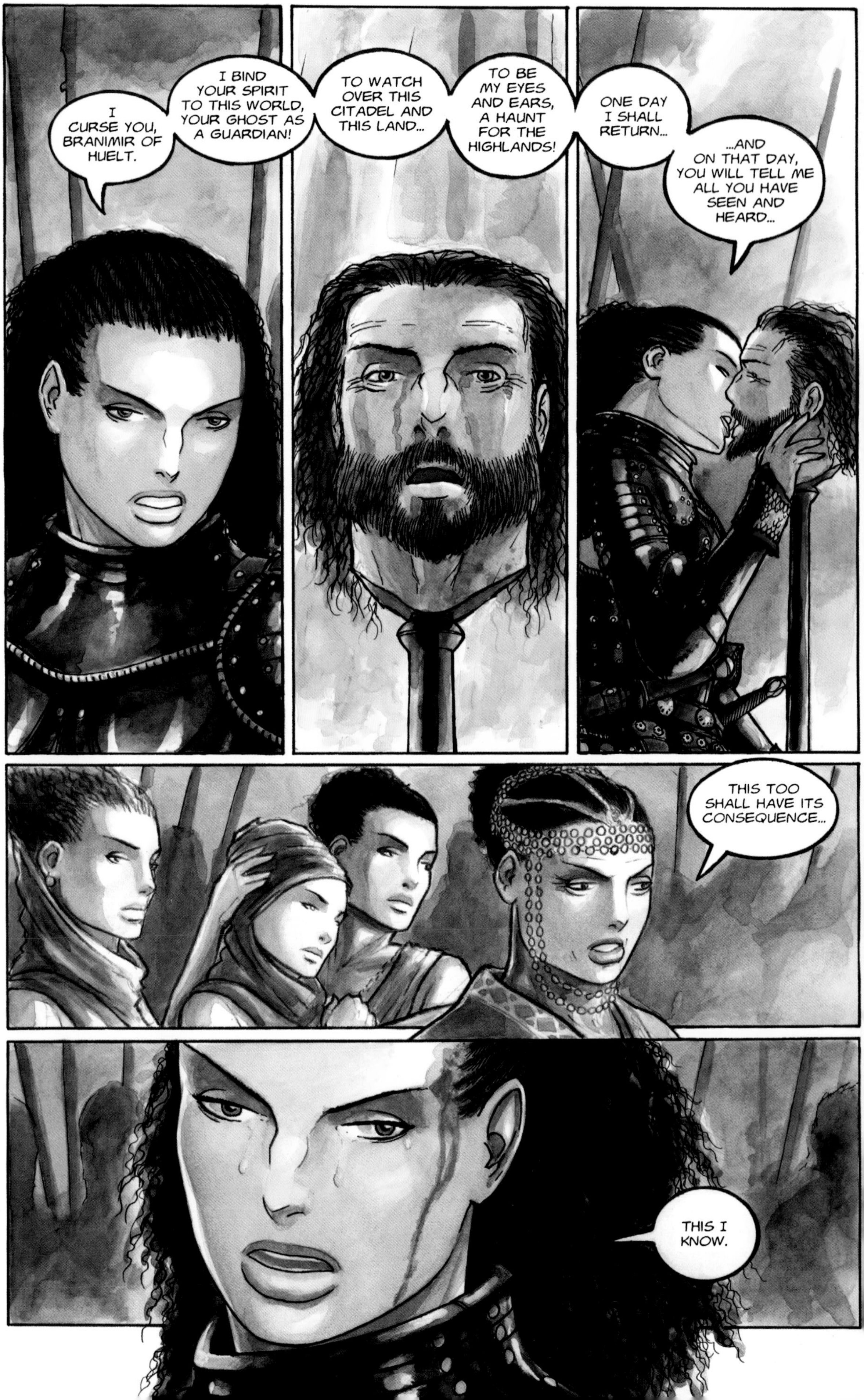
I CURSE YOU, BRANIMIR OF HUELT.
I BIND YOUR SPIRIT TO THIS WORLD, YOUR GHOST AS A GUARDIAN!
TO WATCH OVER THIS CITADEL AND THIS LAND...
TO BE MY EYES AND EARS, A HAUNT FOR THE HIGHLANDS!
ONE DAY I SHALL RETURN...
...AND ON THAT DAY, YOU WILL TELL ME ALL YOU HAVE SEEN AND HEARD...
THIS TOO SHALL HAVE ITS CONSEQUENCE...
THIS I KNOW.

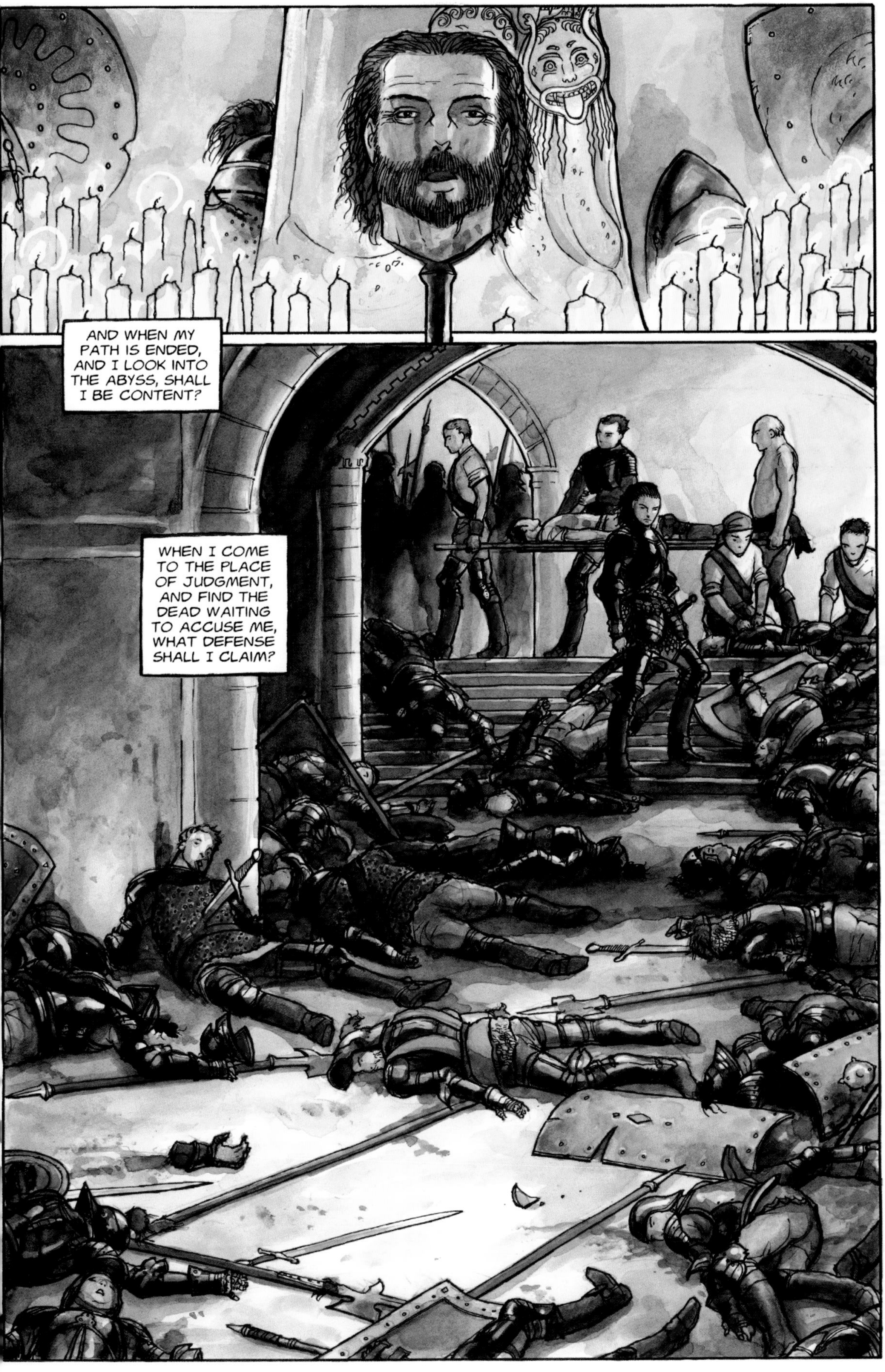
AND WHEN MY PATH IS ENDED, AND I LOOK INTO THE ABYSS, SHALL I BE CONTENT?
WHEN I COME TO THE PLACE OF JUDGMENT, AND FIND THE DEAD WAITING TO ACCUSE ME, WHAT DEFENSE SHALL I CLAIM?

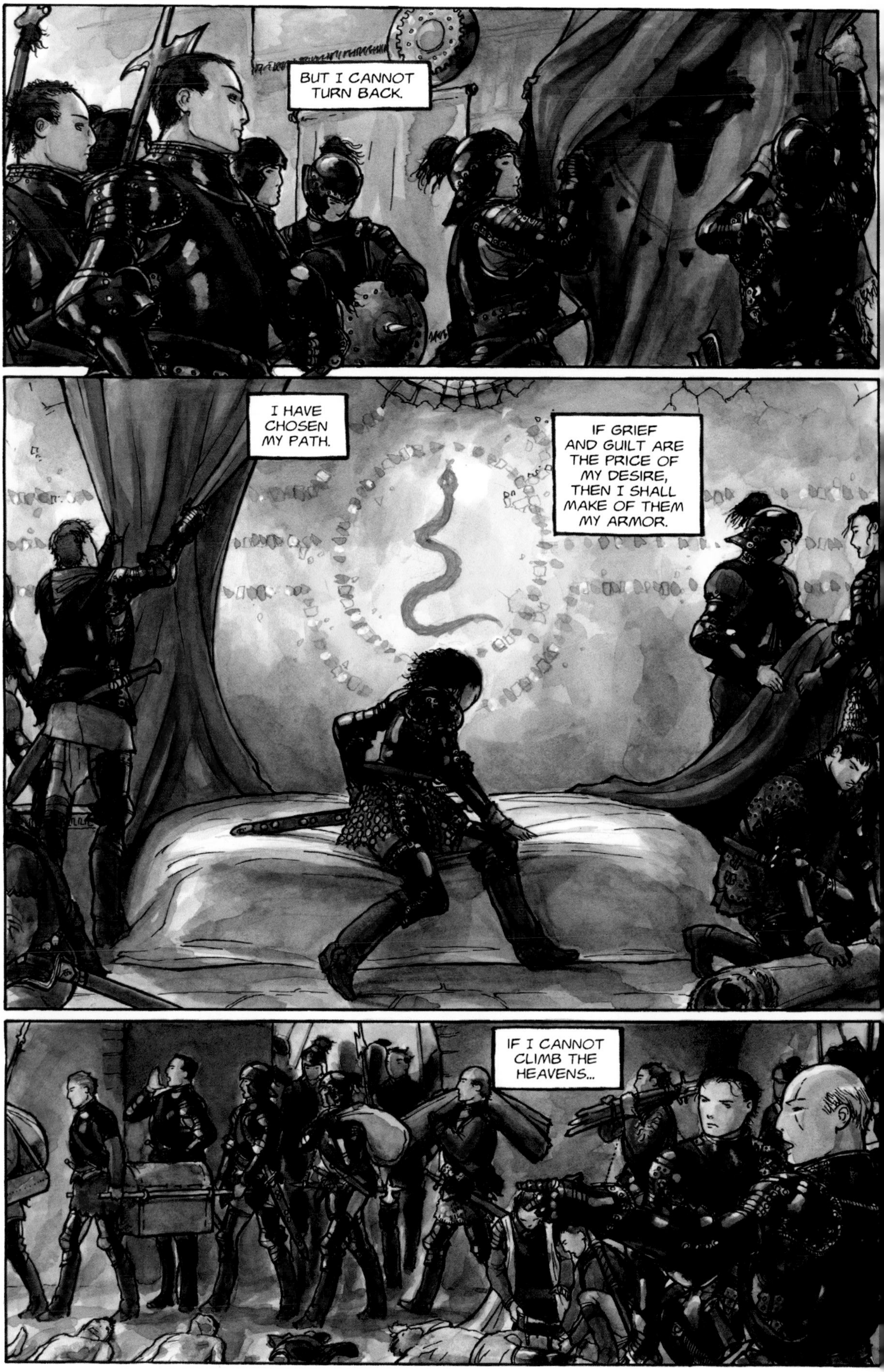
BUT I CANNOT TURN BACK.
I HAVE CHOSEN MY PATH.
IF GRIEF AND GUILT ARE THE PRICE OF MY DESIRE, THEN I SHALL MAKE OF THEM MY ARMOR.
IF I CANNOT CLIMB THE HEAVENS...

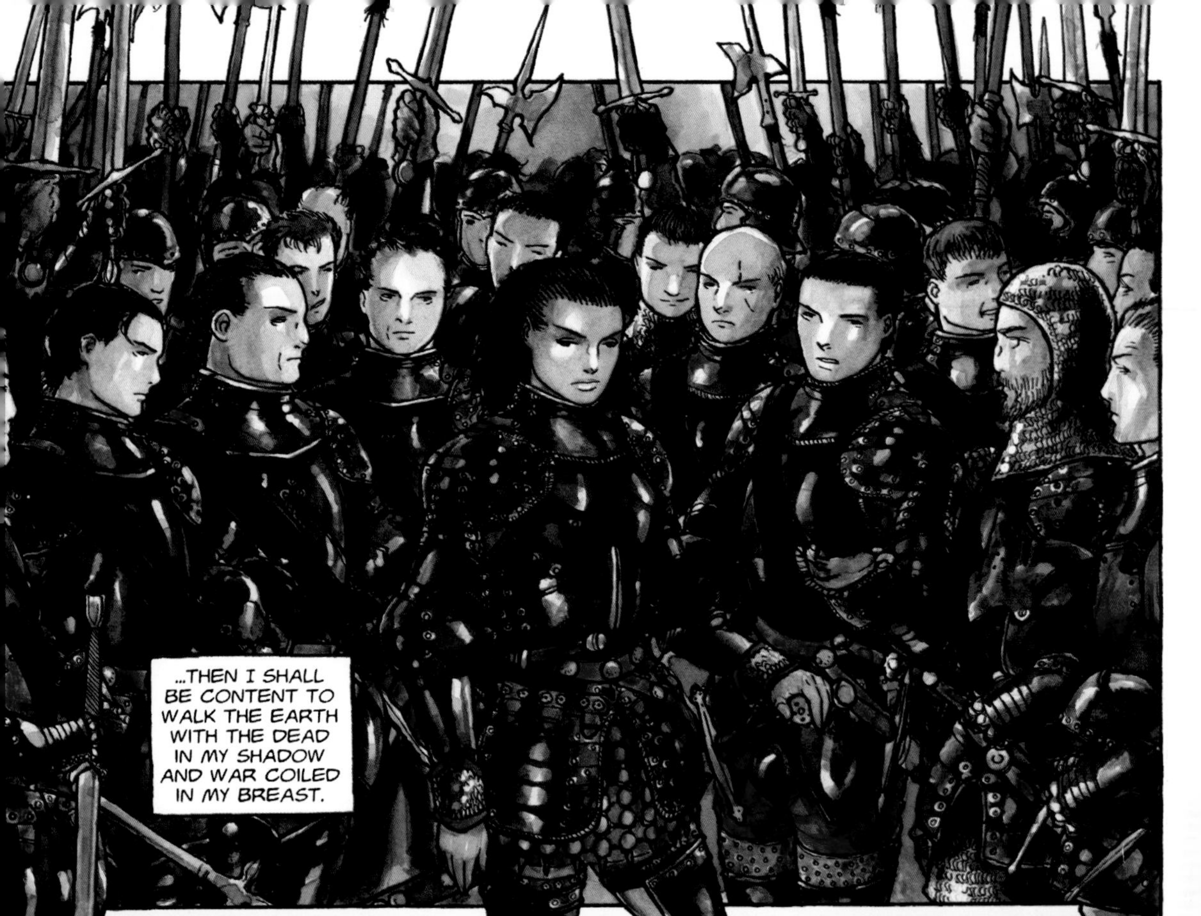
...THEN I SHALL BE CONTENT TO WALK THE EARTH WITH THE DEAD IN MY SHADOW AND WAR COILED IN MY BREAST.

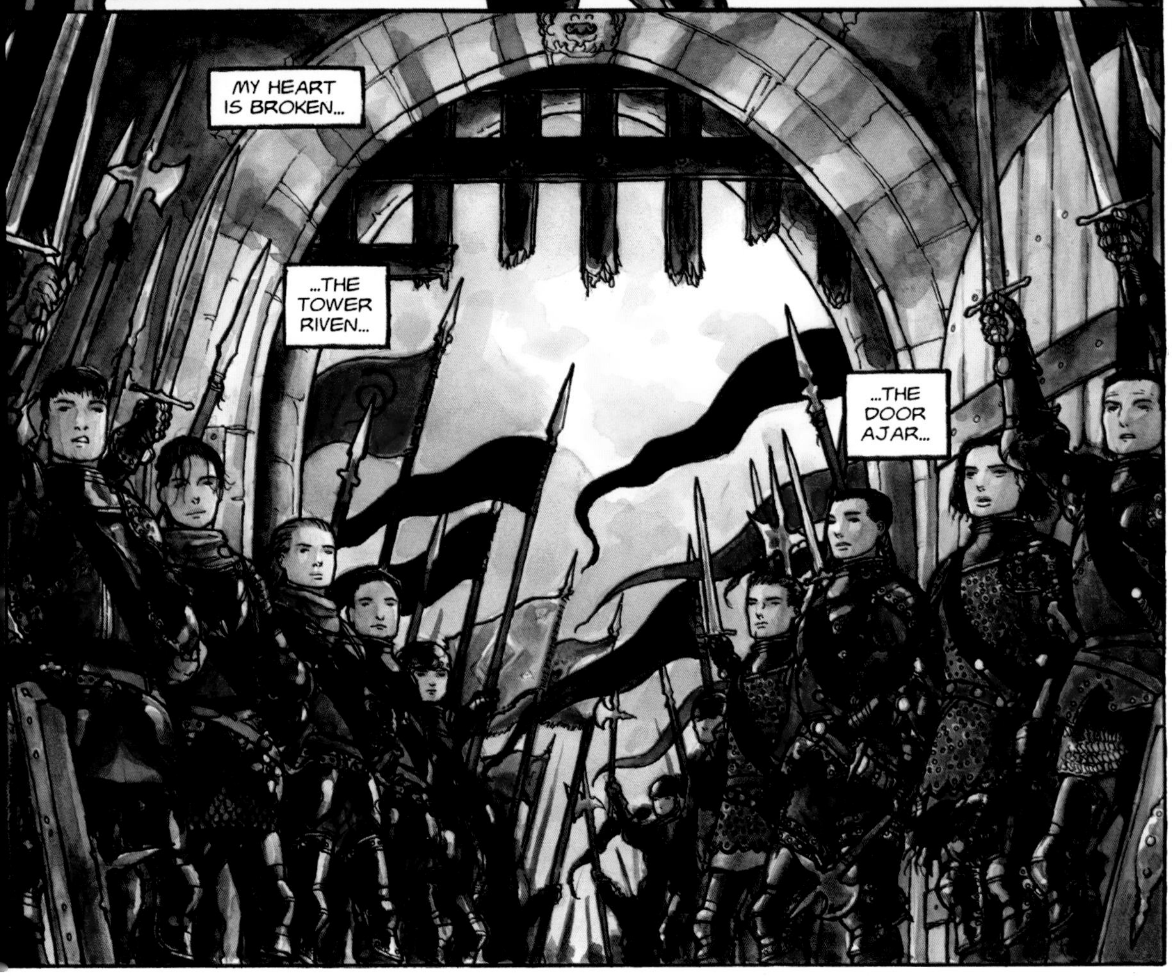
MY HEART IS BROKEN...
...THE TOWER RIVEN...
...THE DOOR AJAR...

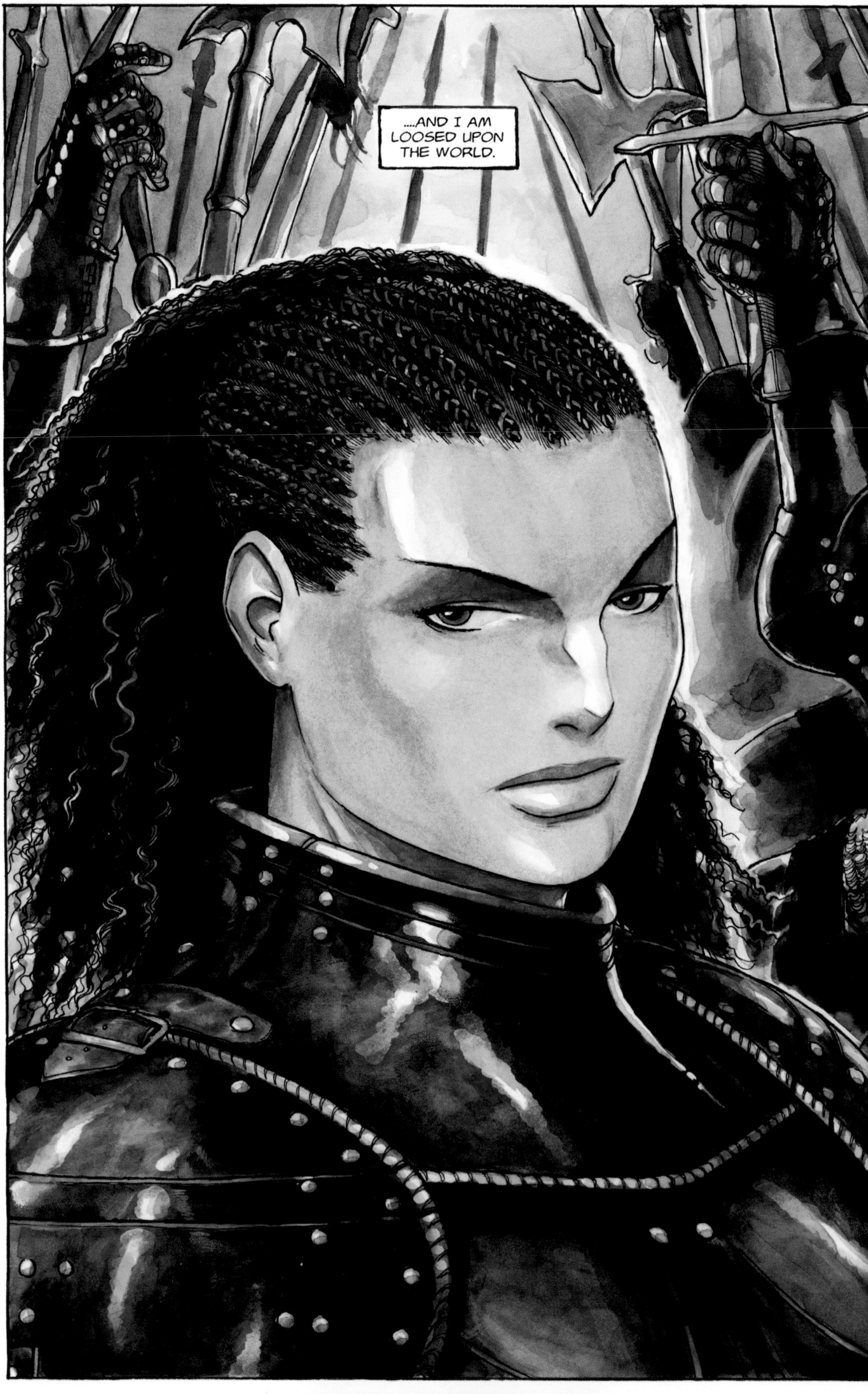
....AND I AM LOOSED UPON THE WORLD.

To Be Continued...

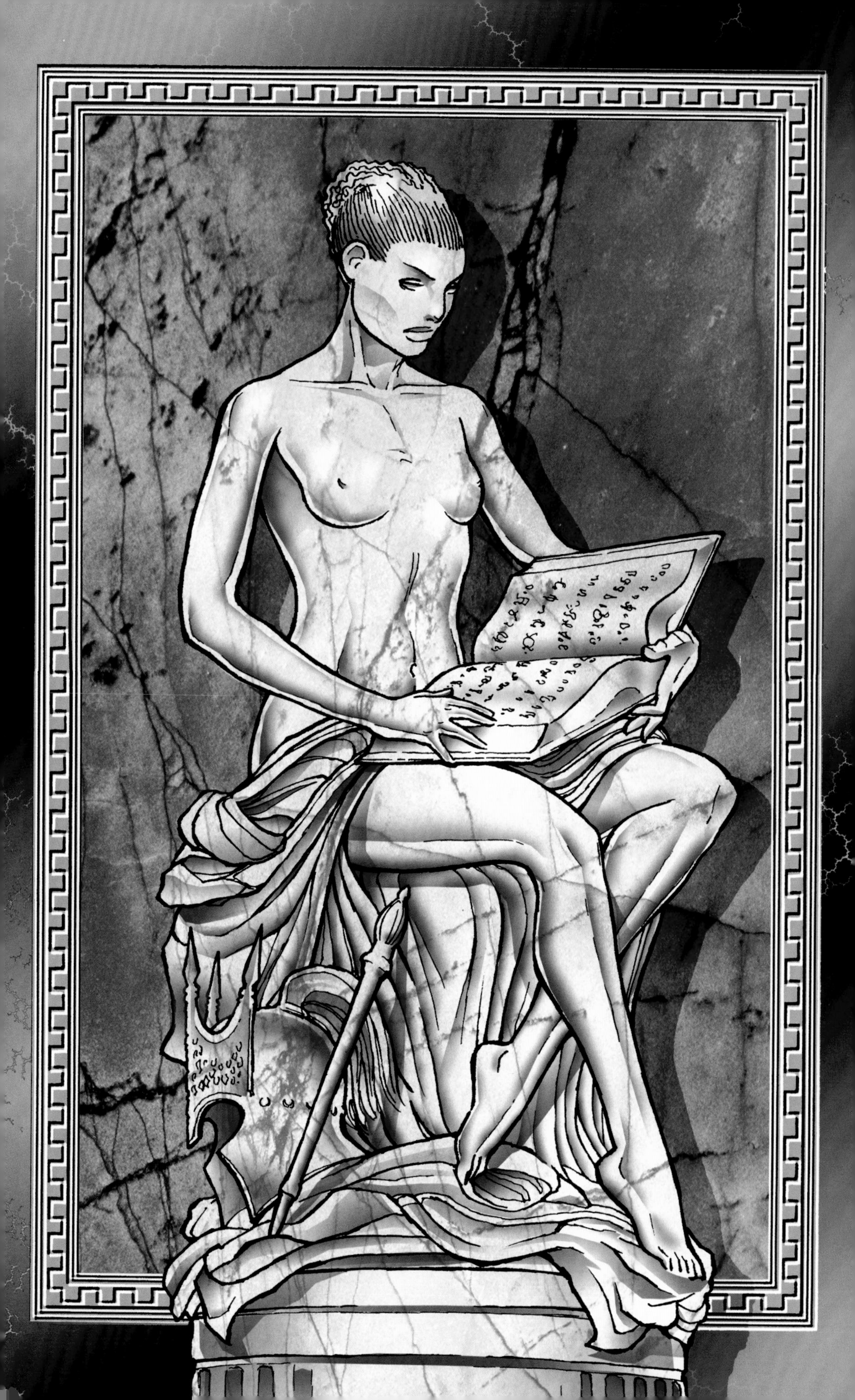

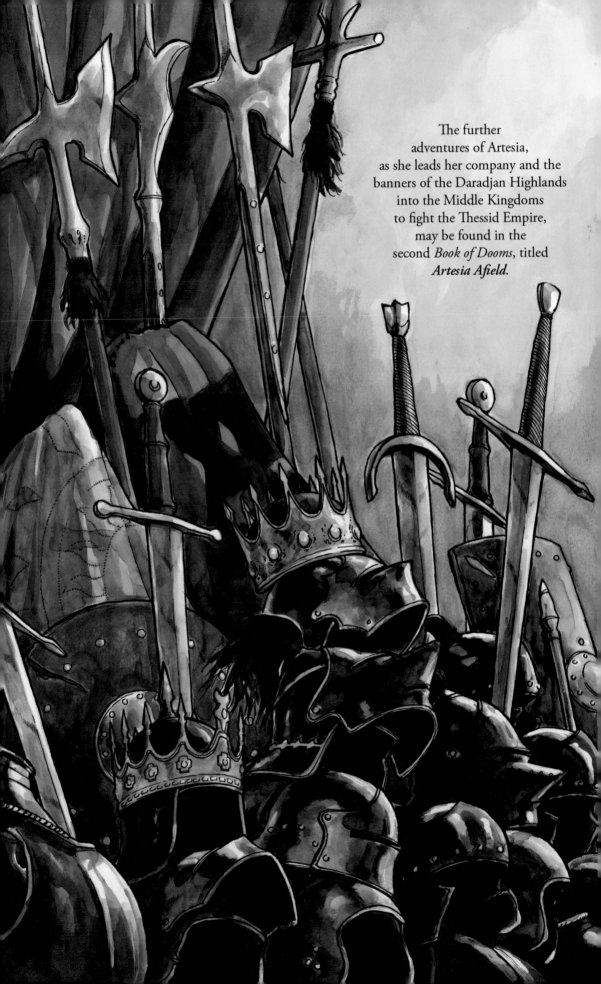

The further
adventures of Artesia,
as she leads her company and the
banners of the Daradjan Highlands
into the Middle Kingdoms
to fight the Thessid Empire,
may be found in the
second *Book of Dooms*, titled
Artesia Afield.

A GUIDE TO **THE DIVINE**

YHERA, QUEEN OF HEAVEN

Yhera is the Goddess of Night, Queen of the Waters, and one of the goddesses of the Moon. She is worshipped by the Daradjan Highlanders, amongst others, as the Creatrix, the divine origin of all that is. She is the Great Goddess of language, sovereignty, rulership, wealth, wisdom, love, fertility, protection, and war. Yhera is known by countless names and epithets, so as *Yhera Cosmopeiia* she is the divine World Spirit, as *Yhera Luna* she is the Goddess of the Moon and sister to *Adjia* and *Djara*, as *Yhera Chthonia* she is the primordial earth and sister of *Geniché*, as *Yhera Tredéa* she is the protective goddess of all life, as *Yhera Anath* she is the goddess of war, and as *Yhera Invictus* she is the undefeated Queen of Victory.

GENICHÉ, QUEEN OF THE UNDERWORLD

Geniché was once Goddess and Queen of the Earth, the giver of life, and, with her sister *Geteema*, the mother of all within *Yhera*'s creation. The Earth was once her garden, and she ruled it as a Paradise until, in a moment of grief and anger, she abandoned the world and fled into darkness. She created the Underworld and spoke the First Law, mandating that all born of her Earth must follow her into Death. The cause of her grief has been shrouded in mystery.

ADJIA LUNA, THE MOON HUNTRESS

Adjia Luna, sometimes called *Adjiana*, is one of the three goddesses of the Moon, along with her sisters *Yhera* and *Djara*. She is the goddess of transformations, of birth, growth, maturity, maternity, and death. She is also the goddess of transitional places and moments – as *the Huntress*, she is the goddess of the space between man and animal, between culture and nature; as *the Dreamer*, the giver of good visions and dreams, the goddess of the space between consciousness and unconsciousness, the Heavens and the Earth.

DJARA LUNA

Djara, sometimes known as *Urgale* or *Morgale*, is the Moon goddess of Death and Darkness; she is the queen of ghosts and dark magic, the giver of lunacy and nightmares, the keeper and revealer of secrets. Many of her dark brood serve *Geniché* as guardians and guides to the dead. She is most commonly worshipped like her twin sister *Adjia* as the goddess of crossroads, both literal and figurative, though she is often invoked in secret by anyone using curse magic or divinatory magic, as she acts as an aid to both.

GETEEMA

Sister to *Geniché*, Geteema is the monstrous Queen of the Dark Earth. She is sometimes known as *the Dragon Mother* and *the Mother of the Giants*, and her children include *Irré the Black Sun, Amaymon the Whisperer, Vani the Mountain King, Heth the Sea King*, and many others. Out of jealousy she sent many of her children to destroy ancient Ürüne Düré, and she herself consumed the body of *Agdah Cosmopeiia*, after which *Yhera* imprisoned her in the Underworld.

AGDAH COSMOPEIIA, THE YEAR-GOD

The God of the Shining Sky, Agdah Cosmopeiia is the god of the year-cycle: the growths of spring, the harvests of the fall, and the deprivations of the winter. Worshipped as *Agdah Helios*, he is the Cosmos Sun, the Sun as the source of life. As *Ammon Agdah* he is the Keeper of the Animals or the Household Protector, the guardian of herd and hearth, giver of fertility, luck, and household prosperity, and sometimes the lord of forests and wild animals, and as such is almost always portrayed as having an animal's head or horns or antlers. He taught the peoples of the world the arts of survival after *Geniché* abandoned the Earth. As *Agdah Cosmopeiia*, he was slain by *Geteema* in defense of Düréa, but later restored to Heaven.

DAEDEKAMANI

A son of *Yhera*, Daedekamani is considered by many the first magician and creator of the magical arts, especially alchemy; he created the first magical runes, and gifted them and the secrets of their use to mankind, particularly to his descendants amongst the ancient Golans. Daedekamani is a wanderer, and so is often considered a patron of travelers as well as as a guide to the dead.

SEEDRÉ, GUARDIAN OF THE DEAD

A son of *Geniché*, Seedré was the first to follow his mother to the Underworld and became the Judge of the Dead. He watches over the corporeal remains of the deceased, sends *Djara*'s daughters to guide them on their journey, and judges them when they appear before him in the Underworld. He is sometimes called *Osidred*.

ILLIKI HELIOS, THE SUN-BULL

Illiki is the Sun-Bull, a son of *Agdah Cosmopeiia* and *Ami the Morning Star*. He lived for a time in Ürüne Düré, until it was lost beneath the sea. He was the father of *Islik* the Divine King. He is worshipped in his guise as *the Spring Sun* as the bestower of progeny and the promoter and protector of vegetation and crops, an archetype of divine kingship; as *the Winter Sun,* he is the dying god with knowledge of the Underworld, cast from the Heavens by his half-brother *Irré* the Black Sun. He was later restored, either by *Yhera* or by his son *Islik*.

IRRÉ, THE BOW-BEARER

Half-brother to *Illiki Helios,* whom he usurped for a time, Irré is the Black Sun, bringer of unbearable heat, drought, and the blinding intensity of both darkness and light. Irré is the bow-bearing god of plague and fire; he is the Black Goat, a god of war, struggle, disaster, disorder, the desert and the wilderness. He is often held responsible for illness, disease, and sudden death, and so is worshipped in a propitiatory manner to prevent or reverse such events; more positively, Irré is a protector of entrances, and so is invoked in the defense of buildings and cities against fire and siege.

HATHHALLA

The Devouring Fire of the Sun, Hathhalla is worshipped as the lion-headed goddess of battle and vengeance. Hathhalla is the goddess of the Sun's righteous strength, and at *Yhera*'s behest she imprisoned *Irré* in the Underworld after he cast down her brother *Illiki Helios*. Some believe her to be a guise of *Halé*, the Goddess of Slaughter.

AMI-AND-DIEVA, THE MORNING AND EVENING STARS

Twin daughters of *Yhera*, Ami and Dieva are the Maidens of Dawn and Dusk, respectively. Ami is a goddess of love, and is associated with fertility and fraternity in their more romantic and socially approved aspects; Dieva is a goddess of sexuality, and is often associated with licentiousness and immorality. They are worshipped singly, as a pair, or as the single entity *Amadieva* the Sun Maiden (the strong sun of the morning and the weak sun of the evening).

ISLIK, THE DIVINE KING

Islik is a demigod son of *Illiki Helios*, the Sun-Bull. He was the first of the Illian Dragon Kings, the founder of the Sun Court, and ruled as King of the Earth. After his father was cast down by *Irré*, Islik was usurped by *Ishraha the Rebel*, who cast him into exile. After wandering the world for 21 years, he returned to reclaim his throne, and after imprisoning Ishraha in the Underworld, Islik ascended to the Heavens and became King of both Heaven and Earth. His worshippers believe that rather than descending to *Geniché*'s Underworld, they ascend to the Heavens to Islik's Palace after they die.

AGALL

Agall is a demigod son of *Agdah Cosmopeiia*. Equally famous for his considerable temper as for his strength and courage, he is worshipped as the First Hero. The Sacker of Cities, he fought alongside *Geteema*'s children at the destruction of Ürüne Düré. Though already old, he joined *Islik* in exile as the Black Sail, and helped him regain his throne.

THE GORGONÆ: MOGRAN, HALÉ, AND MÉDURE

The Gorgonæ are the Triple War Goddess, daughters of *Djara*, worshipped singly and in combination. Mogran, the Riot Goddess, is the goddess of terror, confusion, and dissension; Halé, the Goddess of Slaughter, is the goddess of (mindless) rage and berserker fury; and Médüre, the Cunning One, is the goddess of warlike skill and heroic valor. They are kept chained in the Underworld, and only *Yhera Anath* or her general, *Ariahavé*, may set them loose. Amongst the Palatians and the Thulamites, they are known as the *Wargarad*.

ARIAHAVÉ

Ariahavé is *Yhera*'s brightest and most rebellious daughter. Known as the Civilizer, she is the protectress of cities and citadels and their citizens and defenders; she is the patroness of civilization and its heroes. After *Geniché* abandoned the Earth, she taught the lost peoples of the world the arts of society -- agriculture, poetry, spinning, pottery, music, and mining. She is also the chief war goddess of the Palatians, her most dedicated adherents.

BRAGE THE SMITH

Brage, also called *Abrage, Bragea,* and *Braphagos* is the first smith, the creator of the arts of metal-working; he is the fire-god of hearth, kiln, and foundry. He is the creator of a rune-system that bares his name, and a series of wondrous magical artifacts, some of which may still be found throughout the known world. For a time Brage lived amongst the Düréans, and he fell in love with the Galéan Queen *Surtara.* They eloped to the Isle of Khael, and their daughters became the Oracle Queens of Khael.

ACHRE

A daughter of *Brage,* Achre rebelled rather than undergo the ritual to become an Oracle Queen of Khael and lose her eyesight. She crippled Brage, drove him into the Underworld, and escaped the Isle. In her wanderings Achre was adopted by *Ariahavé* the Civilizer, who had been her secret tutor on the Isle of Khael. Achre bound the great Dragon of the Pallithanes and, as the mother of *Archaia,* is the demi-goddess ancestress of the Palatians.

ARCHAIA

The daughter of *Achre,* tutored by *Ariahavé,* Archaia is the founder of the city of Palatia and built its Seven Gates. She bore three daughters, **Divinrhada, Vargate,** and **Baséa,** who founded the three most ancient Houses of Palatia. With her daughters, she sailed to war against *Geteema*'s children, and was slain in defense of Düréa.

THULA

A daughter of *Geniché,* Thula is the demi-goddess ancestress of the Thulamites, the snake-queen fire-stealer who took the secrets of magic and civilization from the Düréans and the Otherworld for her descendants. She and *Achre* dueled with both weapons and dance to a standoff, and according to some stories she performed magics that allowed her to bear a child by *Achre.* Thula sailed to defend Ürüne Düré against *Geteema*'s children, though she had herself weakened its defenses. She is known variously as *the Forked Tongue, the Mother of Heroes,* and *the Fire-Queen.*

DALL AND PULMA

Twin daughters of *Thula,* Dall and Pulma were placed by Thula in the care of *Ami* and *Dieva* as infants, and they made the Heavens their first home. They used their mother's stolen magics to bind horses, fought by her side at the sinking of Düréa, and later they returned to the Heavens and now appear as the Twins constellation.

CERAM

A son of *Thula,* Ceram is the demi-god ancestor of the Ceraics, exiled by his mother after he refused to aid the Düréans. He is called the Thunderer, and his father is said to have been *Illiki* the Sun-Bull, seduced by *Thula* in Ürüne Düré during her raid there, making him the half-brother of *Islik.* Ceram hunted Islik and the Four Kings in Exile when they passed through the great deserts of the Midlands.

VANI

Demi-god ancestor of the mountain-dwelling Vanimorians, Vani is the son of *Ammon Agdah* and *Geteema;* he is often depicted as having either an eagle or vulture head. He is called the Mountain King, and brings the Spring thaw. Worship of Vani spread considerably during the Vanimorian dominance of the Thessid-Golan Empire, but with the rise of the Isliklids (who champion *Irré*), his worship has largely retreated back into the mountains.

LIGRID, THE TEMPTRESS

A daughter of *Geteema,* Ligrid is the Queen of Licentiousness and Perversity; she is often thought of as either a rival to *Dieva,* Dieva's secret tutor, or even as a guise or mask of Dieva. While Dieva's sexuality

is generally socially acceptable, Ligrid is the breaker of taboos and the corruptor of flesh and spirit.

AMAYMON, THE WHISPERER

The Prince of Intrigue and Secret Power, Amaymon is the dark rule-breaker. He is the son of *Geteema* and *Daedekamani,* though his father rejected him and denied his paternity. Amaymon is now his father's greatest rival and enemy. He is the god of secret knowledge, bribery, corruption, and assassins, worshipped by those who want something for nothing. He counseled *Irré* to overthrow *Illiki Helios* and *Ishraha* to begin his rebellion against *Islik* the Divine King, thus beginning the War in Heaven.

ISHRAHA, THE REBEL ANGEL

A demigod son of *Irré,* Ishraha was a faithful general to *Islik* after his ascent to the Sun Throne of Illia and the creation of the first Sun Court. After Irré cast down *Illiki Helios,* Ishraha led a rebellion against Islik and usurped the throne, casting Islik and his loyal followers into exile. Islik later returned to claim his rightful realm, casting Ishraha into a prison in the Underworld before ascending to the Heavens.

THE DÜRÉANS

In the difficult years following Geniché's abandonment of the Earth, amongst the peoples of the world wandering lost in confusion were three tribes of the Moon's descendants. They were the *Améans,* descended of Adjia Luna and her Companions; the *Numéans,* descended of Urige, daughter of Yhera Luna; and the *Galéans,* descended of the Gorgonæ, the triple daughters of Djara Luna.

Ammon Agdah showed them how to survive in the harsh new wilderness that had overtaken Geniché's gardens, and then Ariahavé one by one brought the three tribes across the sea to an isle. Ariahavé taught them the arts of the world, and showed them many of her mother's secrets: beauty and magic, love and war, building and unbuilding. They built a great city on the isle, and planted great gardens in its palaces. The three tribes of the Moon named the isle **Ürüne Düré** (usually translated as either *Mountain of Thrones* or *Heart of Thrones*), and in time they were called the **Düréans.**

For a thousand years, Ürüne Düré was the the greatest and most beautiful city on the face of the Earth, rivaled in art and learning only by the cities of the Gola founded by **Hashuwaht** the First King, where Daedekamani taught alchemy to his worshippers and descendants. The Queens of Düréa were fabled for their wisdom, beauty, and knowledge, and men and women came from every corner of the world to learn from them. The Düréans sent explorers and colonists to found cities and build great palaces of marble and clay. Bragea the Smith came to live in Ürüne Düré, and set up his great forge there, producing wonders for the Düréan Queens. Illiki the Bull saw the city from the sky above, and came to live there for a time. He ruled from Ürüne Düré as the Bull of Heaven, and the Düréans built temples to him wherever their ships went.

After a thousand years had passed since its founding, the Queens of Ürüne Düré awoke to a bleak vision: Geteema, Goddess of the Dark Earth, had looked upon the treasures of Düréa and had been filled with jealousy, and she was sending her children to destroy it. This came to pass, and an army of demigods, giants, titans, monsters and great heroes led by a dark and fiery Dragon crossed the sea to destroy the Isle and its defenders, who were led by the Düréan heroine **Hannath Hammergreia.** A great siege began, and gods and heroes from across the world came to aid in its defense, but the Last Queens had already foreseen their fate. For thirty-one years the siege raged, but in the end Geteema consumed Agdah Cosmopeiia and drove Illiki Helios back into the Heavens, and her army swept triumphant over Ürüne Düré's great walls. The Last Queens bade Achre of Palatia and Thula of Téthédré and **Oloma** of Sabuta to take the last of the Düréans with them across the sea, out of the doomed city. The last three Queens – **Néma,** Queen of the Numéans, **Evaka,** Queen of the Galéans, and **Hercyna,** Queen of the Améans – performed a final enchantment and the Isle crumbled into the waters, taking the armies of Geteema with it. Ürüne Düré was lost forever beneath the sea, and the Düréans were scattered into the world.

A MYTH OF
THE BLACK HUNTER

Before the dawn of history, one amongst the Race of Men commited a grievous crime, and Geniché abandoned the Earth and withdrew into the Underworld. Different cultures have different myths of the Crime that ended the Age of the Gods, but most believe it was Theft, Murder, or Rape: something that was taken, rather than received as a gift. The unknown perpetrator was cursed by Geniché, Yhera, and Hathhalla with horns as a mark of his crime, and the Horned Man has been a popular scapegoat ever since. Bereft of the presence of Geniché, the Earth, once a Paradise, became a dangerous and desolate wilderness, and the creatures of the world wandered lost in confusion.

 Some amongst Geniché's children chose to follow her into the Underworld. The first was her son **Seedré**, also called Osidred, who became the Judge of the Dead, appointed by his mother to greet the dead at the place of their judgment and listen to the accounts of their accusers, even as he awaited the arrival of the Horned Man. Many of the spirits of the Earth followed after him, as did beasts great and small, and parts of the world were no longer fertile. And many of Djara's dark brood followed her, dark-hearted spirits who became Death Guides and furies, nightmares and carrion eaters, and teemed in the darkness of the Underworld.

Some of Geniché's children stayed behind to help the peoples of the world in their struggle to survive their harsh new environs. Others stayed behind to hurt them, blaming them for their mother's decision to abandon the Earth. One such was her youngest son, who grew angry that the world had driven his mother into exile. His brother, Ammon Agdah, had forgiven the Race of Men, and was now helping the lost peoples of the world to survive, but Geniché's youngest could not forgive them. He looked up into the sky, and saw Hathhalla sharpening her great axe, and he prayed to her for guidance. She whispered in his ear, and he fashioned a huge barbed spear out of an ancient oak and summoned a great steed, and he began to hunt across the Earth.

Wherever he went, he would fall upon the lost peoples of the Earth with a great roar, taking the still-living heads of those he speared as trophies to dangle from hooks, and casting a compulsion upon others to make him join his vengeful quest. In time his first name was forgotten, and he came to be called **the Black Hunter**, and his mad entourage was called **the Wild Hunt**, and they were a plague upon a desolate world.

The Wild Hunt raged across the Earth for long centuries, and one day the Black Hunter spied three tribes gathering upon an isle, and sought to hunt there. The Wild Hunt jumped the Silver Scale Sea and landed upon the shores of Ürüne Düré, but the goddess Ariahavé leapt from the skies and drove them back across the sea, barring them from returning. Ariahavé taught the way to defeat the Black Hunter to the Düréans. They in turn taught Achre and Thula, Ceram and Oloma, King Hashuwaht and Agall together, Cewert, Surep; in time, a thousand heroes from across the world learned the way to defeat the Black Hunter and one by one they did so, until he roared only in the dark places of the Earth where even heroes rarely went. Finally the Düréan Queen **Hannath Hammergreia** sought him out, and though he killed her once, she returned from the dead as was her wont and the tables were turned, and the Black Hunter became the hunted. She caught him and banished him to the Underworld.

When Geniché found her youngest son finally returned to her, she summoned Hathhalla from the Heavens, and sent Hathhalla as an emissary to her sister Yhera, to ask that her son be allowed one night of the year to hunt upon the world. Hathhalla brought her request to the Queen of Heaven, and after long thought Yhera relented and commanded that the Black Hunter be loosed upon the world the night before the Day of the Law, which marked the coming of Death, to hunt those that strayed from shelter.

So now once a year, at the beginning of winter, the Wild Hunt rides and the peoples of the world must seek shelter: behind door or gate, in house or city (protected by *Ammon Agdah* and *Ariahavé*); nearby blessed hearthstone or campfire (protected by *Ammon Agdah, Yhera Parage,* or *Ariahavé Parage*); or within a magic warding. All others are fair game for the Hunt.

 But sometimes the Wild Hunt breaks loose from the Underworld, and rides out unannounced into the world.

A YEAR OF
THIRTEEN MOONS

Three primary calendrical systems are used throughout the Known World. The oldest is the Düréan Lunar Calendar, which divides the year into a cycle of thirteen full moons that appear over the course of 364 days. Each moon cycle lasts 28 days, and is divided into four seven-day weeks. The Düréans marked the first day of the year on the anniversary of the return of Ami and Dieva from the Underworld, announcing the return of Helios. Traditionally, the months of the year are **First Moon** (*Arisa-luna*), **Spring Moon** (*Nisa-luna*), **Axe Moon** (*Labra-luna*), **Green Moon** (*Tamaz-luna*), **Bull Moon** (*Auros-luna*), **Twin Moon** (*Diana-luna*), **Scarab Moon** (*Rab-luna*), **Harvest Moon** (*Elul-luna*), **Red Moon** (*Marina-luna*), **Judgment Moon** (*Hannan-luna*), **Scorpion Moon** (*Urgala-luna*), **Twilight Moon** (*Daradana-luna*), and **Last Moon** (*Annua-Luna*).

The Düréan Lunar Calendar is essentially the official Festival Calendar of the Cult of Yhera, and is still used, sometimes with different names, in Khael, Palatia and its territories, by the Ceraic and Oceraic nomads of the Midlands, and in parts of the Far West and Far North. The Düréans dated their calendar from the founding of Ürüne Düré, and according to the scribes of Khael the current Lunar year is 2616 (usually marked with a 'd' to indicate the Düréan Calendar, as in d2616). The Palatians begin the dating of years from the founding of the City of Palatia Archaia, and mark their dates with a 'p,' so for them the current year is p1640.

Almost as old as the Düréan Lunar Calendar is the Golan Celestial Calendar, based upon the cycle of the Star Signs. The appearance of a new Sign in the Heavens marks the beginning of a new month. The Signs of the Celestial Calendar are **The Ram** (*Nisanu*), **The Bull** (*Ayargu*), **The Sky Twins** (*Hasiggisah*), **The Scarab** (*Dam'uzu*), **The Sun Lion** (*Lebargu*), **The Maiden** (*Urigu*), **The Scales** (*Tashru*), **The Sphinx** (*Djarahsvan*), **The Archer** (*Hanun'at*), **The Dragon** (*Tiamet*), **The Star-Child** (*Shebetae*), and **The Serpent** (*Adaral*).

The Celestial Calendar is the official secular calendar of the Thessid-Golan Empire and the neighboring Queendom of Amora-and-Meretia, though they both use the Imperial Avellan Calendar as the official Divine King liturgical calendar. The dating of Celestial years began with the institutionalization of the calendar by King Hashuwaht, and generally mark the current date as c2432 (with a 'c' to indicate the Celestial Calendar). Official Imperial annals in Thessid-Gola are generally dated from the ascent of Akkalion to the Emperor's throne, 446 years ago, though some in the Empire insist on dating recent years from when he fell into the Gray Dream, 406 years ago.

 The third primary calendar is the Imperial Avellan Calendar, created and instituted by the Court of Dauban Hess, the Golden Emperor (at the time the Court was located in Avella, in Thessidia). The year begins on the anniversary of the Divine King's return to Illia from exile, when Islik emerged from his ordeals in the Underworld to regain his throne (corresponding to the 4th day of the First Moon in the Düréan Lunar calendar). The year is divided into twelve months based upon the anniversaries of various heroic deeds performed by the Divine King: ten months to mark His Ten Victories (**Telesium, Sirenium, Myradéum, Arathéum, Ceranum, Midéadad, Édorum, Hemodium, Mortium** and **Illianum**), one month to mark his reign on earth (**Emperium**), and one month to mark his ascension to the Heavens (**Ascensium**). The Imperial Avellan Calendar functions as the official liturgical calendar of Divine King worship.

The Imperial Avellan Calendar is also the official secular calendar throughout Sun Court Divine King lands, including the Hemapoline League of Cities (comprising the Isle of Illia, where the Sun Court is located, and the Hemispian Peninsula), the Middle Kingdoms, and amongst the priestly hierarchy of the Phoenix Court of the Thessid-Golan Empire. The calendar was backdated from the time of Dauban Hess to the ascension of Islik the Divine King into Heaven. The current year (marked with an 'i' to indicate the Imperial Avellan Calendar) is generally recorded as i1472.

 In the Highlands of Daradja, both the Lunar Calendar and the Imperial Avellan Calendar of the Middle Kingdoms are used, as is the Avellan Year, currently i1472.

The events of this book take place beginning on the 26th day of Green Moon.

DRAGON KINGS & EMPERORS

Islik was born a half-mortal, the demigod son of *Illiki Helios,* the Sun-Bull, and *Herrata* the Blessed, a daughter of the line of the ancient hero *Myrcalion,* was born on the isle of Illia, sometimes called the Isle of the Sun, standing as it does between the Silver Scale Sea and the great Golden Sea of the East. He ascended to the throne of Illia and established his Sun Court soon after reaching manhood. As King of Illia he warred against the barbarian warlords of the Hemispian Peninsula, and eventually brought those lands under his control. Tributes were sent to him from the Gola and Galia, and he was then called for the first time King of the Earth.

Islik was overthrown by *Ishraha,* the Rebel Angel, who usurped his throne and cast him into exile. For 21 years, Islik wandered the world with *Agall*, *Coromat* of Vanimoria, and *Jala* of Samarappa as the four **Kings in Exile**, traveling beyond the Midlands and finally even into the Underworld. He performed Ten Victories during his journeys to prove his right to the throne, the last of which was casting Ishraha into Hell. After siring many sons he ascended into the Heavens into a new palace of his own making. There Islik became the Divine King of both Heaven and Earth, at least according to his followers.

His descendants and followers held near-divine power in his name throughout Illia and Hemispia. The greatest of them were called **Dragon Kings** in the manner of days of old, for they seemed to have in them the powers of the ancient followers of **Cewert**, the great hero of Hemispia, but without having to kill dragons and giants to gain their powers as Cewert had taught; such power was simply their birthright as the heirs of Islik.

DAUBAN HESS

In time, however, the Dragon Kings of Illia and Hemispia fell to squabbling, and war rent the land until **Dauban Hess**, a descendant of Islik, unified them again under his own banner and was hailed as the Conqueror King. Some said that Islik had come down from Heaven to sire Dauban Hess himself, so great was his power.

Dauban Hess consolidated Illia and Hemispia, and then struck out into the world. He conquered Amora with ease, and then the ancient courts of the Gola welcomed him with open arms, and he established his court at the city of Seker. There he was told of **Nymarga the Tyrant,** the great lord of Thessidia, by rumor a son of Ishraha. Nymarga had taken power in the West, and was being hailed as the Worldly Tyrant.

Divine King seers proclaimed Nymarga a son of Ishraha and Ligrid, the Temptress Queen. So in i221 Dauban Hess led his armies out of the Gola into Thessidia, and began a great war, the war between the Conqueror King and the Worldly Tyrant. Twenty years passed in bloody conflict on a scale not seen since the War in Heaven, until Dauban Hess slew Nymarga in Tir-en-Tiel and took his crown. Nymarga's body was cursed by priests of the Divine King and entombed in salt.

Dauban Hess conquered Thessidia and Vanimoria, far into the West to Metea and Samarappa and the lands of the Ghal, where he drove out the **Isliklidae,** False Pretenders who claimed descent from Islik as he did, before returning to conquer Dania. He received tribute from Khael, and in all the known world only a minor city-state, Palatia, refused to recognize him as the Golden Emperor of the World.

Dauban Hess moved the Sun Throne of Illia to Millene and established his own political court in Avella, capital of Thessidia, ruling over the largest empire in history. He tired of court life, however, and soon left on a great expedition to the East to find the Dawn, where Helios the Sun rises each day. He was never heard from again.

THE WORM KINGS

Before sailing into the Golden Sea, Dauban Hess had appointed a series of great Kings who held power over his territories, each given a Dragon Throne as a sign of their authority in his name. As time passed without word from the Emperor, some of the Kings declared themselves powers in their own right, and fell into squabbling. After divinations seemed to reveal the death of Dauban Hess, a split emerged between the generals appointed by Dauban Hess and the Dragon Kings of Illia, Hemispia and Dania, who held power as hereditary monarchs of the ancient Sun Court. None could hold the Golden Empire together on their own, and soon the Empire broke into many pieces, ruled by **the Successor Kings.**

Worship of the Divine King suffered a schism. In the east and in Dania, where Dauban Hess had kept Dragon Kings in power, the principle of inherited kingship was championed by those who reinstated **the Sun Court** in Illia. In the south and west, the Successor Kings of Thessid-Gola proclaimed their allegiance to **the Phoenix Court** at Millene in response, and asserted non-hereditary claims on kingship, being for the most part generals appointed to power.

As it was once the Imperial Court of Dauban Hess, the Phoenix Court at first outshone the Sun Court, but in time, the Thessid-Golan Kings fell prey to the subtle influence of magic inherited from Nymarga's rule in Millene. Since rule by appointment could not guarantee the lasting legacy of an inheritance passed on to descendants after death, some of the rulers of the Phoenix Court grew increasingly interested in enchantments to extend their lives. The use of alchemy and sorcery increased, as did the worship of dark Forbidden Gods amongst the Successor Kings of the Phoenix Court. They became twisted and corrupt shadows of their former selves, and their bodies rotted but did not die, and they were called **the Worm Kings.** They waged war against the Sun Court, warring against the Dragon Kings, Amora, Khael, and Palatia, even as rebellion swept Thessid-Gola.

A Worm King fleet sacked the Oracle City, on Khael, and in so doing brought about their doom. They were cursed by the Oracle Queen with her dying breath, and their capital of Millene disappeared in a volcanic maelstrom, taking with it the original Sun Throne and plunging the world into the *Winter Century.*

After the destruction of Millene, Thessid-Gola disintegrated. Vanimoria and the Gola, now called Grand Sekeret, went their separate ways. New kings and priests came to power in Thessidia, and they led the great purge of Worm King influence from the new Phoenix Court. They rejected the title of King, and called themselves *Emirs,* ruling by appointment in the Phoenix Court tradition. Throughout the world, the last of the Worm Kings were hunted to their deaths, though the hunt took centuries. The last known Worm King, **Githwaine**, was found disguised in Uthed Dania, and there **Erlwulf**, called by some the last true Dragon King, was slain in its pursuit. Githwaine was unmasked and destroyed, and Uthed Dania was blighted and became *Lost Uthedmael.*

THE LION EMPEROR

In time a new power rose in Thessidia, the young emir **Akkalion**, scion of a princely house untainted by a Worm King past. A great warlord, he led his armies into Grand Sekeret, but after conquering the land he submitted himself to the testing of the Golan Great Schools, and so was hailed as the Thessid-Golan Emperor. He reconstituted the Phoenix Court in Sekeret, and then turned west and conquered Vanimoria, Metea and Ramoristan, intent on reestablishing the Golden Empire of Dauban Hess.

He was unable to conquer Samarappa from the Isliklids, who had returned to rule the West, and Akkalion returned from his conquests having learned humility. He conquered Amora and received tribute from the Sun Court cities of Illia and Hemispia. He turned then to the land of Dania, now called the Four Kingdoms of Dania, Auria, Atallica, and Maece. He landed with a great fleet in Maece, and there was met by the **Watchtower Kings** of the coast, backed by inland allies. The night before their battle Akkalion was overcome by a strange dream from which he did not awake, and in the morning Irré, the Black Sun, rose in the sky; bereft of their Emperor, the demoralized Thessid army was driven into the sea.

The Black Day Battle marked the end of the Empire's expansion. Akkalion was taken back to his capital, Avella, but his mind remained trapped in his dream. The Sun Court lands of Illia-and-Hemispia, organized now into the Hemapoline League of Cities, ceased their tributes, and the Queens of Amora, backed by the upstart city-state of Palatia, threw out their Thessid overlords. Power in the Empire fell first to the Phoenix Court and the priests of the Emperor's own cult, but eventually a Sultan was appointed to speak in the Emperor's stead and lead the Imperial emirs.

TALES OF
THE WITCH-QUEEN

Of the three goddesses of the Moon, the most feared is *Djara Luna*, the goddess of the waning and Dark Moon, when the Moon disappears from the Heavens and travels the distant and secret paths of the Otherworld and the Underworld. When the Moon is dark, the door between the worlds is open and may be passed through by those who know the way, and by the unwary. Since before time Djara has walked the paths of darkness, and she is said to have known Death even before Geniché first pronounced her Law. Djara built the Underworld from her dreams and held its throne in readiness until Geniché descended to become Queen of Death as she had been Queen of Life.

Despite her dark and secret ways – or perhaps because of them – Djara has a great unnumbered brood, both by unnamed consorts and by her own magics. Her children include Sleep and Doom, who serve Yhera herself, and Din and Discord, who serve the Gorgonæ. Angels of death and dooms, nightmares, furies, death guides and guardians, haunts and other frightening spirits – almost all of the inhabitants of the dark and secret parts of the Underworld and the Heavens are her children, according to the *Corpus Divinica Düréa*, the first codified book of stories about the gods.

Of her children, all but four were born into the Otherworld and claim the Otherworld as their proper domain. Her four children born in the worldly sphere were four daughters: **Annaft**, who dwells on an isle in the Golden Sea where Ami the Morning Star first comes to call each day; **Hemwayne**, also called the Sand Queen, who dwells in an oasis of the Ulik Desert and leaves no footprints in the dunes; **Memyra**, who dwells on a wooded isle of the Panoch Sea, north even of Palatia; and **Urgrayne**, who dwells upon a lofty crag in the Harath Éduin mountains.

Urgrayne has haunted the world since before human memory. Though she is called *the Witch-Queen of the Harath Eduins* and makes her residence in those mountains by all report, folktales tell of her presence throughout the Midland steppes and deserts, the mountains of Metea and Vanimoria (where she is called *Geteema's midwife*), and even into the distant Kessite kingdoms (where she is called *the Seer of Kings*). Amongst the Isliklids, who migrated from Kessite lands in the Far West to the Dain Eduins, fighting and then joining the Thessid Empire along the way, she is reportedly called *the Pathfinder*.

Legends say that Urgrayne and her sisters were active in the courts of Ürüne Düré. In more recent times Urgrayne has been rarely seen, and is more often spoken of in folktales and popular stories in which she is encountered at night by travelers on the road. According to these folktales, Urgrayne appears riding an ornamented sled drawn by a team of black horses, accompanied by armed and armored knights who never speak or show their faces. Some tales say that her bodyguards are merely hollow suits of armor that have been enchanted with the semblance of life; other tales claim that her bodyguards are men who have gazed upon her face and form and become enchanted by the sight of her, leaving their former lives to exist solely on the sustenance of her presence. Several ballads based on such tales – *the Erl and the Witch Queen, the Knight of Thorns and the Witch Queen,* and the more recent (and some say, historical) *Lord Malcolm and the Witch Queen* – are popular throughout the region.

Amongst the Highland Clans, by both legend and local report, are self-proclaimed members of **the Witch's Host**, who claim some connection to Urgrayne; they claim her blessing is a mark of fortune for their chieftains, captains and priestesses. She is described as their patron and protector, though no clear benefit seems to result from this association. Some claim she directs their actions in secret, but no evidence of this has ever been found. The warlords who fought Dauban Hess' legions long ago and the leaders of the Highland companies that fought the Empire at the Black Day Battle were all from the Witch's Host, according to popular lore.

Even less certain is her influence upon practitioners of magic throughout the Middle Kingdoms. The Divine King order of Agall, dedicated to their hero-patron's hatred of unlicensed practitioners of the magical arts, have long held that Urgrayne is the titular and actual head of a vast network of evil-doers. They have blamed her and her agents as the frequent cause of disease, pestilence, drought, rebellion, and sedition throughout the Middle Kingdoms.

CITADEL KING
& HIGHLAND CLAN

The Danian Highlands, which include the Harath and Dain Éduin mountain ranges, comprise some of the worst terrain in the region of the Silver Scale Sea. According to legend, the Highlands were once green and prosperous in the days of Geniché's Eden, but became blighted and desolate with her absence from the world. The original inhabitants of the Highlands were descendants of **Queen Dara,** daughter of Yhera, and called themselves *Daradjans.* Under barbaric kings and queens they led an isolated life, though they are recorded as amongst the defenders of Düréa at the Isle's fall.

After the fall of Düréa, the Daradjan warriors who returned brought with them Düréan refugees, who were granted lands and accepted as subjects of the realm of Daradja by Queen **Lanys.** Her hospitality and openness angered some amongst the mountain folk, who rejected the newcomers and began to refer to themselves as *Highlanders* (to distinguish themselves from the newer lowland arrivals to Daradja).

Though never a cause of outright violence, this schism continued to the point where even today the term *Highlander* is only applied to those that claim direct descent from the original Daradjans, while the term *Daradjan* is used for anyone who lives in the Highlands regardless of bloodline or origins. Düréans who fled the sinking of the Isle, Danians and Aurians from the lowlands, Déskédrans and Téthédrans from the north, Galians and Vanimorians who settled there during Dauban Hess' brief rule, Hemispian adventurers who hunted Githwaine, even slaves and servants of the Isliklid who have fled the Dain Eduins – all have over time mixed with the original peoples of the land, and come to be called Daradjans, though the realm of Daradja ceased to exist centuries ago in any meaningful political sense after the four daughters of **Arathea** plunged her realm into civil war, fighting to control the four Great Citadels of Daradja: An-Athair, Finleth, Dara Dess and Heth Moll.

The stone citadels that dot the region, built by the ancient Daradjans and their most lasting physical legacy, have long fallen into the hands of different competing factions. In addition to the four Great Citadels, at least twenty minor citadels of ancient provenance (and perhaps hundreds more castles, keeps, and towers of more recent construction) serve as seats of local power. The rulers of the ancient citadels generally claim the title of King or Queen, though the usage of such titles is far more informal than the strict hierarchies of the Middle Kingdoms. The only title of rank for high-born landholders acknowledged throughout the whole of the Highlands is **lord**; lords acting in a martial capacity who can muster a full *banner* – a military unit of at least 20 mounted soldiers – are called **banner lords**. Other titles (the ancient Danian *erl*, the Hemispian *baron*, the Imperial title of *dux* or *duke*) are claimed on occasion, but are not common.

The Highlanders that claim direct descent from the ancient Daradjans long ago established themselves as the **Highland Clans**, the First Children of Dara, and claim the status of exiles in their own land. The Clans generally eschew the politics of the region's other inhabitants, and dwell in the most desolate areas from the Dain Eduins to Pela's Gap. Twenty-eight Clans are generally acknowledged, though that number is in dispute as several of them are factions that have split off from larger Clans. By tradition the Clans' military might has been the Free Companies, standing bodies of mercenaries that seek service with clan chieftains in times of strife, the oldest of which were formed around i1065 to follow King **Cynan** to fight at the Black Day Battle. Eight Highland Companies of some history – the **Marauders**, the **Blackhearts**, the **Long Claws**, the **Leatherskins**, the **Bronzehearts**, the **Blackwings**, the **Silverwings**, and the **Ironclads** – currently serve the King of Dara Dess.

Many consider the Citadel Kings and Free Companies of Daradja to be little better than brigands and pirates, and indeed many of them have either risen from such pasts or slunk into those careers in times of trouble and want. The Highlands have long been a gathering ground for bandits and worse, in particular for criminals and exiles banished "over the mountains" from the Middle Kingdoms. Some brigand bands have elaborate histories, such as the **Cyr Faira Mal**, who have seemingly haunted the Vale of Skulls since the dawn of time, and the **Bloody Hundred**. The northern coast of Daradja is dotted with seaside citadels and fortified ports that act as the home base for fierce pirates.

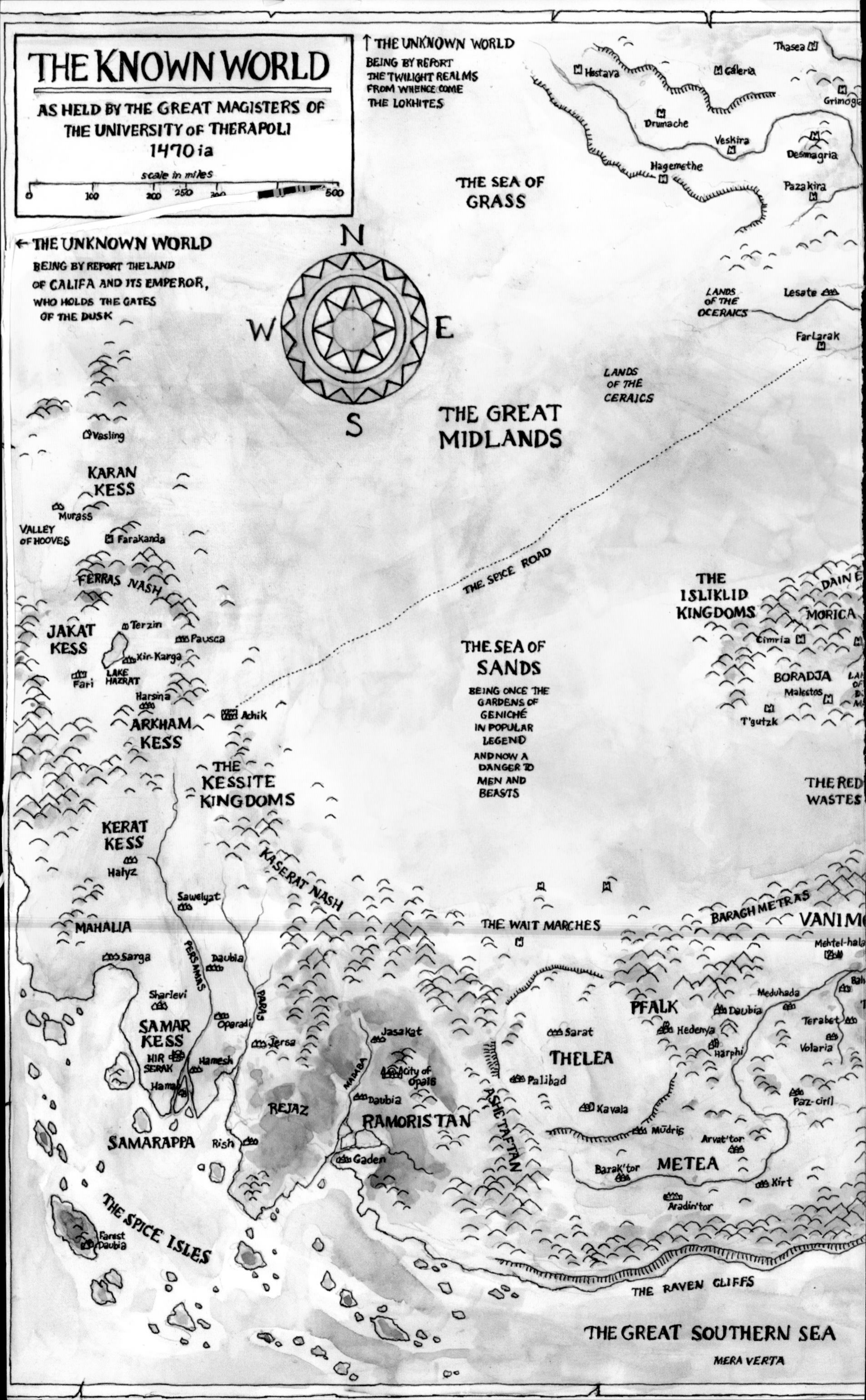

THE KNOWN WORLD
AS HELD BY THE GREAT MAGISTERS OF THE UNIVERSITY OF THERAPOLI 1470 ia
scale in miles
0 100 200 250 300 500
THE UNKNOWN WORLD
BEING BY REPORT THE TWILIGHT REALMS FROM WHENCE COME THE LOKHITES
THE UNKNOWN WORLD
BEING BY REPORT THE LAND OF CALIFA AND ITS EMPEROR, WHO HOLDS THE GATES OF THE DUSK
N
W
E
S
THE SEA OF GRASS
Hastava
Caleria
Thasea
Grimogia
Drumache
Veskira
Desmagria
Hagemethe
Pazakira
LANDS OF THE OCERAICS
Lesate
FarLarak
LANDS OF THE CERAICS
THE GREAT MIDLANDS
Vasling
KARAN KESS
Murass
VALLEY OF HOOVES
Farakanda
FERRAS NASH
THE SPICE ROAD
JAKAT KESS
Terzin
Pausca
Kir-Karga
LAKE HAZRAT
Fari
Harsina
ARKHAM KESS
Achik
THE KESSITE KINGDOMS
THE SEA OF SANDS
BEING ONCE THE GARDENS OF GENICHÉ IN POPULAR LEGEND
AND NOW A DANGER TO MEN AND BEASTS
THE ISLIKLID KINGDOMS
MORICA
Cimria
BORADJA
Malestos
T'gutzk
THE RED WASTES
KERAT KESS
Halyz
KASERAT NASH
Sawelyat
MAHALIA
Sarga
PERSAMAS
Daubia
PARAS
THE WAIT MARCHES
BARAGHMETRAS
Mehtel-hala
Sharlevi
SAMAR KESS
Oparadi
HIR SERAK
Hama
Hamesh
Tersa
Jasakat
MABABA
City of Opals
Daubia
REJAZ
RAMORISTAN
ASHE TAFTAN
PFALK
Sarat
Daubia
Meduhada
Hedenya
Terabet
Volaria
Harphi
THELEA
Palibad
Kavala
Paz-ciril
Mudris
Arvat'tor
SAMARAPPA
Rish
Gaden
Barak'tor
METEA
Kirt
Aradin'tor
THE SPICE ISLES
Farest Daubia
THE RAVEN CLIFFS
THE GREAT SOUTHERN SEA
MERA VERTA

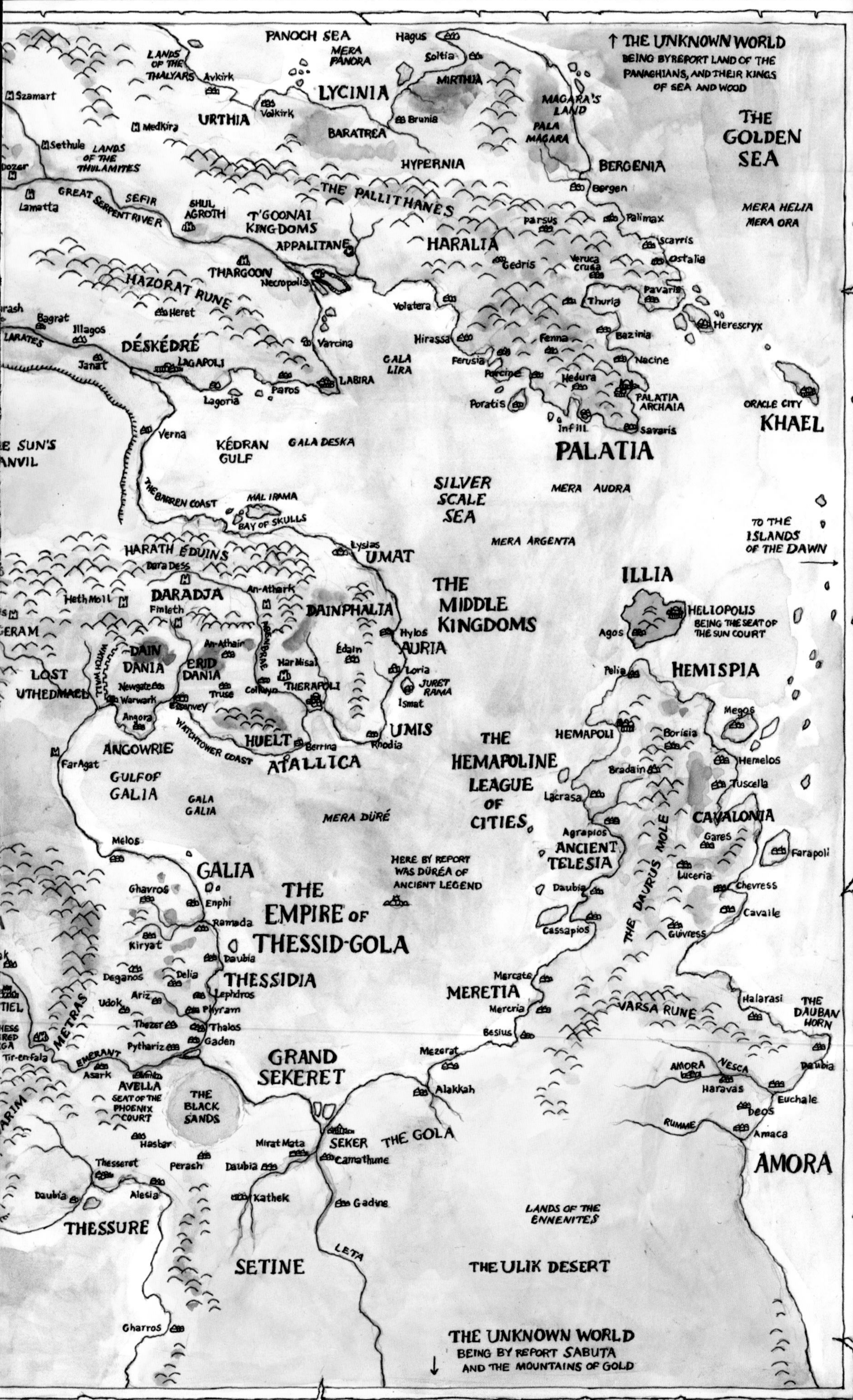
PANOCH SEA
Hagus
MERA PANORA
Soltia
LANDS OF THE THALYARS
Avkirk
LYCINIA
MIRTHIA
↑ THE UNKNOWN WORLD
BEING BY REPORT LAND OF THE PANACHIANS, AND THEIR KINGS OF SEA AND WOOD
Szamart
Volkirk
URTHIA
Medkira
Brunia
MAGARA'S LAND
PALA MAGARA
THE GOLDEN SEA
BARATREA
Sethule
LANDS OF THE THULAMITES
Dozer
HYPERNIA
BERGENIA
Bergen
Lamatta
GREAT SERPENT RIVER
SEFIR
SHUL AGROTH
T'GOONAI KINGDOMS
THE PALLITHANES
MERA HELIA
MERA ORA
Parsus
Palimax
APPALITANE
HARALIA
Scarris
Ostalia
Gedris
Veruca Crusa
THARGOON
Necropolis
HAZORAT RUNE
Pavaris
Heret
Volatera
Thuria
Bagrat
Illagos
Herescryx
LARATES
DÉSKÉDRÉ
Varcina
Hirassa
Bazinia
Fenna
Janat
LAGAPOLI
GALA LIRA
Ferusia
Nacine
Porcine
Hedura
Paros
LABIRA
Lagoria
PALATIA ARCHAIA
Poratis
ORACLE CITY
KHAEL
Infill
Savaris
Verna
THE SUN'S ANVIL
KÉDRAN GULF
GALA DESKA
PALATIA
SILVER SCALE SEA
MERA AUDRA
THE BARREN COAST
MAL IRAMA
BAY OF SKULLS
TO THE ISLANDS OF THE DAWN →
MERA ARGENTA
Lysias
HARATH ÉDUINS
UMAT
Dara Dess
ILLIA
THE MIDDLE KINGDOMS
An-Athark
Heth Moll
DARADJA
Fimleth
DAINPHALIA
HELIOPOLIS
BEING THE SEAT OF THE SUN COURT
GERAM
Hylos
Agos
An-Athair
AURIA
DAIN DANIA
ERID DANIA
Edain
WITCH WALL
Loria
Pelia
HEMISPIA
LOST UTHEDMAEL
Har Misal
JURET RAMA
Newgate
Truse
Colluyn
THERAPOLI
Ismat
Warwark
Essenvey
Megos
Angora
WATCHTOWER COAST
UMIS
THE HEMAPOLINE LEAGUE OF CITIES
HEMAPOLI
Borisia
ANGOWRIE
HUELT
Berrina
Rhodia
ATALLICA
FarAgat
Hemelos
Bradain
GULF OF GALIA
Tuscella
Lacrasa
GALA GALIA
MERA DÜRÉ
CAVALONIA
Agrapios
Gares
Melos
ANCIENT TELESIA
Farapoli
HERE BY REPORT WAS DÜRÉA OF ANCIENT LEGEND
GALIA
Luceria
Ghavros
Chevress
Enphi
THE EMPIRE of THESSID-GOLA
Daubia
THE DAURUS MOLE
Cavaile
Ramada
Cassapios
Glivress
Kiryat
Daubia
Delia
Deganos
THESSIDIA
Mercato
Lephdros
MERETIA
Udok
Ariz
Phyram
VARSA RUNE
Halarasi
THE DAUBAN HORN
METRAS
Merceria
Thezer
Thalos
Besius
Pytharez
Gaden
EMERANT
GRAND SEKERET
Mezerat
AMORA
NESCA
Daubia
Tir-en-Fala
Asark
Alakkah
Haravas
AVELLA
SEAT OF THE PHOENIX COURT
THE BLACK SANDS
Euchale
Deos
RUMME
Amaca
Mirat Mata
SEKER
THE GOLA
Hasbar
Camathume
AMORA
Thesseret
Perash
Daubia
Alesia
Daubia
Kathek
Gadine
LANDS OF THE ENNENITES
THESSURE
LETA
SETINE
THE ULIK DESERT
Gharros
THE UNKNOWN WORLD
BEING BY REPORT SABUTA AND THE MOUNTAINS OF GOLD
↓

ACKNOWLEDGMENTS

I wish to express my thanks to the folks at Sirius Entertainment who first gave *Artesia* a home: Robb Horan (and Brenda), Larry Salamone, my former editor Mark Bellis, and the ever-resourceful Keith Davidsen. My thanks as well to Mark McNabb of McNabb Studios for his invaluable prepress and design work on the first two *Artesia* series; to Lisa Webster (& Tim) and Wendy Wellington for their help on the original www.artesiaonline.com, and to Jeremy Mohler and Dustin Dade for their work on the new sites; to Michael, Bob, and Paul (and family) at PrintSolutions in Englewood; to Kristin, Jessica, and everyone at Brenner Printing; to Robert Conte and Stephen Boomgard at Regent Publishing Services; to Filip Sablik, Robert Randle, Mark Herr, Jim Kuhoric, Patricia Moore, Andrew Smith, Chana Goldberg, Karen Huddler, Janice Wilhelm, Bill Schanes, and the other fine folks at Diamond Comics and Diamond Books; to Steve Wieck, Ned Cosker, and Craig Grant at DriveThruRPG and DriveThruComics; and to Brian Petkash and Liz Fulda at Sphinx Group.

Thanks also to Dawn Murin and Robert Raper at Wizards of the Coast; Jim Pinto; and Becky Jollensten, Rich Thomas, and Mike Chaney at White Wolf Publishing and its Swords & Sorcery studios, for occasionally providing me employment outside of a world of my own making.

For their occasional encouragement, comments, criticisms, conversation, and continual example over the years, my thanks to John Kovalic, Joe Linsner, Eva Hopkins, Voltaire, Jill Thompson, Brian Azzarello, Mark Crilley, Jason Alexander, Mike Norton, Sherard Jackson, Michael Kaluta, Kevin Tinsley, Dave Napoliello, Thomas Harlan, Arvid Nelson, Alec Peters, Chris Gossett, Carla Speed McNeil, Alex Smits, Joe Koch, Dave Elliot, Kensuke Obayashi, Dave Forrest, Christian Beranek, Marshall Dillon, Dave Lewis, David Petersen, Julia Petersen, Marvin Mann, Jennifer Rodgers, Russell Collins, Sean Wang, Peggy Twardowski, Julie Haehn, Joe Martin, Mike Lee, Janet Young, Luke Crane, Chris Moeller, and Ray Lago, amongst others.

As always, my thanks to my brother John, Lillian, Hide, Michael & Naomi (and Noah and Eli and Maya), John & Heather (and Colombine), Aki & Tammy (and Gordo and Tyler), Patti, Liz, Alice, Ray & Lucy (and Winston), Vera, Al & Kaoru, David & Wendy, David C., Marc & Lisa (and Scott and Patrick and Gregory), Mikey & Meg, Dennis & Kelly, my father, and Joe Scott, who got the ball rolling on this world, and Chris and Aimee (and Spencer and Chloe), whom I still hold, much to their continued seeming bemusement, as my Ideal Readers.

A Select Bibliography of books that have influenced the writing of the *Artesia* series
and the content of the Known World:

-- Roberto Calasso, *The Marriage of Cadmus and Harmony*, Alfred A. Knopf, 1993.
-- Joseph Campbell, *The Hero with a Thousand Faces*, Princeton/Bollingen, 1949.
-- Yves Bonnofoy (compiler) and Wendy Doniger (translator), *Mythologies*, University of Chicago Press, 1991.
-- J.G. Frazer, *The Golden Bough*, 12 volumes, Macmillan, 1935.
-- Marcel Detienne and Jean-Pierre Vernant (translated by Paula Wissing), *The Cuisine of Sacrifice Among the Greeks*, University of Chicago Press, 1989.
-- Christopher A. Faraone, *Talismans & Trojan Horses: Guardian Statues in Ancient Greek Myth and Ritual*, Oxford University Press, 1992.
-- Christopher A. Faraone and Dirk Obbink, editors, *Magika Hiera: Ancient Greek Magic & Religion*, Oxford University Press, 1991.
-- Jennifer Larson, *Greek Heroine Cults*, University of Wisconsin Press, 1995.
-- Neil Forsyth, *The Old Enemy: Satan & The Combat Myth*, Princeton University Press, 1987.
-- Carlo Ginzburg, *Ecstasies: Deciphering the Witches' Sabbath*, Pantheon Books, 1991.
-- Barbara Ehrenreich, *Blood Rites: Origins and History of the Passions of War*, Metropolitan Books, 1997.
-- Bruce Lincoln, *Death, War, and Sacrifice: Studies in Ideology and Practice*, University of Chicago Press, 1991.
-- Antonia Fraser, *Boadicea's Chariot: The Warrior Queens*, Weidenfeld and Nicholson, 1988.
-- John Keegan, *The Face of Battle*, Viking Press, 1976.
-- Victor Davis Hanson, *The Western Way of War: Infantry Battle in Classical Greece*, Hodder & Stoughton, 1989.
-- Donald W. Engels, *Alexander the Great and the Logistics of the Macedonian Army*, University of California Press, 1978.
-- Malcolm Vale, *War and Chivalry: Warfare and Aristocracy in England, France, and Burgundy at the End of the Middle Ages*, University of Georgia Press, 1981.
-- J. R. Hale, *War and Society in Renaissance Europe, 1450-1620*, Johns Hopkins University Press, 1985.
-- Sydney Anglo, *The Martial Arts of Renaissance Europe*, Yale University Press, 2000.
-- Mary Gentle, *The Book of Ash*, four volumes, Avon, 1999.
-- George R.R. Martin, *A Song of Ice and Fire*, four volumes so far, Bantam Spectra, 1996 - present
-- Jacqueline Carey, Kushiel's Legacy: *Kushiel's Dart, Kushiel's Chosen, Kushiel's Avatar*, TOR, 2001-2003.